From Dryden to Jane Austen

From Dryden to Jane Austen

Essays on English Critics and Writers, 1660-1818

Hoyt Trowbridge

UNIVERSITY OF NEW MEXICO PRESS

Albuquerque

Library of Congress Cataloging in Publication Data

Trowbridge, Hoyt.
   From Dryden to Jane Austen.

   Includes bibliographical references and index.
    1. English literature—18th century—History
and criticism—Addresses, essays, lectures.
2. English literature—Early modern, 1500–1700—
History and criticism—Addresses, essays, lectures.
3. Criticism—Great Britain—Addresses, essays,
lectures. I. Title.
PR442.T7   820'.9'004   76-21490
ISBN 0-8263-0430-3

Library of Congress Catalog Card Number 76-21490
International Standard Book Number 0-8263-0430-3
First edition

For Margery

Contents

Preface

These essays were composed over a long period of time—some forty years—and include pieces written in both the earliest and the most recent stages of their author's professional life. Ten of them are reprinted from various journals or other standard vehicles of scholarly communication. Credit to the original publisher is given at the foot of the first page of each of these essays, and I am grateful to the university presses and other copyright holders who have given permission to reprint them. Chapters 3, 4, 13, and 14 were written during the last two or three years and have not been previously published.

For several of the earlier pieces, I have revised the quotations and footnotes to take advantage of better texts of the works and correspondence of Swift, Pope, Gay, Dr. Johnson, and others, which have become available since the essays were first written. I have also made a few superficial stylistic changes, to conform to the more informal conventions which have developed in scholarly writing over the years, and in a few cases I have added references to secondary sources, published after the first appearance of those essays and agreeing or disagreeing with their theses and arguments. Otherwise, they are all reproduced here exactly as they were first written.

Considered as a whole, the collection does not claim to present a comprehensive interpretation of either the criticism or the literature of the period it covers. In preparing it for the printer, however, I have been interested to observe several continuities of subject, method, and interpretive problems and issues, which give it some degree of unity. One of the most pervasive is the use of intellectual history and philosophic texts to clarify the meaning and bearing of many of the works discussed. The value of a solid grounding in philosophy for students of literature is a lesson I have been preaching to my students and colleagues for a long time, though for the most part without conspicuous success. Another recurrent theme is a long-standing preoccupation with method both in scholarly interpretation of works written in past ages and in those works themselves. An example of the first is the running battle in the earliest essays against the concept of "preromanticism," which dominated eighteenth-century studies during the first third or even half of this century. The fundamental defect of that approach, as I say in discussing Hurd's *Letters on Chivalry and Romance* (Chapter 9), is "the methodological bias resulting from an unhistorical imposition of nineteenth-century issues and categories on eighteenth-century writings." Few scholars would use such an approach today, but the general principle remains valid and has much wider application. My views on the need to take account of method as well as doctrine in interpreting intellectual works of the past are most explicitly expressed near the end of Chapter 12, on probable reasoning in Johnson's *Preface to Shakespeare*. It was from the early writings of Richard McKeon of Chicago, especially his classic essay "Literary Criticism and the Concept of Imitation in Antiquity" (*Modern Philology* 34 [1936], 1-35), that I first came to understand the inadequacy of purely doctrinal readings of such works. It seems to me a pity that so few other non-Chicagoans have profited from McKeon's theory and practice as an intellectual historian.

Probable reasoning is only one kind of method among many, but it is one that was more widely understood and put to use in the seventeenth and eighteenth centuries than most scholars have recognized. In rereading the essay on Dryden and the rules (Chapter 2), I was struck by the early date at which I first became interested in it. Though I do not mention the fact in any of these essays, the case of Dryden is particularly intriguing, because it antedates Locke's influential treatment of the subject in the *Essay concerning Human Understanding*. Dryden lived for ten years after publication of the *Essay* (1690), but his kind of probabilism is wholly classical, derived ultimately from Aristotle and more directly from Cicero. I do not expect to pursue the subject further, but some enterprising graduate student might write an excellent dissertation comparing the interpretations of probable reasoning by Glanvill, Boyle, and other spokesmen for the Royal Society, before Locke, with the logical treatises of Isaac Watts (1725) and Jean Pierre de Crousaz (1741), which were written under Locke's influence. As the essay on Gilbert White (Chapter 13) goes some way to show, the question is a fundamental one for the history of science as well as for eighteenth-century aesthetics, criticism, historiography, social theory, and philosophy.

If I have any regret in reviewing these essays, it is that I could not include more studies like those on *The Shepherd's Week* (Chapter 5), Pope's *Eloisa to Abelard* (Chapter 6), and the novels of Jane Austen (Chapter 14), which use historical evidence for purposes of critical interpretation and evaluation. At various times I have thought a good deal about doing something similar with Fielding, Goldsmith, and the poems of William Collins or George Crabbe, but so far these ideas have come to nothing. Perhaps I may still be able to work out one or two of them.

It has been a pleasure to work with Elizabeth Hadas Heist, my able and amiable editor at the University of New Mexico Press. I am also very grateful to the university itself for its generous sabbatical leave policy and to the Faculty Research Allocations Committee for travel grants that helped make it possible for me to work during several extended periods at major research libraries in this country and in London and Oxford.

My wife, to whom the book is dedicated, has lived with me through all the ups and downs and turns and twists of personal and professional life for these forty years and more. I owe far more than I can say to her support, understanding, and patience.

PART ONE

The Father of English Criticism

1

Dryden on the Elizabethans

Dryden's *Essay on the Dramatic Poetry of the Last Age* was published in 1672 as an appendix to *The Conquest of Granada*. In the epilogue to the second part of the play, Dryden had committed himself to some unfavorable opinions of the Elizabethan playwrights:

> Wit's now arriv'd to a more high degree;
> Our native language more refin'd and free.
> Our ladies and our men now speak more wit
> In conversation, than those poets writ.[1]

It was to defend this "bold *Epilogue*," with its praise of Restoration refinement and its disparagement of Elizabethan crudity, that Dryden wrote the *Essay*.[2] It is not one of his best or most important critical works, but it has a good deal of interest for students of his thought. It is one of three essays which Dryden devoted to the discussion of Elizabethan drama, and as such it is central to an understanding of his critical opinions. It has, I think, been frequently misunderstood.

Dryden has often been accused of inconsistency, especially in his attitude toward Shakespeare, and the *Essay on the Dramatic Poetry of the Last Age* has been cited as one of the clearest instances of his critical instability. In studies of Dryden the essay is commonly contrasted, much to its disadvantage, with the *Essay of Dramatic Poesy,* published in 1668,

Reprinted with permission of the Department of Publications, University of Iowa, from *Philological Quarterly,* 22 (1943), 240-50. Originally published under the title "Dryden's *Essay on the Dramatic Poetry of the Last Age.*"

a little less than five years before. The earlier piece was an eloquent defense of the Elizabethans; the later essay, it is said, was a severe and sweeping attack upon them.

The usual interpretation of the *Essay on the Dramatic Poetry of the Last Age* is amusingly (though callously) summed up in Saintsbury's remark that the Rose Alley ambuscade of 1679, in which Dryden was severely beaten by hired bullies, exacted a sufficient and suitable atonement for the sins of this piece. It seemed to Saintsbury a shameful departure from Dryden's usual modesty and good taste.[3] The same judgement has been more soberly stated by other students. Margaret Sherwood, in her monograph of 1914, noted in this essay a "marked change of attitude" since the *Essay of Dramatic Poesy*. She contends that Dryden had come increasingly under French influence and had turned away from his former allegiance to Shakespeare; a patronizing tone crept into his writing, and the Elizabethans, once highly praised, were now "severely scored."[4] This conception of the essay is most fully developed in W. E. Bohn's comprehensive study of Dryden's critical development. Bohn divided Dryden's career as a critic into five contrasted periods. The *Essay of Dramatic Poesy* is the most important and most representative work of the first of these periods, when Dryden, with "superb enthusiasm," boldly took his stand upon his literary instincts, which favored the Elizabethans.[5] The *Essay on the Dramatic Poetry of the Last Age* belongs to Dryden's second period. In this phase of his career, Bohn wrote, Dryden's mood had entirely changed:

> The literature of the former age is to be examined sceptically, coldly, in the manner of contemporaneous English philosophy; there are to be no fond enthusiasms here. . . . In the *Essay of Dramatic Poesy* Dryden loved Shakespeare: here there is no talk of love; instead we are to have a scientific impartiality.

Once free and inquiring, Dryden had become a critical conformist. Identifying himself with the nobility and the court, he now defended the literature of the court, the polished and artificial heroic play, and scorned both the lower classes of the present and the "sturdy, human, romantic English literature of the past."[6] Like Saintsbury and Sherwood, Bohn interpreted the *Essay on the Dramatic Poetry of the Last Age* as a general attack upon the Elizabethan dramatists and contrasted its "carping" and "fault-finding" with the enthusiastic praise given to their work in the *Essay of Dramatic Poesy*.

This interpretation seems to me to involve a radical misunderstanding of Dryden's purpose in the *Essay on the Dramatic Poetry of the Last Age,* and therefore a fundamental misconception of its import. As I should construe it, the essay was not intended as a general attack upon the Elizabethans. It is concerned only with limited and relatively superficial aspects of their work—especially their language, a topic which was not treated in the *Essay of Dramatic Poesy*—and its criticism of the Elizabethans on this score did not involve a retraction of Dryden's former praise of their plays on other grounds. If this interpretation is sound, the two essays are not contradictory, and in this case, at least, we may absolve Dryden from the charge of critical instability and inconsistency which has so often been made against him.

Dryden's larger purpose in all his critical writings was to improve the art of his own time; he was concerned that "poetry may not go backward, when all other arts and sciences are advancing."[7] He believed that the essential requirement for artistic advance was the establishment of an objective standard of aesthetic judgment, some criterion or measure of value by which poets might improve their performance and the public might guide its taste. Without such an objective standard, Dryden believed, the poet was governed by chance and the audience by mere caprice.[8]

This standard was to be embodied partly in a system of well-founded artistic rules and partly in a just criticism of the most important models. Rules and models were alike necessary, if art was to go forward; but some rules are false or insignificant, and no human work is perfect. In both it was essential to distinguish the true and valuable from the false and unworthy. In all his critical essays Dryden was endeavoring either to sift and clarify the rules, the "grounds of criticism" as he called them in the preface to *Troilus and Cressida,* or to apply them in the judgment of great models.

In the *Essay of Dramatic Poesy* and in the *Essay on the Dramatic Poetry of the Last Age* (as also in the preface to *Troilus*), his materials were the plays of Shakespeare, Fletcher, and Jonson. Both essays were intended to contribute to the advancement of letters by separating what is truly admirable in the Elizabethan poets—the most important models an English dramatist could have—from the elements in their work which are inferior and not to be imitated. The two essays share this common purpose, but they make different points. In one, taking Elizabethan drama in the large, Dryden tried to isolate and define its special merits; in the other he was concerned with a particular kind of fault or weakness in these same plays. In the main, there is little overlapping between them.

The specific subject of the *Essay on the Dramatic Poetry of the Last Age* is clearly and explicitly stated at the beginning. It is not a general treatment of Elizabethan drama. Dryden limits his subject to certain definite elements in the works of Shakespeare, Fletcher, and Jonson: namely, to their language and wit. He assumed, as his generation usually did, that English society had improved since the last age; he analyzes the nature of this general social improvement and argues that poetry, as an imitation of nature, must naturally have benefited from it:

> It is therefore my part to make it clear, that the language, wit, and conversation of our age, are improved and refined above the last; and then it will not be difficult to infer, that our plays have received some part of those advantages.[9]

His purpose was to show that in these particular qualities, though not by any means in every respect, the plays of his own age were superior to those of the Elizabethans.

This limitation of the subject rests upon a basic theoretical distinction, which Dryden made not only here but in many other places, between the age and the individual talent. He believed that the poet is dependent in many ways upon his age, which gives him his education, his language, his models (both in real life and in art), and above all his audience. As he had written in the epilogue which he was defending in the *Essay,*

> They, who have best succeeded on the stage,
> Have still conform'd their genius to their age,

and the characteristics of a poet's time must always influence the nature of his performance. As a poet may profit from the advantages of his age, so he may suffer from its defects; times differ, and the artist's achievement is necessarily limited, modified, or increased by the circumstances of his period. But in Dryden's view (which in some ways closely resembles that of Taine), no work of art is entirely the product of its age; if it were, all the works of any particular period would be alike and of equal value. Art is the product of at least two factors, the age and the poet's own genius, and the artistic value of any poem or play is determined by variations in these two causal factors. Where an equality of genius may be assumed, the works of a better age will necessarily be finer; and conversely, a poet of great talent, though working in a bad age, may produce poems superior to those of a more polished period in which there is no comparable native gift.[10] A work of art may have merits due to its age together with faults due to a failure or mediocrity of talent; it may on the other hand have all the beauties of genius qualified by the defects of an inferior period. Homer and Shakespeare were Dryden's standing examples of the latter situation, and it is notable that he consistently preferred this type of poet to the more sophisticated and polished but less richly endowed talent of a Virgil or Corneille.[11]

In the *Essay on the Dramatic Poetry of the Last Age* Dryden was concerned only with the first of these two factors—that is, with the qualities of Restoration and Elizabethan plays which reflected the general level of culture and social intercourse in the two ages. He hoped to show that in these qualities, as abstracted from those which are the product of individual talent, the writers of his own age had an advantage which just criticism ought to recognize and which, in the interests of poetry itself, writers ought to exploit. The other factor is briefly touched upon only in the last two paragraphs of the essay.

Dryden's comparison between the Elizabethan age and his own falls into three main parts: language, wit, and conversation. The improvement in language is divided under two headings, the rejection of "improper" old words and the admission of "proper" new ones. Dryden felt that his argument on this point would have been stronger if there had been some absolute standard of propriety to which he could refer; but, as he remarked elsewhere, England lacked even a fixed grammar, the indispensable basis of linguistic rule.[12] In the absence of any definite standard, he could prove the errors of the Elizabethans only by quoting examples; the best proof that they were truly improper was the fact that writers would no longer commit them. He therefore quotes from Ben Jonson many instances of obscurity, redundancy, false syntax, and "ill placing of words." Such faults, Dryden says, are of course still commoner in Shakespeare and Fletcher than in Jonson, who was "the most correct of that age." The age was ignorant in many things; Dryden cites in particular the "lameness" of Elizabethan plots. He ascribes these faults not to the poets but to their age; these writers lacked the benefits of enlightened conversation, and their audience, knowing no better, did not encourage them to write more correctly.[13].

On the addition of new words, Dryden states that "our tongue has been beautified by the three fore-mentioned poets," though still further refined by Suckling and Waller. In this respect the only advantage of the Restoration poet was to come later in a process of cumulative improvement; the point is small and Dryden does not put much weight upon it.[14]

The second main division of his argument is the improvement in "wit." Dryden uses the term both in a wider sense, to denote artistic propriety, the adjustment of expression to thought, and also in a narrower sense to signify "sharpness of conceit," as in comic repartee.[15] Shakespeare and Fletcher, with all their talent, were extremely uneven and careless; but Jonson, though weaker than they in fancy, was "the most judicious of poets." His fancy, directed so often to the description of folly and vulgarity, was "not so much or noble" as theirs, but "he always writ properly, and as the character required." If this is wit, Jonson had as much of it as any poet.[16]

In the stricter sense of the term, Fletcher was the wittiest of the Elizabethans. Dryden considered Fletcher's Don John to be the best picture of a gentleman in any of the plays of the last age; yet even this character "speaks better" and is more vigorously maintained in the Restoration adaptation. Wit, that is "sharpness of conceit," was not Jonson's talent, and when he tried to write wittily he was forced either to borrow from the ancients or to fall into "meanness of expression," especially puns. But this was then the mode of wit—"the vice of the age, and not Ben Jonson's." In the wit of all three writers Dryden found something vulgar, something "ill-bred and clownish," which reflected the conversation of the authors and the bad taste of their uncourtly age.[17]

The third part of Dryden's argument deals with conversation, "the last and greatest advantage of our writing." The Restoration court, largely because of the king's example, was more polished than that of Elizabeth and James. There was less gallantry in the former age, and poets did not then keep such good company as they do now:

> I cannot, therefore, conceive it any insolence to affirm, that, by the knowledge and pattern of their wit who writ before us, and by the advantage of our own conversation, the discourse and raillery of our comedies excel what has been written by them.[18]

With this summary Dryden completes the defense of his main thesis. His claim for his own age, though debatable, is not an extravagant one. Concretely summarized, it amount to this: the Restoration playwrights, improving upon a model originally given them by Fletcher, excelled the Elizabethans in witty comedy and in grammatical propriety; they excelled Fletcher and Shakespeare, though not Jonson, in correct plotting and stage decorum. Dryden credited these advantages to a general advance in the level of taste and social manners.

Up to this point, the essay has dealt almost exclusively with those aspects of the Elizabethan plays which the poets owed to their age; Dryden has hardly touched upon the positive merits, peculiar to each poet, which proceeded from their own talent. In the remaining paragraphs, having fully established his main contention, Dryden briefly but clearly analyzes the various special talents of the three chief Elizabethan playwrights. These remarks round out the discussion by showing that defects of language and wit by no means tell the whole story; in addition to the faults which he had defined and illustrated, these poets had many admirable qualities. The last two paragraphs of the essay draw up a balance between the faults of their age and the beauties of their genius.

Dryden states that he admires the "beauties and the heights" of Shakespeare, the quickness and easiness of Fletcher, especially in witty comedy and in scenes of love, and finally the accuracy of Jonson's judgment in "the ordering of his plots, his choice of characters, and maintaining what he had chosen to the end." These were the talents peculiar to those writers, the qualities that made them admirable and worthy of imitation; in these various aspects they are severally excellent and to be applauded. To balance these virtues, all three had certain deficiencies. Dryden could not condone Shakespeare's carelessness, Fletcher's redundancy of matter and incorrectness of language, or Jonson's use of "Cobb and Tib"—that is, of low or "mechanic" characters—in his comedies of humor. The essay closes with a general summation in which Dryden once more ascribes to the "gallantry and civility of our age" the special and limited advantages which his contemporaries possessed over their predecessors. Though not better poets, they had extrinsic advantages which allowed them, in some respects, to compose more pleasing plays.[19]

If we compare these judgments with those made in the *Essay of Dramatic Poesy* five years before, it will be evident, I think, that Dryden's opinions had undergone no radical change. Some allowance must be made for the dialogue form of the earlier essay, and also for the different specific purposes of the two pieces; but if such allowances are made there is no contradiction between them.

In the *Essay of Dramatic Poesy* Dryden's purpose had been to "vindicate the honour of our English writers, from the censure of those who unjustly prefer the French before them."[20] The case for French drama was strongly and persuasively presented by Lisideius; he defended it largely on grounds of greater regularity and formal perfection. Having done justice to the French in this part of the dialogue, Dryden evidently felt free in the reply of Neander, his own spokesman, to defend the merits of the Elizabethans with all possible force—indeed to overstate on some points.[21] Yet even here he allowed Neander to admit substantially the same faults he was to recognize in his own person five years later in the other *Essay*.

Neander, the defender of the English, fully accepts the negative criticisms which had been advanced by Lisideius; it is true, he concedes, that the French "contrive their plots more regularly, and observe the laws of comedy, and decorum of the stage (to speak generally), with more exactness than the English."[22] He admits also that Fletcher is irregular and careless and that Shakespeare is extremely uneven:

I cannot say that he is every where alike; were he so, I should do him injury to compare him with the greatest of mankind. He is many times flat, insipid; his comic wit degenerating into clenches, his serious swelling into bombast.[23]

Neander defends them, in spite of these confessed faults, on grounds of superior ''liveliness''—Shakespeare for his greatness and variety of characters, Fletcher for his representation of love and his ''quickness of wit in repartees.''[24] These are precisely the same beauties and faults which Dryden ascribes to these poets in the *Essay on the Dramatic Poetry of the Last Age:* tragic elevation and grandeur in Shakespeare, comic quickness and ease in Fletcher, qualified in both by carelessness, luxuriance, and impropriety.[25]

Jonson's characteristic faults and virtues, as Neander defines them, are of a different kind. In general, Neander finds Jonson's greatest merit in his skillful and elaborate plotting, ''the copiousness and well-knitting of the intrigues.'' Jonson was an English Virgil, ''the pattern of elaborate writing,'' and the most correct of English poets. Neander defends him against the claims of French comic writers because his plays, as regular as any of theirs, had in addition a greater variety of plot and characters. On the other hand, Jonson's talent was narrower than Shakespeare's or Fletcher's. His genius, Neander says, was too sullen and saturnine to treat love gracefully; his wit, too, was inferior to that of Beaumont and Fletcher—though one could not say he lacked wit entirely, he ''was frugal of it.'' His special talent was for ''humour'' and in this kind he particularly delighted to represent ''mechanic people.''[26] As in the *Essay on the Dramatic Poetry of the Last Age,* Jonson's virtue is correctness and technical skill; his talent, in both essays, is said to be primarily for comedy of humor; he lacks or is frugal of wit, and his comic butts are usually low and vulgar—the ''mechanic people'' of 1668, the ''Cobb and Tib'' of 1672. Jonson's genius, like that of Fletcher and Shakespeare, is defined in the same terms in the earlier and in the later essay, and he is praised and blamed in both for the same talents and the same limitations.

The only criticism of the Elizabethans which was not anticipated in 1668 is that directed against their language; in the *Essay of Dramatic Poesy,* Dryden's comments on this point were limited to the observations that Shakespeare's language had become a little obsolete and that Jonson's idiom was too much Latinized.[27] But the omission of a more extensive treatment of this question is to be explained partly by artistic and partly by logical considerations; we cannot infer from its absence that Dryden did not then recognize grammatical faults in the Elizabethans, nor, alternatively, that he saw them but considered them of no significance. He must have recognized these faults, which were plain to any eye, but he omitted them either because they were inappropriate to the dialogue he was composing or because they were irrelevant to the issues discussed in it. A discussion of Elizabethan grammar would certainly have overloaded a debate already sufficiently complex, and the question is not in any case one which could plausibly be treated in a dialogue; it is quite unsuited to the level of generalization demanded in a conversation among gentlemen on a boating excursion. Furthermore, questions of grammatical propriety were irrelevant here, just as a discussion of *liaison des scènes* or the unity of action would have been irrelevant in the essay of 1672. If it had been introduced into the dialogue, the grammatical criticism of 1672 could not have affected the conclusions, based upon quite other grounds, which were reached in 1668; and by the same token the defense of Shakespeare in the dialogue, founded as it was upon his lively representation of great characters and great passions, could not remove the objections raised against his language in the later essay. No change of opinion or attitude can be inferred from the absence of grammatical analysis in the earlier piece and its presence in the later one.

The two essays, then, are obviously designed to make different points, but they are not contradictory; where they overlap they are in agreement, and where they cover different ground they are complementary. The *Essay on the Dramatic Poetry of the Last Age* is not to be understood as a revision of its more brilliant predecessor; it is rather a supplement, footnote, or appendix. Its point is confessedly of second-rate importance, and is one which may be added to the broader and more significant conclusions of the *Essay of Dramatic Poesy* without in any way retracting them.

As I remarked at the beginning of this essay, Dryden's defense of his "bold *Epilogue*" is not one of his most interesting or most important pieces. He himself evidently did not think highly of it, for it was omitted from some copies of the second edition of the *Conquest of Granada* (1673), and from all other editions during his lifetime.[28] Bohn suggests that Dryden probably withdrew the essay because he was ashamed of its carping and fault-finding—a view to which Saintsbury might also have subscribed.[29] It seems more likely that he felt it to be platitudinous, a somewhat pointless documentation of the obvious. Would anyone in Dryden's generation deny that Shakespeare and Jonson committed many grammatical solecisms? And was it likely that any Restoration playwright would imitate them in this? The whole essay may have seemed to Dryden supererogatory; the point was sound enough but not worth making. He may have found, too, that his contemporaries, misunderstanding his intentions as they have since been misunderstood by other readers, considered him to have turned against his Elizabethan masters. From this charge, at least, I think we may freely absolve him. In 1672, just as before that time and after it, Dryden admired those poets, this side idolatry, as much as any.

Notes

1. W. P. Ker, ed., *Essays of John Dryden,* (Oxford: Clarendon Press, 1926), I, 161.
2. Ibid., p. 162.
3. George Saintsbury, *History of English Criticism* (Edinburgh: W. Blackwood, 1925), pp. 123-24.
4. Margaret Sherwood, *Dryden's Dramatic Theory and Practice* (New Haven: Yale University Press, 1914), pp. 27-29.
5. William E. Bohn, "The Development of John Dryden's Literary Criticism," *PMLA,* 22 (1907), 67-75.
6. Ibid., pp. 93-100.
7. *Essay on the Dramatic Poetry of the Last Age,* Ker, I, 163.
8. Among many other places, see especially Ker, I,120-21, 179; II,16-17, 133-34, 136-37, 225-26.
9. *Dramatic Poetry of the Last Age,* Ker,I,163. Cf. Preface to *An Evening's Love* (1671), ibid., pp. 134-35, 138-41.
10. See for example the comparison of Ovid and Chaucer in Dryden's *Preface to the Fables,* Ker, II, 254-57.
11. Virgil's age was more favorable to poetry than any other in the world's history, according to Dryden (Ker, II, 25, 135, 214), and the *Aeneid* is the most perfect of poems (ibid., pp. 12-14, 128). Homer was superior, however, in invention and design (ibid., pp. 148-49), and his genius, which was "violent, impetuous, and full of fire," was more congenial to Dryden and more pleasing to the reader (ibid., pp. 251-54). On Shakespeare see ibid., I, 68, 78-79, 224-28; II, 4-6, etc.
12. *Original and Progress of Satire,* Ker, II, 110.
13. Ker, I, 164-70.
14. Ibid., pp. 170-71.
15. Cf. Ker, "Introduction," I, lvii.
16. Ibid., pp. 171-72.
17. Ibid., pp. 172-75.
18. Ibid., pp. 175-76.
19. Ibid., pp. 176-77.
20. Ibid., p. 27.
21. Especially in attacking the coldness and long-windedness of French tragedy; see ibid., pp. 71-72. Cf. Pierre Legouis, "Corneille and Dryden as Dramatic Critics," in *Seventeenth Century Studies Presented to Sir Herbert Grierson* (Oxford: Clarendon Press, 1938), pp. 280-81.
22. Ker, I, 67.
23. Ibid., p. 80.
24. Ibid., pp. 78-81.
25. Ibid., pp. 172, 176-77.
26. Ibid., pp. 78-83; cf. pp. 172-74, 177.
27. Ibid., pp. 81-82.
28. Ibid., p. lxxiv.
29. Bohn, p. 97, note. For a recent judgment on this old essay, see Robert D. Hume, *Dryden's Criticism* (Ithaca and London: Cornell University Press, 1970), pp. 94, 95, 228.

2

The Place of Rules in Dryden's Criticism

A fundamental task in the interpretation of any literary critic is to determine the nature and status of the general criteria which lie behind his judgments of specific works and writers. Discussion of Dryden's criticism has largely turned upon this question. The critics of the neoclassical period—the writers, let us say, from Ben Jonson to Samuel Johnson—are agreed in general to have been characterized by their use of "rules," that is to say, of objective norms or canons, established by reason, which they applied in the judgment of particular works of art. Did Dryden share this faith in rules, or did he appeal to other criteria, perhaps subjective and antirational? If he did make use of rules, we should inquire also as to their derivation and status—the sort of reasoning by which they were supported and the kind and degree of validity which he supposed them to possess.

To the first of these questions, three answers have been suggested. The clearest example of the first answer is to be found in George Saintsbury's *History of Criticism*. According to Saintsbury, Dryden was the Shakespeare of criticism. He judged poems as Shakespeare wrote them, by "aiming at delight, at truth, at justice, at nature, at poetry, and letting the rules take care of themselves." If at times he seems to have appealed to critical rule and system, he did so only in deference to fashion and fools. In the last analysis, Dryden judged poems simply by his own impression, by his own intuition of poetic quality.[1]

Reprinted, with permission of the University of Chicago Press, from *Modern Philology,* 44 (1946), 84-96.

In his *Life of Dryden,* Dr. Johnson tells a very different story. Writing some eighty years after Dryden's death, Johnson knew that many changes had taken place during the intervening period. He seems to have feared that Dryden's doctrines and judgments might seem commonplace to the sophisticated reader of 1780. We ought to remember, Johnson says, that in Dryden's time these ideas were new. In that age, sound principles of criticism were known to few: "Audiences applauded by instinct, and poets perhaps often pleased by chance." It was Dryden who first taught the English to criticize by rule: "Dryden may be properly considered as the father of English criticism, as the writer who first taught us to determine upon principle the merit of composition." Dryden's great achievement, Johnson believed, had been to establish a groundwork of critical standards and principles, upon which other men had continued to build; for a criticism by instinct or intuition he substituted a criticism by law.[2] This is the exact opposite of Saintsbury's view.

The third solution combines the two above. A representative instance is Margaret Sherwood's discussion in her essay on Dryden's theory of drama. In her opinion Dryden had no consistent position. He wavered continually between French rules and English freedom, judging at one time by the canons of rationalism, at another by subjective impression or intuitive response.[3] This is the answer given by most students of Dryden's thought; few have been able to find any single criterion underlying the variety of his critical opinions and judgments.

The second question, though almost as important as the first, is much less frequently considered. The most relevant discussion is that of L. I. Bredvold, who represents Dryden as a Pyrrhonist, a skeptical antirationalist. In religion the natural expression of this philosophy is "fideism," an attack upon natural reason in the interests of revelation and ecclesiastical authority. In politics the same distrust of reason leads to a defense of tradition and authority—in Dryden's case, to a moderate constitutional Toryism. His thought in these two fields is consistent both in its distrust of reason and in the conservative conclusions to which such distrust leads.[4] In criticism, according to Bredvold, Dryden's thought is unsystematic and tentative; as a Pyrrhonist, he distrusted reason and was always ready to change his mind. Appealing at one time to the rules, at others to nonrational criteria, his criticism is essentially unstable and inconsistent. In so far as he did make use of rules, their status was that of hypotheses or provisional generalizations, tentatively held and easily dropped in favor of other criteria.[5] In criticism, as in religion and politics, Pyrrhonic skepticism or antirationalism is the continuing substratum beneath the surface contradictions that gives unity and integrity to Dryden's thought.

These, then, are the questions with which we are concerned, together with some of the solutions that have been offered by scholars and critics. The evidence to be presented here is drawn primarily from a single work, Dryden's *Defence of an Essay of Dramatic Poesy;* it will be supplemented, however, by material from other critical essays by Dryden and, in connection with Bredvold's thesis, by evidence drawn from some of Dryden's sources and from the writings of his contemporaries. I will not attempt here to analyze Dryden's practice as a critic; my purpose is to recover his theory of criticism and to define its nature, as he himself conceived it.

The *Defence* was written in 1668 as a reply to the preface to Sir Robert Howard's play *The Duke of Lerma,* which, in turn, was an attack upon Dryden's *Essay of Dramatic Poesy*. Considered as a whole, the *Defence* is not of first-class importance. The main point at issue was the propriety of rhyme in serious plays—a question of considerable practical importance at the time but of comparatively minor theoretical interest. Howard was an amateur, a fourth-rate poet whose views were too superficial to have much intrinsic value,[6] and Dryden's rebuttal is largely devoted to *ad hoc* satire on Howard's frequent obscurities, mistranslations, grammatical faults, and errors of reasoning. The *Defence* nevertheless contains, in two or three passages, a serious and reasoned treatment of certain crucial theoretical questions. For all his superficiality, Howard had raised some fundamental problems, which Dryden considered more fully in his reply than he had occasion to do in any of his later works. These passages give the essay a unique value and interest for the student of his critical thought.

Howard speaks in his preface as a friend of reason but an enemy of dogmatism; he accuses Dryden of attempting to establish laws by dictatorial fiat. In poetry he defends liberty of taste and opinion against the rules:

> . . . Nor do I condemn in the least any thing of what Nature soever that pleases, since nothing cou'd appear to me a ruder folly than to censure the satisfaction of others; I rather blame the unnecessary understanding of some that have labour'd to give strict rules to things that are not Mathematical, and with such eagerness persuing their own seeming reasons that at last we are to apprehend such Argumentative Poets will grow as strict as *Sancho Pancos* Doctor was to our very Appetites; for in the difference of *Tragedy* and *Comedy,* and of *Fars* it self, there can be no determination but by the Taste; nor in the manner of their Composure; and who ever wou'd endeavour to like or dislike by the Rules of others, he will be as unsuccessful as if he should try to be perswaded into a power of believing, not what he must, but what others direct him to believe.[7]

For Howard, evidently, there was no middle ground between mathematical demonstration and the anarchy of uncontrolled individual preferences; if, therefore, the rules were not susceptible to demonstration, it followed that taste alone could be the guide. The poet must be free to dress his play ''in such a fashion as his fancy best approves'' and the audience, by the same token, to judge the result by its own satisfaction. The poet might preserve the unities if he liked, might rhyme or not as pleased him best; and the audience was to respond according to its taste. Howard's argument, denying the possibility of a criticism by rule, left all questions of better and worse in poetry to be determined by personal preference. It was for this reason that his preface needed a serious refutation.

In opposing this antinomian view, Dryden makes three important claims: first, the negative contention that taste—mere liking or disliking—cannot be taken as the criterion of poetic value; second, as the positive counterpart of this contention, that it is possible to ground the rules on objective principles and to support them by reasoned arguments; and, finally, that such principles are not dogmatic, since they are not claimed to be demonstrative. In short, there is a middle ground between individual taste and arbitrary law, and it is in this area that sound criticism ought to operate. Taken together, these three propositions constitute Dryden's general position as to the function and status of rules in criticism.

✠✠✠

Dryden's first argument, against the validity of taste as a criterion, is made in reply to Howard's statement that ''in the difference of *Tragedy* and *Comedy,* and of *Fars* it self, there can be no determination but by the Taste.'' After noting the ambiguities of this proposition, Dryden replies to what he takes to be its sense—''that betwixt one comedy or tragedy and another, there is no other difference but what is made by the liking or disliking of the audience.'' This statement, which seems to reject all objective standards, Dryden flatly denies:

> The liking or disliking of the people gives the play the denomination of good or bad, but does not really make or constitute it such. To please the people ought to be the poet's aim, because plays are made for their delight; but it does not follow that they are always pleased with good plays, or that the plays which please them are always good. The humour of the people is now for Comedy; therefore, in hope to please them, I write comedies rather than serious plays: and so far their taste prescribes to me: but it does not follow from that reason, that Comedy is to be preferred before Tragedy in its own nature; for that which is so in its own

nature cannot be otherwise, as a man cannot but be a rational creature: but the opinion of the people may alter, and in another age, or perhaps in this, serious plays may be set up above comedies.[8]

This argument rests upon the assumption that the value of a work of art is entirely independent of opinion. Each work and each kind has an unchanging intrinsic value, which would be the same "were there neither judge, taste, nor opinion in the world," and the function of criticism is to judge each in accordance with its real worth. But, since this real value is not determined by opinion, the liking or disliking of the people cannot be the criterion by which it is judged. Taste can have no authority, for real value "cannot be otherwise" than it is, while taste is constantly changing; to depend upon taste is to be at the mercy of whim and caprice. In order to be valid, therefore, criticism requires an external rule, some standard or measure which is independent of opinion.

Those who believe (with the majority) that Dryden's thought was radically inconsistent, varying without pattern from year to year, may find this passage unconvincing as evidence of Dryden's permanent views. If, as the *Defence* certainly shows, Dryden believed in 1668 that uncontrolled taste had no authority in criticism, this fact would not necessarily prevent an appeal to taste in his other writings. On this point, however, Dryden's position did not change; he returns again and again to the assertion that taste in itself has no validity or authority but must always be checked and guided by some objective criterion of poetic worth.

His attack upon the taste of the people as we see it in the *Defence* is repeated in many other works. In the *Essay of Dramatic Poesy* itself, he had already said emphatically, "If by the people you understand the multitude, the *hoi polloi*, 'tis no matter what they think; they are sometimes in the right, sometimes in the wrong: their judgment is a mere lottery."[9] In the prefaces to *An Evening's Love* (1671) and to *All for Love* (1678), he again expresses his contempt for the popular audience; their applause is valueless, he says, because "the crowd cannot be presumed to have more than a gross instinct, of what pleases or displeases them."[10] The same attitude is shown in the dedication of *The Spanish Friar,* during the 1680s, and again in the *Discourse on Satire* in the 1690s, the last decade of Dryden's life.[11] The reason for this contempt, though clear in all these passages, is most explicitly stated in the preface to *Troilus and Cressida* (1679), when he attacks "that audience which loves Poetry, but understands it not."[12] Having no ground but instinct, the people's opinion proves nothing as to the real merit of a poem or play.

Although the theoretical basis of these remarks seems clear, they might perhaps be discounted as an expression of mere class prejudice. But the same idea appears elsewhere in a more general form, without application to any particular social class. Dryden distinguishes in several places between a "blind admirer" and a true critic.[13] The blind admirer, whether in the stalls or in the upper gallery, is distinguished from a true critic by his lack of understanding. Such men, though often enthusiastic lovers of poetry, judge it without discrimination, by a mere "gross instinct" of what pleases. They know what they like, as we say, but cannot explain why. Such men are to be found in all parts of society; a lack of principle, though characteristic of the mob, is to be found in every class. The true critic, by contrast, not only loves poetry but understands it, too; he is able to defend his inclination by his reason, because he admires not "blindly" but "knowingly."[14] As a result, his views are likely to be both sound and convincing; in the long run, since they are grounded on principle, they will win out. Such views, Dryden says, are "of God."[15]

This idea is most fully developed in the dedication of Dryden's *Aeneis* (1697), where he adapts from the French critic De Segrais an analysis of the reading public into three groups. The classification is based upon capacity for true judgment, which is assumed to depend not on sensitivity or enthusiasm but on understanding and a grasp of principle. The first two groups, having either no principles or very inadequate ones, have but little capacity of right judgment. The third and highest group, which is also the smallest, includes the "best judges," the *judices natos*. This is the part of the audience which Virgil, in common with all true poets, had particularly wished to please:

> . . . the most judicious: souls of the highest rank, and truest understanding. These are few in number; but whoever is so happy as to gain their approbation can never lose it, because they never give it blindly. Then they have a certain magnetism in their judgment, which attracts others to their sense. Every day they gain some new proselyte, and in time become the Church.[16]

Their judgments are sound and enduring because they are never given blindly, out of mere taste, instinct, or subjective impression. The essence of true criticism, as distinguished from a blind enthusiasm for poetry, is an appeal beyond taste to the enduring criteria of reasoned principle.

The second of Dryden's arguments against Howard is a proof that objective criteria can actually be established. Howard had claimed that "the general rules laid down for Playes" were wholly undemonstrable and groundless, because "the great foundation that is laid to build upon is nothing, as it is generally stated."[17] If Dryden's attack on taste was to stand, it was necessary to defend the ground or foundation on which the rules were to rest. He had shown that they were necessary, if critical judgment was to conform to real literary value; he must now show that they are possible.

Dryden's proof is based upon the nature of an art, as he conceived it:

> . . . let us consider what this great foundation is, which he says is nothing, as it is generally stated. I never heard of any other foundation of Dramatic Poesy than the imitation of Nature; neither was there ever pretended any other by the Ancients or Moderns, or me, who endeavour to follow them in that rule. This I have plainly said in my definition of a play; that it is a just and lively image of human nature, &c. Thus the foundation, as it is generally stated, will stand sure, if this definition of a play be true; if it be not, he ought to have made his exception against it, by proving that a play is not an imitation of Nature, but somewhat else, which he is pleased to think it.
>
> But 'tis very plain, that he has mistaken the foundation for that which is built upon it, though not immediately: for the direct and immediate consequence is this; if Nature be to be imitated, then there is a rule for imitating Nature rightly; otherwise there may be an end, and no means conducing to it.[18]

This argument assumes that an art is a skill directed to some end and that the existence of an end implies some means of attaining it. Rules of poetic production, formulating the means appropriate to attain the poet's end, are therefore inherent in the nature of poetry as an art; and these same rules provide the standards by which the products of his art are to be judged. If the end is to imitate nature, this aim constitutes the foundation upon which the rules, as means to that end, may be erected.

This argument, like that against the validity of uncontrolled taste, appears in Dryden's later works as well as in his reply to Howard. The conception of an art, which provides the major premise of this argument, is to be found almost everywhere in his critical writings. It is implied, for example, in his use of the term "artificial" in praise of a poet's work, or "inartificial" in condemnation.[19] It appears also in the familiar distinctions between nature and art, genius and skill, or fancy and judgment. With other critics of the neoclassical period, Dryden assumes that good poetry cannot be composed without genius, a creative power implanted in the poet by nature; but he always contends that true poetry requires, in addition, the judgment to "manage" this power, to apply it with skill to the task at hand.[20]

The same idea of art is expressed metaphorically in several places. Dryden compares the poet to a gunsmith or watchmaker, a wrestler, a physician, and an architect or builder.[21] The inference drawn from all these analogies is the

necessity of skill; and in the last two, more specifically, of skill based on
theoretical insight or knowledge. As Dryden says in the preface to *An
Evening's Love,* the writer of farce—a type of the bad poet—is like a
mountebank doctor, a mere "empiric"; for even if he succeeds, it is by
inferior means and without understanding what he does. The good poet, on
the other hand, is like the true physician: he understands the principles of his
art, the reasons for what he does and the causes of his success. "What the one
performs by hazard, the other does by skill."[22] Or, again, in condemning
plays written without a plan, Dryden says that poets who succeed in such
undertakings "ought to have sacrificed to Fortune, not to the Muses."[23] To
succeed by chance is no credit to an artist, for discrimination in the choice of
means is inherent in the very definition of an art. For Dryden, if not for some
critics of later times, a poet without art is a contradiction in terms.

In its complete form, as a proof of the existence of standards, Dryden's
argument against Howard reappears in his *Parallel of Poetry and Painting*
(1695). In this essay, which was prefixed to Dryden's translation of Du
Fresnoy's poem *De Arte Graphica,* Dryden commends his author as "one who
perfectly understood the rules of painting; and the surest to inform the
judgment of all who loved this noble art."[24] Taking Du Fresnoy's rules as
authoritative for painting, Dryden presents an extended parallel between the
sister arts: first, in their ends and their kinds, which are the same or very
similar, and then in their means, which are analogous. The comparison is
fruitful because both are arts and because, as such, they proceed by parallel
paths toward a common goal: "I must now consider them, as they are great
and noble arts; and as they are arts, they must have rules, which may direct
them to their common end."[25] The end in both arts is to please, and the
general rule for attaining it is the imitation of nature, which is "justly
constituted as the general, and indeed the only, rule of pleasing, both in
Poetry and Painting."[26] Upon this general rule, as a foundation, the more
specific rules are grounded; they formulate the various subordinate or
particular causes by which the artist's purpose may be effected:

> Having thus shewn that imitation pleases, and why it pleases in both
> these arts, it follows, that some rules of imitation are necessary to obtain
> that end; for without rules there can be no art, any more than there can be
> a house without a door to conduct you into it.[27]

In the *Parallel,* as in the *Defence,* Dryden argues that both poetry and
criticism—both performance and judgment—are founded on rational
principles. Considered by one as rules of production, by the other as standards
of evaluation, these principles were essential to the perfection of both. Poetry
deserved to be called an art when it achieved its purpose by rationally

determined means, and criticism was sound when it judged the poet's performance by the appropriateness of these means to the chosen end. If poetry were not an art, there could be no such standards in criticism; but, since it is an art, its rules provide the canons of a rational artistic judgment.

It was Dryden, according to Dr. Johnson, who first established this view in England. Before his time, "audiences applauded by instinct, and poets perhaps often pleased by chance," but Dryden "taught us to determine upon principle the merit of composition." This conception of his historic mission is confirmed by Dryden himself in the *Discourse on Satire,* published in 1693. Looking back some twenty-five years to his apprentice days in criticism, Dryden says that in the *Essay of Dramatic Poesy* he had tried to draw "the outlines of an art, without any living master to instruct me in it." In England at that time, the art of poetry had been praised but not studied:

> Shakespeare, who created the stage among us, had rather written happily, than knowingly and justly, and Johnson, who, by studying Horace, had been acquainted with the rules, yet seemed to envy to posterity that knowledge, and, like an inventor in some useful art, to make a monopoly of his learning.[28]

It was a primitive time—"before the use of the loadstone, or knowledge of the compass." Dryden's achievement, as he himself conceived it, had been to teach those arts to his countrymen: to show, both by example and by argument, that rules were essential to poetry and that in these same rules might be found the objective criteria of a sound and reasonable criticism. Dr. Johnson's discussion is, in fact, hardly more than a paraphrase of Dryden's own statement in the *Discourse on Satire*.

If this conclusion has been denied by many students of Dryden, the reason probably lies in a gratuitous assumption that rules are inherently opposed to the true spirit of poetry. When Saintsbury wrote that Dryden aimed at delight, truth, justice, nature, and poetry and let the rules take care of themselves, he obviously assumed that rules were incompatible with these positive qualities. But Dryden's view was very different. To him delight was the end of poetry, the imitation of nature its most general and basic means; the more specific rules were simply less general means to the same end. They were not incompatible with delight, nature, or poetry; they were, in fact, an important source of these effects. Without them, in his view, poetry was not an art, and criticism had no criteria.

More generally, Saintsbury's misunderstanding of Dryden may be ascribed to his failure to transcend the limitations of his own critical position. As Dorothy Richardson has shown, Saintsbury was a part of the "art for art's sake" movement; his views were formed under the influence of Pater and

Swinburne, Gautier, Baudelaire, and Flaubert.[29] He often seems to have valued the older critics insofar as they anticipated his own ideas, and he sometimes found these ideas where they did not actually exist. This was the case, I think, in his treatment of Dryden. Saintsbury himself believed that the best, if not the only, criterion of poetry was "that immediate and magical effect on the senses of the mind—that direct touch of the poetic nerve,"[30] and he read this impressionism into Dryden. The wish, it seems, was father to the thought.

❧❧❧❧

The third and last part of Dryden's reply to Howard brings us to our second main question. Assuming that rules are necessary in criticism, what is the intellectual status of these criteria? On what sort of evidence do they rest? Can they be established demonstratively, or do they admit some degree of uncertainty? On this problem we part company with Saintsbury and Johnson, since they did not discuss it, and turn to Professor Bredvold, whose conception of Dryden as a skeptic has a direct bearing on the question.

According to Howard, Dryden wanted to govern poetry by dictatorial prescription. "Things that are not Mathematical," in Howard's opinion, ought to be governed wholly by fancy or individual preference; Dryden's attempt to judge poetry by rule constituted a dogmatic infringement of the poet's liberty. But Dryden denies any dictatorial intention. He had made no claim of certainty for the rules laid down in the *Essay of Dramatic Poesy*. It was a "sceptical dialogue," presenting several different views, with the reasons which could be offered in support of each, but making no attempt either to reconcile these views or to judge among them:

> He is here pleased to charge me with being magisterial, as he has done in many other places of his preface; therefore, in vindication of myself, I must crave leave to say, that my whole discourse was sceptical, according to that way of reasoning which was used by Socrates, Plato, and all the Academics of old, which Tully and the best of the Ancients followed, and which is imitated by the modest inquisitions of the Royal Society. That it is so, not only the name will show, which is *an Essay*, but the frame and composition of the work. You see it is a dialogue sustained by persons of several opinions, all of them left doubtful, to be determined by the readers in general; and more particularly deferred to the accurate judgment of my Lord Buckhurst, to whom I made a dedication of my book.[31]

Of course Dryden had his own convictions, which were voiced in the *Essay* by his spokesman Neander, but these convictions were not forced upon the reader. His own views, like those of the other speakers, were presented as "problematical," and the reader was expected, with Lord Buckhurst, to determine the issue "in favour of which part you shall judge most reasonable."[32] Dryden considered his position reasonable, but he did not claim that its validity had been conclusively established.

The distinction which Dryden had in mind here is illustrated concretely in connection with his argument, already quoted above, in support of the existence of rules: "If Nature is to be imitated, then there is a rule for imitating Nature rightly; otherwise there may be an end, and no means conducing to it." He then goes on:

> Hitherto I have proceeded by demonstration; but as our divines, when they have proved a Deity, because there is order, and have inferred that this Deity ought to be worshipped, differ afterwards in the manner of the worship; so having laid down, that Nature is to be imitated, and that proposition proving the next, that then there are means which conduce to the imitating of Nature, I dare proceed no further positively; but have only laid down some opinions of the Ancients and Moderns, and of my own, as means which they used, and which I thought probable for the attaining of that end.[33]

Dryden distinguishes in this passage between two degrees of certainty, the demonstrative and the probable. Although the existence of rules of some sort seemed to him demonstrable, the arguments in support of particular rules were all of a merely probable order. They were to be received, therefore—as he says elsewhere in another connection—"with a doubtful Academical assent, or rather an inclination to assent to probability."[34] Thus he agrees with Howard that mathematical certainty is unattainable in criticism, but he contends that individual fancy is not the only alternative. Rejecting both taste and demonstration, he finds a mean between the extremes in the realm of probable arguments. Since the rules are confessed to be merely probable, his position could not fairly be called dogmatic; on the other hand, since they had sufficient plausibility to justify assent, he also avoided the opposite extreme of anarchic individualism.

The source of this view, according to Bredvold, is the skeptical tradition which descended from Pyrrho of Elis through Sextus Empiricus and Cicero to Montaigne, Charron, Sir Thomas Browne, and others, and so to Dryden and his contemporaries. Bredvold shows that Dryden was acquainted with this tradition and that he makes use of skeptical arguments against reason in several of his works, especially in the religious and political writings. I believe, however, that Dryden's position can and should be dissociated quite clearly from that of historic Pyrrhonism; while he agreed with the skeptics at some points, he differed from them at others. The true source of his "problematical" way of thinking, in my opinion, lies in a quite different quarter.

It is important, first of all, to distinguish between two types of skeptical philosophy: the "probabilism" illustrated in ancient times by Carneades, and the more thoroughgoing skepticism of Pyrrho and Sextus Empiricus.[35] This distinction is much emphasized by Sextus, our chief source of information about Greek skeptical thought. In the opening chapter of the *Hypotyposes,* he differentiates three main types of philosophic system: the Dogmatic, including Aristotle, Epicurus, and the Stoics; the Academic, illustrated by Cleitomachus and Carneades; and the Pyrrhonic or truly skeptical. As he explains in a later chapter, the Academic philosophers were skeptical as far as they denied that things can be "apprehended" or known with certainty. But they differed from the Pyrrhonists in recognizing several degrees of uncertainty, ranging from the improbable (or seemingly false) to the probable, the probable and tested, and, finally, the probable, tested, and "irreversible." On this basis, using probability as the guide of life, a man might reasonably assent, in practice, to many things that were not "apprehensible." From the point of view of Sextus and the extreme Pyrrhonians, the Academic writers were dogmatists in disguise.[36]

This distinction is collapsed by Cicero, who identifies not only the later Academics but even Socrates and Plato with the skeptical sect. As against the dogmatic stoicism of his opponents, Cicero represents himself (in the *Academica*) as a skeptic; his guiding principle, however, is not a Pyrrhonic suspension of all belief but an Academic probabilism. As he says:

> Nor between us and those who suppose themselves to know [i.e., the Stoics and other dogmatists] is there any difference, except that they do not doubt that those things which they defend are true, while we accept many probabilities which are easily followed, but which we can scarcely claim to affirm.[37]

Near the close of the dialogue, in a passage which throws much light on Dryden's views, Cicero refutes the claim of Lucullus that without certainty there can be no basis for the arts. Although their principles cannot be "apprehended"—and must therefore be considered to be uncertain—Cicero contends that probable knowledge is quite sufficient for the arts. "We abolished,'' he says, ''what never existed, leaving, however, what was enough for them.''[38]

It is obvious, from his reply to Howard, that Dryden understood skepticism in Cicero's sense. Whether or not he knew Sextus, he did not distinguish, as Sextus did, between Academicism and true Skepticism. His *Essay of Dramatic Poesy* was skeptical, he says, because it was constructed ''according to that way of reasoning which was used by Socrates, Plato, and all the Academics of old, which Tully and the best of the Ancients followed, and which is imitated by the modest inquisitions of the Royal Society.''[39] He concedes, as Cicero does, that certainty is unattainable in criticism, but he contends, in opposition to Howard, that probabilities are sufficient for the establishment of rules. To Dryden, skepticism meant, at most, the probabilism of Cicero and the Academy; though skeptical in one sense, since he denied that demonstrative certainty could be attained in literary criticism, he was clearly not a Pyrrhonist in the sense defined by Sextus.

But Dryden must be dissociated in some degree even from Cicero and the probabilists. His critical method was formulated in terms of a distinction between demonstrative and probable reasoning. As with the parallel Ciceronian distinction between ''apprehension'' and probability, the immediate consequence of this disjunction is to establish probable arguments as a legitimate mode of reasoning; in this respect Dryden agrees with Cicero and the Academics against the Pyrrhonists. But Dryden's distinction did not eliminate all intellectual certainty; on some questions, even outside mathematics, demonstration seemed to him possible. In theology, as we have seen, he counted the argument from design as a demonstration; and in criticism, while particular rules were always merely probable, the existence of rules in general seemed to him certain.[40] For Cicero, on the other hand, certainty existed nowhere; no proposition could be ''apprehended,'' and all arguments were merely probable. At this point Dryden differs radically from skeptics of all varieties.

The source of Dryden's way of reasoning should be sought, therefore, in some other tradition. The most plausible origin, in my opinion, is to be found in the logical treatises of Aristotle. Aristotle distinguishes in many places between ''science'' and ''dialectic.'' The method of science, as elaborated in the *Analytics,* is demonstration, which provides, with intuitive reason, the only grounds of certain knowledge; the method of dialectic, a process of reasoning from probable premises, yields only tentative or approximative results.[41] The appropriate method, in each department of inquiry, is determined by the nature of its subject matter; dialectic, though an inferior method, is necessarily and properly employed in the sciences which deal with variable things. Thus ethics, for example, must be content with probabilities:

> We must be content, then, in speaking of such subjects and with such premisses to indicate the truth roughly and in outline, and in speaking about things which are only for the most part true and with premisses of the same kind to reach conclusions that are no better. In the same spirit, therefore, should each type of statement be *received;* for it is the mark of an educated man to look for precision in each class of things just so far as the nature of the subject admits; it is evidently equally foolish to accept probable reasoning from a mathematician and to demand from a rhetorician scientific proof.[42]

In a loose sense, as denying the possibility of an ethical "science," this statement might be called skeptical. Its effect, however, is the opposite of skeptical; for it saves demonstrative certainty in some fields, while at the same time justifying probable arguments and tentative or approximative results in others.

This distinction is preserved, through various transmutations, in the main tradition of modern logic. In the handbooks of the early seventeenth century, it is sometimes phrased as a distinction between Science and Opinion; the former employs demonstration, which "consisteth of necessary, certaine, and infallible Propositions, and of such things as cannot be otherwise," but the method of proof in matters of opinion is the "Dialecticall Syllogisme," which is "made of probable and credible Propositions." Opinion does not give rise to certainty but is "knowledge of things casuall, which may be sometime false, sometime true."[43] In a somewhat different form, the distinction is preserved even in the antischolastic "new" logics of Dryden's maturity. It appears in the *Port-Royal Logic,* a classic of the Cartesian reformation in philosophy, as a weapon against both Pyrrhonism and Academicism. True reason, the authors say,

> places all things in the rank which belongs to them; it questions those which are doubtful, rejects those which are false, and acknowledges, in good faith, those which are evident without being embarrassed by the vain reasons of the Pyrrhonists, which never could, even in the minds of those who proposed them, destroy the reasonable assurance we have of many things.[44]

Another formulation, obviously influenced by Locke, is given to the distinction by Isaac Watts, a generation later:

Where the Evidence of the Agreement or Disagreement of the Ideas is so strong and plain, that we cannot forbid nor delay our Assent; the Proposition is call'd *certain,* as *every Circle hath a Centre; the World did not create it self. An Assent to such* Propositions is honour'd with the name of *Knowledge.*

But when there is any Obscurity upon the Agreement or Disagreement of the Ideas, so that the Mind does not clearly perceive it, and is not compell'd to assent or dissent, then the Proposition, in a proper and philosophical Sense, is call'd *doubtful* or *uncertain;* as *the Planets are inhabited; the Souls of Brutes are mere Matter; the World will not stand a thousand Years longer;* Dido *built the City of* Carthage, &c. Such *uncertain* Propositions are call'd *Opinions.*[45]

It is notable that Watts illustrates demonstration by geometry and, in theology, by a version of the argument from design: *"the World did not create it self."*

The philosophers and scientists of Dryden's period make active use of the distinction between demonstrative and probable proofs; they, too, employ it for an explicitly antiskeptical purpose. Meric Casaubon, for example, describes rational belief as a mean between the "vicious extremities" of credulity and incredulity—between superstition and skepticism. Sound reasoners distinguish between probability, the "ordinary grounds of reason," and "certain knowledge, or science," which is grounded on the knowledge of causes; employing each type of evidence as it is appropriate, human reason is able to discover truth in all things natural, civil, and divine.[46] Closer to Dryden are Glanvill and Boyle, the apologists for the Royal Society. Like Dryden, these men called themselves skeptics; however, they preserve certainty—in some fields and under proper safeguards—by a distinction between demonstrative and probable arguments. A probabilist in natural science and in many other fields of thought, Glanvill specifically admits demonstration in mathematics and in divinity: "Our religious *foundations* are fastened at the pillars of the *intellectual* world, and the grand *Articles* of our Belief as demonstrable as *Geometry.*"[47] A similar conclusion is defended by Locke in Book IV of the *Essay concerning Human Understanding.* True "knowledge," which is certain, may be attained either by direct intuition or by demonstration; where these are impossible, the mind must depend upon probability as the ground of "judgment" or "assent." Like Dryden, Glanvill, Boyle, and Watts, Locke does not limit demonstration to mathematics: though knowledge is admittedly "very short and scanty," demonstration is possible wherever the agreement of two ideas with some third, intermediate idea can be intuitively perceived.[48] According to Locke, this definition permits a demonstrable foundation for the rules of morality, as well as certain knowledge of the existence of God.[49] Here he claims rather more for demonstration than many of his contemporaries were willing to do.

In general, these statements differ markedly both from Aristotle's formulation and from each other; they disagree as to the nature of demonstration and also as to the spheres of its legitimate application. On the essential point, however, they are closer to each other and to Aristotle than they are to any version of the skeptical or academic philosophies; though un-Aristotelian in several respects, all these writers distinguish between probable and demonstrative proofs and use the distinction to guarantee certainty in some fields of thought. Their debt to Aristotle is explicitly acknowledged by Boyle and Tillotson,[50] and it seems equally clear in Glanvill, Locke, and Dryden.

Whatever the source of Dryden's method of reasoning, it is not skeptical in spirit or intent. His criticism, as Johnson recognized, is a criticism by rule. In this field, as in religion and politics, his fundamental aim was to establish some kind of objective standards as a check against the anarchy of individual preference and opinion. In opposition to the antinomianism of Howard, he argued that sound criticism requires the use of objective rules or canons, grasped by the understanding and supported by reasoned arguments; he found these rules in the means which reason and experience had shown to be conducive to the ends of poetry.[51] He agreed with Cicero that certainty can never be attained in criticism but that probability is a sufficient basis for the arts; the rules, therefore, are tentative or hypothetical and are to be accepted with a "doubtful academical assent." Here we may agree with Bredvold. But this conception of critical method is formulated by Dryden in terms of a distinction between demonstration and probability. For him, as for many others in his time, this distinction was antiskeptical in intention and effect; by recognizing degrees of knowledge, proportional to the nature of evidence, they were able to save reason from the attacks both of the Pyrrhonists and the Academics. In criticism, we must conclude, Dryden believed that rational principles were both necessary and possible: literary evaluation, as he understood it, was a process of rational judgment, which determined the merit of works and writers by the application of probable rules.

Notes

1. George Saintsbury, *A History of Criticism and Literary Taste in Europe* 2d ed. (London and Edinburgh: W. Blackwood, 1905), II, 388-89.

2. Samuel Johnson, *Lives of the English poets,* ed. G. B. Hill (Oxford: Clarendon Press, 1905), I, 410-11; cf. also p. 366.

3. Margaret Sherwood, *Dryden's Dramatic Theory and Practice* (New Haven: Yale University Press, 1914), pp. 27-29, and passim.

4. L. I. Bredvold, *The Intellectual Milieu of John Dryden* (Ann Arbor: University of Michigan Press, 1934), especially pp. 11-15, 70-72, 108-10, 115-20, 132-34.

5. L. I. Bredvold, *The Best of Dryden* (New York: T. Nelson & Sons, 1933), pp. xxxiv-xxxviii.

6. For a similar judgment of Howard compare Paul Spencer Wood, "The Opposition to Neo-Classicism in England between 1660 and 1700," PMLA, 43 (1928),190-91. For other and generally more favorable opinions see D. D. Arundell, *Dryden and Howard* (Cambridge: Cambridge University Press, 1929), pp. ix-xi; Paul Hamelius, *Die Kritik in der englischen Literatur des 17. und 18. Jahrhunderts* (Leipzig, 1897), p. 48; and James E. Routh, *The Rise of English Classical Criticism* (New Orleans, 1915), p. 22.

7. J. E. Spingarn, ed., *Critical Essays of the Seventeenth Century,* (Oxford: Clarendon Press, 1908), II, 106-7.

8. W. P. Ker, ed., *Essays of John Dryden* (Oxford: Clarendon Press, 1926), I, 120-21.

9. Ibid., p. 100.

10. Ibid. pp. 195, 135-36.

11. Ibid., I,246, and II,50-51.

12. Ibid., I,221, 226.

13. Ibid., pp. 138, 196.

14. Ibid., II,115.

15. Ibid., pp. 225, 258.

16. Ibid., pp. 223-26.

17. Spingarn, II,108.

18. Ker, I,123.

19. Ibid, p. 49.

20. Ibid, p. 220; cf. also pp. 8, 106-7, 228-29; II,45, 92-93, 138, and passim.

21. Ibid., I, 147, 220, 136, 46.

22. Ibid., p. 136.

23. Ibid., p. 46.

24. Ibid., II, 115.

25. Ibid., p. 133.

26. Ibid., p. 137.

27. Ibid., p. 138.

28. Ibid., pp. 16-17.

29. Dorothy Richardson, "Saintsbury and Art for Art's Sake in England," PMLA, 59 (1944),243-60.

30. Quoted in ibid., p. 259, n.74.

31. Ker, I, 124. Cf. Phillip Harth, *Contexts of Dryden's Thought* (Chicago: University of Chicago Press, 1968), Ch. i, "The Sceptical Critic;" and Dryden, *Works,* Vol. XVII, ed. Samuel H. Monk and A. E. Wallace Maurer (Berkeley and Los Angeles: University of California Press, 1970), p. 348.

32. Ker, I, 23-27 ("Epistle Dedicatory").

33. Ibid., p. 123.

34. Dryden, "Life of Plutarch," in *Works,* XVII, 253.

35. Bredvold recognizes this distinction (*Intellectual Milieu,* p. 18) but does not apply it in his

analysis of Dryden. "Pyrrhonic" and "skeptical" are used throughout his study as synonymous terms. That Dryden did make a distinction between them is clear from another passage in the "Life of Plutarch," where he contrasts "the *Pyrrhonians,* or grosser sort of *Scepticks,* who bring all certainty in question" and the Academists, who avoided such a pessimistic and negative epistemology by "inclining the ballance to that hand, where the most weighty reasons, and probability of truth were visible." *(Works,* XVII, 249)

36. Sextus Empiricus *Hypotyposes* i.33, 220-35; cf. also Montaigne, "Apologie de Raimond Sebond," *Essais,* ed. Pierre Villey (Paris, 1930), II, 337-39, 455-57; Antoine Arnauld, *Port-Royal Logic,* Part IV, Ch. i; and David Hume, *Enquiry concerning Human Understanding,* Ch. xii.

37. "Nec inter nos et eos, qui se scire arbitrantur, quicquam interest, nisi quod illi non dubitant quin ea vera sint, quae defendunt, nos probabilia multa habemus, quae sequi facile, adfirmare vix possumus." (Cicero *Academica priora* ii.3, 8)

38. "Sed quo modo tu, si nihil comprehendi posset, artificia concidere dicebas neque mihi dabas id, quod probabile esset, satis magnam vim habere ad artis, sic ego nunc tibi refero artem sine scientia esse non posse. An pateretur hoc Zeuxis aut Phidias aut Polyclitus, nihil se scire, cum in eis esset tanta sollertia? Quod si eos docuisset aliquis quam vim habere disceretur scientia, desinerent irasci: ne nobis quidem suscenserent, cum didicissent id tollere nos, quod nusquam esset, quod autem satis esset ipsis relinquere." (Cic. *Acad. pr.* ii. 47, 146)

39. Ker, I, 124. Dr. Johnson, with characteristic precision, describes the *Essay* as "artfully variegated with successive representations of opposite probabilities" *(Lives,* I, 412). Even when only one line of argument is presented, Dryden often makes clear that the evidence is not conclusive; his opinions are "set not up for a standard to better judgments," and those who think differently are free to present their reasons (Ker, II, 81-82; cf. I, 190, and II, 53, 248).

40. Ker, I, 123; cf. also *Conquest of Granada,* Part II, Act IV, sc. iii *(Works,* ed. Walter Scott and George Saintsbury (Edinburgh: W. Paterson, 1882-93), IV, 190): "By reason man a godhead may. discern/ But how he would be worshipped cannot learn" (cited by Bredvold, *Intellectual Milieu,* p. 117). Elsewhere, however, he states that we have "the highest probabilities" for religion, but can demonstrate nothing ("Life of Lucian," *Works,* XVIII, 66; cf. preface to *Religio Laici*).

41. Aristotle *Prior Analytics* i.1. 24a22-b16; *Posterior Analytics* i. 1. 71a5-11, 71b9-23; *Topics* 100a29, 104a8; *Nichomachean Ethics* vi. 3. 1139b 18-36; and passim.

42. *Eth. Nich.* (Oxford trans.) i. 3. 1094b18-28.

43. M. Blundevile, *The Arte of Logick* (London, 1617), Book V, Chaps. xvii, xx, xxi. Cf. also Thomas Spencer, *The Art of Logick* (London, 1628), Part II, Chaps. liv, lv; Robert Sanderson, *Logicae Artis Compendium,* 4th ed. (Oxford, 1640), Chap. xvii; Gerard Vossius, *De Logices et Rhetoricae* (1668), Chap. xiii.

44. *The Port-Royal Logic,* trans. Thomas S. Baynes, 8 ed. (Edinburgh: Sutherland and Knox, n.d.), pp. 4-5; cf. pp. 299-308.

45. Isaac Watts, *Logick,* 4th ed. (London, 1731), p. 175; see also pp. 253-59, and passim.

46. Meric Casaubon, *Of Credulity and Incredulity* (London, 1668), pp. 6-7.

47. Joseph Glanvill, *Scepsis Scientifica,* ed. John Owen (London: Kegan Paul, 1885), pp. 179-80. See also "Of Scepticism, and Certainty," pp. 44-51, and "The Agreement of Reason and Religion," pp. 5-6, 20, and passim, in *Essays on Several Important Subjects in Philosophy and Religion* (London, 1676). Cf. Robert Boyle, "The Reconcileableness of Reason and Religion," *Theological Works,* ed. Richard Boulton (London, 1715), I, 417-29; and John Tillotson, "Preface," *Works,* 8th ed. (London, 1720), fol. B1v-B2r; cf. also p. 585. Harth's admirable first chapter, which defines Dryden's skepticism very much as it is defined here, particularly stresses the resemblance between Dryden's empirical and probabilistic conception of method in literary criticism and the beliefs of Glanvill, Boyle, and other spokesmen for the Royal Society about method in the natural sciences. *(Contexts of Dryden's Thought,* pp. 8-15, 30-31)

48. John Loche, *Essay concerning Human Understanding,* ed. A. C. Fraser, (Oxford: Clarendon Press, 1894), Book IV, Chaps. i-iii and xiv-xvi.

49. Ibid., Chap. iii, pp. 208, 212; cf. also Chap. x.

50. See the passages cited above, n.47.

51. Cf. John C. Sherwood, "Dryden and the Rules: The Preface to *Troilus and Cressida,*" *Comparative Literature,* 2 (1950), 73-83; idem, "Dryden and the Rules: The Preface to the *Fables,*" *JEGP,* 52 (1953),13-26; and "Precept and Practice in Dryden's Criticism," *JEGP,* 48(1969),432-40.

3

Perception, Imagination, and Feeling in Dryden's Criticism

The preceding essay, though written long ago, still seems to me to present a valid account of one side of the critical process as Dryden understood and practiced it: its *reasoned* aspect, the intellectual or rational side. But criticism surely must have another component, not touched on in that essay. In all ages, men have reasoned about literary works in reaching conclusions about their aesthetic value, but their first impact upon the critic, as on any ordinary reader or theatergoer, is more direct and immediate. Like other art objects, a literary work is a particular, concrete thing, which we necessarily experience, in the first instance, through our nonrational faculties, the responsive powers of perception, imagination, and emotion. Dryden recognized this fact, of course, and in judging any work throughout his long career as a critic, he always incorporates as primary data impressions of it which arise from these nonintellectual sources. Any account of the critical process as he conceived it must be incomplete, therefore, if this side of it is not adequately described. That is the missing element which I should like to supply here, isolating it so far as possible from the reasoned aspect and explaining the reciprocal relations between the two parts of the total process.

The three kinds of nonrational response will be taken up in turn, following the order given in the title. The procedure will be inductive, beginning each division or subdivision of the subject with a review of passages in which Dryden reports direct perceptual, imaginative, or emotional responses and reserving for the ends of the sections any limiting or qualifying concepts derived from the reasoned aspect of his criticism.

✠✠✠

In the interest of aesthetic sanity, it is well to distinguish clearly between literal and figurative statements about the role of perception in our experience of any of the arts. Literally speaking, the only senses which can be involved in our response to literature are hearing and sight. The first is necessarily involved because words—the distinctive vehicle, medium, or "means of imitation" in literary art—are sounds, which are or can be arranged by the poet in audible patterns, perceived by us through the ear. Because all literary works, including those written in prose, can always be read aloud, they are audible in a strictly literal meaning of the term. In this respect, as many aestheticians have observed, literature is akin to music; certainly no one would deny that the sound of the words, as we hear them, is an essential element in our experience of literature.

Literature is visible in the same strict sense in only one of its many forms: drama when performed in a theater. A theater audience does literally see the play, responding to the "spectacle," as Aristotle called it, which is provided by the stage setting, properties, and lighting, by the costumes, postures, movements, and facial expressions of the actors, and the like. In this one genre, therefore, as aestheticians once again have not failed to note, literature is akin to the visual arts of painting, sculpture, and architecture, in which the eye is the primary channel of experience. In the theater, of course, the audience not only sees the action unfolding before its eyes but also hears the words spoken by the actors. On that ground, some theorists have argued that performed drama is the most intense and comprehensive form of literature. Since no musical composition can be seen and no painting can be heard, it might even be contended that drama has greater power over the senses than any other art.

Dryden, as I say, was well aware of these commonplace observations and distinctions. In his critical writings, he regularly records impressions derived from perception. Hearing is basic in his response to all forms of literature, including those written in "the other harmony of prose,"[1] and sight in the literal sense is important in discussing dramatic works, designed for theatrical performance.

A word is a meaning attached by convention to a sound. In discussing the style of writers, whether ancient or modern, Dryden habitually applies three criteria of excellence, variously expressed as "apt, significant, and sounding,'' ''proper, sounding, and significant,'' or simply as ''significant and sounding'' (I, 15, 164, 248; II, 62). The aptness or propriety of words, as well as their significance or meaningfulness, are qualities predicated of language in its semantic dimension; such judgments are rational, depending on knowledge of the particular language being used and on inferences concerning the appropriateness of the words chosen to the intended meaning and the context. Whether a word is ''sounding,'' on the other hand, is a question concerning its phonetic character, which only the ear can judge. When words are marshaled in a series, it is the sense of hearing that perceives in them patterns of rhythm and rhyme, discriminating them as harmonious or ill-sounding, smooth or harsh, majestic or thundering, and these perceptual judgments are accompanied by varying degrees and kinds of pleasure or pain (I, 19, 118, 223-24, 227, 247, 268, etc.). Stichomythic repartee in a play is certainly not natural, Neander concedes in the *Essay of Dramatic Poesy*, but we delight in its quickness and wit, to which rhyme adds ''the last perfection.'' ''The cadency and sweetness of the rhyme leaves nothing in the soul of the hearer to desire'' (I, 103-4).

The role of hearing in Dryden's criticism can be most fully illustrated from his many discussions of Virgil. In more than thirty years of critical writing, from the preface to *Annus Mirabilis* (1667) to the preface to *The Fables* (1700), he almost never mentions the Roman poet without referring to the sweetness, harmony, and nobility of his versification (I, 55; II, 251). In the *Discourse on Satire* (1693), for example, he compares the versification of Virgil, Horace, and Juvenal:

> But versification and numbers are the greatest pleasures of poetry: Virgil knew it, and practiced both so happily, that, for aught I know, his greatest excellency is in his diction. In all other parts of poetry, he is faultless; but in this he placed his chief perfection. . . . When there is anything deficient in numbers and sound, the reader is uneasy and unsatisfied; he wants something of his complement, desires somewhat which he finds not: and this being the manifest defect of Horace, 'tis no wonder that, finding it supplied in Juvenal, we are more delighted with him. (II, 86)

The harmony of Virgil's numbers gave Dryden much trouble when he translated the *Aeneid*; their sweetness will not be drawn out into another language, and the wretched translator, being tied to his author's thoughts, ''must make what music he can in the expression; and for this reason, it cannot always be so sweet as that of the original'' (Dedication of the *Aeneis* [1697], II, 223, 228, 233).

As we noted above, the ear discriminates among the auditory effects of different works and writers, and these effects are accompanied by pleasure or pain, by different degrees and kinds of satisfaction or dissatisfaction. At the opposite extreme from Virgil, who is always musical, are bad poets like Holyday or Stapleton, pedantically attempting to translate Juvenal or Persius literally, line by line. Their crabbed verses not only offend the ear but do not even convey the meaning clearly:

> He [Holyday] was forced to crowd his verses with ill-sounding monosyllables, of which our barbarous language affords him a wild plenty. . . . His verses have nothing of verse in them, but only the worst part of it, the rhyme; and that, into the bargain, is far from good. But, which is more intolerable, by cramming his ill-chosen, worse-sounding monosyllables so close together, the very sense which he endeavors to explain is become more obscure than that of his author. . . . In Holyday and Stapleton, my ears, in the first place, are mortally offended; and then their sense is so perplexed, that I return to the original, as the more pleasing task, as well as the more easy. (*Discourse on Satire*, II, 113)

More complex auditory discriminations are made in Dryden's characterization of the *Faerie Queene* stanza, which he considers to be ill-chosen, yet "so numerous, so various, and so harmonious" that only Virgil and Waller have surpassed Spenser as makers of verses; or in his well-known description of Chaucer's verse, which is not harmonious to us, but has "the rude sweetness of a Scotch tune in it, which is natural and pleasing, though not perfect" (I, 28-29; II, 258-59). Butler's Hudibrastics, on the other hand, "give us a boyish kind of pleasure. It tickles awkwardly with a kind of pain, to the best sort of reader" (II, 105). The best sort of reader, in this context, is one with a sensitive and discriminating ear.

Even more striking as an example of Dryden's perceptual discriminations is his differentiation of the versification of Virgil and Ovid in the preface to *Sylvae* (1685). Two authors may be equally sweet and yet very different, he says, for "there is a great distinction to be made in sweetness, as in that of sugar and that of honey." If a translator is to convey some sense of his author's unique talent and character as a writer, as he should do, he must be aware of such subtle differences of manner and try to duplicate them in his translation. Virgil's verse is energetic, majestic, and perpetually varied, while Ovid's is smooth and sweet, but monotonous: "he is always, as it were, upon the hand-gallop, and his verse runs upon carpet ground" (I, 254-55). Repeating this comparison twelve years later in the dedication of the *Aeneis* (1697), Dryden says that Ovid's versification "cannot so properly be called sweet, as luscious'' (II, 215). But most translators level out these distinctions. Finding it difficult enough to achieve a tolerable degree of smoothness and harmony in their English numbers, they make the two poets sound ''so much alike, that, if I did not know the originals, I should never be able to judge by the copies which was Virgil, and which was Ovid.'' If a poet must have a ''musical ear,'' that capacity is equally necessary for the translator or critic; in the audible dimension of literature, ''the ear must preside'' for all three of them (I, 254, 268, 277).

These assertions may seem to claim an ultimate and independent authority in criticism for auditory perception, but that was not Dryden's view. Words are not merely sounds; they also carry meanings. If the ear must preside in our response to the phonetic dimension of language, rational judgment is required both to interpret the meanings correctly and to determine the appropriateness of the sounds to the sense. Dryden defines poetic wit as ''a propriety of thoughts and words; or, in other terms, thoughts and words elegantly adapted to the subject'' (*Apology for Heroic Poetry*, I, 190; cf. 270). Virgil, whose writings inspired that definition (I, 256), knew how to manage his vowels to best advantage, disposing them ''as his present occasions require''; the very sounds of his words ''have often somewhat that is connatural to the subject,'' and the majesty of his versification is not only immediately pleasing to the ear but suited to the grandeur and nobility of his thoughts (II, 216, 233; I, 17).[2]

The Horatian principle of propriety—that expression must be governed by thought, style by its subject, sound by sense—was so deeply ingrained in Dryden's thought that he had some difficulty, when he first attempted in the 1680s to write opera libretti, in reconciling the demands of that half-musical, half-literary form to his usual aesthetic assumptions. In the preface to *Albion and Albanius* (1685), an opera on which he collaborated with the French composer Grabut, he flounders about a good deal, seeking some way to save that fundamental rule. The recitative parts do not stretch it too far, but the *''songish part''* exacts a harmonious sweetness, to which the words must be accommodated; it ''must abound in the softness and variety of numbers; its principal intention being to please hearing rather than to gratify the understanding.'' It may seem preposterous, he says, that ''rhyme, on any consideration, should take the place of reason,'' but the writer of an opera must follow the laws laid down by the Italians, who first brought the new form to perfection. Even so, the librettist's command of language can do much to lessen the difficulty, if not to avoid it completely. ''The chief secret is the choice of words; and, by this choice, I do not here mean elegancy of expression, but propriety of sound, to be varied according to the nature of the subject.'' In practice, Dryden finds that the poet and the composer can often bring their distinct arts into harmony by a mutual compliance, one sometimes sacrificing potential beauties of meaning and verbal style to accommodate to the auditory beauties of the music, the other sometimes adjusting the sound to suit the thoughts and feelings expressed by the poet's words. He pays Grabut a warm tribute for his share in this collaborative effort:

> And let me have the liberty to add one thing, that he has so exactly expressed my sense in all places where I intended to move the passions, that he seems to have entered into my thoughts, and to have been the poet as well as the composer.

Though by no means satisfied that they have fully succeeded, he does feel that between them they have given their auditors some degree of the pleasures proper to both arts, and the best judges have applauded their achievement (I, 270-78).

Since sight, in a literal sense, enters into our experience of literature only in the theater, Dryden has fewer occasions to record visual impressions than he does to speak of auditory responses and discriminations. In two interesting passages, however, he links sight and hearing as the two sensory channels through which we experience a drama. The first passage recognizes that a play is addressed to those senses but treats the fact as neutral, because Dryden has a different kind of point to make; in the second passage, the sensory appeal of a drama is basic to its total effect. .

In the dedication of the *Aeneis*, Dryden compares epic with tragedy. Apparently because Homer preceded the Greek tragic poets by several centuries, he asserts that narrative poetry was earlier historically than dramatic forms:

> For the original of the stage was from the Epic Poem. Narration, doubtless, preceded acting, and gave laws to it: what at first was told artfully, was, in process of time, represented gracefully to the sight and hearing.

In a passage in the *Essay of Dramatic Poesy,* to be discussed later, Neander says that tragedy, being shown rather than told, gives the audience a more lively image of human nature than an epic poem does (I, 101). In the *Dedication,* however, Dryden does not pursue further the implications of his distinction between the narrative and dramatic methods, but instead goes on to discuss some of the "laws" carried over from the earlier kind to the later: the unities of action and time, the emotional and ethical effects. Far from arguing that the direct effect of drama upon the senses makes it more powerful than nondramatic forms, he contends that the epic poem is superior because of its greater length and comprehensiveness: "out of one Hercules were made infinity of pigmies," and "there is more virtue in one heroic poem than in many tragedies" (II, 156-59).

In the preface to *Tyrannic Love,* much earlier in his critical career (1670), Dryden places the emphasis the other way, stressing the power of a drama over the senses of hearing and sight, and the emotional and imaginative responses which they draw forth. He is arguing that religious subjects are not beyond the scope of dramatic poetry, which can serve piety as well as morality:

> By the harmony of words we elevate the mind to a sense of devotion, as our solemn music, which is inarticulate poesy, does in churches; and by the lively images of piety, adorned by action, through the senses allure the soul; which while it is charmed in a silent joy of what it sees and hears, is struck at the same time with a secret veneration of things celestial, and is wound up insensibly into the practice of that which it admires.[3]

Here the experience of an audience in the theater is described as totally nonrational, a direct sensory response of the ear to the harmony of words, analogous in effect to organ music in a church, and of the eye to the visible images conveyed by the appearance and movements of the actors on the stage. These not only allure and charm the soul with sensual joy but carry with them an appropriate emotional effect, elevating the mind to feelings of devotion, veneration, and admiration. In the final clause, Dryden even suggests that the intensity of the experience will continue to echo in the mind, motivating congruent behavior in real life, after the audience has left the theater. It is his most extreme and eloquent statement of the theater's power over our minds, the almost magical spell it can cast upon our senses and feelings.

However eloquent, such an account can hardly represent Dryden's full understanding of the way we respond to works of literary art, for even in seeing and hearing a performed drama, the most sensory of all the genres, something else must be involved in the process. His analogy between the effects of church music and the auditory effects of a verse play with a religious subject implies a difference as well as a resemblance: if instrumental music is "inarticulate," because it lacks words, the play is not. An audience watching a performance of *Tyrannic Love* responds not only to the visual appearance of the actress playing the part of St. Catherine and to the audible harmonies of the verses she speaks, but also to the meanings that her words express, from which the watchers infer her thoughts and feelings, her character and her pitiful situation. The "image of piety" produced in their minds by the play is the effect of a complex psychological process in which sensory perception, emotion, and intellection are simultaneously at work.

From other passages, in fact, we know that Dryden believed the sensual allure of the theater to be a danger, which can easily seduce and pervert sound critical judgment:

> In a play-house, everything contributes to impose upon the judgment; the lights, the scenes, the habits, and, above all, the grace of action, which is commonly the best where there is the most need of it, surprise the audience, and cast a mist upon their understandings; not unlike the cunning of a juggler, who is always staring us in the face, and overwhelming us with gibberish, only that he may gain the opportunity of making the cleaner conveyance of his trick.

Such charms are too often false beauties, "Delilahs of the theatre," no more lasting than a rainbow; "when the actor ceases to shine upon them, when he gilds them no longer with his reflection, they vanish in a twinkling" (Dedication of the *Spanish Friar* [1681], I, 245-46).[4]

Here, once again, we come upon Dryden's dividing line between the rational and the irrational aspects of the critical process. As we saw in the preceding essay, he thought that the mere liking or disliking of a play or a poem by a reader or critic proved nothing whatever as to its real artistic value. We begin to criticize, as Dryden understood criticism, only when we can "defend our inclination by our reason." Rational judgments, based on a true understanding of the ends intended by the poet and the means he has employed to achieve them, are the only opinions that are "of God," and in time become the church (II, 115, 223-26, 258). In the dedication of the *Spanish Friar,* after recognizing the hypnotic effect of the lights, scenes, and habits, he goes on to assert once again the same fundamental conviction. "Nothing but truth can long continue," he says, and to fix a lasting admiration we must judge the "hidden beauties of a play," which depend upon the propriety of thoughts and words, their suitability to the occasion, the subject, and the persons—questions which even the most discerning critic may be unable to answer under the powerful, though transient, enchantments of the theater (I, 245-49). What I did not make clear in my earlier essay is that those enchantments, perceptual and affective, provide data which a critic cannot ignore. They are Delilahs when they are not justified by real dramatic substance, offering nothing but a cheap gilding to cover the poet's ineptness.

But when they support and enhance the realization of the playwright's intention, they are true beauties, deserving the applause of the most rigorous critic.

❦❦❦

In turning from perception to imagination, we enter a trickier terrain, in which it is easy to go astray. An initial difficulty, though not a very serious one, concerns Dryden's use of the terms "imagination" and "fancy." In his important article " 'Distrust' of Imagination in English Neo-Classicism," Donald F. Bond asserts flatly that the two terms were used interchangeably throughout the seventeenth and eighteenth centuries.[5] Jensen's dictionary glosses the two terms as normally synonymous in Dryden's usage, but points out that in the early preface to *Annus Mirabilis* (1667) "imagination" is used synonymously with "wit" as a term referring to the poetic act or faculty as a whole, under which "invention," "fancy," and "elecution" are three parts, aspects, or "happinesses."[6] In a note on the same passage, Watson observes that this usage is eccentric, both for Dryden and for his contemporaries and successors.[7] Although the passage should be kept in mind as an exception, it seems safe to accept Bond's generalization as broadly correct; certainly there is nothing in Dryden's theories of either poetry or criticism that anticipates the distinction between imagination and fancy which is so fundamental in the aesthetics of Wordsworth and Coleridge.

Historians of criticism have had much to say about seventeenth- and eighteenth-century conceptions of the role of imagination in the creative process,[8] but they seldom discuss the functions it was thought to have in a reader's or a critic's reactions to literature. Recently, however, both Jensen and John M. Aden have recognized in their dictionaries that Dryden assigns an important role to that nonrational faculty in the process through which literary works are experienced and judged, as well as in that through which they are produced. Aden includes separate entries on "Fancy (Responsive)" and "Imagination (Responsive)," both of which are illustrated by quotations, supplemented by cross-references to other pertinent passages in Dryden's critical writings.[9] Jensen recognizes the same fact in one of his definitions of the term "Imagination," as used by Dryden: "The faculty (in a member of an audience or in a reader) which receives images and forms ideas and images corresponding to the quality of what is seen or heard . . . . Although the imagination here is receptive, it is not passive."[10]

The critical vocabulary current in the seventeenth and eighteenth centuries does not make a terminological distinction between the productive and the responsive imagination, since both were regarded as activities of the same faculty, covered in general English usage by the same term, but it was widely supposed that images formed in the mind of a reader were a vital part of ordinary literary experience. Dr. Johnson, for example, defines "imagery" in one of its senses as "representations in writing; such descriptions as force the image of the thing described upon the mind" (*Dictionary:* "Imagery," def. 4). Addison is even more explicit in his definition of the "secondary" pleasures of the imagination, which "flow from the ideas of visible objects, when the objects are not actually before the eye, but are called up into our memories, or formed into agreeable visions of things that are either absent or fictitious" (*Spectator,* no. 161). For Addison, life itself offers many "pleasures of the imagination" in this sense, but the specific subject of his series of essays is the imaginative delight arising from descriptions of objects and persons in poetic fictions. In *The Author's Apology for Heroic Poetry and Poetic License* (1677), Dryden himself calls this power "imaging":

> Imaging is, in itself, the very height and life of Poetry. It is, as Longinus describes it, a discourse, which, by a kind of enthusiasm, or extraordinary emotion of the soul, makes it seem to us that we behold those things which the poet paints, so as to be pleased with them, and to admire them. (I, 186; *On the Sublime* xv)

He hopes that his own poems will have this power over the minds of his readers; as he says in a passage quoted by Johnson, "I wish there may be in this poem any instance of good imagery" (I, 187).

In his judgments on other men's works, Dryden repeatedly uses imagery or imaging as a fundamental criterion of poetic excellence, especially in nondramatic works which "paint" people, places, and things, but do not present them for direct perception by the eyes and ears. Both Aden and Jensen quote or cite a number of examples, though they do not mention two which seem to me especially striking and representative. In the very early preface to *Annus Mirabilis,* Dryden says of Virgil:

> . . . When action or persons are to be described, when any such image is set before us, how bold, how masterly, are the strokes of Virgil! We see the objects he presents us with in their native figures, in their proper motions; but so we see them, as our own eyes could never have beheld them so beautiful in themselves. . . . See his *Tempest,* his *Funeral Sports,* his *Combat of Turnus and Aeneas:* and in his *Georgics,* which I esteem the divinest part of all his writings, the *Plague,* the *Country,* the *Battle of Bulls,* the labour of the *Bees,* and those many other excellent

images of Nature, most of which are neither great in themselves, nor
have any natural ornament to bear them up; . . . but the very sound of his
words have often somewhat that is connatural with the subject; and while
we read him, we sit, as in a play, beholding the scenes of what he
represents. (I, 16-17)

We are not actually in a theater, literally beholding these things, but the
images they stir in our minds are as vivid as if we actually saw them; through
the poet's art in selecting and heightening, they may indeed be much more
beautiful.

Ovid and Chaucer are other nondramatic poets who have the power to fill
the imagination with vivid pictures. Comparing them as descriptive poets,
Dryden says in the preface to *The Fables:*

For an example, I see Baucis and Philemon as perfectly before me as if
some ancient painter had drawn them; and all the Pilgrims in the
Canterbury Tales, their humors, their features, and the very dress, so
distinctly as if I had supped with them at the Tabard in Southwark. Yet
even there too the figures of Chaucer are much more lively, and set in a
better light; which though I have not time to prove, yet I appeal to the
reader, and am sure he will clear me from partiality (II, 255-56).

In these passages describing the response of readers or critics to nondramatic
works, Dryden implicitly defines the imagination in the same way that
Addison later defined it explicitly: as an image-making power of the mind
which forms agreeable visions of things that "are not actually before the
eye." As we can see from his appeal to his readers at the end, he assumes that
their imaginations will be as active as his own in reading Ovid, Chaucer, or
Virgil. They will make similar imaginative discriminations, and will be
delighted in proportion to the liveliness of their own impressions.

In watching a play, of course, we do literally behold the scenes which the
poet represents. One might think, then, that there was no need for imagination
in our response to a drama we are seeing and hearing in the theater. As a
number of passages show, however, Dryden believed that the imagination of a
theater audience is awake and active, though its role is more complex and less
easily defined in this kind of literary experience than it is in the experience of
nondramatic poems.

Among other passages illustrating his fourth definition of "imagination,"
Jensen cites three in the *Essay of Dramatic Poesy*. We may use the same
passages, together with one more from the same essay, to clarify further

Dryden's conception of the functions of the imagination in the criticism of drama. The terrain here is tricky indeed, for the four passages are assigned to different speakers, occur at different stages of the overall argument, and reach different conclusions. They are alike, however, in that all of them are reasoned arguments based upon a common premise, Lisideius's definition of a good play, which was accepted early in the debate by all four speakers as the "standing measure of their controversy." The operative criteria are two pairs of complementary terms, the "just" and the "lively," which are attributes of the "image of human nature" presented by a play, and "delight" and "instruction," which are the effects of that image on the audience (I, 35-36).[11] In Dryden's rhetorical, audience-oriented kind of theory, the second pair states the ends or purposes of a drama, the first pair the means by which the ends are achieved.[12] The four passages are pertinent to our interests because they all recognize that the response of the audience, from which the delight and instruction arise, involves perception, imagination, and emotion.

The first two passages, spoken by Lisideius and Neander in the climactic debate on the relative merits of French and English dramaturgical principles and practices, concern the use of "relations," narrative reports of events taking place offstage. In Lisideius' argument, the implied definition of the imagination, as it operates in the audience's response to those parts of a drama's action that are related, is the same Addisonian one that we have seen Dryden using in his criticism of nondramatic writers. In Neander's reply, the definition is broadened in order to account for our response to the whole dramatic action, the enacted as well as the narrated events.

Arguing that French dramatists use relations skilfully, managing them "with better judgment and more à propos than the English do," Lisideius applies to drama the distinction between showing and telling, representing and describing, which Neander repeats later in differentiating between the epic and dramatic methods of storytelling. Represented events are perceived by the eyes and ears, while those which are related must be imagined by the theater audience from details given in the relator's description. A well-written, well-recited narration can produce a lively effect in the minds of the hearers, but in general direct sensory perception is more vivid and intense. For that reason, the poet should dramatize those events in his story which have the greatest appeal for the spectators, in order to maximize the effect, and should narrate events which would be incredible or too horrifying if actually seen, so as to mitigate the disbelief or shock of the audience. Although Lisideius praises the French for their address in the use of relations, he generously concludes by citing several commendable examples in Jonson and Fletcher (I, 62-65).

Neander's reply to this part of Lisideius' defense of the French is equally fair and moderate. He agrees that tumultuous or incredible actions should be narrated rather than shown, and he has no quarrel with the reasons Lisideius has given for that rule. He is not quite ready to abandon all dramatizations of battles and deaths, at least on the English stage, partly because "our countrymen" will scarcely suffer combats and other objects of horror to be taken from them, but partly also for the more philosophical reason that the imagination may have more scope and flexibility than Lisideius assumes:

> For why may not our imagination as well suffer itself to be deluded with the probability of it, as with any other thing in the play? For my part, I can with as great ease persuade myself that the blows which are struck are given in good earnest, as I can that they who strike them are kings or princes, or those persons which they represent.

Here he has clearly passed beyond the narrow but clearly marked limits of the Addisonian definition. The imagination is no longer merely an image-making faculty, responding to verbal clues in passages—whether in dramatic or nondramatic works—that describe persons and events but do not literally show them. Instead, it has become a power of the mind that can "suffer itself to be deluded" by the whole dramatic fiction, as enacted in a theater (I, 74-75).

In this passage Neander comes close to anticipating Dr. Johnson's argument on the unities of time and place in the *Preface to Shakespeare:* "Delusion, if delusion be admitted, has no certain limitation." If we can imagine that a candlelit theater is the plain of Pharsalia and that our old acquaintances are Alexander and Caesar, who is to say that we can't imagine much more?[13] But Neander does not push the argument that far, and he mildly concludes by observing that a judicious dramatist will try to find a mean in his use of relations, not showing too much of the action, as the English are accused of doing, nor too little like the French, ". . . so as the audience may neither be left unsatisfied by not seeing what is beautiful, or shocked by beholding what is either incredible or undecent" (ibid.).[14]

The third passage which Jensen cites to illustrate his definition of the responsive imagination occurs in the final section of the debate, in which Crites attacks the use of rhyme in serious plays and Neander defends it. Crites' argument sounds simpleminded in Neander's summary of it near the beginning of his reply: "You say the stage is the representation of Nature, and no man in ordinary conversation speaks in rhyme" (I, 96). The case Crites makes is actually a good deal more complex and sophisticated than that suggests, for it includes a well-thought-out theory of dramatic illusion, in which the respective roles of judgment and imagination in the response of a theater audience are clearly distinguished and defined. Crites thus implicitly appeals to the broadened conception of the imagination's function which Neander had suggested in his reply to Lisideius.

As Huntley remarks in his admirable analysis of the *Essay's* argument, Crites' reasoning here is consistent with his position on earlier issues, since he "leans more toward the justness of the definition than toward the liveliness."[15] He grants that in watching a play, the audience is not really deluded. The play is still known to be a play, the dialogue among several persons is understood to be the labor of one poet, and we know perfectly well that the scenes representing cities and countries are not really such, but only painted on boards and canvas; our fancies submit willingly to the pretense that everything we see is real, knowing that we are to be deceived and desiring to be so. In short, we are still in our wits and remain rational creatures (I, 92-93).

Here again Dryden comes very close to Johnson's account of dramatic illusion:

> The truth is, that the spectators are always in their senses, and know, from the first act to the last, that the stage is only a stage, and that the players are only players. . . . It will be asked, how the drama moves, if it is not credited. It is credited with all the credit due to a drama. It is credited, whenever it moves, as a just picture of a real original; as representing to the auditor what he would himself feel, if he were to do or suffer what is there feigned to be suffered or to be done. . . . Imitations produce pain or pleasure, not because they are mistaken for realities, but because they bring realities to mind.[16]

Justness of representation is accepted by Johnson as a basic evaluative criterion, as it is by Crites, but Johnson defines "nature" differently and uses the standard for a different argumentative purpose. Nature is conceived throughout the *Preface* as the general or universal attributes of reality, including, of course, the realities of human nature and the human condition. In his main argument to prove Shakespeare's excellence as a dramatist, Johnson had already shown that in all their constitutive parts—the plots, the characters, their thoughts and feelings, and the style through which the substantive elements are expressed—the plays do depict "just representations of general nature," fictitious analogues of actual human experiences.[17] In discussing dramatic illusion, however, his purpose is not to judge the excellence of any body of writings, but rather to explain a psychological phenomenon—how audiences can be moved by dramatized fictions which they never believe to be real. Taking it for granted that any good play will meet the standard of justness, he rejects the traditional solution of the problem, a temporary and voluntary delusion of the fancy, by redefining belief or "credit": we do not believe, even for a moment, that the fiction is a reality, but we accept it and are moved by it because it "brings realities to mind," making us feel as we would feel in similar real-life situations.

Crites' purpose is different from Johnson's. The question he raises is a narrow, technical one: whether the use of rhyme, as a device of style, is legitimate in serious plays. He does not argue toward a theory of the audience's state of mind in watching a play, as Johnson does, but instead accepts as a starting point the traditional view which Johnson refutes: although we are not literally deluded, we voluntarily allow our imaginations to be deceived while we watch the play. His line of argument is still further separated from Johnson's by his contention that the audience's imaginative assent needs to be supported by as close a correspondence as possible between the reality represented and its fictional analogue. While we gladly assent to the deception, it must be based upon a just resemblance, verisimilitude, and probability of truth. The mind of man, Crites says, "does naturally tend to, and seek after truth; and therefore the nearer anything comes to the imitation of it, the more it pleases." The basic premise underlying all dramatic fictions is the supposition that they represent people acting and speaking extempore, without premeditation; their dialogue is the effect of sudden thought.[18] Crites does not deny that their thoughts and language may be heightened to some degree beyond what would be likely in real life, but the style should never too obviously reveal the hand of art. His standard, then, is not absolute resemblance—a demand so palpably impossible that he does not even mention it—but rather as little departure from the model as the limiting conditions of the art permit. It is a matter of degree: the grosser the lie, the weaker the belief; the more improbable the fiction, the more grudging the imaginative assent. Conversely, of course, the closer to truth and nature, the greater will be the imaginative response, and consequently the pleasure. Applying this relativistic standard to the question at issue, Crites concludes that rhyme departs too grossly and improbably from the norms of actual speech, even in serious plays, but blank verses are legitimate; he admits that no one speaks them extempore, but "as nearest nature, they are still to be preferred" (I, 90-93).[19]

Jensen does not cite any part of Neander's reply to Crites, because the word "imagination" in his fourth sense nowhere occurs in it, but the passage does have an important indirect bearing on the subject. Neander's purpose is to show that "in serious plays where the subject and characters are great, and the plot unmixed with mirth . . . rhyme is there as natural and more effectual than blank verse." As Huntley points out in his summary, the term "natural" in

Neander's statement of his thesis applies the criterion of justness in Lisideius' definition of a good play, while "more effectual" picks up the complementary criterion of liveliness, to which Crites makes no reference in his attack on rhyme.[20]

Accepting Crites' rule that the best style is that which is "nearest nature," Neander offers two arguments to show that dialogue written in rhyme may be just and natural. The first is that a good dramatic poet, whether writing in prose, blank verse, or rhyme, will be able to observe the norms of conversational speech through his skill in the choice and placement of words; bad poets, lacking that skill, will be unable to imitate idiomatic speech in any medium (I, 94-96). The second argument, without abandoning the "just," adds the "lively" by redefining "nature" to take account of generic differences in subject, style, narrative method, and effect:

> I answer you, therefore, by distinguishing betwixt what is nearest to the nature of comedy, which is the imitation of common persons and ordinary speaking, and what is nearest the nature of a serious play: this last is indeed the representation of nature, but 'tis nature wrought up to an higher pitch. . . . Tragedy, we know, is wont to image to us the minds and fortunes of noble persons, and to portray these exactly; heroic rhyme is nearest nature, as being the noblest kind of modern verse. . . . [Tragedy and epic have the same high and noble subject], only the manner of acquainting us with those actions, passions, and fortunes is different. Tragedy performs it *viva voce,* or by action, in dialogue; wherein it excells the epic poem, which does it chiefly by narration, and therefore is not so lively an image of human nature. (I, 100-102; cf. I, 154).

The criterion of liveliness shifts the argumentative focus from the relation between a poem and its model to the effectualness, its impact on the audience. Naturalness, for Crites the sole and final standard, is thus subordinated by Neander to delight and instruction, the ends to which just representation is merely the means. The representation must still be natural, but liveliness, as one of the chief sources of our delight, becomes a second and more ultimate value.

As I said in beginning my discussion of the four passages in the *Essay of Dramatic Poesy,* they are all reasoned arguments, and as such are representative examples of the rational dimension of Dryden's criticism. On the other hand, it is also clear that the imaginations of the four speakers, like those of any other reader or spectator, are always actively responding to the works they discuss—sometimes forming images in the mind's eye, sometimes yielding imaginative belief to the whole dramatic fiction—and that these responses provide data that are essential to critical evaluation. The just and the lively, as criteria of poetic excellence, are premises accepted by all the speakers and appealed to, under varying interpretations, in all their reasonings on the many questions they debate. But the liveliness of a poem is an attribute which cannot be demonstrated by reasoned argument. As the harmony of a poet's verse can be judged only by the ear, so the liveliness of the image of life conveyed by any kind of poem must be perceived, imagined, or felt. That is why criticism cannot do without these nonrational responses, as Dryden well knew and never forgot.

☙❧☙❧

It should already be apparent that Dryden is unabashedly guilty of that heinous critical heresy, the "affective fallacy."[21] To him, if not to some twentieth-century theorists, it seemed obvious that one of the basic aims of every literary work is to give delight. In Dryden's psychology of the audience, all the perceptual and imaginative effects that we have been discussing carried with them correlative affective reactions. The harmony or disharmony of a poet's verses, perceived by the ear, gives us pleasure or pain, leaves us satisfied or uneasy, gratifies or frustrates our desires. As we watch a serious play on a religious subject, our souls are allured by what we see and hear and at the same time are struck with a sense of devotion, a secret veneration for things celestial. We respond with pleasure and admiration to the images aroused in the fancy by the descriptions of great poets, and a wide range of emotions is stirred in our minds by the dramatic fictions to which we gladly give imaginative assent. Since all the ancient and modern critical systems known to Dryden assumed that the emotional effects produced by poetry are crucial to the solution of problems of aesthetic value, he would surely have been astonished and bewildered by a theory which denied that such effects occur, or contended that they were irrelevant to critical judgment.

The many affective responses which Dryden records in his critical writings may be roughly divided into two kinds, those which express liking or disliking, a favorable or unfavorable response to writers or works, and others that record more specific emotional reactions, varying according to a poem's subject and purpose. The first can be disposed of quite quickly, but the second is more complex.

Liking or disliking is expressed through the many approximate synonyms or antonyms of "pleasure" such as "delight," "charm," "liking," "satisfaction," "inclination," "partiality," "relish," and the like (I, 69,

113-15, 120, 252;II, 195, 225, and passim). In extreme cases, Dryden uses the language of love and hate to convey feelings of this kind. Speaking of one of the bad poets who will certainly be celebrating the sea victory in very ill verses, Crites quotes Virgil's famous line:

> "All I would wish," replied Crites, "is that they who love his writings, may still admire him, and his fellow poet: *Qui Bavium non odit,* &c., is curse sufficient."

Lisideius caps the quotation with another: *"Nam quos contemnimus, eorum quoque laudes contemnimus"* (I, 33).[22] Dryden himself finds Ovidian conceits and jingles "nauseous" in a serious poem, and he "abhors" the brutal actions of Achilles in the *Iliad* (II, 159, 256). Elsewhere, however, he declares himself for Homer and Tasso, "and am more in love with Achilles and Rinaldo than with Cyrus and Oroondates" (I, 157). The most famous of all such emotive statements is at the conclusion of Neander's comparison between Jonson and Shakespeare in the *Essay:* "I admire him, but I love Shakespeare" (I, 83). Speaking in his own person, Dryden says almost the same thing in comparing Juvenal and Horace in the *Discourse on Satire:* "And who would not choose to be loved better, rather than to be more esteemed?" (II, 87).

One of the contraries of "to please" is "to bore," "to put to sleep." Horace said that even Homer sometimes nodded, and Dryden thought that the same thing was true of the greatest modern poets: Shakespeare is "many times flat, insipid," and Milton's *Paradise Lost* has "flats amongst his elevations, when 'tis evident he creeps along sometimes for above an hundred lines together," though we forgive them both, because they offer so much that does please and move us greatly (I, 80, 268). Among several causes which can make a play or a poem boring, Dryden most often mentions a lack of novelty, variety, or surprise. In the *Essay of Dramatic Poesy,* Eugenius says that the plots of classic drama could arouse only "a yawning kind of expectation," because their outcomes were already known; the appetites of the audience were "cloyed with the same dish, and, the novelty being gone, the pleasure vanished; so that one main end of Dramatic Poesy in its definition, which was to cause delight, was of consequence destroyed." Later in the debate, Neander observes the same defect in the French playwrights. Their verses are "the coldest I have ever read," because many of the speeches, like protracted declamations, tire us with their length; as with the tedious visits of bad company, "we are in pain till they are gone." He also praises Jonson for his variety of characters and skillfully contrived underplots, which entertain the spectators with new and unexpected things whenever the main design is in danger of growing tiresome. He says, too, that verses which become monotonous cannot be good:

> . . . nothing that does *perpetuo tenore fluere,* run in the same channel, can please always. 'Tis like the murmuring of a stream, which not varying in the fall, causes at first attention, at last drowsiness. Variety of cadences is the best rule; the greatest help to the actors, and refreshment to the audience. (I, 46-47, 58, 71, 88, 96)

Neander's complaint that French dramatists are often cold and insipid is repeated in the preface to *All for Love*. Their care not to offend makes them tiresome: ''But as the civilest man in the company is commonly the dullest, so these authors, while they are afraid to make you laugh or cry, out of pure good manners make you sleep.'' The metaphor of satiation from too much of one dish expresses one of Dryden's standing complaints against Ovid, who ''sometimes cloys his readers, instead of satisfying them,'' because he never knew when to give over. Dryden even defends, rather halfheartedly, his mingling of serious and comic plots in the *Spanish Friar* by appealing to the need for variety. In the present mood of the English theater audience, ''the feast is too dull and solemn without the fiddles,'' though yielding to its fickle taste is probably a mistake; for this once, Dryden chose ''to break a rule for the pleasure of variety'' (I, 194, 234, 249). If the power to please an audience is an ultimate aesthetic value, as it is for him, one of the most damaging things a critic can say about a poem is that it is boring.

Although delight is an ultimate value, Dryden believed that it had no critical authority unless it arose from artistic causes actually present in the poetic work being judged. A poem may please some people, or even a whole age, without being intrinsically and objectively of any great value. In a passage from the *Defence of an Essay of Dramatic Poesy* (1668), quoted in Chapter 2 above to document this same point, Dryden says:

> The liking or disliking of the people gives the play the denomination of good or bad, but does not really make or constitute it such. To please the people ought to be the poet's aim, because plays are made for their delight, but it does not follow that they are always pleased with good plays, or that the plays which please them are always good. (I, 120-121)

Most actual audiences have little more ''than a gross instinct, of what pleases or displeases them.'' Their feelings are whimsical, capricious, and perpetually changing, and their judgment is ''a mere lottery,'' sometimes right, sometimes wrong. But a poem that is truly good or truly bad is so ''in its own nature,'' and its real value never changes, because it ''cannot be otherwise.'' This true value can be grasped only by the ''best judges,'' the *judices natos,* those who never give their approbation ''blindly,'' out of mere subjective impression or uncritical enthusiasm, but always ''knowingly,'' from an understanding of poetry and a grasp of its principles (I, 100, 135-36, 195, 221, 226, 246; II, 50-51, 115). Most precisely phrased, Dryden's standard is not delight simply and without qualification, but ''what ought to please,'' ''what should delight a reasonable audience'' (I, 179, 209; II, 40, 136-37). The line of demarcation between the rational and irrational aspects of criticism, and the primacy of the former over the latter, could not be more unequivocally stated.

The second kind of emotional response to literature, as briefly noted above, is more specific than a generalized pleasure or displeasure, liking or disliking. We may begin with several miscellaneous responses which are mentioned only once or twice in discussing particular poets or works. A unique instance is the religious emotions of awe, devotion, and reverence of which Dryden speaks in the preface to *Tyrannick Love.* In two places, where he seems to be thinking primarily of Seneca, he speaks of horror and detestation as effects produced by representations of lust, cruelty, revenge, and ambition. He condemns such effects as improper to tragedy (I, 54, 143)—a judgment which implies a concept of ''proper pleasure,'' an important general principle, which will be discussed more fully below. The responses mentioned in Dryden's comparison between Horace and Juvenal in the *Discourse on Satire* are even more interesting, because they illustrate clearly the connection in his aesthetic theory between delight, as the general end which all poems seek to achieve, and the more specific emotional effects aroused by a particular genre. The pleasure Horace gives him is but languishing, Dryden says, but Juvenal has a more vigorous and masculine wit, writes in a more numerous and sonorous style, and expresses thoughts and emotions that are sublime and lofty:

> . . . He gives me as much pleasure as I can bear; he fully satisfies my expectation; he treats his subject home: his spleen is raised, and he raises mine: I have the pleasure of concernment in all he says; he drives his reader along with him; and when he is at the end of his way I willingly stop with him. (II, 84)

If it seems surprising that Dryden should speak of ''spleen'' as not only a proper but a sublime and noble effect of satire, his meaning becomes clearer further on in the *Discourse,* when he says that ''Juvenal always intends to move your indignation, and he always brings about his purpose,'' and that in his vehement attacks on tyranny we are better pleased with ''a zealous vindicator of Roman liberty than with a temporising poet, a well-mannered court-slave. . ." (II, 95, 87).

Another miscellaneous effect is a vaguely defined "softness and tenderness," which he mentions in several different connections. He defends his own verses addressed to the Duchess of York, which produce such an effect, on the ground that they achieved what he endeavored; because they are addressed to a lady, "I affected the softness of expression, and smoothness of measure, rather than the height of thought" (I, 18-19). In a better-known passage, he objects to Donne's amorous verses because he "perplexes the minds of the fair sex with nice speculations of philosophy, when he should engage their hearts, and entertain them with the softness of love" (II, 19). One of the arguments advanced by Eugenius in the *Essay* for the superiority of the moderns is that there are few love scenes in ancient drama: "their tragic poets dealt not with that soft passion, . . . whose gentleness would have tempered them, which is the most frequent of all passions, and which, being the private concernment of every person, is soothed by viewing its own image in a public entertainment" (I, 54). Here Eugenius contends that other poetic purposes, unattempted by the ancients, are as legitimate as the ends which their poets pursued and their critics endorsed. It is an important point for defining Dryden's whole attitude toward the poetry and criticism of the ancients, and we shall return to it later in discussing his "Heads of an Answer to Rymer."

Effects having wider application than these miscellaneous responses may be illustrated by the emotions aroused by comedy and tragedy, which Dryden expresses under varying but always contrasted terms. We have already mentioned "laugh or cry," perhaps the simplest of such discriminations. Another example is his explanation of the continuing popularity of Beaumont and Fletcher, because "there is a certain gaiety in their comedies, and pathos in their more serious plays, which suits generally all men's humours." Elsewhere, emphasizing the defects of the Elizabethan playwrights, he says that many plays by Shakespeare and Fletcher are "so meanly written that the comedy neither caused your mirth, nor the serious part your concernment." In the preface to *The Mock Astrologer,* similarly, he says that the value of a play lies not in the story but in the workmanship: "He who works dully on a story, without moving laughter in a comedy, or raising concernment in a serious play, is no more to be accounted a good poet, than a gunsmith of the Minories is to be compared with the best workman of the town." When he first conceived the subject of his *Spanish Friar,* he tells Lord Haughton in his dedication of the play, "I found, or thought I found, somewhat so moving in the serious part of it, and so pleasant in the comic, as might deserve a more than ordinary care in both.'' Speaking of the same play in another essay fourteen years later, he still finds the comical parts ''diverting'' and the serious ''moving,'' though he confesses that the double plot is an unnatural mingle (I, 81, 147, 165, 244; II, 147). The unnaturalness of the combination is a reasoned conclusion, but the fact that the different parts of the play do still divert and move can be known only from the emotional effects that they continue to produce. A final, balanced judgment of the play would have to recognize the truth both of the reasoned conclusion and of the felt effect.[23]

One of Dryden's key terms, ''concernment,'' has already appeared in several passages previously quoted. It is regularly used to distinguish the effect of serious kinds from that of comic writings; as we have seen, comedies may be gay, pleasant, or diverting, but he never asserts that they arouse concernment for the characters and their fates. But tragedies, heroic plays, the serious parts of tragicomedies, the satires of Juvenal, the epics of Homer and Virgil, the narratives and dramatic monologues of Ovid all ''move the passions and beget concernment'' (I, 72; cf. I, 53, 57, 63, 65, 72, 166, 224; II, 202, etc.). Through defects of natural gift, acquired understanding, or poetic workmanship, some serious plays fail to do so. In that case, they cannot be good for much artistically, for the primary end, purpose, scope, or design of all such works is to ''move our nature'' by working upon passions, to ''move and stir up the affections'' (I, 212; II, 74; cf. I, 113, 120).

Underlying all of Dryden's references to concernment, and other emotional effects as well, is an assumption that all or most readers respond to the same works in the same way, following psychological laws that govern all mankind. Dryden never attempts to establish these laws in any systematic way, as some later theorists did, but in a few places he does express his belief in the constancy and uniformity of human responses to poetic fictions. Though implied rather than explicitly stated, the uniformitarian assumption seems quite clear in his reply to Rymer's attack on Fletcher's *King and No King*. Rymer had claimed that the play continues to please because of the excellence of the actors, not from any intrinsic merits, but Dryden says that he finds the play moving when read as well as when seen in the theater. He grants the defects of plot which Rymer had so wittily urged, but thinks that even in a play that is admittedly imperfect there must be lesser degrees of nature, which arouse at lease some faint emotions in us, ''for nothing can move our nature, but by some natural reason, which works upon passions. And since we acknowledge the effect, there must be something in the cause.'' The effect, of course, is the ''moving'' which he feels in his own mind as he reads; the reason or cause is Fletcher's depiction of characters, feelings, and thoughts within the play. In speaking of ''us'' and ''we'' and ''our,'' Dryden is tacitly assuming that his response is not eccentric, but would be felt by everyone sharing in "our nature" (I, 213).

The same assumption is fully explicit in his preface to Ovid's *Epistles*, when he appeals to his readers to consult their own feelings:

> If the imitation of Nature be the business of a poet, I know no author who can justly be compared with ours, especially in the description of the passions. And to prove this, I shall need no other judges than the generality of his readers; for, all passions being inborn with us, we are almost equally judges when we are concerned with the representation of them. Now I will appeal to any man, who has read this poet, whether he finds not the natural emotion of the same passion in himself, which the poet describes in his feigned persons? (I, 233)

In the *Parallel of Poetry and Painting*, finally, he ventures for once on a broad psychological generalization, which he credits to his ingenious young friend, Mr. Walter Moyle. In their noblest genres, Dryden says, both arts are "imitations of the passions, which always move, and therefore consequently please; for without motion there can be no delight, which cannot be considered but as an active passion" (II, 137-38).

In these passages Dryden anticipates two later developments in English and European criticism. James Malek draws attention to the first of them when he observes of the *Parallel:*

> . . . Dryden is not primarily interested in the psychological causes of aesthetic effects; instead, he makes assumptions about universal human traits on which generic rules of art can be based. Comparative discussions in which explanations of aesthetic effects in terms of natural causes play a significant role did not appear in England before the publication of such Continental works as Jean Baptiste Du Bos's *Réflexions critiques sur la poësie et sur la peinture* (1719), but Dryden's discussion of the impressions of time and place in poetry and painting contains the germs of causal explanations of aesthetic effects.[24]

Dryden's assumption that the responses of audiences are governed by universal human traits, even though it is not worked out in detail or supported by empirical evidence, is a fundamental one within his own system, because it provides a theoretical warrant for reasoning either from effects on audiences to their causes within poems or in the opposite direction, from the causes to their natural psychological effects.

The second development which Dryden anticipates in these passages is that which culminates in Hume's essay, "Of the Standard of Taste" (1757).

Hume argues that in aesthetics, as in ethics, general principles are founded on sentiment rather than on reason, but that a standard of taste—"a rule by which the various sentiments of man may be reconciled; at least, a decision afforded, confirming one sentiment, and condemning another"—may be found in "general observations, concerning what has been universally found to please in all countries and all ages." Responses which conform to "the common sentiments of human nature" are valid, while those which are eccentric, arising from a defective or unhealthy state of the responsive organs, are to be rejected. Dryden does not accept the first clause of this double conclusion, but he does anticipate the second. His uniformitarian assumption, implicit in his appeals to his readers to confirm or deny the responses he reports by consulting their own perceptual, imaginative, and emotional reactions, provides an objective check, observable through experience, against subjectivism and eccentricity.

Though no more important than "concernment" in Dryden's critical vocabulary, "admiration" requires a more elaborate exposition. It is an interesting term historically. Unknown to any ancient system of criticism, it entered the lexicon of modern literary discussion at least as early as the time of Francesco Robortello, the first full-scale commentator on the *Poetics* (1548).[25] Jensen mentions Scaliger and Sidney as other Renaissance theorists who use the term, and he cites specific examples in Hobbes and Rymer;[26] it can also be found in Corneille, Boileau, Rapin, and other French critics of Dryden's period. In the notes to his fine edition of Dennis, another contemporary in whose critical writings the word figures prominently, E. N. Hooker says that there seem to have been two hypotheses as to the causes within a work that produce admiration in the audience, some theorists emphasizing elements of the marvelous or supernatural, others the nobility and grandeur of heroic character and deeds.[27] Though not contradictory, the two views did produce differing critical conclusions.

Some critics of the sixteenth, seventeenth, and eighteenth centuries treat admiration as one of the effects of tragedy (e.g., Robortello), but others find it more characteristic of epic poetry (e.g., Rapin). Dryden reports admiration as part of his emotional response to both forms, though in some passages he treats it as especially the effect of heroic poetry. He does not limit himself to either of the theories mentioned by Hooker, but in different contexts speaks of several causes of admiration. In many places, he pairs "admiration" with "concernment," as joint effects of the same genre or work.

In three passages Dryden speaks of "admiration" as one of the effects produced by tragedy, serious plays, or quasi-tragic poems like the *Metamorphoses* and *Heroides*. In the *Defence of an Essay of Dramatic Poesy*, replying to Howard's claim that there is no difference between tragedy, comedy, and farce except ''what is made by the taste only,'' Dryden contends that the genres differ objectively and essentially—''in their natures''—and would do so ''were there neither judge, taste, nor opinion in the world.'' They are radically unlike in subject matter, style, and purpose, ''for the action, character, and language of Tragedy, would still be great and high; that of Comedy, lower and more familiar; admiration would be the delight of one, and satire of the other'' (I, 120). Two passages in the *Essay* itself link admiration with concernment and compassion as ends of serious literary forms. Eugenius says that the Latin *Medea* ''moves not my soul enough'' to be a work of Ovid's,[28] as some had contended, because his nondramatic writings showed that he had a genius for the stage and ''a way of writing so fit to stir up a pleasing admiration and concernment, which are the objects of a tragedy, that had he lived in our age . . . no man but must have yielded to him.'' Both the principle and its application are still further extended when Eugenius goes on to praise a scene in Seneca's *Troades* for raising a high degree of compassion in a reader, and certain unidentified plays by Shakespeare and Fletcher for their excellent love scenes, which arouse compassion and other soft, gentle emotions (I, 53-54). Later in the debate, Lisideius asserts that the ''end of tragedies or serious plays, says Aristotle, is to beget admiration, compassion, or concernment.'' Attacking the ancients for lack of variety and surprise in their plots and the English for intermingling mirth and compassion in the same drama, he claims that the former ''move but little concernment in the audience,'' and that the author of a tragicomedy ''must ruin the sole end and object of his tragedy, to introduce somewhat that is forced in, and not of the body of it.'' Since mirth and compassion are incompatible things, ''the poet must of necessity destroy the former by intermingling of the latter'' (I, 57-58).

Although Dryden speaks often of admiration as one of the effects intended by writers of tragedies or serious plays, he associates it still more closely with epic poetry and its various branches. The proper wit of a heroic or historical poem, he says in the preface to *Annus Mirabilis,* chiefly consists in ''the delightful imagining of persons, actions, passions, or things.'' His images in that poem are patterned after those of Virgil, though he cannot promise that they will be as fine:

> Such descriptions or images, well wrought, which I promise not for mine, are, as I have said, the adequate delight of Heroic Poesy; for they beget admiration, which is its proper object. (I, 14-18)

Homer, he says elsewhere, is even more effectual in raising admiration: ''To cause admiration is, indeed, the proper and adequate design of an Epic Poem; and in that he has excelled even Virgil'' (II, 13). Well-wrought images are one of the causes of admiration, but there are others; some are aspects of heroic style, some of its elevated subject matter. Similitudes, which can be used only sparingly in dramatic dialogue, are much more proper to the epic: ''But this figure has a contrary effect in heroic poetry; there it is employed to raise the admiration, which is its proper business'' (II, 202). Still another cause, one of the two mentioned by Hooker, is the character of the hero: ''The shining quality of an epic hero, his magnanimity, his constancy, his patience, his piety, or whatever characteristical virtue his poet gives him, raises first our admiration,'' which in turn makes us want to imitate those virtues in our own lives (II, 159). The other contemporary theory as to the cause of admiration, which Hooker ascribes especially to Le Bossu, is that it arises primarily from elements of the marvelous or extraordinary in the epic. For Dryden, this is yet another source of admiration, especially in heroic poems or heroic plays, which raise the imagination and stir admiration by ''those gods and spirits, and those enthusiastic parts of poetry, which compose the most noble parts of all their writings'' (I, 152-54; cf. I, 187; II, 137-38). These different explanations are not at all inconsistent, for they all reflect Dryden's lifelong belief that heroic poetry, among all the genres, requires the highest powers in the poet, imitates nature and human life in their grandest and most beautiful forms, expresses them through the most elevated language, and produces in its audience the most intense and noble delight and instruction. That is why ''a heroic poem, truly such, is undoubtedly the greatest work which the soul of man is capable to perform'' (II, 154; cf. I, 154).[29]

The emotional vocabulary we have been considering so far—''concernment,'' ''admiration,'' and less frequent responses such as ''horror,'' ''indignation,'' or the soft and gentle feelings aroused by scenes of love— is a modern invention, adopted by Dryden from Italian and French theorists of the sixteenth and seventeenth centuries, but unknown to ancient critics. In ''pity'' and ''fear,'' however, we come upon terms which are central to the aesthetic philosophy of that ancient affective critic, Aristotle. If we are to understand the role of these two responses in Dryden's critical practice, it will be necessary to clarify a much more fundamental question, which we have already skirted several times—the underlying relationship between his whole system and that set forth in the *Poetics*.

At some points, Dryden seems to follow Aristotle quite closely. Pity is defined by Aristotle as the emotion we feel for someone suffering undeserved misfortune. If a tragic action is to arouse that feeling, he argues, its movement should be from good fortune to bad and the hero should be neither eminently

virtuous nor an utter villain, but rather a character between the two extremes:
"a man who is not eminently good and just, yet whose misfortune is brought
about not by vice or depravity, but by some error or frailty" (*Poetics* xiii).
Defending his characterization of Antony in *All for Love,* Dryden says:

> All reasonable men have long since concluded, that the hero of the poem
> ought not to be a character of perfect virtue, for then he could not,
> without injustice, be made unhappy; nor yet altogether wicked, because
> he could not then be pitied. I have therefore steered the middle course;
> and have drawn the character of Antony as favourably as Plutarch,
> Appian, and Dion Cassius would give me leave; the like I have observed
> of Cleopatra. (I, 191)

In the preface to *Troilus and Cressida,* he repeats that "it is necessary that the
hero of the play be not a villain; that is, the characters, which should move our
pity, ought to have virtuous inclinations, and degrees of moral goodness in
them," and in the *Parallel of Poetry and Painting* he says again that "the
grounds of pity for their misfortunes" will be lacking if the protagonists are
either thoroughly wicked or wholly perfect:

> Sophocles has taken the just medium in his Oedipus. He is somewhat
> arrogant at his first entrance, and is too inquisitive through the whole
> tragedy; yet these imperfections being balanced by great virtues, they
> hinder not our compassion for his miseries. (I, 210-14; II, 125-36)

It seems rather ludicrous to speak of Oedipus as too inquisitive, and Aristotle
certainly never suggests that trait as the hamartia of Sophocles' great tragic
hero, but in recommending a mean between virtue and villainy as the best way
to raise pity, Dryden and the Stagyrite are not far apart.

Another concept which Dryden took over from the *Poetics* is that of
"proper pleasure." Both he and Aristotle believed that poems can be
classified into distinct genres, and that each kind is designed to produce a
definite sort of emotional effect, which is the source of its special pleasure. In
judging a poem's artistic excellence, Aristotle applies two criteria: its beauty
as a constructed object and its power or working, its capacity to produce the
intended emotions in the minds of the audience. Under the second criterion,
the poem's value is proportional to its success in arousing the appropriate
passions—in making us "laugh or cry," for example, as Dryden says the
French dramatists are too well-mannered to do.

But Dryden's way of discriminating and defining the genres is different
from Aristotle's. As he explicitly acknowledges in the *Essay of Dramatic
Poesy* and again in the *Discourse on Satire,* his generic formulations are

sometimes merely descriptions, or lists of traits, rather than complete, watertight, formal definitions. Aristotle's definitions are much more precise and systematic, because the genus of all poems, and indeed of the products of all the fine arts, is imitation, while the differentiae are found in the object, manner, and means of imitation. Stated in terms of matter and form, the matter of a poem is diction or language, while its form is derived from the object of imitation—primarily from the plot or action, which is the organizing principle or "soul" of a poem, and secondarily from the imitated characters and their thoughts. For Dryden, the basic differentiae are the subject and the style or expression, a disjunction derived not from Aristotle but from Horace and the Roman rhetoricians. It has many far-reaching consequences, the most basic of which is that it inverts the Aristotelian relation between matter and form: the matter becomes that which is imitated or expressed, and form becomes the expression. The vagueness and generality of Dryden's formulation of the genres also follow from this disjunction. When he substitutes "serious play" for "tragedy," thus broadening the boundaries of that kind so as to bring heroic drama within its scope, he can do so because both are written in an elevated style and represent subjects that are above common life. In the same way, the vaguer term "heroic poesy" often replaces "epic," and it is so broadly conceived that it can include such diverse forms as a historical poem like *Annus Mirabilis,* the satires of Juvenal, and Denham's *Cooper's Hill,* all three being "branches" of the heroic in virtue of certain traits of subject and style, while differentiating features are disregarded (I, 7, II; II, 108, 149). Another example is Dryden's treatment of Ovid's *Heroides,* discussed elsewhere in this volume, as dramatic poems of tragic quality and effect.

Since the genres are so loosely defined, Dryden's statement of their effects also becomes vaguer, less precise, and more fluid. An emotion so general as "concernment" becomes the business of all serious forms, and "admiration" may be effected both by plays and by any of the branches of heroic poetry, though in a higher degree by epic poems (or heroic plays, which imitate them) because of their more perfect heroes, greater opportunities for the marvelous, and more figurative style. The precisely defined "pity" and "fear" of the *Poetics* are converted into "admiration, compassion, and concernment," a transmutation which would certainly have astonished Aristotle. Dryden does continue to use the Aristotelian terms, though with profound changes in their meaning and application.

The case of pity is somewhat analogous to that of admiration, except that the relative position of the two genres, heroic poesy and serious drama, is reversed. In the epic kind, Homer is "more capable of exciting the manly

passions than those of grief and pity,'' but his depictions of the grief of Priam
and Hecuba show that he was also ''ambitious enough of moving pity,'' and
did so very effectively. As for Virgil, the episode of Nisus and Euryalus
arouses both compassion and admiration, and the passionate grief of Dido
when deserted by Aeneas is ''one of the greatest beauties of his poem'' for the
same reason (II, 13, 143, 195). Even so, Dryden speaks much more
frequently of the power of drama to arouse compassion. It is the effect chiefly
aimed at by Sophocles and Euripides, by Shakespeare and Fletcher, and by
Dryden himself in *All for Love* and *Troilus and Cressida* (I, 191-92, 210, 212,
220; II, 125-36). This difference of degree between the emotional responses
typically raised by the two major genres is perhaps implied when he says in
the *Parallel* that in a tragic or epic poem, as in a painting, the hero must be the
principal subject, outshining all the others: ''he is the chief object of pity in
the drama, and of admiration in the epic poem'' (II, 143). Both forms are
capable of raising admiration and compassion, but heroic poetry tends more
toward the first, tragedy toward the second.

''Fear'' has an ambiguous role in Dryden's treatment of the emotional
effects of drama. When he offers a full definition of tragedy, as in the preface
to *Troilus and Cressida,* he follows both Aristotle and the French theorists in
making fear and pity coequal effects of the genre (II, 207, 208, 210, 212,
220), but in reporting his own response to particular tragedies or other serious
works he mentions compassion frequently but seldom speaks of fear. His
separation of the inseparable Aristotelian twins is evident in his discussion of
Oedipus, which gives due weight to pity, but says nothing at all about fear. He
seems very far from Aristotle when he says that ''Shakespeare generally
moves more terror, and Fletcher more compassion,'' ascribing the difference
to the tempers and talents of the two English dramatists: ''the first had a more
masculine, bolder and more fiery genius; the second, a more soft and
womanish.'' Why he should have deemphasized fear, while retaining it as a
legitimate purpose and effect for some writers and works, is a puzzling
question to which I don't know the answer. It may be that he thought of fear as
included under the broader term ''concernment,'' as he suggests in the
''Heads of an Answer to Rymer.'' Perhaps he did not fully understand
Aristotle's concept of fear, though it is very fully and lucidly defined in the
Rhetoric.

Since we have reviewed the concepts of pity and fear in Dryden's treatment
of tragedy, it would seem natural to consider his interpretation of tragic
catharsis as well. Actually, the subject hardly seems relevant to our concerns
here, since his discussions of it in the preface to *Troilus and Cressida* and the
dedication of the *Aeneis* do not report any direct nonrational responses to

literature, like the perceptual, imaginative, and emotional effects we have been talking about, but instead present an abstract intellectual theory—and a secondhand one at that. His interpretation turns upon instruction and delight as the two chief ends of all poetry:

> To instruct delightfully is the general end of all poetry. Philosophy instructs, but it performs its work by precept; which is not delightful, or not so delightful as example. To purge the passions by example, is therefore the particular instruction which belongs to Tragedy. Rapin, a judicious critic, has observed from Aristotle, that pride and want of commiseration are the most predominent vices of mankind; therefore, to cure us of these two, the inventors of Tragedy have chosen to work upon two other passions, which are fear and pity. We are wrought to pity by their setting before our eyes some terrible example of misfortune, which happened to persons of the highest quality; for such an action demonstrates to us that no condition is privileged from the turns of fortune; this must of necessity cause terror in us, and consequently abate our pride. But when we see the most virtuous, as well as the greatest, are not exempt from such misfortunes, that consideration moves pity in us, and insensibly works us to be helpful to, and tender over, the distressed; which is the noblest and most god-like of moral virtues. (I, 209-10)

In spite of Rapin's ascription of this moralistic interpretation to Aristotle, there is nothing at all like it anywhere in his writings. He nowhere asserts that pride and want of commiseration are men's most predominant vices, that the pity and fear aroused by tragedy have an ethically therapeutic effect, or that the causes of pity and fear are examples of misfortune, from which we infer that no man is exempt from disasters, and consequently that we must avoid pride and hardheartedness. Like other sixteenth- and seventeenth-century attempts to make some kind of sense of the brief and enigmatic references to catharsis in the *Poetics,* Rapin's explanation gives meaning to the term by integrating it within a framework of theory that is not Aristotelian at all. From Dryden's postulation of delight and instruction as the ends of poetry—and consequently as the ultimate premises of any aesthetic argument—it should be apparent that the bases of the theory are derived not from the *Poetics* but from Horace and the Roman rhetorical tradition.

We may begin to draw together some of the scattered and tangled threads of this survey by considering one piece of evidence that has not yet been discussed, the ''Heads of an Answer to Rymer'' which Dryden jotted down in 1677 or 1678 on the endpapers of his presentation copy of Thomas Rymer's *Tragedies of the Last Age* (1677).[30] This document has been much discussed by scholars since the essays by Walcott (1936) and Hathaway (1943),[31] but it seems to me that they all distort the meaning and significance of Dryden's intriguing notes by failing to grasp their relationship to his usual assumptions and methods as we have been trying to reconstruct them from the whole body of his critical writings. The editors of the California edition (1971) come closest to recognizing these connections when they say of Dryden's references to Aristotle:

> Implicit in such statements is a point of view that Dryden had expressed through Eugenius and Neander in *Of Dramatick Poesie*. Thus *Heads of an Answer* throws light back on the *Essay* and helps us to realize—what indeed few can have doubted—that Eugenius and Neander express Dryden's fundamental position as a reader, a theorist, and a practicing dramatist. (*Works,* XVII, 416)

But the editors' headnote and commentary do not fully define just what that fundamental position is.

Rymer's little book (it is less than sixty pages long in Zimansky's edition)[32] is written in the form of a letter, addressed to Fleetwood Shepheard. He warns at the beginning that his friend must not expect him to lay his reasons together in form and method: ''You know I am not cut out for writing a *Treatise,* nor have a *genius* to *pen* any thing *exactly;* so long as I am *true* to the *main sense* before me, you will pardon me in the rest'' (pp. 20-21). It is characteristic of him that he should announce in his first paragraph that he will treat three plays by Beaumont and Fletcher, two by Shakespeare, and one by Ben Jonson, yet break off after covering the first three with only a glancing reference to *Othello* and *Cataline,* because he finds that he has already written enough to fill a volume and hesitates to burden Shepheard with further scribbling (pp. 17, 75-76). In spite of this studied disorder, his basic argument is quite simple and clear, not at all difficult to follow.

His most fundamental premise is the Horatian doctrine that poetry must delight, profit, and move the audience. As he observes in concluding the essay, his reasoning turns mainly, but not exclusively, on pleasure:

> Some would blame me for insisting and examining only what is apt to *please,* without a word of what might profit.
> 1. I believe the end of all Poetry is to *please.*
> 2. Some sorts of Poetry please without profiting.

3. I am confident whoever writes a Tragedy cannot please but must also profit; 'tis the Physick of the mind that he makes palatable. (p. 75)

Early in the essay he makes a distinction between history and poetry, very much like Sir Philip Sidney's in the *Apology for Poetry*, to which he refers intermittently throughout. The philosopher Socrates, setting up for morality, instructed in a pleasant, facetious manner; Sophocles and Euripides, with the same end in view, "were for teaching by *examples*, in a graver way, yet extremely *pleasant* and *delightful*." Finding that history, being bound to fact in particular cases, "was neither proper to *instruct*, nor apt to *please*," the ancient dramatists improved upon history by presenting "something more *philosophical*, and more *accurate*," a world that is "more *exquisite* and more *perfect* than History," a picture of human life that is "better and more beautiful" than empirical reality (pp. 22-23, 27, 36, 41, 61). The actual world is brazen, as Sidney says, and "the poets only deliver a golden."

Throughout his destructive analysis of the three Fletcherian plays—*Rollo, A King and No King,* and *The Maid's Tragedy*— Rymer moves back and forth, almost at random, between two operative criteria: the natural, probable, or reasonable, as the measure of a drama's depiction of reality; and the pleasing, instructive, or moving, as the standard for its effect upon the audience. In accordance with the principle that poetry presents a golden world, "nature" is conceived as characterized by order and harmony, "whereby the causes and effects, the vertues and rewards, the vices and their punishments are proportion'd and link'd together" (p. 75). It is from this principle that he derives his two most notorious rules, decorum and poetic justice. Whatever may be the case in history and real life, in poetry all women are modest, all kings are kingly; in that world, no servant may kill a master, a woman who kills a man must be his social superior, and "all crown'd heads by *Poetical right* are *Heroes*," who can never be accessories to a crime, still less commit murder themselves, and of course would never droll and quibble with buffoons, as Arbaces does in the comic parts of *A King and No King* (pp. 64, 65, 42, 44). "Poetical justice"—a term coined by Rymer, though the concept is everywhere in seventeenth-century French critical theory[33]—follows in much the same way from the principle that poetry presents a "more *exquisite* and more *perfect*" world than history shows. Continuing his remarks about Sophocles and Euripides, Rymer says that in history they saw virtue oppressed and wickedness on the throne, the same end often happening to the righteous and the unjust: "they saw these particular *yesterday-truths* were imperfect and unproper to illustrate the *universal* and *eternal* truths by them intended." They concluded, therefore, that justice should always be exactly administered in their plays, no crimes left unpunished and all virtues rewarded in proportion to their merit (pp. 22, 26-28, 32, 75).

In this first aspect of his argument, Rymer's reasoning is much like that of Crites in the *Essay of Dramatic Poesy*. There are differences, of course; Crites has a much more literal conception of the nature to be imitated by poetry,[34] and he puts a good deal of stress on the observation of the three unities, which Rymer passes over as "the *mechanical part* of Tragedies," not worth discussing when substantive value is lacking (p. 18). But they are alike in basing their judgments on nature, truth, and probability.

When he turns to his second criterion, Rymer sounds more like Lisideius or Neander, both of whom shift the argumentative focus, as we noted, to the effect of drama upon the audience. Rymer avowedly derives his principles from the practice of the ancients and the rules of Aristotle and Horace, which common sense confirms as just and reasonable (pp. 18, 20). As Dryden had done before him and would continue to do after publication of *The Tragedies of the Last Age,* Rymer incorporates a number of Aristotelian doctrines, sometimes drastically transformed, within a theoretical matrix that is essentially Horatian. As we have already seen, he takes his start from pleasure and profit, the two ends of all poetry. In tragedy, as a distinct genre, the delight arises from a drama's power to "move or concern," the poet's care to "engage the affections, take along the heart, and secure the good will of the Audience" (pp. 57, 48). Tragedy is specifically designed to arouse the emotions of pity and fear—compassion for those suffering undeserved misfortune and terror for ourselves—when we feel that the example dramatized by the poet teaches a lesson pertinent to our own lives. If we are to feel pity for a character, he or she must not be monstrous, "a Bitch, or *Polecat,*" like Seneca's Phaedra, but predominantly good, struggling like the Phaedra of Euripides to overcome her illicit passion, neither wicked nor absolutely innocent (pp. 50-57). The profit of tragedy comes from its useful moral lessons and its purging of the passions, "the Physick of the Mind," correcting our human corruptions and reforming our manners (pp. 19, 27, 43, 61, 75).

All of these principles, Rymer exuberantly contends, are grossly and flagrantly violated by the plots and characters of the three Fletcherian plays. He admits that they continue to be the most applauded English tragedies of the last age, but since they lack all intrinsic merit either as representations of nature or as instruments of delight and instruction, the pleasure they have given in the theater can only be ascribed to their comic parts, which are highly diverting, and to the acting of Mr. Hart and Mr. Mohun. Empirics in poetry may appeal to experience to prove that the plays please, but a distinction must be made between essentials and accidentals, between "what *pleases naturally in it self*" and what pleases because of the actors, dancers, and stage machines:

> These say (for instance) a *King* and no *King, pleases*. I say the *Comical* part *pleases*. I say that Mr. *Hart pleases;* most of the business falls to his share, and what he *delivers,* every one takes upon *content;* their *eyes* are prepossest and charm'd by his *action,* before ought of the *Poets* can approach their *ears;* and to the most wretched of *Characters,* he gives a lustre and *brillant* which dazles the *sight,* that the *deformities* in the Poetry cannot be perceiv'd. (p. 19; cf. p. 74)

Since Zimansky's edition of Rymer (1956), several scholars have recognized, as some earlier commentators did not, that Dryden's "Heads of an Answer to Rymer" outlines a possible counterargument against some of Rymer's critical conclusions, but does not attack his principles.[35] Dryden grants that the author of the *Tragedies of the Last Age* is learned, gives an impressive account of ancient drama, and presents a model of tragedy that is "Excellent, and extream Correct" (*Works,* XVII, 191-92)—a judgment that he later repeats in the preface to *Troilus and Cressida* and in letters to Dorset and Dennis.[36] In the "Heads" he explicitly accepts almost all of Rymer's basic premises: the ends of poetry are to delight and instruct; tragedy achieves both by moving pity and terror, which cannot be done unless the play represents human life justly and naturally; the protagonist should be neither wholly guilty nor wholly innocent; tragedy profits by purging the passions and reforming manners. Dryden's reply is made from within the same realm of discourse as Rymer's, basically the same doctrinal system.

Dryden's rough notes sketch out four possible lines of argument against Rymer's praise of the ancients and denigration of the Elizabethans. The first two had been anticipated, though by different speakers, in the *Essay of Dramatic Poesy* ten years earlier. One repeats a point made by both Eugenius and Neander: the lack of variety and surprise in ancient drama, the narrowness of its plots and fewness of persons, its circumscribed image of life, which makes it less delightful than the English plays ("Heads," pp. 186, 189, 192; cf. Eugenius in the *Essay of Dramatic Poesy,* I, 46-49; Neander, pp. 73, 78; and preface to *All for Love,* p. 200). The assumption that novelty and surprise are sources of delight in poetry, the lack of them a cause of boredom and sleep, is to be found everywhere not only in Dryden's criticism but in almost all the theorists and critics of the seventeenth and eighteenth centuries.

The second argument is an appeal to experience, refuting Rymer's scornful rejection of that defense as the refuge of "*Stage-quacks* and *Empiricks*" in

Poetry.''[37] Rymer concedes that Fletcher's plays had been warmly applauded, but ascribes their success to the excellent acting of Mohun and Hart, which blinded the audience to the deformities of the poetry. The favorable response of Restoration theater audiences is restated by Dryden in more emphatic terms: '' 'Tis evident those Plays which he arraigns have mov'd both those Passions [pity and terror] in a high degree upon the Stage.'' He was well aware of the hypnotic spell which can be cast over our senses and feelings in the theater, as we have seen, and he knew that ''the lights, the scenes, the habits, and, above all, the grace of action'' could impose upon our judgment (I, 245-46). But he does not think that the good acting of Mohun and Hart can explain the success of Fletcher's plays. For one thing, the parts have been played by many other actors, and always with the same result: ''the Event has been the same, that is, the same Passions have been always mov'd.'' Experience also shows that the plays are moving when read, as he says again later, from the evidence of his own response to them (Preface to *Troilus and Cressida*, I, 212). Here he appeals to others to confirm the fact by consulting their own feelings: ''I dare appeal to those who have never seen them acted, if they have not found those two Passions mov'd within them.'' The ''general Voice'' must certainly carry more weight than Rymer's single testimony, and if the effect has been felt by most audiences and readers, there must be some cause to explain it, within the plays as written. Though action may add grace and life in performance, there must be ''something of Force and Merit in the Plays themselves, conducing to the Design of Raising those two Passions'' (p. 187). Hume thinks that this argument ''might be employed today against any attempt to improve television programs'' (p. 112), but it is saved from Nielsen-rating logic not only by the uniformitarian assumption which clearly underlies it but also by the closely reasoned argument from effect to cause. It is a way of reasoning always central to Dryden's method as a critic.

The first two arguments sketched out in the ''Heads'' should not surprise any attentive reader of Dryden, since they are paralleled elsewhere in his criticism and are fully consistent with his usual assumptions and methods. The third is more surprising. The argument is first raised, in the form of a question to be resolved, in the third paragraph of the ''Heads.'' Anyone wanting to answer Rymer, he says, ''ought to prove two things; First, That the Fable is not the greatest Master-Piece of a Tragedy, tho' it be the Foundation of it.'' After stating the second thing an answerer ought to prove, he gives a first brief solution to the problem:

> *Aristotle* places the Fable first; not *quoad dignitatem, sed quoad fundamentum;* for a Fable never so Movingly contriv'd, to those ends of

his, Pity and Terror, will operate nothing on our Affections, except the Characters, Manners, Thoughts, and Words are suitable. (p. 185)

He returns to the question at the very end of his notes:

Rapin attributes more to the *Dictio,* that is, to the Words and Discourses of a Tragedy, than Aristotle has done, who places them in the last rank of Beauties; perhaps only last in Order, because they are the last Product of the Design, of the Disposition or Connexion of its Parts, of the Characters, of the Manners of these Characters, and of the Thoughts proceeding from those Manners.

Rapin's Words are Remarkable:

'Tis not the admirable Intrigue, the surprizing Events, and extraordinary Incidents that make the Beauty of a Tragedy, 'tis the Discourses, when they are Natural and Passionate.

So are *Shakespear's.* (pp. 192-93)[38]

The issue is pertinent to Rymer because the *Tragedies of the Last Age* rests its case against Fletcher almost wholly on his treatment of plot and character, which Rymer assumes to be the most essential elements in any narrative, the primary source of its beauties or defects.

It is not really surprising that Dryden should misread Aristotle's proofs of the primacy of plot, as he clearly does here, since he quite often distorts the meaning of Aristotle's terms, propositions, and arguments by reformulating them within the framework of an entirely different aesthetic philosophy. Whether his downgrading of plot is compatible with Horace and the rhetoricians is a more complex question. In some respects he is clearly reasoning within that tradition; the word "suitable" in his first statement of the argument is, of course, Horace's criterion of propriety, and in the second statement Dryden is using the standard rhetorical analysis of a piece of writing into three parts, *inventio, dispositio,* and *dictio.* In that tradition, however, expression is always subordinated to thought, *verbum* to *rem,* so that, in a narrative poem, plot or fable—that is, the subject as designed and ordered by the poet—should be first not only *quoad fundamentum* but *quoad dignitatem* as well.

The passage Dryden quotes from Rapin is quite misleading as an expression of the general theory developed in the *Reflections* as a whole. In the first part of the treatise, "Of Poesie in General," Rapin discusses in a series of chapters the subject and design, the fable and its ordonnance (Chs. xiv-xxiv), then the manners (Ch. xxv), the thoughts or sentiments (Ch. xxvi), and finally the expression or language (Ch. xxvii). This is clearly a descending order of importance, for he says several times that the plot is the "soul" and the

"greatest Beauty in the productions of *Wit*" (pp. 146, 173), while the manners
and passions provide the next greatest delight of Poetry (p. 174). Rapin follows
the same sequence even in the chapter from which Dryden quotes the statement
that the discourses, not the events and incidents, make the beauty of a tragedy.
Rapidly listing the many faults of modern tragedy, he begins with the subjects
and the contrivance, then moves systematically from characters and manners to
thoughts, and finally to expression (Part II, "Of Poesie in Particular," Ch. xxi,
pp. 212-14). Rapin certainly believes, as everyone in the rhetorical tradition
does, that in a perfect poem all the parts must be beautiful in themselves as well
as proportioned to the other parts (pp. 167, 178-80, 195-97, 200), and consequently that low words, improper language, expressions without majesty, and
discourse without life, such as Rapin finds in modern tragedies, are a very serious
defect (p. 212). But to say that lofty words and noble expressions take precedence
over the thoughts, manners, and plot in making "the *Beauty* of a *Tragedy*" (p.
213) is surely inconsistent with the fundamental principles of Rapin's critical
theory. If he is not grossly inconsistent, the statement should be understood as no
more than a passing hyperbole, in a context stressing the importance of style, to
express the fact that this part, too, must be great and moving.

Dryden's usual position on the priority among the parts is essentially the
same as Rapin's, as we can readily see, among many other passages, from a
statement about style in his last critical work, the preface to *The Fables:*

> Now the words are the colouring of the work, which, in the order of
> nature, is last to be considered. The design, the disposition, the manners,
> and the thoughts, are all before it: where any of those are wanting or
> imperfect, so much wants or is imperfect in the imitation of human life,
> which is in the very definition of a poem. Words, indeed, like glaring
> colours, are the first beauties that arise and strike the sight; but, if the
> draught be false or lame, the figures ill disposed, the manners obscure or
> inconsistent, or the thoughts unnatural, then the finest colours are but
> daubing, and the piece is a beautiful monster at best. (II, 253)

In the preface to *Troilus and Cressida*, written within two years after he jotted
down his "Heads of an Answer to Rymer," he specifically applies the same
Horatian orthodoxy to tragedy: the plot is the foundation of a play, and the
groundwork is that which is most necessary, since the firmness of the whole
fabric depends upon it; "yet it strikes not the eye so much, as the beauties or
imperfections of the manners, the thoughts, and the expressions" (I, 213). But
what strikes the eye first or most vividly can hardly be the part of greatest
dignity and worth, if plot is the foundation of all—first *quoad fundamentum,*
as he concedes even in the "Heads."

I think we must grant not only that Dryden misrepresents Rapin by lifting the sentence he quotes from its context, but also that his attempt to elevate the importance of *dictio,* if strictly construed to refer to style or expression as distinguished from all aspects of content, is really impossible to reconcile with his Horatian principles. There are other aspects of his thought, however, which may not fully justify this line of argument, but which make it more intelligible that he should propose it as a reasonable possibility. In the *Essay,* in the "Heads," and later in the *Grounds of Criticism in Tragedy,* Dryden states as a fact, known through both personal experience and observation of theater audiences, that the plays of Fletcher and Shakespeare do arouse emotions appropriate to serious plays. If so, there must be some causal explanation within those works. If Rymer's arguments have shown that the cause can hardly be ascribed to the faulty, improbable plots of the plays, then it must be found in some other component part. In his first statement of the argument, in the "Heads," Dryden suggests that if plot is eliminated, characters, manners, thoughts, and words still remain. In the restatement of the argument at the end of the notes, he seizes upon Rapin's term, "discourses," as perhaps the most plausible explanation. The term has a convenient and tempting ambiguity, because it may refer either to the words as words, which are *dictio* in the strict sense, or to the words as speeches expressive of character and thought, which are parts of *inventio,* second only to plot in the hierarchy of parts. The final sentence of the "Heads" completes this argument by elimination: Shakespeare's plays do please and move concernment, and the most likely explanation is that his "discourses" are "Natural and Passionate." They are, that is to say, both "just" and "lively," faithful to the actualities of human life and character and also capable of moving "admiration, compassion, or concernment." If Dryden cheats a little in exploiting the ambiguity of "discourses," is it not to his credit that he should refuse to yield on a fact known through experience, and should stubbornly keep searching for its rational explanation?

The last line of argument suggested in the "Heads" is the most fully developed of them all. It first appears, in the fourth paragraph of the notes, as the second thing that an answer to Rymer ought to prove: "Secondly, That other Ends, as suitable to the Nature of Tragedy, may be found in the *English,* which were not in the *Greek*" (p. 185). He first suggests that Aristotle, knowing only the ancient dramatists, may have defined tragedy too narrowly when he limited its ends to the stirring of pity and fear. In a true definition of tragedy, he says, the ultimate end is to reform manners and bring us to virtue; pity and fear are not properly ends, but rather the means Aristotle recommends for achieving that moral purpose:

If then the Encouragement of Virtue, and Discouragement of Vice, be the

proper End of Poetry in Tragedy: Pity and Terror, tho' good Means, are
not the only: for all the Passions in their turns are to be set in a Ferment;
as Joy, Anger, Love, Fear, are to be used as the Poets common Places;
and a general Concernment for the principal Actors is to be rais'd, by
making them appear such in their Characters, their Words and Actions,
as will interest the Audience in their Fortunes.

He grants that, in a broader sense of the terms, "pity" may comprehend
concernment for the good and "terror" detestation for the bad; but this widened
definition will then admit many additional new passions as legitimate effects of
tragedy. If the English have raised those other passions, as well as pity and fear,
should we not consider whether they may have "answer'd this End of Tragedy, as
well as the Ancients, or perhaps better?" If Aristotle had known Shakespeare and
Fletcher, he might well have come to that conclusion himself: "for Aristotle drew
his Models of Tragedy from *Sophocles* and *Euripides;* and if he had seen ours,
might have chang'd his Mind" (pp. 186-87, 191).

Thinking, no doubt, of modern heroic plays, both French and English,
Dryden especially emphasizes love as a passion scarcely attempted by the
ancients, except in the isolated case of Phaedra, but undoubtedly fit for
tragedy because it is a "Heroic Passion" (p. 186). Here he appeals again to
Rapin for support: "Rapin confesses that the *French* Tragedies now all run
upon the *Tendre,* and gives the Reason, because Love is the Passion which
most Predominates in our Souls" (p. 190).

In this quotation, as in the one on the relative importance of plot and style
which we considered above, Dryden has misconstrued Rapin by lifting a
sentence out of its argumentative context. Rapin does state, as a fact about
modern drama, that the French plays turn upon gallantry and "bend all their
Subjects to *Love* and *Tenderness*" (Part II, Ch. xx, p. 210). He suggests that
the fact may be explained, if not excused, by traits of national character; the
French are naturally gallant, and it is understandable that playwrights should
want to appeal to those sentiments:

> *Gallantry* moreover agrees with our *Manners,* and our Poets believ'd that
> they could not succeed well on the *Theatre,* but by sweet and tender
> *Sentiments;* in which, perhaps, they had some reason: For, in effect, the
> Passions represented become deform'd and insipid, unless they are
> founded on *Sentiments* conformable to those of the *Spectator.*

But Rapin cannot approve this *"New System* of *Tragedy."* It may suit with our
national humor, but it degrades tragedy "from that *Majesty* which is proper to
it, to mingle in it *Love,* which is of a Character always *Light,* and
little suitable to that *Gravity* of which *Tragedy* makes Profession."

Recognizing that this austere view will be unpalatable to French poets and most of the audience, especially the women, he says that he "is not hardy enough to declare my self against the Public," and does not dare to "presume so far on my own *Capacity* and *Credit,* to oppose my self of my own Head against a usage so established." Nevertheless, he cannot help thinking that the new system is a sign of modern degeneration, our lack of the strength needed "to sustain an *Action* on the *Theatre* by moving only *Terror* and *Pity*" (pp. 209-12). Far from supporting Dryden's attempt to broaden the definition of tragedy and defend the raising of "all the Passions in their turns," Rapin's chapter explicitly condemns that line of defense.

In his extensive and thoughtful discussion of the "Heads of an Answer to Rymer," Robert Hume accurately describes the notes as an attempt to reconcile Rymer's principles with Elizabethan dramatic practice.[39] This effort was doomed to failure from the beginning, Hume thinks, because the only convincing line of defense of Shakespeare and Fletcher would be to recognize that their plays are radically different in kind from those of the ancients and the seventeenth-century French playwrights, as Elder Olson has argued in *Tragedy and the Theory of Drama,* and consequently that the standards of French theory and practice—Rymer's principal source—are inapplicable to Elizabethan drama; it must be judged by quite different criteria.[40] Dryden, seeking to maintain the standards of classical theory and practice but to extend them to include other subjects, emotional effects, and poetic purposes, is "willing to see the differences only in terms of degree and development." His failure to draw a distinction of kind between Elizabethan tragedy and the tragedies of the Greeks inevitably leads him into inconsistencies and confusions, "dubious conclusions" and "logical contradictions." Dryden's rebuttal of Rymer "founders" on the irreconcilability of the dramatic practice of the Elizabethans with the current theory of literature, which Dryden accepts.[41]

It may well be that Olson's way of defending the Elizabethans would be more convincing, *sub specie aeternitatis,* than the lines of argument sketched in Dryden's "Heads." But if we interpret and judge those arguments in their own terms, within the framework of doctrine and method which Dryden constructed and used throughout his critical career, they do not seem at all confused or inconsistent. Olson is a modern Aristotelian, following a method which sharply and clearly differentiates poetic kinds, their effects, and the criteria which are appropriate in evaluating them. Dryden sincerely believed that he took his lights from Aristotle and Horace, but we have seen here, again and again, that he never was an Aristotelian in Olson's sense. He is an analogizer, arguing from universal principles like "delight" and "instruction" that are applicable not only to all forms of poetry but to other arts as well. He does make differentiations of kind, in subordination to the more general laws which are common to all, but his definitions of the genres are formulated in a different manner. They are broader, looser, and more flexible than Aristotle's, allowing differences of degree, admitting such odd collocations as the inclusion of *Cooper's Hill* and Juvenal's *Satires* as branches of heroic poesy, and transmuting pity and terror into concernment, admiration, and compassion. In such a system of criticism, it is entirely legitimate to argue that pity and fear, though good means of achieving the ends of tragedy, are by no means the only legitimate ones. One could even believe that if Aristotle had known our plays as well as those of Sophocles and Euripides, he "might have chang'd his Mind."

ℭℭℭ

As we come to the end of this long journey through difficult country, I believe that several general findings can be asserted with a good deal of assurance.

1. It was not one of the main purposes of this study to defend the stability and consistency of Dryden's critical thought, as it was in both of the preceding essays. It should be evident, however, that the body of doctrines and methods we have explored constitutes a coherent intellectual whole. It has many facets and is highly flexible; it may be turned to many critical uses. In different argumentative contexts, different aspects of the theory may be dominant: the unity and beauty of the work itself, the proportionality of its parts, the probable causal links which bind beginning, middle, and end together; the temper and talent of the poet, considered as the producer of a work of art; the justness and naturalness of the work's representation of human actuality; its power to arouse intense and vivid effects in the minds of its readers or spectators. But these are all parts of a single system, whose essential elements are at least potentially present from the beginning of Dryden's critical career, and which vary hardly at all to the end of it.

2. To describe Dryden's critical theory and practice as "Aristotelian"—or, for that matter, to say the same of either Rymer's or Rapin's—is not only to mistake the true historical affiliations of their kind of criticism but to commit a far more serious error of interpretation, a radical distortion of its essential structure and mode of operation as an aesthetic and critical system. Both its genesis and its definition are clearly to be found in a later and very different species of theory, in Horace, Cicero, and Quintilian, and in the Renaissance editors and commentators who reinterpreted the *Poetics* in the light of that Roman rhetorical tradition.

3. The whole system is affective, in the extended sense that it everywhere assumes that poems have perceptual, imaginative, and emotional effects on

readers and critics, and that these nonrational responses are crucial in judging the artistic merit of writers and works. If we use the convenient classification of critical species developed by M. H. Abrams in *The Mirror and the Lamp,* Dryden's belongs to the "rhetorical" or "pragmatic" kind, oriented toward the audience, which conceives a work of art as a construction designed to produce certain psychological effects and judges its value by its success in doing so. Rational theory provides the major premises of critical judgment, but the minor premises, connecting general principles with particular cases, must be supplied by the actual responses which can be observed in readers or audiences and felt by good critics. He reports such responses in all his critical essays, prefaces, and dedications, because in a system such as his they are primary data for sound aesthetic evaluation.

4. Dryden's way of reasoning is also radically teleological and intentionalistic. The two alleged "fallacies" are inseparably interlocked and mutually supportive, since in his view the poet's most basic intention is to give delight by writing a poem which will satisfy his audience's eyes and ears, fill their imaginations with lively images, and stir in their minds such passions as indignation, concernment, admiration, compassion, terror, or other specific emotional responses. To do so is the end or business of poems, and the purpose, goal, object, or design of poets.

5. Dryden's way of criticizing does not "end in impressionism and relativism," as Beardsley and Wimsatt claim that all affective systems do. It is true that he trusts his own ears, eyes, fancy, and feelings. But he has, within his system, three excellent reasons for trusting those responses, without falling into subjectivism or impressionism. The first one is that he is a *poet;* if he is a good one, as he hopes and believes, then he has by definition the delicacy of perception, energy of imagination, and sensitivity of feeling, combined with good artistic judgment, which the poet needs at least as much as the critic does. The second reason is that he believes himself to be a good *critic,* a reasonable reader who can validate his nonrational responses by the reasoned aspect of his critical judgments. He understands poetry, its ends and means, its rules and beauties; when he loves or hates a poem, he can defend his inclination by his reason. The warrant for that belief is more than thirty years of wide-ranging critical thought. The third and most fundamental reason for trusting his own responses to poems and plays is that he is a *man.* Because he shares in our common nature, he can be confident that others will be moved as he is by works of art. When he appeals to his readers to consult their own sensations, fancies, and emotions, as he does repeatedly, he tacitly assumes the constancy and uniformity of human responses to life and art. The validity of anyone's individual reactions can be confirmed or denied by checking them against those of others; they are right and natural if they agree, wrong and

worthless if they do not. As suggested earlier, we have in this assumption at least the germ of the standard of taste which Hume developed with so much precision and elegance half a century after Dryden's death.

6. Dryden's principles, terminology, and analytical categories are essentially the same as those of Rymer, Rapin, and most of the other theorists of his time. His uniqueness—and I believe his greatness as a critic—lies not in his doctrines but in certain characteristics of his habitual way of reasoning. In the first place, his treatment of the poems he discusses is far more comprehensive and flexible than that of Rymer and most other critics of that age. He can and does take account of all the manifold aspects under which a work of art can be considered, and he moves easily and without contradiction from the "just" to the "lively," "delight" to "instruction," effect to cause, or cause to effect. In the second place, Dryden is saved from the excesses of Rymer, Le Bossu, Dacier, and others by his well-thought-out assumptions about method in criticism. They are empirical and probabilistic. Rymer thought that the rules he applied were so self-evident to common sense that they are as "convincing and clear as any demonstration in *Mathematicks*."[42] But Dryden was a "sceptical critic" in the sense so lucidly defined by Phillip Harth in the admirable first chapter of *Contexts of Dryden's Thought*. The "diffidence and scepticism" which he ascribes to himself in several well-known passages is not a Pyrrhonic suspension of all belief, which would deny the possibility of either science or criticism, but a *"Scepsis Scientifica,"* like that expounded and practiced by Glanvill, Boyle, Sprat, Hooke, and other spokesmen for the Royal Society. It is an essentially optimistic epistemology, which asserts that truth in most things is within the reach of human understanding, but only if it is pursued in a modest, undogmatic spirit, taking the word of no authority on trust, grounding all generalizations on observed facts, and reaching conclusions that are not "clear as any demonstration in *Mathematicks*" but tentative and provisional, at best no more than probable.

Two monuments of that method and attitude are the *Essay of Dramatic Poesy* and the "Heads of an Answer to Rymer"—the first "so artfully variegated with successive representations of opposite probabilities,"[43] the other with its liberating faith that our perceptual, imaginative, and emotional responses as readers or spectators provide experiential evidence that may overthrow very plausible abstract arguments, that even Aristotle might have changed his mind if he had known the plays of Shakespeare and Fletcher, and that a responsible critic can explore many possible lines of reasoning without supposing that any of them could end in demonstrative certainty. But the whole body of his critical writing gives eloquent testimony to his lifelong commitment to the spirit of free inquiry, which such principles not only permit but require.

Notes

1. Dryden, *Preface to the Fables,* in *Essays,* ed. W. P. Ker (Oxford: Clarendon Press, 1926), II, 249. Citations within parentheses in the text will be to this edition except where otherwise noted. A few essays not reprinted by Ker will be cited from other editions.

2. See also the passages cited under "Propriety" by John M. Aden, *The Critical Opinions of John Dryden* (Nashville: Vanderbilt University Press, 1963), p. 198, and by H. James Jensen, *A Glossary of John Dryden's Critical Terms* (Minneapolis: University of Minnesota Press, 1969), p. 95.

3. Preface to *Tyrannic Love,* in Dryden, *Of Dramatic Poesy and Other Critical Essays,* ed. George Watson (London: J. M. Dent & Sons, 1962), I, 139.

4. Robert D. Hume, *Dryden's Criticism* (Ithaca: Cornell University Press, 1970), says of this passage that Dryden "was almost startlingly devoid of the theatrical sense we would expect of a professional playwright," and that he really preferred to have his plays read rather than performed (pp. 58-59). It is true that in Dryden's opinion a valid judgment was more likely to be made by a critic who had read a play as well as seen it, but it does not follow that he lacked theatrical sense or did not like to have his plays performed.

5. Donald F. Bond, " 'Distrust' of Imagination in English Neo-Classicism," in *Essential Articles for the Study of English Augustan Backgrounds,* ed. Bernard N. Schilling (Hamden, Conn.: Archon Books, 1961), p. 297, n.33. Bond's essay originally appeared in *PQ,* 14 (1935),54-69.

6. Jensen, pp. 50-52, 63-64. See also Frank L. Huntley, *On Dryden's "Essay of Dramatic Poesy"* (Ann Arbor: University of Michigan Press, 1951), p. 15.

7. Watson, I, 98,n.3.

8. Bond's discussion is limited to the role of the imagination in the production of intellectual and imaginative works, though several of the writers he quotes do speak of the effects of such works on the minds of audiences or readers. John M. Aden's essay, "Dryden and the Imagination: The First Phase," *PMLA,* 74 (1959),28-40, and the reply of Robert D. Hume, "Dryden on Creation: 'Imagination' in the Later Criticism," *RES,* n.s. 21 (1970),295-314, are both concerned only with the poet's imagination, not with that of readers and spectators. The same can be said of Murray Bundy, "Invention and Imagination in the Renaissance," *JEGP,* 29 (1930),535-45, and of my own article, "Joseph Warton on the Imagination," Ch. 8 below.

9. Aden, *Critical Opinions,* pp. 108, 134-35.

10. Jensen, def. 4, p. 64.

11. See the lucid analysis of Lisideius's definition by Huntley, pp. 22-23.

12. In describing Dryden's criticism as rhetorical and audience-oriented, I am using the convenient classification of critical species developed by M. H. Abrams in *The Mirror and the Lamp* (New York: Oxford University Press, 1953), Ch. 1. See also R. S. Crane, "English Neoclassical Criticism: An Outline Sketch," in *Critics and Criticism, Ancient and Modern,* ed. R. S. Crane (Chicago: University of Chicago Press, 1952), pp. 372-88, esp. pp. 375, 377-78.

13. Samuel Johnson, *Preface to Shakespeare,* in *Works of Samuel Johnson,* Vol. VII *Johnson on Shakespeare,* ed. Arthur Sherbo (New Haven: Yale University Press, 1968), pp. 76-77.

14. In their discussion of relations, both Lisideius and Neander follow Horace (*Ars Poetica,* 11. 180-87) and Pierre Corneille (*Discours de trois unités,* in *Oeuvres,* ed. Charles Marty-Laveaux [Paris: Librairie Hachette, 1862-1922], I, 100-101).

15. Huntley, p. 51.

16. Johnson, *Preface to Shakespeare,* pp. 77-78.

17. Ibid., pp. 61-71.

18. In the preface to *Annus Mirabilis,* Dryden had said earlier that dramatic dialogue is "supposed to be the effect of sudden thought" (I, 15).

19. Earlier in the debate, Crites states the rule for unity of time in a similarly relativistic way. He does not contend that the fictional time should be identical with performance time, but rather that it "should be proportioned as near as can be to the duration of that time in which it is represented." He thinks the outer limit should be a twenty-four-hour natural day (I, 38-39).

20. Huntley, pp. 53-54.

21. W. K. Wimsatt and Monroe C. Beardsley, "The Affective Fallacy," *The Verbal Icon* (Lexington, Ky.: University of Kentucky Press, 1954), pp. 21-39; the essay was originally published in 1949. One of the oddest things about the very strange argument by which Wimsatt and Beardsley support their thesis is that they make no effort at all to show that the aesthetic theories of Plato, Aristotle, and Longinus, which they recognize to be affective, are formally or materially fallacious, or that their doctrines "end in impressionism and relativism," as they say all such theories do.

22. Virgil *Eclogues* iii.90; the second quotation has not been identified.

23. Dryden's final comment on the *Spanish Friar* is that "The faults of that drama are in the kind of it, which is tragi-comedy. But it was given to the people: and I never writ any thing for myself but Antony and Cleopatra" (II, 152). His ultimate judgment of the mixed genre is the same as that of Lisideius in the *Essay* (I, 57-58; cf. I, 166).

24. James S. Malek, *The Arts Compared: An Aspect of Eighteenth-Century British Aesthetics* (Detroit: Wayne State University Press, 1974), p. 22.

25. See Bernard Weinberg, "Robortello on the *Poetics,*" in Crane, *Critics and Criticism,* pp. 319-48.

26. Jensen, p. 20. See also J. E. Gillet, "A Note on the Tragic 'Admiratio,' " *Modern Language Review,* 13 (1918), 233-38.

27. E. N. Hooker, ed., *The Critical Works of John Dennis* (Baltimore: Johns Hopkins University Press, 1939-43), I, 455. Cf. H. T. Swedenberg, Jr., *The Theory of the Epic in England, 1650-1800* (Berkeley and Los Angeles: University of California Press, 1944), pp. 47, 51, 64-65, 195.

28. Dr. Johnson says that Dryden "might have determined the question upon surer evidence, for it is quoted by Quintilian as the work of Seneca," but it is like Dryden to have confidence in his own impressions; his remarks about the coldness or insipidity of most French drama are very similar, though he does not use them as a basis for determining authorship, as he does here.

29. See the interesting essay by H. T. Swedenberg, Jr., "Dryden's Excessive Concern with the Heroic," in *Essays in English Literature of the Classical Period Presented to Dougald MacMillan,* ed. Daniel W. Patterson and Albrecht B. Strauss (Chapel Hill: University of North Carolina Press, 1967), pp. 12-26.

30. I will follow the text of the "Heads" given in *The Works of John Dryden,* Vol. XVII, ed. Samuel H. Monk and A. E. Wallace Maurer (Berkeley and Los Angeles: University of California Press, 1971), pp. 185-93. Page references will be given within parentheses in the text.

31. Fred G. Walcott, "John Dryden's Answer to Thomas Rymer's *The Tragedies of the Last Age,*" *PQ,* 15 (1936),194-214; Baxter Hathaway, "John Dryden and the Function of Tragedy," *PMLA,* 58 (1943),665-73; the reply to Hathaway by E. N. Hooker, *PQ,* 23 (1944), 162-63; Curt A. Zimansky, *The Critical Works of Thomas Rymer* (New Haven: Yale University Press, 1956), pp. xxxiii-xxxvi; George Watson, "Dryden's First Answer to Rymer," *RES,* n.s. 14(1963),17-23; Robert D. Hume, "Dryden's 'Heads of an Answer to Rymer': Notes toward a Hypothetical Revolution," *RES,* n.s. 19(1968), 373-86; idem, *Dryden's Criticism,* pp. 103-23; the California edition of Dryden, IX,411-17; Joan C. Grace, *Tragic Theory in the Critical Works of Thomas Rymer, John Dennis, and John Dryden* (Rutherford, N.J.: Fairleigh Dickinson University Press, 1975), pp. 113-17.

32. All citations of Rymer will refer to Zimansky's edition, with page numbers given within parentheses in the text.

33. Zimansky, pp. xxviii-xxix.

34. Dean T. Mace, "Dryden's Dialogue on Drama," *Journal of the Warburg and Courtauld Institute,* XXV (1962),87-112, and Hume, *Dryden's Criticism,* pp. 190-203, especially emphasize the contrast between Crites' literal conception of nature and the concept of "heightened" nature defended by Lisideius and Neander. In the *Parallel of Poetry and Painting,* following the quasi Platonist Bellori, Dryden says that both epic poetry and historical painting

imitate perfect beauty and ideal form, though he interprets the concepts as ideas existing only in the mind of the artist, synthesized from the scattered, imperfect beauties found in individuals. In tragedy, comedy, and portrait painting, however, he says that an imitation of ideal form is impossible, because their perfection lies in "their likeness to the deficient faulty nature" (II, 123).

35. Zimansky, pp. xxxiii-xxxvii; Hume, *Dryden's Criticism,* pp. 107-17; California ed., IX, 411-16.

36. *The Letters of John Dryden,* ed., Charles E. Ward (Durham, N.C.: Duke University Press, 1962), pp. 13-14, 71-72.

37. Zimansky, p. 19. In the preface to *An Evening's Love* (1671), Dryden himself had attacked writers of farces as mere "empirics": they are like mountebank doctors, who may sometimes succeed by chance, but who have no knowledge or understanding of what they do. Good poets and dramatists, on the other hand, are like true physicians: they understand the principles of their art, the reasons for what they do and the causes of their success (I, 136).

38. Cf. Réné Rapin, *Whole Critical Works* (London, 1706), II, 204. All page numbers given within parentheses in the text refer to Vol. II of this edition.

39. Hume, *Dryden's Criticism,* p. 120.

40. Ibid., pp. 111-12. Elder Olson, *Tragedy and the Theory of Drama* (Detroit: Wayne State University Press, 1961), Chs. 7-9.

41. Hume, *Dryden's Criticism,* pp. 108, 109, 111-13, 115, 116, 117.

42. Rymer, "Preface to Rapin," Zimansky, pp. 2-3.

43. Samuel Johnson, "Life of Dryden," *Lives of the English Poets,* ed. G. B. Hill (Oxford, 1905), I, 412.

PART TWO

———— ⚘ ————

The Scriblerians

4

Swift and Socrates

In Swift's prose writings, poems, and letters there are some thirty explicit references to Socrates and almost as many more to works and ideas of Plato. These allusions occur over a period of forty years, from the "Ode to the Athenian Society" in 1692 and Swift's first political tract, *A Discourse of the Contests and Dissensions between the Nobles and the Commons in Athens and Rome* (1701), to a piece of light verse written in 1732 and a letter to Pope dated 1 May 1733. The major works have their fair share of such references, with three in *A Tale of a Tub* and two in *Gulliver's Travels,* Books III and IV. Swift had a seal with a head of Socrates, used among other things to countersign a holograph draft of his will, and his library included two sixteenth-century folio editions of Plato's works in Greek (both with Latin translations), one of which he had annotated.[1] His interest in Socrates and Plato, as men and thinkers, was lifelong.

It is not likely that Swift devoted much time to studying the writings of Plato after his early formative years, though he continued to remember a few key passages long afterward.[2] His many allusions to both Plato and Socrates are for the most part quite conventional, citing facts and ideas familiar to most educated persons of his period. The references do show, however, that some facts or legends about the life and character of Socrates, along with a small number of Platonic concepts and propositions, formed part of that vocabulary of ideas, distinctions, historical examples, and symbols on which he drew for a variety of uses throughout his career.

Considered as empirical data, these references provide a body of evidence, limited yet significant, from which some inferences may be drawn as to Swift's intellectual convictions on several subjects, and which may also shed light on the interpretation of particular works and passages whose meaning and bearing have been debated by scholars. As I shall try to show, the allusions are especially pertinent to determining his attitude toward the freethinkers, among whom he includes the deists; his position on the place of reason both in religion and in morality; and the interpretation of Gulliver's Fourth Voyage.

✣✣✣

We may begin by reviewing rapidly a miscellaneous group of examples, some of them quite trivial in content, which will give us some notion of the main components of his conception of the two great Greeks, the sources from which they were drawn, and the diverse functions they serve in both ironic and nonironic writings.

Several references occur in minor works attacking freethinkers, "modern" writers generally, and the Whigs, all favorite objects of satiric ridicule. In the phrase, "All the Philosophers in the World, from the Age of *Socrates* to ours," for example, Swift is mocking the "refined Way of Speaking" in the attack on the rights of the church by the freethinker Tindal, and when he says that Lord Carteret is credibly reported to have sometimes quoted passages out of Plato and Pindar, he is laughing at Whiggish dissatisfaction with the lord lieutenant's singular taste for the classics, a regrettable weak side resulting from his "old unfashionable Academick Education." The ironical vindication of Lord Carteret also includes one of two allusions to an apocryphal tale that "Socrates, a Heathen Philosopher, was found dancing by himself at Four-score" and that "a King called Caesar Augustus (or some such Name) used to play with Boys; whereof some might possibly be Sons of Tories." Swift had cited the same two examples, long before, with a similar ironic implication, in a letter written to Archbishop King in 1708.[3]

There are two references to the comic treatment of Socrates by Aristophanes in the *Clouds*. According to the putative author of the introduction to *A Tale of a Tub* (1704), "the Philosopher's Way in all Ages has been by erecting certain *Edifices in the Air* . . . not excepting even that of Socrates, when he was suspended in a Basket to help Contemplation."[4] In his "Answer to a Scandalous Poem" (1732), a whimsical reply to a *jeu d'esprit* by Thomas Sheridan in which women are compared to clouds, Swift speaks on behalf of the affronted clouds. The poem is "scandalous" from their point of view, because they find the analogy insolent and degrading. Among other proofs of their immense superiority, the clouds cite Socrates:

Tis known, that Socrates the wise
Ador'd the Clouds as Deityes.
To us he made his dayly pray'rs,
As Aristophanes declares;
From Jupiter took all dominion,
And dy'd defending his opinion.[5]

Similarly facetious, though more closely related to historical fact, is a reference in *A Tritical Essay upon the Faculties of the Mind* (1707). One of Swift's many parodies of the writings of Grub Street moderns, the essay is a jumbled collection of trite topics and stale quotations which never mentions its ostensible subject, the faculties of the mind. It absurdly brackets Aristotle, said to have drowned himself because he could not explain the ebb and flow of the tides, with Socrates, who "was pronounced by the Oracle to be the wisest Man in the World," although he said he knew nothing (*PW*, I, 247).[6] Assuming that Socrates' assertion proves the oracle wrong, the modern author thinks that both of his examples illustrate the worthlessness of all ancient thinkers.

A Letter of Advice to a Young Poet (1721) is another ironic attack on the moderns. Among other outrageous precepts, it recommends that Scripture be studied as "a Fund *of* Wit, and a Subject *for* Wit," in accordance with the practice of all modern poets, and that the aspiring neophyte should encumber himself as little as possible with the "Pedantry of Learning," since flowers of wit "ought to spring, as those in a Garden do, from their own Root and Stem, without Foreign Assistance" (*PW*, IX, 328-33). In the following passage the "forementioned Author" is Sir Philip Sidney, whose *Defense of Poesy* is humorously cited throughout the letter:

Some of the old Philosophers were Poets (as according to the forementioned Author, *Socrates* and *Plato* were, which however is what I did not know before) but that does not say, that all Poets are, or that any need be Philosophers, otherwise than as those are so call'd who are a little out at the Elbows. . . . Nor must it be forgotten that Plato was an avow'd Enemy to Poets, which is perhaps the Reason why Poets have been always at Enmity with his Profession; and have rejected all Learning and Philosophy for the sake of that one Philosopher. As I take the matter, neither Philosophy, nor any part of Learning, is more necessary to *Poetry* (which if you will believe the same Author is *the sum of all Learning*) than to know the Theory of Light, and the several Proportions and Diversifications of it in particular Colours is to a good Painter. (*PW*, IX, 332)

Whether the letter was written by Swift himself or by someone consciously imitating his style, as Herbert Davis thinks possible,[7] its playful use of Plato in an ironical attack on modern wits makes the same point against them that Swift made most memorably in the fable of the Spider and the Bee. The whole piece is very much in the vein of the earlier *Battle of the Books,* the Digressions in *A Tale of a Tub,* and the contemptuous treatment of the ignorant and irreverent young gentlemen of wit and pleasure in the *Argument against Abolishing Christianity.*

Squire Bickerstaff mentions Socrates twice in his *Predictions for the Year 1708.* To emphasize the great gulf between ignorant pretenders like Partridge and the true noble art of astrology, he claims that the latter "hath been in all Ages defended by many learned Men; and among the rest, by Socrates himself; whom I look upon as undoubtedly the wisest of uninspired Mortals" (*PW,* II, 142). He also cites Socrates to show that in some cases "the Stars do only *incline,* and not force the Actions or Wills of Men":

> A Man may, by the Influence of an over-ruling Planet, be disposed or inclined to Lust, Rage, or Avarice; and yet by the Force of Reason overcome that evil Influence. And this was the Case of *Socrates.* (*PW,* II, 144)

The allusions seem to reflect the engaging mixture of folly and dignity that made the character of Isaac Bickerstaff so appealing to Swift's contemporaries. The claim that Socrates was a defender of astrology must have been meant to seem patently absurd, since both Xenophon and Cicero had said—as we shall see later in another context—that the great historical achievement of Socrates was to turn men's thoughts from the study of the planets to an examination of the ethical problems of their own daily lives. As such, the claim is in keeping with Bickerstaff's laughable obsession with the astrological art and his conception of himself as a man of learning and a responsible scientist. On the other hand, it is to his credit that he thinks Socrates "the wisest of uninspired Mortals" and that he should protect his religious orthodoxy by reconciling the influence of the stars with freedom of the will, at least in such a rare instance of rational self-control as Socrates provides.

Somewhat different from the preceding examples, since it turns upon a Platonic myth rather than on tales about Socrates the man, is an allusion in the *Examiner,* no. 31 (8 March 1708), to the speech of Aristophanes in the *Symposium,* which traces the origin of love to divided man's eternal search for his other half. In Swift's refinement of the myth, a second slicing of mankind produces hatred, faction, and parties, which "not only split a Nation, but every Individual among them, leaving each but half their Strength, and Wit, and Honesty, and good Nature" (*PW,* III, 101-2). He uses the same idea, without explicitly referring to Plato, in one of his birthday poems to Stella, which characteristically mixes realistic deflation, parody of conventional love-compliment, and backhanded praise. Because her years and size have doubled since he first knew her, he comically wishes that she and his love might both be halved:

> Oh, would it please the Gods to split
> Thy Beauty, Size, and Years, and Wit,
> No Age could furnish out a Pair
> Of Nymphs so gracefull, Wise and fair
> With half the Lustre of Your Eyes,
> With half your Wit, your Years and Size:
> And then before it grew too late,
> How should I beg of gentle Fate,
> (That either Nymph might have her Swain,)
> To split my Worship too in twain. (*Poems,* II, 722)

A few allusions refer to specific Platonic doctrines. In discussing the books in Swift's library, Harold Williams says: "It may seem strange that Swift, who never concealed his contempt for abstract metaphysics, should discover a genuine feeling for Plato, as he undoubtedly did. It was probably the political philosophy that appealed to him."[8] The content of Swift's allusions to Plato do not confirm this conjecture, but he did refer twice to two Platonic propositions about government: the assertions in the *Republic* that in a city composed entirely of good men, "to avoid office would be as much an object of contention as to obtain office is at present," and that the strongest inducement for a good man to take office is the realization that "he who refuses to rule is liable to be ruled by one who is worse than himself."[9] The earlier of Swift's references to these statements, in the *Discourse of the Contests and Dissensions . . . in Athens and Rome* (1701), was written before he had left the Whig Party to join the Tories under Harley and Bolingbroke, and his purpose is to defend Whig leaders threatened with impeachment. In ancient times, he says, men of virtue and abilities were discouraged from public service by demagogic impeachments of men like Miltiades, Aristides, Phocion, and Pericles himself:

This was so well known in *Greece,* that an Eagerness after Employments in the State, was looked upon by wise Men, as the worst Title a Man could set up; and made *Plato* say, *That if all Men were as good as they ought; the Quarrel in a Commonwealth would be, not as it is now, who* should *be Ministers of State, but who should* not *be so.* And Socrates is introduced by Xenophon severely chiding a Friend of his for not entering into the publick Service, when he was every way qualified for it (*PW,* I, 224-25).[10]

Some Advice to the October Club (1712) was written in a very different rhetorical situation, after Swift had left the Whigs, though again his purpose was to oppose vindictive treatment of political opponents. The October Club, a sizable group of country Tories described by Trevelyan as "Jacobite when drunk and Hanoverian when sober,"[11] was troublesome to the Tory ministers because, as Swift wrote to Stella, they "drive things on to extremes against the Whigs, to call the old ministry to account, and get off five or six heads."[12] His letter to them is a piece of straight political rhetoric, entirely without irony. Writing as an anonymous "Person of Honour" and addressing members of the club in a conciliatory tone as "true Lovers of our Constitution in Church and State," Swift hoped to persuade them that Harley should be trusted and that pressing him for purges would only play into the hands of the common enemy. In this context, Swift's reference to the Platonic penalty for refusing to serve the state is shrewdly calculated, at the climax of his argument, to arouse fears that the government might fall without achieving the much-desired peace. It might then be succeeded by a new Whig ascendancy of insatiable malice toward the church, the monarchy, and everyone opposed to its venomous schemes:

> In such a Juncture, I cannot discover why a wise and honest Man should venture to place himself at the Head of Affairs, upon any other regard than the Safety of his Country, and the Advice of *Socrates,* to *prevent an ill Man from coming in.* (*PW,* VI, 79)

Both here and in the *Contests and Dissensions,* Swift's allusions to the discussion between Socrates and Thrasymachus in the first book of the *Republic* show less interest in Plato's political philosophy than in the satirical or rhetorical potentialities of a striking and memorable notion, still carrying a penumbra of favorable Socratic connotation but totally isolated from its original intellectual setting.

We may conclude this preliminary survey with two further instances, both in nonironic writings. In *The Sentiments of a Church-of-England Man* (1711; written 1708), Swift argues for a moderate position, opposed to the extremes of both Whigs and Tories on the great issues of religion and government. He uses Plato and Socrates to support his warning on the dangers of religious schism:

> And I think it clear, that any great Separation from the established Worship, although to a new one that is more pure and perfect, may be an Occasion of endangering the publick Peace; because, it will compose a

Body always in Reserve, prepared to follow any discontented Heads, upon the plausible Pretexts of advancing true Religion, and opposing Error, Superstition, or Idolatory. For this Reason, *Plato* lays it down as a Maxim, that *Men ought to worship the Gods, according to the Laws of the Country;* and he introduceth *Socrates,* in his last Discourse, utterly disowning the Crime laid to his Charge, of teaching new *Divinities,* or Methods of Worship. (*PW,* II, 11-12)[13]

This conservative maxim, obviously a fundamental one for Swift's whole outlook on the most heated controversies of his age, will appear again later in this essay, when we examine his reply to the freethinker Anthony Collins.

The latest of all his allusions to Socrates and Plato occurs in a long letter to Pope, in which he comments briefly on the newly published first epistle of the *Essay on Man:*

What is, is best, is the thought of Socrates in Plato, because it is permitted or done by God. . . . I have retained it after reading Plato many years ago. (*Corr.,*IV,153)

Here, as in his other references to specific Platonic passages, it is not the dialectical arguments that he remembers, but only a few separable propositions or maxims. Some of them, as we have seen, are little more than materials for whimsical jokes, instruments of satiric deflation, or conveniences in rhetorical persuasion. A few, however, were of lasting importance to him as confirmation, from an admired non-Christian source, of ideas which were essential elements in his own philosophy of religion, ethics, and government.

❦❦❦

I have remarked that it was to Bickerstaff's credit that he considered Socrates to have been "the wisest of uninspired mortals." In a number of other references, Swift himself takes Socrates as a model of wisdom and virtue. Some of these allusions occur in playful or satirical contexts, but they all present Socrates as one of the admirable worthies of human history, who have shown by their thoughts and acts what men at their best are capable of. Two modern students of Swift, J. C. Maxwell and M. M. Kelsall, have discussed some of the wider issues raised by these passages.

The trial and death of Socrates, as recorded in Xenophon's *Memorabilia* and Plato's *Apology, Phaedo,* and *Crito,* held a special appeal for Swift, as they have for many others over the centuries. In his list of admirable and contemptible human actions—"Of Mean and Great Figures Made by Several Persons" (undated)—Socrates is one of those who made great figures:

"Socrates, the whole last Day of his Life, and particularly from the Time he took the Poison to the Moment he expired" (*PW,* V, 83). His accuser Anytus naturally represents the opposite ethical extreme, as Swift indicates in replying (1728) to an objection against his severe criticism of the lately deceased Chief Justice Whitsed for his part in the controversy over Wood's halfpence:

> . . . a most foolish Precept, that *de mortuis nil nisi bonum;* so that if *Socrates,* and *Anytus* his Accuser, had happened to die together, the Charity of Survivors must either have obliged them to hold their Peace, or to fix the same Character on both.[14]

To Swift, always given to simple black-and-white moral contrasts, Anytus is as much a pattern of evil as Socrates is of wisdom, courage, and serenity of mind.

In several other places Swift lists men of extraordinary moral character. A facetious example is the reference in *A Tale of a Tub* to Socrates, Pythagoras, and Aesop as men outwardly ugly who were misjudged because "transitory Gazers have so dazzled their Eyes, and fill'd their Imaginations with the outward Lustre, as neither to regard or consider, the Person or the Parts of the Owner within" (*PW,* I, 40). Swift probably had in mind Alcibiades' description of Socrates, in the *Symposium,* as a mask of Silenus, ugly outside but when opened revealing divine and golden images within.

In another jest in the Dedication of the *Tale,* Socrates is bracketed with other famous men of antiquity. The Bookseller, putative author of the Dedication, tells how the Grub Street writers, when he had asked for "Hints and Materials, towards a Panegyrick upon your Lordship's [Prince Posterity's] Virtues," had brought him ten sheets of stale commonplaces, which they claimed to have ransacked from "the Characters of *Socrates, Aristides, Epaminondas, Cato, Tully, Atticus,* and other hard Names, which I cannot now recollect" (*PW,* I, 14). Two of the same worthies, Socrates and Cato, are mentioned with more serious intent in "To Stella, Visiting Me in My Sickness." If she wishes to attain "True Honour," which comprehends all the virtues described by moralists, she must:

> Ask no Advice, but think, alone,
> Suppose the Question not your own:
> How shall I act? is not the Case,
> But how would *Brutus* in my Place?
> In such a Cause would *Cato* bleed?
> And how would *Socrates* proceed?
>
> (*Poems,* II, 724)

If she follows this rule, Stella will be enrolled, like heroes and heroines of old, among her "Brethren of the Skies."

Brutus, Cato, and Socrates appear again in the most seriously intended of these lists of worthies, in the Glubbdubdrib episode of Gulliver's Third Voyage:

> I had the Honour to have much Conversation with Brutus; and was told that his Ancestor *Junius, Socrates, Epaminondas, Cato* the Younger, Sir *Thomas More* and himself, were perpetually together: a *Sextumvirate* to which all the Ages of the World cannot add a Seventh. (*PW,* XI, 196)

Epaminondas, Cato, and More had all been included, along with Socrates, among those admirable men who made great figures by some particular actions or circumstances of their lives; Cato was the best of the Romans, according to Swift, and Sir Thomas More was "the only man of true virtue that ever England produced."[15] In this sextumvirate of the truly good, Swift's small company of secular saints, Socrates held a secure and unquestioned place.

Two of these passages—those from the poem to Stella and from the Third Voyage—are briefly discussed in an essay by J. C. Maxwell, published some years ago in *Scrutiny*.[16] Linking these references with the fable of the Spider and the Bee in the *Battle of the Books,* Maxwell argues that all three illustrate the "flimsiness" of the Augustan image of antiquity, an arbitrarily selective construction, incompatible with a truly historical attitude toward the past. It would be impossible, he says, to form any clear idea of what the ancients stand for in the *Battle:* " 'honey and wax,' 'sweetness and light,' are the merest counters." Brutus, Cato, and Socrates are similarly vague and remote, "bloodless stock figures of 'virtue,' " who carry with them a certain traditional prestige and emotive potency, but who have no definite or positive symbolic content. They are used by Swift to serve his totally destructive purpose, the scornful damnation of contemporary civilization. In this last remark, Maxwell echoes the *Scrutiny* party line on Swift, of which Leavis's essay, "The Irony of Swift," is the best-known expression.[17]

If a truly historical attitude toward the past is one of total detachment and neutrality, we can readily agree that Swift's view of the ancients is unhistorical. He sees the past through the eyes of a moralist, distinguishing good men and great actions from bad and mean ones, always seeking for models and standards which can help to guide us, as he advises Stella, in the ethical decisions of our own lives. Swift, of course, would have denied vehemently that his many attacks on the values and practices of a corrupt society were destructive in either purpose or effect. From the point of view of the satiric victims, satire is no doubt destructive by definition, since its purpose is to attack and expose their follies and vices. But why should the

critic take up their cause? Do Maxwell and Leavis want to defend the values
of a godless, mercenary, power- and pleasure-seeking society? And if Leavis
is entitled to his Great Tradition—one which is, incidentally, just as moralistic
in its way as Swift's, and much more arbitrarily selective—why should not
Swift have his?

I don't know why Maxwell finds the Bee and the Sextumvirate vague and
empty of content. The meaning of ''honey and wax'' is lucidly expounded not
only by the Bee but by Aesop as well: they are the sweetness of art and
beauty, the light of reason and truth. Both are derived from a diligent and
humble search through nature and the best thought of the past, and are made
available to men in all ages through *''our* Wings *and our* Voice''—the
imaginative flights and the language of great poets, both the ancients and their
latter-day admirers and allies (*PW,* I, 149-51). Socrates, Brutus, and Cato
may seem bloodless to Maxwell, but in Swift's imagination they were alive as
truly wise and virtuous men, whose thoughts and acts had been recorded and
attested by ancient historians and biographers. In satiric attack, their function
is to reveal by contrast the pride and tawdriness of ''modern'' society and
men; their affirmative moral value is to show that we do not have to live by the
stupid and vicious standards of such a society. Though all the ages of the
world cannot add a seventh to the noble Sextumvirate, they are a lasting proof
that human beings can live wisely and virtuously if they only will. Even today
the Six may serve as models and norms, to help us attain True Honour in the
moral decisions of our own lives.

Kelsall, too, discusses the Sextumvirate and their relation to Swift's
attitude toward the ancients, but he raises an entirely different critical problem
from the one Maxwell addresses—the meaning and function of the
Houyhnhnms in *Gulliver's Travels.* Connecting the Sextumvirate with the
Utopias of Plato and Sir Thomas More, Kelsall uses those associations as
evidence against the ''soft'' or anti-Houyhnhnm interpretation of the Fourth
Voyage.[18] In choosing his Sextumvirate, Swift was ''once again paying
tribute to the ancients.'' The heroes, as historical examples, embody
traditional ideals of fortitude, temperance, and public-spirited benevolence, to
which Plato had given classic expression in the guardians of the *Republic.*
Both the heroes and the guardians would have been perfectly at home in the
land of the noble horses:

> In its ideal picture of the Guardians the *Republic* depicts a race of men
> morally of basically the same breed as the horses (Platonic metaphysics
> we may omit as certainly not Socratic) and individually of the same
> mould as Swift's heroes. . . . The horses represent an ideal, therefore,
> which is completely traditional. It may be paralleled not only in the ideal

community of Plato (and of More), but also in the actual lives of the sextumvirate, whether their ideals were Socratic, Stoical, or Christian.

This traditional ideal, which identifies virtue with reason, is philosophically defended by Plato and other ancient thinkers, is fictionally presented in the Utopians of More and the Houyhnhnms of Swift, and is validated as humanly possible by the great actions of the historical Sextumvirate.[19] If these equations are correct, Swift surely cannot have intended the Houyhnhnms to be taken as objects of satiric attack.

Other scholars have advanced other kinds of internal and external evidence for rejecting the ''soft'' interpretation of the Fourth Voyage, some of which are doubtless more fundamental and conclusive,[20] but I think Kelsall's line of reasoning has some merit as adding still further weight to the case for the ''hard'' interpretation, which takes the Houyhnhnms as Swift's satiric norm, the rational ideal against which the moral worth of Gulliver and all men may be measured. I believe, in fact, that Kelsall's argument can be extended and strengthened by observing a further, more specific parallel between the guardians and the Houyhnhnms.

Swift himself suggests such a parallel in a key passage in the Fourth Voyage, when he says that his Houyhnhnm master ''agreed entirely with the Sentiments of *Socrates,* as *Plato* delivers them; which I mention as the highest Honour I can do that Prince of Philosophers'' (*PW,* XI, 267-68). The basis of this agreement, of course, is that in Houyhnhnmland, as in Plato's republic, reason governs both within the individual and in the state:

As these noble *Houyhnhnms* are endowed by Nature with a general Disposition to all Virtues, and have no Conceptions or Ideas of what is evil in a rational Creature; so their grand Maxim is, to cultivate *Reason,* and to be wholly governed by it (*PW,* XI, 267).

If virtue is identified with reason, it follows that a rational being can be recognized by the ethical quality of his behavior. As Plato's guardians exhibit the ''marks of a philosopher,'' so the Houyhnhnms carry the ''marks of a rational creature.'' The noble horses, ''so orderly and rational, so acute and judicious'' (*PW,* XI, 226), are shown by all their actions, as well as by Gulliver's praises, to be just, temperate, teachable, courteous, cleanly, and gentle. As shown in the sixth book of the *Republic,* the moral qualities of Plato's philosopher-guardians are virtually identical. Philosophic minds, those which love truth and seek knowledge, must inevitably possess many other excellences:

He whose desires are drawn toward knowledge in every form will be

absorbed in the pleasures of the soul, and will hardly feel bodily
pleasure—I mean, if he be a true philosopher and not a sham one. . . .
Such a one is sure to be temperate and the reverse of covetous; for the
motives which make another man desirous of having and spending, have
no place in his character. . . . Can he who is harmoniously constituted,
who is not covetous or mean, or a boaster, or a coward—can he, I say,
ever be unjust or hard in his dealings?

    . . . Then you will soon observe whether a man is just and gentle, or
rude and unsociable; these are the signs which distinguish even in youth
the philosophical nature from the unphilosophical. . . . And must not
that be a blameless study which he only can pursue who has the gift of a
good memory, and is quick to learn—noble, gracious, the friend of truth,
justice, courage, temperance, who are his kindred?[21]

Kelsall observes parenthetically that in recognizing an analogy between the
guardians and the Houyhnhnms, we need not commit Swift to an acceptance
of Platonic metaphysics. The point deserves emphasis, for it is fundamental to
a correct understanding of Swift's relation to Plato. The Fourth Voyage is a
satirical fiction, not a philosophical treatise. In the *Republic* the marks of a
philosopher are logical conclusions within an elaborate dialectical framework;
the traits of the Houyhnhnms are signs and effects of their imputed fictional
character as rational animals. Swift not only ignores the reasoning through
which these and other Platonic conclusions are reached, but also eliminates
everything abstruse and technical in the philosophical system developed in the
Republic. In *Gulliver's Travels* we hear nothing of the five forms of the state
and of the soul; nothing of the Idea of the Good, "which is the author of
science and truth, and yet surpasses them in beauty"; nothing of the
distinction between being and becoming, the immutable and the fluctuating;
nothing of reason as the faculty, above the region of hypotheses and images,
which ascends to first principles. The complex epistemology of the "divided
Line" is reduced to a commonsense distinction between knowledge and
opinion. "Temperance" is defined in the *Republic* as "the agreement of the
naturally superior and inferior, as to the right to rule of either, both in states
and individuals," but the temperance of the Houyhnhnms is simply a decency
and moderation in fulfilling bodily needs.[22] The noble horses are wise and
good in an unanalyzed, everyday meaning of those words, but they are far
from being philosophers as conceived by Plato. Finally, the purpose of the
Fourth Voyage is not to discover philosophical truth, nor even to teach it;
rather, its aim is rhetorical: to convince its readers that pride in their supposed
rationality is wholly unwarranted, since the pittance of reason allotted to

human beings is used by most of us only to "aggravate our *natural* Corruptions, and to acquire new ones which Nature had not given us."

Fundamental though these differences are, they do not invalidate Kelsall's association of the Houyhnhnms with the Sextumvirate and the guardians, nor do they weaken its probative force as evidence that Gulliver's veneration for the horses cannot have been ironically intended. All that either Kelsall or I would contend is that Swift invented the Houyhnhnms as a fictional embodiment, within a devastating attack upon human pride, of the same principle which Plato defended in the *Republic* and elsewhere and which Socrates exemplified in his life and death—that reason and virtue are inseparable.

✠✠✠

Swift's reply to Anthony Collins's *Defence of Free-Thinking* includes a fairly extensive passage about Socrates and Plato, a longish paragraph on the former and a shorter one on the latter. Within the context of the body of evidence we are reviewing here, the chief significance of these references lies not in their intellectual content, but rather in their exemplification of Swift's consistently held and well-thought-out policy in dealing with the anti-Christian writers of his age, those *"Atheists, Deists, Socinians, Anti-Trinitarians,* and other Subdivisions of *Free-Thinkers"* whom he attacks with so much scorn and contempt in the *Argument against Abolishing Christianity* (*PW,* II, 36). The rationale behind his policy is explicitly spelled out in a number of Swift's other writings, but its operation in practice can best be understood by a three-way comparison between the book he attacks, his reply, and another answer to Collins, the *Remarks on a Defence of Free-Thinking* by Richard Bentley, which reflects a very different conception of the most effective method of counterattack against the swarming freethinkers and other contemporary enemies of Christianity and the church.

Anthony Collins (1676-1729) was a man of respectable background, educated at Eton and King's College, Cambridge, who inherited a good estate in Essex and, after leaving London in his late thirties, served as justice of the peace and deputy lieutenant and treasurer for the county. He was a friend of Locke's in the years just before the philosopher's death, and also of the French skeptical scholars Le Clerc and Des Maizeaux. He is identified as a deist in Sir Leslie Stephens's account of him in the *Dictionary of National Biography,* described in fact as "the most conspicuous of the deist writers who took the line of historical criticism."[23] Several of his works do have a somewhat deistical cast, as one can gather from titles like *Essay concerning the Use of Reason* (1707) and *Discourse on the Grounds and Reasons of the Christian Religion* (1724). Even in these works, however, his assumptions and arguments are by no means exclusively deistic and historical, and in many of his other writings, including the *Discourse* which Swift attacked, there are no specifically deistic doctrines or modes of reasoning. The common element which does run through everything he wrote is hostility to Christian beliefs, the practices and laws of the English church, and especially the Anglican clergy. Reading pieces like his *Letter to Mr. Dodwell* (1707), against Samuel Clarke's arguments for the immortality of the soul, or *Priestcraft in Perfection* (1709), contending that the alleged authority of the church in controversies of faith is based on a fraudulent clause in the Thirty-Nine Articles, or *Defence of the Divine Attributes* (1710), attacking a sermon on predestination by Archbishop King, one feels that Collins is a man driven by an irrational hatred, who continually probes his opponents' intellectual and historical position for possible points of weakness to be attacked by any arguments or evidences that fall to hand.

Not to prejudge the case, however, let us summarize his defense of freethinking as factually and neutrally as we can, leaving Bentley and Swift to bring out its intellectual tone and quality. In the original edition, the *Discourse of Free-Thinking, Occasioned by the Rise and Growth of a Sect Call'd Free-Thinkers* (London, 1713) is a book of 178 octavo pages. It is written in the form of a letter, but since the writer and the recipient are both unnamed and neither is assigned any real or feigned traits of individual character, the epistolary device seems to have no rhetorical purpose or effect. The anonymity, which extends to the printer and bookseller as well, is perhaps meant to be given some meaning and force, for in the final sentence of the book Collins implies that anyone associated with the *Discourse* is almost sure to be persecuted. If his friend thinks the book worth publishing, he should conceal his connection with it: "For I think it Virtue enough to endeavour to do good, only within the bounds of doing your self no Harm" (p. 178). The author must have been almost immediately known, however, because Swift ascribes the work to Collins in the title of his reply.

Collins begins by asserting that *"self-evident Truths"* are the principles of knowledge and the foundation of all reasoning.[24] Men who deny what is self-evident are in a "Distemper'd State of Mind," so that they must follow either some disordered fancies of their own or, more commonly, the "Dictates of artificial designing Men or crack-brained Enthusiasts," who arrogantly "presume to be *Guides* to others in Matters of *Speculation*." Freethinking, he says, is one of those "Subjects too evident to be made plainer, and which ought to be admitted on the first Proposal," but since the designing men and their dupes are beyond the reach of reason, while all others need no instruction to see the truth in this matter, he has "not the least hopes of doing any good" by his treatise (pp. 3-4). The implications of the key terms in this opening flourish—"artificial designing Men," *"Guides,"* Matters of *Speculation"*—are not fully clear here, but Collins gives definite meaning to them in the body of the work and sums them up explicitly in a mirroring passage at the very end:

> . . . I look upon it as impossible to name an *Enemy* to *Free-Thinking,* however dignify'd or distinguish'd, who has not been either Crack-brain'd and Enthusiastical, or guilty of the most Diabolical Vices, Malice, Ambition, Inhumanity, and sticking at no means (tho ever so immoral) which he thought tended to God's Glory and the Good of the Church; or has not left us some marks of his profound Ignorance and Brutality. (pp. 177-78)

Between these anticlerical framing passages, the *Discourse* is divided into three main sections. The first, beginning with a definition of freethinking, offers five numbered arguments to prove that it is every man's right to think freely, and that freethinking is beneficial to individuals and to society. The second gives seven arguments proving that the duty and right to think freely is not limited to secular subjects but includes *"those Points of which Men are deny'd the Right to* think freely: *such as,* of the Nature and Attributes of God, the Truth and Authority of the Scriptures, *and* of the Meaning of Scriptures" (p. iii). The last section answers six objections alleged against freethinking. The first of the three parts is the briefest, only twenty-seven pages (5-32). The second is sixty-seven pages long, fifty-three of which are devoted to the last of its seven arguments, taken from "the conduct of the Priests, who are the Chief Pretenders to be Guides to others in matters of Religion" (pp. 46-99). In the final section, after covering the first five objections in nineteen pages, Collins spends the last third of his book, sixty pages (118-78), in arguing from a long series of historical instances that freethinkers, far from being *"the most infamous, wicked, and senseless of all Mankind,"* as the priests claim, have actually included the men most renowned in history for wisdom and virtue. The list of freethinkers begins with Socrates and Plato and impudently ends with Archbishop Tillotson, "whom all *English Free-Thinkers* own as their Head" (p. 171).

The force of the concluding section as an argument in defense of freethinking obviously depends upon the reader's acceptance of Collins' claim that all those eminent men actually were freethinkers, in his sense of the term. A broad basis for the claim is laid at the very beginning of the work in his definition of freethinking, so general as to include any thought whatever:

By *Free-Thinking* then I mean, *The Use of the Understanding, in endeavouring to find out the Meaning of any Proposition whatsoever, in considering the nature of the Evidence for or against it, and in judging of it according to the seeming Force or Weakness of the Evidence.* (p. 5)

With this definition as a major premise, Collins offers a minor premise for each of the thinkers he lists by quoting statements from their works or ascribed to them by historians and other witnesses. All the passages cited concern "Matters of *Speculation,*" as he calls them—that is, religious beliefs, attitudes, and practices.

His discussion of Socrates, one of the briefer passages in the long list, illustrates the pattern of his reasoning clearly. He begins:

SOCRATES, the divinest Man that ever appear'd in the Heathen World, and to whose Virtue and Wisdom all Ages since have done justice, was a very great *Free-Thinker.*

To support this assertion he offers three lines of argument. First, Socrates disbelieved the gods and common creeds of his country and was offended by attributions of "*Repentance, Anger,* and other *Passions* to the Gods, and talk of *Wars and Battels in Heaven,* and of the *Gods getting Women with Child,* and such-like fabulous and blasphemous Storys." Rejecting these fables and thinking for himself, Socrates "obtain'd a just Notion of the Nature and Attributes of God, exactly agreeable to that which we have receiv'd by Divine Revelation, and became a true *Christian.*" He was recognized as such by Justin Martyr, who said that, since Christ is "*nothing else but* Reason," anyone who lives by reason is a Christian; and by Erasmus, who said that Socrates's words to Crito, just before taking the poison, are so wonderful that one wants to cry out, "Sancte SOCRATES, ora pro nobis." Secondly, Xenophon tells us that Socrates could not have made "Notions, or Speculations, or Mysterys, any parts of his Religion," because he said that men were fools to make inquiries into heavenly things. Finally, Socrates suffered the common fate of freethinkers, in being calumniated as an atheist and put to that "Punishment for Free-Thinking, which Knavery and Folly . . . are ever ready to inflict on all those who have the Honesty and Courage to endeavour to imitate him" (pp. 123-26).

Moving on to Plato, Collins says that he was more cautious than Socrates, never talking publicly against the gods and religion of his country, but was nevertheless a true freethinker, who "thought himself into Notions so contrary to those which were received or known in *Greece,*" that he often seems to anticipate truths of the Gospel. Celsus, in fact, contended that Christ borrowed his doctrines from Plato, though Origen defends our blessed Lord on the ground that He not only had no Greek but was ignorant even of Hebrew letters. Celsus himself recognized the agreement between Platonism and Christianity, and the Platonist Amelius said of St. John the Evangelist, *"By* JOVE *this* Barbarian *is of our Master* PLATO's Opinion!" It was natural, therefore, that many Platonists became Christians, many Christians Platonists, and that zealous Christians, in their ardor to convert the heathen world, should have forged a number of spurious texts under Plato's name, including the thirteenth letter to Dionysius (pp. 126-28).

Bentley's *Remarks upon a Late Discourse of Free-Thinking* (1713)[25] is obviously the work of a scholar, thoroughly at home among the writings Collins cites, with an expert's command of the languages in which they are written, their authenticity and textual history, their sources and occasions, and their place in the history of thought. He carries this learning more lightly than one might expect from the blustering, dogmatic Bentley of the *Battle of the Books* and the *Dunciad*. His commentary is written in the form of a letter, and he was sufficiently familiar with literary developments in his time to understand the conventions of the epistolary form and to invent—and sustain with considerable skill—the persona of an imaginary writer, one Phileleutherus Lipsiensis. This author is a German Lutheran, neither English nor Anglican but a scholar and a Christian, very much in the humanist tradition of Erasmus, Colet, and More. He explains his knowledge of the English language by a long stay at Oxford in the past, and his happening to see Collins' book by his friendship for an English traveler, who had brought a copy with him to Leipzig as a gift (p. 3).

In a brief prefatory letter to his friend F. H. (Francis Hare), to whom the whole of the *Remarks* is addressed, he says that as a lifelong lover of freedom, "train'd up and exercised in *Free Thought* from my Youth," he had looked forward eagerly to reading Collins's book, and perhaps even to being admitted some day, as a "humble Foreigner Brother, *a Free-thinker of* Leipsic," to membership in the "Rising and Growing" society that Collins alludes to in his title. He soon found, however, that the specious show of freethinking is actually nothing but a cover for the inculcation of atheistical opinions. Instead of seeking membership in Collins's club, therefore, he has decided to write some Remarks which will express a humane scholar's judgment of the ability and sincerity that have gone into Collins's ramshackle composition (pp. 4-6).

In the eighty-two octavo pages of Bentley's commentary there are fifty-three separate Remarks, each dealing with a specific passage in the *Discourse*. He does not follow Collins all the way through to the end, but breaks off after a fairly extensive exposition of Collins's treatment of Cicero, the eighth of the wise and virtuous freethinkers listed in the concluding argument from historical instances (Collins, pp. 135-40; Bentley, pp. 68-82). Here I shall discuss only five of the Remarks, 3-5, 45, and 46, which are representative of the whole and also especially pertinent to our interests here.

The third, fourth, and fifth Remarks analyze Collins's definition of freethinking, already quoted above. Bentley's first observation is that the definition is so universal and extensive that it comprehends the thought of the whole human race, even fools, madmen, and children, for they too "use what *Understanding* they have; and judge as things *seem*." Freethinking in this inclusive sense, he says, is as early as the creation of Adam (p. 13), and defending the right to it is needless, since no religion or sect has ever denied it:

> 'Tis as necessary to the Rational Mind, as Respiration is to the Vital Body. Without this all Religions that were, are, or may be, are equally commendable. Christianity itself depended on it at its first propagation; the Reformation was grounded upon it, and is maintain'd and supported upon the same bottom. (p. 15)

But Collins does not really mean to identify freethinking with all thought, or with rational thought. The term "free" does not even appear in the definition, but the true meaning of the word, as Collins uses it, can be gathered from the characterizing marks or signs by which he distinguishes free from unfree thought. Among other things, to be free is to be self-assured, ready to speculate on "any Proposition whatsoever" without regard to one's ability or knowledge. To be free is to be bold, rash, arrogant, presumptuous, to have "an inward Promptness and Forwardness to decide about Matters beyond the reach of their Studies." Another mark of freethinking is to be "against the Current of common Doctrine," "in *opposition* to the rest of Mankind." It is plain throughout the *Discourse*, Bentley says, that the specific difference defining freedom for Collins—its essential requisite—is singularity, whim, and contradiction, together with a strong propensity to the paradoxical and perverse and a pathological tendency toward jealousy, mistrust, and surmise against all those who differ from his views. The fact is that Collins and his friends really care nothing about free thought in any intelligible definition of the term, but instead are dogmatic atheists, who rail at all "Guides" but set themselves up as guides to a "glorious Gospel" of their own:

> That the Soul is material and mortal, Christianity an imposture, the Scriptures a forgery, the Worship of God superstition, Hell a fable, and Heaven a dream, our Life without Providence, and our Death without hope like that of Asses and Dogs. . . . If all your *Free-thinking* does not center in these Opinions, you shall be none of their Family. . . . That's the only *Free-Thinking*, to *think* just as They do. (pp. 10-16)

It may have been a mistake, rhetorically speaking, for Bentley to make such strong assertions so early in his Remarks, before he has begun his detailed examination of particular passages in the *Discourse*. But perhaps these opening charges may be taken not as propositions he claims to have proved from Collins's almost empty definition, but as what was to be proved by the cumulative weight of the Remarks to follow. However that may be, Bentley's analysis of Collins's pages on Socrates and Plato offers much evidence to support the charges made in Remarks 3-5.

Bentley begins Remark 45 by repeating the claim, already made in his fifth Remark, that Collins makes singularity—disagreement with majority opinion—the characteristic mark of freethinking. If what he really meant by it was rational judgment, based on an impartial weighing of evidence for and against, he would have included in his list of freethinkers not only Socrates, but Constantine, all the early converts from paganism, and the many martyrs who died rather than renounce the truths they had come to believe. But for Collins, now that Christianity is established, freethinking consists in contradicting everything those sincere and courageous men had come to accept (pp. 30-31).

Bentley does not comment either on Collins's assertion that Socrates became a Christian or on his final "proof," from the fact that he was condemned as an atheist and put to death. He does reply at some length to the two other proofs: that Socrates' freethinking is manifested in his dislike for attributions of human traits and actions to the gods, and that he did not make speculations or mysteries any part of his religion. Collins documents the first by citing Plato's *Euthyphro* and the second by paraphrasing a passage from Xenophon's *Memorabilia*.[26] To the scholarly Phileleutherus Lipsiensis, it is evident that Collins has played fast and loose with both passages.

If we check Collins's statements against the texts themselves, we find the passage in the *Euthyphro,* when interpreted in context, does not unequivocally commit Socrates to disbelief in the gods and creeds of his time and country. Questioned by Socrates, Euthyphro says that he thinks it just and pious to bring an indictment for murder against his own father, since both Saturn and Jove are said to have punished their fathers for crimes. Socrates says that he *"assents with some difficulty"* (Bentley quotes the Greek) when he hears such things said of the gods; he asks whether Euthyphro thinks it true that "there are really Wars, and Enmities and Battles among the Gods, and many other such matters, as Poets and Painters represent?" When Euthyphro acknowledges that he does think these things true, Socrates does not pursue the question further, but moves on into his real subject, an inconclusive search for the definitions of piety and impiety, the essences of the holy, the right, and their opposites. It is true, Bentley's Remark goes on, that Socrates doubted the "poetical" religion of his time, but he never opposed the "civil" religion and always advised his followers to govern themselves in matters of worship by the custom of the country; he himself often offered prayers and made sacrifices. The fact that he was indicted for disbelieving the gods is no proof that he did so; Collins may condemn him all over again, but Socrates did not plead guilty to the charge (pp. 30-31).

The religion of Socrates is, of course, a complex and difficult question, on which whole books have been written. One may well feel that Collins was not entirely wrong in the matter, and that Bentley has at most convicted him of oversimplifying the problem by treating ambiguous evidence as if it were conclusive. One wonders, in fact, why Collins should have mentioned the *Euthyphro* at all, when he could have cited Books II and III of the *Republic,* in which the critical analysis of Homer's representation of the gods offers much more explicit and undeniable evidence. Anyone wanting to defend Collins would have to concede, however, that Bentley is correct in saying that Collins takes disagreement with prevailing creeds as the definitive sign of freethinking.

In the last two paragraphs of Remark 45, Bentley notes that Collins's references to the *Euthyphro* and the *Memorabilia* distort both texts. In the platonic passage, Socrates does speak of stories about wars in heaven, but he says nothing of God's repentance or anger, not a word of Gods getting women with child. These intrusions into the text are obviously intentional, foisted upon Plato in order to make "Scoffs and Contumelies upon the Scripture"—gibes at the language used in the Old Testament and in Revelations, which everyone recognizes to be metaphorical, and sneers at the doctrine of the Incarnation as "fabulous and blasphemous Storys." In Xenophon the phrase which Collins translates as "heavenly things" (Bentley again gives the Greek) really means the celestial bodies, their appearance, causes, and motions; Socrates turned his speculations from the physics of the heavens to "Morality and human Life." If Collins's unscrupulous mistranslation is replaced by the correct meaning, his argument can be reduced to an absurd syllogism: *"Because* Socrates *did not cultivate Astronomy, but Ethics; therefore he had no Mysteries in his Religion."* From both of these instances, Phileleutherus says, we may "take the measure of our Writer's veracity" (pp. 33-35).

Stephen says of the *Remarks* that they reflect in every paragraph the "contempt of a powerful reasoner for a shuffling caviller, of a thoroughly trained and deeply learned critic for a mere dabbler in literature, and the hatred of a theologian for a man who holds a different opinion."[27] In the last clause of this judgment, I'm afraid that Sir Leslie shows the bias of his own nineteenth-century style of skeptical freethinking, but it is true that Bentley not only exposes the technical irresponsibility of Collins's use of sources but also expresses the moral outrage felt by a deeply committed Christian toward a writer with neither reverence for God nor a decent respect for the opinions of sincere and thoughtful men, whether ancient or modern, pagan or Christian. This complex of feelings is especially clear in Remark 46.

On the purely technical side, Bentley-Phileleutherus once again has no difficulty in showing that Collins is "put hard to his shifts, and forc'd to make several doubles" when he tries to bring Plato into the club of freethinkers. The shifts and doubles include further mistranslations, this time from Celsus and Amelius; citation of the latter at "second or fifth hand," as shown by his misrepresentation of the whole drift and tone of Amelius's comment on St. John; and another false charge of priestly forgery, Plato's thirteenth epistle. Phileleutherus defends the authenticity of the letter by citing external evidence from the testimony of ancient scholars, going back two hundred years before the Christian era, and by showing that circumstantial references within the letter itself are "apt and proper to the Writer and to the Date." On a small scale, the passage is a model of valid scholarly reasoning on a question of attribution.

In the course of documenting these technical defects, Bentley also repeatedly explicates Collins's sly gibes at Christianity. When we read the words *defends very well* and *our Blessed Lord* in the passage about Origen, we are to expect "some smart piece of Burlesque," which we immediately get in the sneering insinuation that Christ was illiterate. In a similar way, it is not Amelius but Collins who makes a banter on St. John the Evangelist by calling him "this Barbarian." Amelius uses the term neutrally, to mean nothing more pejorative than "this non-Greek," and his paraphrase of the opening passage of the Fourth Gospel is wholly admiring. The source of such distortions is not merely incompetence and ignorance—they are intentional and venomously malicious. The mind which could produce them is not only dishonest but radically corrupt and vicious.

Both Plato and the Platonist Amelius were pagans, but Bentley believed that wise and good men in all ages, even without the great gift of revelation from God himself, have been able to know that there is but one God, who rewards those who diligently seek him. That is the first article of Bentley's faith, too, though he owes it not to Plato but "to God the common Author of Nature, and Father of rational Light." Bentley feels indignant contempt for Collins, but toward ancient non-Christians who truly lived by that rational light, he has the same kind of veneration that Erasmus so movingly expressed when he called upon Socrates to pray for us. The words of Amelius deserve to be written in letters of gold, as St. Augustine said long ago, and Bentley

would far rather *"have my soul be with"* Plato and Socrates than with men
like Collins, who trample the pearls that are cast before them and do their best
to tear to pieces all those who try to help them see the inestimable value of
those gifts (pp. 35-42). Surely these judgments spring from something more
worthy of respect than a theologian's hatred for a man who holds a different
opinion.

We know from a reference in the *Journal to Stella* that Swift conceived the
"little whim" of writing a reply to Collins in January 1713, composed it in a
few days, and arranged for its publication very shortly afterward.[28] In the
original edition, it is a slim pamphlet of twenty-eight duodecimo pages, less
than a third the length of Bentley's *Remarks* and only a sixth as long as
Collins's *Discourse*. It sold for fourpence, though Swift had hoped that it
might cost only three.

The method of attack Swift adopts for his exposure of Collins differs *toto
caelo* from that used by Bentley, each of them choosing the method most
natural for his own temper and talent. Bentley invented an imaginary
spokesman, Phileleutherus, who is detached from all merely parochial English
interests and passions by virtue of being a German and a Lutheran, living in
faraway Leipzig, but who is also a Christian scholar so much like Bentley that
he can present with complete dramatic propriety the same kinds of analysis,
argument, and proof that Bentley himself would have used in writing in his
own person. His rhetoric convinces because he is a learned man of
independent mind whose orthodox faith is not only deeply felt but also firmly
based on solid intellectual foundations. Swift chooses instead the methods of
parody, impersonation, and irony which he was "born to put to use."

Although this explanation of their choice of methods is surely valid and
adequate for both Bentley and Swift, I believe that Swift's choice has a
further, though not contradictory, reason in certain convictions he held about
men's duties in matters of intellectual controversy, whether religious or
political, and also about the most effective ways of counterattack against the
enemies of Christianity in his time. The first set of beliefs, fundamental to his
whole conception of man and sublunary life, is most fully and unequivocally
expressed in two nonsatiric, nonironic pieces of writing, his "Thoughts on
Religion"—private reflections not originally intended for publication—and
his sermon "On the Trinity," which he delivered to his congregation at St.
Patrick's. His conception of the best way to deal with the freethinkers is
clearly stated in the same sermon and in two other nonironic works, his
"Thoughts on Free-Thinking" and the *Letter to a Young Gentleman, Lately
Enter'd into Holy Orders*.

In Swift's view, man is an imperfect creature, endowed by God with certain limited powers adapted to his life in an imperfect world. One of these gifts is a mind capable of reasoning on questions, both philosophical and practical, which concern his status and duties as a distinct kind of being and the problems arising in his daily life on this earth. One of man's first duties, as a creature made by and dependent on a supernatural power, is to use to the best of his ability the mind God has given him. Consequently, as Swift says in the opening reflections of his "Thoughts on Religion":

> I am in all opinions to believe according to my own impartial reason; which I am bound to inform and improve as far as my capacity and opportunities will permit. It may be prudent in me to act sometimes by other men's reason, but I can think only by my own. If another man's reason fully convinceth me, it becomes my own reason. To say a man is bound to believe is neither truth nor sense. (*PW*, IX, 261)

He says the same thing in his sermon:

> It must be allowed, that every Man is bound to follow the Rules and Directions of that Measure of Reason which God hath given him; and indeed he cannot do otherwise, if he will be sincere, or act like a Man. (*PW*, IX, 161)

Men should reason, however, with a humble awareness of the severe limitations inherent in our imperfect rational powers. The intellect of man is not angelic or divine, but mundane; there are many things, both mysteries like that of the Trinity and the causes of many natural phenomena, which we could not fully understand unless we had faculties far superior to those God has chosen to give us (*PW*, IX, 164-65). Our ability to reason is no more than a potentiality, which must be informed and improved by education, and men differ widely in the degree to which they possess it; all of us have some capacity, but none has much. Finally, our reasonings are easily and frequently distorted by irrational forces in our nature: "*Reason* itself is true and just, but the *Reason* of every particular Man is weak and wavering, perpetually swayed and turned by his Interests, his Passions, and his Vices" (*PW*, IX, 166). Each of us must follow the rules and directions of that measure of reason God has given us, but self-critically, with care that our thinking should be sincere and impartial, always remembering the many causes which may seduce us into error.

When intellectual issues have civil implications, no power or authority can take from us that liberty of conscience which consists in possessing our own thoughts and opinions, but how far we may "publicly act in pursuance of those opinions, is to be regulated by the laws of the country.'' As a member of the commonwealth, every man ought to be ''content with the possession of his own opinion in private, without perplexing his neighbor or disturbing the public.'' Three degrees should be distinguished in our liberty of thought and expression: the freedom to judge for ourselves, which is absolute, and the freedoms to communicate our thoughts to others or even to try actively to convert them to our views, which are not absolute and undeniable, but subject to restraint by considerations of social effect and public policy. Both in the private ''Thoughts'' and in the public sermon, Swift says that such restraints apply equally to matters of religious and of constitutional controversy; because of their public consequences, it is entirely proper that attacks upon either the forms of belief and worship or the forms of government established by any society should be governed by laws and magistrates, and that those who attempt to persuade the people to innovations in either field should be ''answerable for the effects their thoughts produce on others.''

Swift's views on the right response to freethinkers are a direct consequence of these principles. He was convinced that such men, while pretending to follow reason, were unwilling to accept the restraints under which our rational faculties have been granted to us. Their reasoning, if it can be called that, is not cautious and humble but bold and arrogant, not sincere and impartial but dishonest and biased. Instead of informing and improving their minds by disciplined study, they use books unscrupulously to give their writings a specious air of learning and distort what other men have thought to suit their own purposes. Those unbelievers could never ''satisfy the general reason of mankind,'' because their arguments are ''miserably defective, absurd, and ridiculous; they strain at a Gnat, and swallow a Camel.'' Their atheistical doctrines go against ''the common Light of Nature as well as Reason; against the universal Sentiments of all civilized Nations,'' and would give offense ''to the Ears even of a sober Heathen'' (''On the Trinity, *PW,* IX., 167).

Such men represent an extreme instance of reason swayed and turned by their interests, passions, and vices. They are motivated not out of zeal for truth, ''but to give a Loose to Wickedness, by throwing off all Religion'':

> . . . When Men are curious and inquisitive to discover some weak Sides in Christianity, and inclined to favour every thing that is offered to its Disadvantage; it is plain they wish it were not true, and those Wishes can proceed from nothing but an evil Conscience, because, if there be Truth in our Religion, their Condition must be miserable. (Ibid., *PW,* IX, 160,166)

Worst of all, they are not content to possess their own infidelity in silence, but carry their freedom of thought to the third and worst degree, following the trade of seducing others:

> . . . their Intent is to overthrow all Religion, that they may gratify their Vices without any Reproach from the World, or their own Conscience; and are zealous to bring over as many others to their own Opinions; because it is some kind of imaginary Comfort to them to have a Multitude on their Side. (Ibid., *PW,* IX, 159, 165)[29]

If the civil powers will not intervene to suppress these efforts to subvert religion, what should be the response of clergymen and others who believe that the salvation of man, both on this earth and eternally, lies in the love of God and following his commandments? Swift's considered opinion, which he repeats in several places, is that it is foolish to "preach against Atheism, Deism, Free-Thinking, and the like," as young divines are too fond of doing. The men themselves are only "three or four Fools, who are past Grace," and attempting to refute their writings by rational arguments is merely "answering Fools in their Folly." It is futile, because what did not arise from reason cannot be put down by reason, and its only effect is to give their ignorant and vicious propaganda an intellectual respectability which it does not deserve ("On the Trinity," *PW,* IX, 167; *Letter to a Young Clergyman, PW,* IX, 77-78). If they are to be answered at all, then, it should be done by holding them up to scornful laughter, exposing their motives and ridiculing their pseudolearning and pseudologic. As Swift's friend Pope says, when law will not or cannot act, the satirist must take over the cause of truth and virtue.

Swift's "little whim" was to reply to Collins in exactly that manner. His titlepage establishes the satiric fiction on which his parodic and ironic attack will be based. The full title, *Mr. C—ns's Discourse of Free-Thinking, Put into Plain English, by Way of Abstract for the Use of the Poor,* accurately states the plan of the work but adds in its very Swiftian final phrase a signal of ironic intent which he had already used for the same purpose, some months earlier, in his *Preface to the Bishop of Sarum's Introduction* (1712).[30] As the titlepage also indicates, the abstract has been made by "a Friend of the Author," who explains in a brief preface that his purpose is to clear away any obstacles that might impede a wider understanding of Collins's "irrefragable Discourse." The appearance of booklearning, given by "a shew of Logick, and multiplicity of Quotations, scattered through his Book," might frighten some well-wishers to infidelity from reading it for their improvement. In compiling his abstract, however, the friend asserts emphatically that he has faithfully "adhered to the very Words of our Author," advancing nothing of his own and adding only a few phrases to smooth and clarify the transitions

(*PW*, II, 27-28). The brilliance of Swift's parodic conception lies in the fact that this claim by the compiler is almost literally true: nine-tenths or more of the words and sentences in *Mr. C—ns's Discourse* are Collins's own.

The reader of Bentley's *Remarks* follows a reasoned refutation of passages quoted or paraphrased from Collins, but the voice heard throughout is that of a third party, Bentley-Phileleutherus, whose arguments the reader weighs and judges by rational criteria, as he would in reading any work of controversial debate. In Swift's ironic parody there is no third party, for he is not present at all; all the words of the piece come either from Collins or from his friend. We hear only one voice, since the few statements added by the abstractor are not distinguished in any way from Collins's own, and that voice expresses not Swift's opinion, but their joint views. The four-penny pamphlet does not analyze, describe, confute, or judge; it *dramatizes* the character and thought of Collins by letting him speak for himself, with just a little heightening and pointing by the clarifying additions of the compiler. The reader responds directly, as he would to the speeches of a character in a comic drama, judging for himself just what kind of thinker this freethinker is. Swift, of course, as the playwright of this drama, is in full control of the process, invisibly guiding the reader's responses by his selection and manipulation of the raw material. The response he wants to arouse is one of contemptuous laughter, but it is more definite than a generalized negative judgment; he has a number of specific points to make about Collins and other freethinkers, which he wants the reader to recognize in the dramatization. The substance of his indictment is virtually identical with Bentley's: that freethinking is merely a transparent cover for atheism, that Collins makes rejection of prevailing creeds the essence of freethinking, that his reasoning is palpably fallacious, and that his book is filled with sneers, supposed to be witty, upon Christian beliefs, the Bible, and the English church and clergy.

Swift's attack does make one point for which there is no parallel in the *Remarks*. When he wrote his reply to Collins, he was at the height of his association with the Harley-Bolingbroke government, and the negotiations leading to the Peace of Utrecht were in their final stages; the peace was formally announced by the queen on May 5. Swift gives the whole *Discourse* a political twist by having the compiler say in his preface that the wise leaders of "our Party," having failed to reestablish their power by political arguments, have determined to open the eyes of the nation by presenting "a short, but perfect, System of their Divinity"—a "brief compleat Body of Atheology," which will subvert the crafty schemes of the Tories to overawe the world by threats of damnation by a supreme power in heaven. The friend of the author is quite sure that "nothing would more contribute to the continuance of the War, and the Restoration of the late Ministry, than to have the Doctrines delivered in this Treatise well infused into the People'' (*PW*, II, 27-28).

This identification of Whiggery with atheism is extended into the main body of the *Discourse* in a passage based on Collins's contention, unusually brazen even for him, that the Society for Propagating the Gospel was actually a society of propagating freethinking. Collins goes on to wish that zealous divines like ''our AT——Ys,'' ''our SW——FTs,'' and others could be sent into foreign parts to execute so glorious a design, instead of continually haranguing upon texts, which they call preaching the Gospel. Then, he says, we would see blessed days, the English church triumphant, and all faction ceased at home. The faithful compiler, adding just enough to point up Collins's sneering tone, anticlerical bias, and political motivation, renders the passage as follows:

> I heartily wish a Detachment of such Divines as Dr. *Atterbury,* Dr. *Smalridge,* Dr. *Swift,* Dr. *Sacheverell,* and some others, were sent every Year to the furthest part of the Heathen World, and that we had a Cargo of their Priests in return, who would spread *Free-thinking* among us; then the War would go on, the late Ministry be restored, and Faction cease, which our Priests inflame by haranguing upon Texts, and falsely call that preaching the Gospel. (*PW*, II, 31)

This attack on the Whigs as patrons of atheism, though no doubt at least half-seriously meant, is not a central element in Swift's exposure of Collins. Its main thrust can be seen from a passage fairly early in the *Discourse* which foreshadows the final long section on eminent freethinkers of the past, including Socrates and Plato. Collins had argued at some length that the right and duty to think freely is not limited to opinions held in private but requires their active propagation. As the compiler renders the passage:

> . . . *Free Thinking* signifies nothing, without *Free Speaking* and *Free Writing.* It is the indispensable Duty of a Free Thinker, to endeavour *forcing* all the World to think as he does, and by that means make them *Free Thinkers* too. You are also to understand, that I allow no Man to be a *Free Thinker,* any further than as he differs from the received Doctrines of Religion. . . . You shall see by and by, that I celebrate those for the noblest *Free Thinkers* in every Age, who have differed from the Religion of their Countries in the most fundamental Points, and especially in those which bear any Analogy to the chief Fundamentals of Religion among us. (*PW*, II, 36-37)

Bentley's treatment of Collins's pages on Socrates, in keeping with his method of sober, reasoned refutation, focuses on Collins's identification of freethinking with the rejection of prevailing creeds, his gibes and flouts against the Virgin Birth, his assertions of the illiteracy of Christ and the barbarism of St. John, and his flagrant violations of scholarly method in the use of sources. Because of the compiler's policy of eliminating any show of book learning, Swift does not attempt to expose the spuriousness of Collins's scholarly pretensions, but he does have his own ways of making the first two points:

> Socrates was a *Free-thinker;* for he disbelieved the Gods of his Country, and the common *Creeds* about them, and declared his Dislike when he heard Men attribute *Repentance, Anger, and other Passions to the Gods, and talk of Wars and Battles in Heaven, and of the Gods getting Women with Child,* and such like fabulous and blasphemous Stories.

As if the implications of this sentence were not clear enough, the compiler now adds one of his small transition-smoothing statements:

> I pick out these Particulars, because they are the very same with what the Priests have in their Bibles, where *Repentance* and *Anger* are attributed to God, where it is said, there was *War in Heaven;* and that the *Virgin* Mary *was with Child by the Holy Ghost,* whom the Priests call God; all fabulous and blasphemous Stories.

Swift's abstract also preserves Collins's last two "proofs" that Socrates was a freethinker, which Bentley passes over without comment: that Socrates became a true Christian and that he met the same fate as other freethinkers. The passage illustrates very clearly the contrast between Bentley's method and Swift's. In the *Remarks,* Bentley spells out the absurd syllogism by which Collins had tried to show that speculations and mysteries had no part in the religion of Socrates. Swift, always a master of mock logic and grotesque nonsequiturs, [31] makes the same point dramatically, by having the compiler add two clarifying sentences, the second and the last; all the rest is in the "very words" of Collins:

> Now, I affirm *Socrates* to have been a true *Christian.* You will ask perhaps how that can be, since he lived Three or four hundred Years before Christ? I answer with *Justin Martyr,* that Christ is nothing else but *Reason,* and I hope you do not think *Socrates* lived before Reason. Now, this true Christian *Socrates* never made Notions, Speculations, or Mysteries any Part of his Religion, but demonstrated that all Men to be Fools who troubled themselves with Enquiries into heavenly Things. Lastly, 'tis plain that *Socrates* was a *Free-thinker,* because he was calumniated for an Atheist, as Free-thinkers generally are, only because

he was an Enemy to all Speculations and Enquiries into heavenly Things. For I argue thus, that if I never trouble my self to think whether there be a God or no, and forbid others, to do it, I am a Free-thinker, but not an Atheist. (*PW*, II, 41-42)

The reader does not need a diagram, because he immediately recognizes for himself the ridiculous illogic of the two enthymemes brought out by the compiler's small additions.

The special rhetorical force of Swift's parodic, dramatizing method is less strikingly evident in his presentation of Collins's proofs that Plato was another freethinker, which is briefer and not nearly as funny. Here again the compiler's policy of eliminating any appearance of book learning requires the omission of almost all the allusions to ancient writers and documents. Origen remains, but Amelius disappears, Celsus becomes a vague "Heathen," and the epistle to Dionysius is generalized as "several Things" forged by zealous priests under Plato's name. Bentley notes that the phrases *defends very well* and *our blessed Lord* function as signals that a smart piece of burlesque is coming, the insinuation that Christ was illiterate. Swift's abstract, which preserves *defends very well* but drops *our blessed Lord,* lets this point go by. The passage does, however, capture quite well Collins's tone of jaunty buffooning impudence:

Plato was a *Free-thinker,* and his Notions are so like some in the Gospel, that a Heathen charged Christ with borrowing his Doctrine from *Plato.* But *Origen* defends Christ very well against this Charge, by saying that he did not understand *Greek,* and therefore could not borrow his Doctrines from *Plato.* However their two Religions agreed so well, that it was common for Christians to turn *Platonists,* and *Platonists* Christians. When the Christians found out this, one of their zealous Priests (worse than any Atheist) forged several Things under *Plato's* Name, but conformable to Christianity, by which the Heathens were fraudulently converted. (*PW*, II, 42)

Though I may seem to have devoted an inordinate amount of space to this detailed comparison of Bentley and Swift with Collins, their common object of attack, I believe that the material has two implications of far-reaching significance for students of Swift's thought and art. The first concerns the close resemblance in substance between Bentley's attack and Swift's, while the second has to do with the sharp contrast between the methods they chose for their replies.

If the points they make against Collins are virtually identical, as we have seen that they are, the reason is that they take their stand on the same ground, sharing the same basic affirmative beliefs about God, the human mind, and the enduring value of the ancients. Although Swift paradoxically casts Bentley as a hero of the "modern" forces in the *Battle of the Books,* it is evident even from the *Remarks* alone—to say nothing of his other writings and the facts of his whole career—that Bentley was not only one of the most eminent classical scholars of his time but also one who revered the best of the ancients at least as deeply as Swift did. Bentley was also a Christian and a rationalist, who believed that God is the "common Author of Nature, and Father of rational Light," and that if we follow that light it will teach us that there is but one God, almighty, omniscient, and merciful, who rewards those who diligently serve him. Because Socrates and Plato knew these things too, Bentley would far rather *"have my soul be with"* them than with men like Collins, who try to convert us to their terrible gospel that the "soul is material and mortal, Christianity an imposture, the Scriptures a forger, the Worship of God superstitution, Hell a fable, and Heaven a dream." However much Bentley and Swift may have differed on Sir William Temple's knowledge of the classics, the authenticity of the *Epistles* of Phalaris, or the date of Aesop's *Fables,* they both believed in the universality of reason, and accepted that synthesis of Christianity with the classics which they inherited from Erasmus and other Renaissance humanists.

The second observation brings us back to the "soft" interpretation of *Gulliver's Travels.* One version of that way of reading the Fourth Voyage, of which Kathleen Williams is a relatively sober example and Martin Kalich one of the most extravagant and bizarre, argues that the Houyhnhnms are deists, whom Swift attacks for assuming that reason provides a sufficient ground for religion, without need for revelation from God. [32] The most cogent objection to this interpretation, which has been forcibly stated by George Sherburn, Ronald Crane, Louis Landa, Phillip Harth, and others, is that no religious issues are raised in the Fourth Voyage.[33] In the treatment of the Houyhnhnms, as Landa says, there is no divine scheme of things, such as we have as a framework for Swift's teaching in his sermons, but instead "a different order of ideas or level of reality, with more limited issues, in which man is considered in terms of his private and public virtues, an appraisal of him as a mundane domestic, political, and social creature."[34] As we will be seeing in the next section of this essay, Swift certainly believed that faith and revealed truth are necessary for salvation. But how the soul may be saved is nowhere in question in *Gulliver's Travels,* which measures modern man and society by a rational standard, showing them to be terribly lacking in the traits on which they pride themselves.

Though Landa's argument seems to me a sufficient answer to readings like those of Williams and Kalich, Swift's way of responding to Collins allows us to add a further point. Swift always refused to acknowledge that deism was an autonomous intellectual position, with its own distinctive principles and modes of reasoning, or that it deserved rational refutation. He lumped the deists together with the atheists, Socinians, anti-Trinitarians, and other subdivisions of freethinkers, all equally contemptible for the perversity of their arguments and all equally motivated by their hatred of all religion, because it put restraints upon their passions and vices. Swift chose to expose Collins by an ironic parody not only because that was his natural bent, the method of attack which he was uniquely gifted to use, but also because of his conviction that any other kind of reply gave the freethinkers an intellectual status they did not deserve. If he had wanted to attack the deists, then, he would never have done so through such amiable, moral creatures as the Houyhnhnms. Surely he would have treated them as he does other freethinkers in *Mr. C—ns's Discourse* or in the *Argument against Abolishing Christianity,* in which even Swift's persona, the nominal Christian, dismisses with scornful contempt the pretensions to wit and learning of Asgil, Tindal, Collins, and the rest of that crew. In Swift's considered opinion, that was much the best way to deal with "three or four Fools, who are past Grace."

⟊⟊⟊⟊

Our final set of references occurs in two closely parallel nonironic works, a sermon on the excellence of Christianity and *A Letter to a Young Gentleman, Lately Enter'd into Holy Orders.* In both, Swift cites Plato and Socrates as representing the farthest reach of human comprehension, unaided by divine revelation. In his admirable study of the religious satire of *A Tale of a Tub,* Phillip Harth has used the *Letter* to define Swift's position on the relation between natural reason and revealed truth, and to establish his affiliations within the tradition of medieval and renaissance Christian thought. Taken together, the two works may also be used to evaluate A. O. Lovejoy's even broader generalizations about eighteenth-century thinking in his well-known essay "The Parallel between Deism and Classicism."

The full title of the sermon is "Upon the Excellency of Christianity, in Opposition to Heathen Philosophy." Preaching on the text, "The wisdom of this world is foolishness with God" (1 Cor. iii, 19), Swift emphasizes the limitations and defects of heathen philosophy, by comparison with the perfection of Christian wisdom. The sermon could almost be described as his *Contra Gentiles,* though he does his best to be just to the ancient philosophers.

Without detracting from the merit of the best ancient thinkers, who were "as wise and good as it was possible for them under such disadvantages," Swift says that their notions of a deity were inadequate, and even "those among them who had the justest conceptions of a Divine Power, and did also admit a Providence," had no conception of trust or dependence upon God. They were unable to agree on the chief good of man and failed to establish any ground for "some happiness, proportioned to the Soul of Man," as a motive for virtue in the conduct of life. Their moral teachings, though containing much truth, suffered "for want of a support by revelation from God," and the greatest examples of wisdom and virtue among them were the result of personal merit and good natural dispositions, not of any doctrines they professed. He concludes by contrasting the contentiousness of heathen moral philosophies with Christian wisdom from above, "first pure, then peaceable, gentle, and easy to be intreated, full of mercy and good fruits, without partiality, and without hypocrisy" (*PW*, IX, 241-50; James iii. 15-17).

Under most of the heads of this general line of argument, either Plato or Socrates is cited as an example. Swift's reasoning is *a fortiori:* whatever is true of these two thinkers, the best of the ancients, must be doubly true of all the rest. To support his contention that heathen wisdom was not highly regarded in primitive Christian times, he says that Christ's treatment of the Pharisees and Sadducees, who followed the doctrines of Plato and Epicurus respectively, shows that the Savior himself had but a low esteem for it (*PW*, IX, 242). The relations of Plato to the younger Dionysius and of Aristotle to Alexander the Great are cited as examples of the worldliness into which even the wisest were likely to fall, when they had no heavenly reward to encourage their progress in virtue (*PW*, IX, 244). Conceding that "there hath been all along in the world a notion of rewards and punishments in another life," Swift says that it never became a settled principle, believed to govern men's actions: even Socrates, in the last celebrated words just before his death, did not "seem to reckon or build much upon any such opinion" (*PW*, IX, 245). To show that the ancient philosophic sects were characterized by confusion and strife rather than peace and gentleness, he states that Diogenes called Socrates a madman, and that the disciples of Zeno and Epicurus, "nay of Plato and Aristotle," engaged in fierce disputes about the most insignificant trifles (*PW*, IX, 250). To illustrate the defects of pre-Christian ethical philosophy, he even claims that "Plato himself, with all his refinements, placed happiness in wisdom, health, good fortune, honour, and riches" (*PW*, IX, 246). Though most of these charges have some basis in fact, the last one is manifestly unfair; wisdom and health were real goods for Plato—wisdom being the final and highest good and health instrumental to it—but he always deprecated the value of honor and riches.[35]

Among all these negative judgments, there are two which are strongly favorable. One refers to our old friends Socrates and Cato, two of the Sextumvirate, in whom fortitude and temperance arrived at the greatest height (*PW,* IX, 249). The other is a tribute to Plato's most sublime moral teaching:

> Plato indeed (and it is worth observing) hath somewhere a dialogue, or part of one, about forgiving our enemies, which was perhaps the highest strain ever reached by man, without divine assistance; yet how little is that to what our Saviour commandeth us? *To love them that hate us; to bless them that curse us; and do good to them that despitefully use us.* (*PW,* IX, 248)

The *Letter to a Young Clergyman* (1721) is not inconsistent with the sermon in distinguishing between pagan and Christian wisdom, but here Swift puts the emphasis the other way. While continuing to recognize the limitations of natural reason and uninspired philosophy, he stresses instead their validity and usefulness within those limits. Supposedly written to the recently ordained cleric by "a Person of Quality,"[36] the letter offers advice, from an intelligent layman's point of view, on the matter, style, and delivery of sermons.

The two principal branches of preaching, the writer of the letter says, are "first to tell the People what is their Duty; and then to convince them that it is so. The Topicks for both these, we know, are brought from *Scripture* and *Reason.*" Communication between a minister and his congregation depends upon their mutual participation in natural reason. The preacher, therefore, needs "tolerable Intellectuals" to begin with, which should be further improved by a "competent Stock of Human Learning, and some Knowledge in Divinity." His auditors will understand and be convinced if the speaker adapts his arguments to their level of comprehension and expresses them in language so plain and simple that even the meanest and most ignorant will be able to follow. The author of the letter strongly disparages attempts to move the passions, and he especially warns his young friend against all ostentation of learning, attempts to explain mysteries, concern with abstruse points of theology, or use of obscure technical language drawn from divinity or any other sophisticated study. The most effective preachers, he believes, are those who depend on "the Fund of their own Reason; advanced, indeed, but not overlaid by Commerce with Books." In addition, of course, they must know the Scriptures, which reveal some religious truths that are beyond the reach of human wisdom (*PW,* IX, 63-81).

Within this larger context, the letter includes three specific references to Plato. Two of them are very brief. Both assert that a preacher's hearers, though not learned, will judge what he says by their own rational faculty, not by any authorities he may cite. Common congregations "will rather believe you on your own Word, than on that of *Plato* or *Homer*," and every plowman is aware of many truths, although he never heard of Aristotle or Plato (*PW*, IX, 75, 76). For the well-educated "Person of Quality," Plato is the prince of philosophers, as Homer is of poets, and his name naturally comes first to mind when an example is needed.

The letter's third, and much more important, reference to Plato and Socrates occurs in three paragraphs of closely argued warning against "the common unsufferable Cant, of taking all Occasions to disparage the Heathen *Philosophers*." In doing so, the Person of Quality draws with precision the boundary between the knowledge attainable by natural human reason and that which is opened to men in Scripture.

To the Christian disparagers of heathen philosophy, including some of the early Church fathers, he concedes three points, all of which he also makes in his sermon. First, the system of morality which could be gathered from the works of pre-Christian thinkers undoubtedly falls short of that delivered in the Gospel. Second, an even greater defect—the "true Misery of the Heathen World"—is the lack of a divine sanction to give unquestionable authority to the philosophers' teachings. Finally, the gentiles were necessarily ignorant of the facts of Christ's birth, life, death, and resurrection, made known to us through the evangelists "to make us wise unto salvation." Their ignorance of these facts does not argue any defect of understanding, however, since the events happened long after their deaths, and belief in them does not fall within the sphere of human wisdom, but is a matter of faith depending on divine authority as laid down in Scripture.

Granting these limitations, Swift finds much to be said for the theological and ethical ideas of the ancient sages. In divinity, valid conclusions had been reached not only by philosophers but by most educated people in those polite and learned ages. They acknowledged and worshiped "one Almighty Power, under several Denominations," and they allowed Him "all those attributes we ascribe to the Divinity." Christ himself did not explain the nature of God more fully, since "human Comprehension reacheth no further," and to know more "would be impossible, without bestowing on us other Faculties than we possess at present." The ethical teachings of the gentile philosophers do fall short of those of the Gospel, but within the limits of human wisdom they are still valid, providing an excellent commentary on the moral part of Scriptural doctrine. As in the sermon, Swift says that the highest reach of heathen thought was to anticipate the Christian virtue of forgiveness, which "is at large insisted on by *Plato*, who puts it, as I remember, into the mouth of *Socrates*."

The advantage of the Christian world over the heathen, then, lies not in any greater power of human understanding, but solely in the possession of certain truths, outside the sphere of human wisdom but divinely revealed and guaranteed, which are absolutely necessary to "make the Knowledge of the true God, and the Practice of Virtue more universal in the World." But other truths, theological and ethical, are shared by both worlds, being the common product of their equal participation in natural reason. The works of the heathen philosophers, therefore, should form a considerable part of a young clergyman's studies; along with the principal ancient orators, historians, and poets, they will enlarge his mind and thoughts, extend and refine his imagination, direct his judgment, lessen his admiration, and increase his fortitude (*PW,* IX, 73-74).

In *Swift and Anglican Rationalism,* Phillip Harth's method is first to establish Swift's position on a particular question or set of questions and then to search through the writings of Swift's predecessors and contemporaries for the closest parallels to Swift's views; a precise definition of his general outlook in divinity and morality thus gradually emerges, inductively, from a series of such comparisons. In his lucid analysis of the *Letter to a Young Clergyman,* [37] Harth shows that the questions it raises concern the value and limits of natural religion and natural law—the theological and ethical truths which are knowable by human reason, unassisted by divine revelation. Natural religion teaches that there is only one God, ascribing to Him the attributes of almighty power, wisdom, and goodness; Swift says that the best of the gentile philosophers had attained knowledge of these truths. Natural law teaches universal ethical principles by which men ought to govern their lives; the bulk of mankind were ignorant of these truths in ancient times, but the philosophers were not. That is why their writings provide an excellent commentary on the moral part of the Gospel, with which they agree in substance, through they fall short in point of certitude. In short, Christian doctrine has two great advantages: it provides a divine sanction, lacking in pagan times, for the truths of natural religion and natural law, and it teaches us further truths, concerning man's supernatural end, which "make us wise unto salvation." [38]

Harth finds the closest parallels to this view in the writings of Swift's great Anglican predecessor, Richard Hooker, and, behind him, in the philosophy of Thomas Aquinas. In this tradition, human reason is capable, without divine aid, of knowing the existence of God, his leading attributes, the immortality of the soul, and the necessity of observing the moral duties prescribed by natural law. Revelation does not reject these truths; it brings them to perfection by repeating them with divine authority, "so that what some may know by reason all may know by faith,'' and by revealing further truths, which cannot be known by natural reason alone. Aquinas and Hooker, going beyond anything directly asserted in Swift's letter, add that even when these saving truths have been made known to men by revelation, our natural reason continues to be needed in religion in order to establish the credibility of Scripture (that it is indeed divine), to interpret it correctly, and to determine laws and usages of the church which are not specifically set forth in the Bible. Thus both teach a middle way, between deism and fideism, in which reason and revelation "together provide the grounds for religion, so that each plays its proper role in the religious sphere and neither can be ignored."[39] Swift implies as much when he says that the topics of Christian preaching are brought, "we know," from Scripture and Reason.

Harth's findings, in my opinion one of the major achievements of modern Swift scholarship, explain and tie together many of the implications of the evidence we have been reviewing in this essay. If the Houyhnhnms embody the same principle that is expounded philosophically in Plato's account of the guardians and illustrated historically in the great actions of Socrates and other members of the Sextumvirate, as Kelsall argues, it is because Swift believed that human reason, though so terribly misused by most of us, is a heavenly gift that we are meant to put to use both in religion and in the moral decisions of our daily lives. Collins and other freethinkers are extreme examples of the distortion of reason by our interests, passions, and vices; Swift believed that it was futile to refute them by rational arguments, because their opinions did not arise from reason but from their desire to escape the restraints that religion put upon their conduct. Bentley did reply to Collins in a reasoned refutation, as Swift did not, but in their basic affirmative beliefs they fully agree: God is "the common Author of Nature, and Father of rational Light" (Bentley), and "every Man is bound to follow the Rules and Directions of that Measure of Reason which God hath given him" (Swift). Both Bentley and Swift believe that if we follow that light, as Plato and the best of the heathen philosophers did, it will teach us that there is but one God, almighty, omniscient, and merciful, who rewards those who diligently search for him, and Scripture reaffirms these teachings with a divine guarantee of their truth. In the *Letter to a Young Clergyman,* similarly, Harth's conclusions explain why Swift advises his young friend to preach directly to the natural reason of his congregation; why he believes in a classically educated clergy, whose innate intelligence has been improved and extended, but not overlaid, by commerce with books; why he despises the common insufferable cant of disparaging the heathen philosophers; and why he venerates Socrates as the wisest and best of uninspired mortals and praises Plato for knowing the true principles of natural religion and for his sublime teaching on forgiveness.

It is now almost half a century since A. O. Lovejoy first published his well-known essay "The Parallel between Deism and Classicism," and I suppose that no one today would accept without some reservations its very sweeping generalizations about eighteenth-century thought.[40] Without attempting any definitive criticism of either his approach or his theses, I believe that we might test the validity of some of his conclusions by comparing them with the evidence we have reviewed here. Lovejoy does not even mention Swift, but the Dean was very much a man of his own time, and if Lovejoy's generalizations are valid, they should presumably apply to him as well as to others.

Lovejoy's ambitious purpose was to analyze the main elements making up the "'characteristic idea-complex which constitutes what is commonly called the 'rationalism of the Enlightenment,' '' and to show that these ideas led to analogous conclusions in theology and aesthetics. Deism, he says, is "simply the application of this complex of ideas to religion," while "the neo-classical theory of poetry, and of the other arts, was in great part the application of the same set of preconceptions to aesthetics." Although he does not say so, the preconceptions which he lists are all assumptions about method, general rules by which the validity of propositions in any substantive field of thought may be judged. Apologizing for the "unlovely language" which he had to invent for stating them, he lists nine such rules, each of which is illustrated initially by its application in religion and then by its consequences in aesthetic theory.

The most obvious and damaging objection to Lovejoy's parallel is his unproved assumption that deism was the dominant, most characteristic form of religious belief during the period under discussion. Whatever may have been the case in France, that was never true in England. It is really very difficult to find more than a handful of writers, among whom the early-seventeenth-century Lord Herbert of Cherbury is probably the clearest example, who developed a coherent rationalistic system of theology, a serious and consistent non-Christian deism or theism. There were philosophers who reasoned about the nature and existence of God, as Descartes, Leibniz, and Locke did, but they were all Christians. There was also a vast army of divines, Catholic and Protestant, whose apologetic and controversial writings were grounded on both rational and Scriptural evidences. But most of those who have been called deists by Sir Leslie Stephen and other historians were men like Collins, Tindal, and Asgil, writers without any consistent intellectual position except an implacable hatred of Christianity and the church. Although Swift may well be suspected of bias in his role as defender of the faith, he was quite right to insist that deism was merely one of several guises assumed by anti-Christian propagandists, intellectually indistinguishable from Socinianism, anti-Trinitarianism, and other branches of freethinking. The deists were no more than a lunatic minority, a few fools, anything but representative of religious thought in Swift's time, or for long afterward.

Turning to Lovejoy's nine methodological preconceptions, I think we can say with considerable assurance that more than half are either irrelevant to Swift or of dubious value in describing his thought. The last two rules, for example, are "rationalistic primitivism" and "a negative philosophy of history." Both are clearly inapplicable to Swift, since he nowhere assumes or contends that the earliest thought is truer than later thought, or that history exhibits a steady decline from pristine intellectual virtue. Three other assumptions seem doubtful or ambiguous as applied to Swift. His belief that "every Man is bound to follow the Rules and Directions of that Measure of Reason which God hath given him" might be said to illustrate Lovejoy's second preconception, "rationalistic individualism," but it is strongly qualified by Swift's emphatic statement that "the *Reason* of every particular Man is weak and wavering, perpetually swayed and turned by his Interests, his Passions, and his Vices." It could be argued that "intellectual equalitarianism" is illustrated by Swift's advice to the young clergyman that he speak from his own natural reason to that of his congregation; he should remember that every plowman is aware of many theological and ethical truths, although he never heard of Aristotle or Plato. But Swift says in several contexts that all men are not intellectually equal, since God has given us reason in different measures; education, too, may advance what we start with. On Lovejoy's fifth rule, "antipathy to 'enthusiasm' and originality," Swift is again in partial but not complete agreement; he vigorously attacks religious enthusiasm in *A Tale of a Tub,* and in the *Letter to a Young Clergyman* he warns against attempts by a preacher to stir the passions of his auditors, but he nowhere uses the originality of an idea or proposition as a proof of its falsity.

The four remaining presuppositions, in my opinion, continue to have some usefulness as descriptions of common attributes of eighteenth-century English thought, including Swift's, though not as explanations. Most students of the period have recognized a considerable degree of truth in the first of Lovejoy's methodological assumptions, "uniformitarianism," and in two of its corollaries, "the appeal to the 'consensus gentium' " and "cosmopolitanism." Both Swift and Bentley clearly assume that, since reason is true, just, and constant, some men in all ages and societies have reached the same conclusions on many important questions. Plato knew as well as we do that there is only one God, the perfection of power, wisdom, and goodness, by whom all things were made, and the ethical teachings of the best ancient philosophers provide an excellent commentary on the moral part of Scripture, because they are as true today as they were then. Conversely, both Bentley and Swift assume that "singularity" is a sign of invalidity. The glorious gospel of the freethinkers must be false, for it goes "against the Current of common Doctrine" and is "in *opposition* to the rest of Mankind" (Bentley). Infidels like Collins could never "satisfy the general reason of mankind," because their doctrines violate "the common Light of Nature as well as Reason" and are contrary to "the universal Sentiments of all civilized Nations" (Swift). The cosmopolitanism of their outlook, similarly, is illustrated not only by their common belief that truth is universal, above all local and temporary variations of custom and manners, but even by so small a detail as Bentley's choice of a persona in his *Remarks* on Collins. As a German and a Lutheran, Phileleutherus Lipsiensis is unaffected by all merely parochial English interests, passions, and prejudices, but as a Christian scholar and man of reason he accepts the same eternal truths that Bentley himself subscribed to.

Also still useful is one further element in the idea-complex which Lovejoy describes. With apologies for the seeming paradox, he calls it "rationalistic anti-intellectualism." It is rational in assuming that truth is attainable by human reason, but antiintellectual in its suspicion of all abstruse doctrines and over-intricate reasoning:

> The presumption of the universal accessibility and verifiability of all that is really needful for men to know implied that all subtle, elaborate, intricate reasonings about abstruse questions beyond the grasp of the majority are certainly unimportant, and probably untrue. Thus any view difficult to understand, or requiring a long and complex exercise of the intellect for its verification, could be legitimately dismissed without examination, at least if it concerned any issue in which man's moral or religious interests were involved. A "system" was a legitimate object of suspicion simply because it *was* a system.[41]

It should be evident that this formulation describes Swift's relation to Plato quite accurately. As we have observed repeatedly, what Swift remembers and values from his early reading of Plato is not the elaborate dialectical arguments, but only a few separable maxims. He was not interested in Platonic metaphysics, and although the Houyhnhnms identify virtue with reason, as Plato does in his account of the guardians, they are not philosophers in Plato's sense. Swift's picture of them omits everything abstruse or technical in the Platonic system, reducing it to a few simple concepts, readily intelligible by anyone and easily stated in the language of everyday life. Swift's theory of preaching, as expressed in the *Letter to a Young Clergyman*, is another manifestation of the same attitude. His persona, the Person of

Quality, is rationalistic in his disparagement of pathetic appeals and in his assumption that communication between a preacher and his congregation depends upon their common possession of natural reason. He is anti-intellectual, in Lovejoy's sense, in his dislike for technical language and his strong disapproval of sermons on abstruse theological questions, attempts to explain mysteries, or ostentatious displays of learning. An effective preacher needs no more than tolerable intellectuals, advanced but not overlaid by a competent stock of human learning and some knowledge in divinity. The truths men need to know are simple and clear, available to all, so that even the meanest and most ignorant can grasp them.

Although Lovejoy's concept of rationalistic antiintellectualism describes quite satisfactorily an attitude that was often expressed in Swift's period, it has no exclusive or distinctive association with the Enlightenment, as he asserts, but was shared by writers in many ages. Especially prominent in the works of Montaigne, Erasmus, More, and other Renaissance humanists, it was also a favorite theme of the ancient Stoics. Socrates himself might be regarded as its ultimate source, since it was he, according to Cicero, who "called philosophy down from the heavens, established her in the cities of men, introduced her into private houses, and compelled her to ask questions about life and morality and things good and evil."[42] Swift was not a Platonist, but in his lifelong belief that philosophy can help men and women to lead a better moral life he was faithful to the spirit of Socrates.

As a final comment on the many allusions to Plato and Socrates that are scattered through Swift's writings, I believe we could say that this whole body of evidence could be taken as an extended gloss on his famous statement to Pope about the misanthropy upon which *Gulliver's Travels* was founded:

> I have got Materials Towards a Treatis proving the falsity of that Definition *animal rationale;* and to show it should be only *rationis capax*. Upon this great foundation of Misanthropy (though not Timons manner) the whole building of my Travells is erected: and I never will have peace of mind till all honest men are of my Opinion: by Consequence you are to embrace it immediately and procure that all who deserve my Esteem may do so too. The matter is so clear that it will admit little dispute. nay I will hold a hundred pounds that you and I agree in the Point. (*Corr.*, III, 103)

If men and women were rational animals, they would be like the Houyhnhnms in mind and behavior, though not in body. They do have some small measure of reason, but its powers are extremely limited and it is easily led astray by their interests, passions, and vices. Most of them spend their lives in a mad pursuit of riches, power, and pleasure, with little regard either for the virtue of their actions or the fate of their immortal souls, and the societies they have built seek the same vicious goals. Small wonder, then, that their whole history shows the bulk of mankind to be "the most pernicious race of little odious vermin that Nature ever suffered to crawl upon the surface of the earth," as the Brobdingnagian king concludes. But if most of us fall woefully short of the Houyhnhnm ideal, we do not have to be Yahoos. A tiny spark of rationality is there in all of us, burning more brightly in some than in others, and it can be fed and strengthened by the right kind of education. If we cultivate it and use it humbly and sincerely, as our maker meant us to do, it can lead us both to a knowledge and love of that maker and to true honor in our life on this earth. In the mind and writings of Swift, Plato was the prince of philosophers, Socrates the wisest and best of uninspired mortals. Although heathen philosophy is far inferior to Christian wisdom from above, Plato's teachings show that human reason, even without divine assistance, can attain truth in both divinity and ethics. All the ages of the world cannot add a seventh to Socrates and the other sextumvirs, but they prove that a life of integrity, temperance, and fortitude is open to all of us. God has made us all *rationis capax,* and therefore *virtutis capax* also. If we behave like Yahoos, the fault is not our maker's but our own.

Notes

1. Harold Williams, *Dean Swift's Library* (Cambridge: Cambridge University Press, 1932), p. 46, and the 1745 Sales Catalogue, pp. 3, 15; cf. T. P. LeFanu, "Catalogue of Dean Swift's Library in 1715, with an Inventory of his Personal Property in 1742," *Proceedings of the Royal Irish Academy,* 37 (1927), Sec. C, no. 13. On the seal see Swift, *Correspondence,* ed. Harold Williams (Oxford: Clarendon Press, 1965), V, 82, and Swift, *Prose Works,* ed. Herbert Davis (Oxford: B. Blackwell, 1939-68), XIII, 200. The two last-named works will be cited hereafter as *Corr.* and *PW,* usually within parentheses in the text.

2. In the letter to Pope, mentioned above, Swift speaks of one Socratic thought, to be discussed below, and adds, "I have retained it after reading Plato many years ago" (*Corr.,* IV, 153).

3. "Remarks upon Tindal's Rights of the Christian Church" (1708), *PW,* II, 30; "A Vindication of his Excellency, John, Lord Carteret" (1730), *PW,* XII, 161; *Corr.,* I, 64. On Swift's relations to Lord Carteret, lord lieutenant of Ireland during a crucial period in the controversy over Wood's halfpenny, see Oliver W. Ferguson, *Jonathan Swift and Ireland* (Urbana: University of Illinois Press, 1962), pp. 113-24. On Socrates' dancing, see Diogenes Laertius *Lives of Eminent Philosophers* II, v, 32.

4. *PW,* I, 33; Aristophanes *Clouds* 218ff.

5. Swift, *Poems,* ed. Harold Williams (Oxford: Clarendon Press, 1937), II, 619-20. Cited hereafter as *Poems,* within parentheses in the text.

6. On the date of this piece, see *PW,* I, xxxv.

7. *PW*, IX, xxiv-xxvii. But cf. Paul Fussell, Jr., "Speaker and Style in *A Letter of Advice to a Young Poet* (1721) and the Problem of Attribution," *RES*, n.s., 10 (1959),63-67; and Cynthia S. Matlack and William F. Matlack, "A Statistical Approach to Problems of Attribution: *A Letter of Advice to a Young Poet*," *College English*, 39 (1968), 627-32.

8. Williams, *Swift's Library*, p. 46.

9. Plato *Republic* (trans. Jowett) I. 347A-D.

10. Xenophon *Memorabilia* III, vii. 1-9. For an excellent analysis of the political ideas in the *Discourse of the Contests and Dissensions*, see R. B. Quintana, *The Mind and Art of Jonathan Swift* (New York: Oxford University Press, 1953), pp. 130-36; cf. Richard I. Cook, *Jonathan Swift as Tory Pamphleteer* (Seattle: University of Washington Press, 1967), pp. 124-26.

11. G. M. Trevelyan, *England under Queen Anne* (1930-48); reprint (London: Fontana Library, 1965), III, 111; for Harley's difficulties with the October Club see *The Lockhart Papers* (London, 1817), I, 322-24.

12. Swift, *Journal to Stella*, ed. Harold Williams (Oxford: Clarendon Press, 1948), I, 194-95.

13. Cf. Plato *Apology* 26-28, and Xenophon *Memorabilia* I. iii. 1-4.

14. "An Answer to a Paper, Called a Memorial," *PW*, XII, 24. Swift had attacked Whitsed in "A Short View of the State of Ireland." On the chief justice's role in the Wood controversy, see Ferguson, pp. 127-28, 196-97.

15. *PW*, II, 2; V, 83-84, 247; VI, 134.

16. J. C. Maxwell, "Demigods and Pickpockets: The Augustan Myth in Swift and Rousseau," *Scrutiny*, 11 (1942), 34-39.

17. F. R. Leavis, "The Irony of Swift," *Scrutiny*, 2(1934), 364-78; reprinted in *The Common Pursuit* (London: Chatto and Windus, 1962), pp. 73-87.

18. James L. Clifford, "The Eighteenth Century," *MLQ*, 26(1965),111-34. Though no doubt oversimplified, Clifford's separation between "hard" and "soft" interpretations of the Fourth Voyage is too convenient and amusing to pass by.

19. M. M. Kelsall, "*Iterum* Houyhnhnm: Swift's Sextumvirate and the Horses," *Essays in Criticism*, 19(1969), 35-45.

20. See, among others, George Sherburn, "Errors concerning the Houyhnhnms," *MP*, 56(1958), 92-97, and cf. n.33 below.

21. Plato *Republic* VI. 485D-487A.

22. Plato *Repub*. IV. 445D; VI. 511B-E; VII. 533E-534A; VI. 509D-511A; IV. 432A.

23. *Dictionary of National Biography*, XI, 363-64. Stephen's very loose use of the term "deist" has led to serious distortions of eighteenth-century religious thought by later historians. Even such responsible scholars as Herbert Davis, *PW*, IV, xvii-xx, and James Sutherland, "Forms and Methods in Swift's Satire," in *Jonathan Swift, 1667-1967*, ed. Roger McHugh and Philip Edwards (Dublin: Trinity College, 1967), pp. 71-72, have followed Sir Leslie in calling Collins a deist.

24. A very clear example of Collins's catch-as-catch-can way of arguing is that here he takes as his starting point this very un-Lockeian proposition about self-evident truths, while in *An Essay concerning the Use of Reason in Propositions, the Evidence whereof Depends upon Human Testimony* (London, 1707) his methodological premise is paraphrased from Locke's statement, in Book IV of the *Essay concerning Human Understanding*, of the criteria by which the probability of testimonies should be weighed (Collins, pp. 3-17; Locke, IV, Ch. xv, para. 4).

25. I have used the third edition, also of 1713, giving page references within parentheses in the text. The British Museum copy of this edition (shelf mark 1120. i. 2) is conveniently bound up with the first edition of Collins's *Discourse*.

26. Plato *Euthyphro* 6A-C; Xenophon *Memorabilia* IV. 7. 1-7.

27. Stephen, *History of English Thought in the Eighteenth Century* (London: Murray, 1927), I, 205; originally published 1876.

28. *Journal to Stella*, II, 603-4.

29. Cf. *Letter to a Young Clergyman*, *PW*, IX, 78, 80. Bentley diagnoses the same motivation for the anti-Christian propaganda of the freethinkers. See Remark 15, p. 31.

30. *PW*, IV, 69. In the *Preface to the Introduction*, Swift makes many of the same points against both freethinkers and Whigs that he made a few months later in the *Discourse*. As usual, he lumps "Atheists, Deists, and Socinians" together, with no distinctions among them (*PW*, IV, 63, 73-74), and he also accuses the Whigs of sponsoring all these heresies: "The Reason why the *Whigs* have taken the *Atheists* or *Free-thinkers* into their Body, is because they wholly agree in the political Schemes, and differ very little in Church Power and Discipline" (*PW*, IV, 84).

31. By far the best account of Swift's use of "spurious enthymemes" and other forms of mock logic is that by John M. Bullitt, *Jonathan Swift and the Anatomy of Satire* (Cambridge, Mass.: Harvard University Press, 1961), pp. 112-23. Bullitt discusses *Mr. C—ns's Discourse*, pp. 97-102.

32. Kathleen Williams, *Jonathan Swift and the Age of Compromise* (Lawrence, Kan.: University of Kansas Press, 1958), Ch. 7, pp. 154-209; Martin Kalich, "Three Ways of Looking at a Horse," *Criticism*, 2 (1960),107-24; idem, *The Other End of the Egg* (New York: 1970).

33. Sherburn, "Errors concerning the Houyhnhnms"; R. S. Crane, *PQ*, 40 (1961), 427-30; Ricardo Quintana, *PQ*, 37 (1958),354-55; Louis A. Landa, *PQ*, 38 (1959),351-53; Phillip Harth, *MP*, 69 (1971),165-69.

34. Landa, pp. 351-52. See also R. B. Quintana, *"Gulliver's Travels:* The Satiric Intent and Execution," in *Jonathan Swift, 1667-1967*, ed. McHugh and Edwards, pp. 78-93: "Swift and Pope were both Christians, but both chose, Swift in *Gulliver's Travels* and Pope in the *Essay on Man*, to keep within a secular, humanistic frame of reference" (p. 89). Cf. John J. McMammon, "The Problem of a Religious Interpretation of Gulliver's Fourth Voyage," *Journal of the History of Ideas*, 27 (1966),59-72.

35. One of the most eloquent of Socrates' many statements of his scale of values is his description of his life's work in the *Apology:* "For I do nothing but go about persuading you all, old and young alike, not to take thought for your persons or your property, but first and chiefly to care about the greatest improvement of the soul" (29D). See also the passages cited below, p. 292, n.18, 19, 20.

36. See Lloyd W. Brown, "The Person of Quality in the Eighteenth Century: Aspects of Swift's Satire," *Dalhousie Review* 48 (1968), 171-84.

37. Phillip Harth, *Swift and Anglican Rationalism* (Chicago: University of Chicago Press, 1961), pp. 32-34.

38. Ibid., p. 34.

39. Ibid., pp. 23-29.

40. A. O. Lovejoy, "The Parallel of Deism and Classicism," in *Essays in the History of Ideas* (Baltimore: Johns Hopkins University Press, 1948), pp. 78-98. For other evaluations of Lovejoy as an intellectual historian, see Ronald S. Crane, "Philosophy, Literature, and the History of Ideas," in *The Idea of the Humanities* (Chicago: University of Chicago Press, 1967), II, 173-87; Roland N. Stromberg, "Lovejoy's 'Parallel' Reconsidered," *Eighteenth-Century Studies* 1 (1968), 381-95; Robert D. Hume, *Dryden's Criticism* (Ithaca: Cornell University Press, 1970), pp. 158-62.

41. Lovejoy, "Deism and Classicism," pp. 85-86.

42. Cicero *Tusculan Disputations* V. 4. 10; cf. *Academica* I. 4. 15.

5

Pope, Gay, and *The Shepherd's Week*

The Shepherd's Week, John Gay's cycle of pastoral eclogues, was published on 15 April 1714.[1] Writing to his friend John Caryll about two months later, Pope represented Gay's poem as an attack on Ambrose Philips, presumably a burlesque of his *Pastorals.* Philips, Pope wrote, had intentionally withheld payment of the subscription money he had collected for Pope's Homer, and it is to this behavior, he said, that "the world owes Mr. Gay's Pastorals."[2]

This letter is so explicit and so well known that none of Gay's critics has failed at least to allude to it, but even in the eighteenth century, when most readers knew of Pope's quarrel with Philips, critics tended to minimize its importance in the interpretation of Gay's poem. There has been a general conviction that Pope's testimony is untrustworthy and may be dismissed, that Gay had no sufficient motive for attacking Philips, and finally that the poem itself does not bear out Pope's statement of its satiric purpose. On these grounds it has been inferred that Pope was either lying or exaggerating, or at best was mistaken; and *The Shepherd's Week* has therefore usually been described in terms quite different from his—as a realistic picture of country life, as a burlesque of pastoral poetry in general, or as a Virgilian parody.

In reply to these objections, it may readily be admitted that Pope was an interested party, and that in writing to Caryll he may have had some reason—whether spite, or vanity, or merely the instinctive mendacity of "one of the most consummate liars that ever lived"[3]—for misrepresenting Gay's

Reprinted with permission of the editor and the University of Washington Press from *Modern Language Quarterly,* 5 (1944), 79-88.

purposes. Beyond this we may even admit that his statement cannot be taken too literally, for we know from a letter he wrote to Swift in December 1713, that Gay's pastorals were begun several months before Philips held up delivery of Pope's subscription money.[4] On the other hand, the statement to Caryll may well have been not a lie but rather a simplification, ascribing to one very recent act of Philips an attitude toward him (on Gay's part and Pope's own) which was actually grounded on many earlier events. In that case Pope's interpretation of the poem might be sound although we rejected his explanation of its immediate motive.

The second objection, Gay's lack of adequate motive, could be removed by showing that he had in fact several reasons both for disliking Philips and for despising his verse; this part of the case will be examined in the paragraphs immediately following. The third objection, that *The Shepherd's Week,* apart from some few incidental gibes, does not carry sufficient internal evidence of a desire to burlesque Philips, can only be refuted by examining the poem itself. This will be done in the third section of this paper.

Without such supporting evidence we should not be justified in accepting Pope's definition of Gay's aims, but if his statement is borne out by the biographical evidence and by an analysis of the poem itself there seems no good reason to continue to reject it. Gay himself left no record of his intentions, and Pope, as one of his most intimate friends, was certainly in a position to know them; it is not reasonable, out of a general suspicion of Pope's veracity, to reject the only direct testimony we have on the purposes for which Gay wrote his poem. At all events, this paper is intended to support Pope's interpretation—in other words, to argue that burlesque of Philips was the basic motive of *The Shepherd's Week* and that the poem is most fully understood in the light of that controlling purpose.

❦❦❦

Ambrose Philips was one of the minor Whig writers of Pope's time, a member of Addison's "little senate" at Button's coffeehouse and author of plays and periodical essays as well as poems.[5] Later known, because of his children's verses, as "Namby Pamby," in the period with which we are concerned he seems to have been generally known as "Pastoral" Philips.[6] His eclogues were published, as Pope's were, in the sixth part of Tonson's *Poetical Miscellanies* (1709).

Pope, whose *Pastorals* had certainly not been underpraised, had no reason to be jealous of Philips's performance, and he shows no evidence of having been so.[7] By 1713 he was deeply engaged in new and quite different projects, and without some special impulse from outside it is unlikely that he would have paid any particular attention to his rival pastoralist. They were by this time acquainted, met frequently at Button's, and were both generally counted as members of the Addisonian group.

From the beginning, however, Philips's Whig friends had been persistent and exaggerated in their praise of his poems. He was complimented in the *Tatler* and half a dozen times in the *Spectator;*[8] elsewhere Welsted and Tickell, both Whig writers, had singled him out for special praise.[9] This advertising campaign reached its climax in the spring of 1713 in a series of five essays on pastoral poetry, probably written by Tickell, in the *Guardian.*[10] Tickell stated that his rules were drawn from the practice of "our countrymen Spencer and Philips" and concluded the series by asserting that Theocritus "left his dominions to Virgil; Virgil left his to his son Spencer; and Spencer was succeeded by his eldest-born Philips." Though Pope was quoted in one of the earlier numbers, he was not mentioned in the concluding essay.

Pope replied to this lopsided estimate by submitting to the *Guardian,* to which both he and Gay were occasional contributors, an anonymous essay (published 27 April 1713), which ironically applied Tickell's critical principles to a direct comparison, ostensibly in Philips's favor, between his *Pastorals* and Pope's own. Tickell, presenting the conventional golden-age theory of pastoral (to which Pope also subscribed), had emphasized simplicity and innocence as the leading characteristics of the form. He argued, however, that these qualities should be adapted to the writer's own country and time. "What is proper in Arcadia, or even in Italy, might be very absurd in a colder country," and the English pastoralist should represent English scenes, dress, superstitions, customs, and sports. Tickell praised Philips for his realistic English settings and commended his Theocritan or "Doric" style.

Pope, ironically accepting these principles and judgments, implied by various devices that Philips's simplicity was tasteless and inane, that he imitated the ancients with excessive "order and method," that his country proverbs were puerile, and that his descriptive passages violated decorum. Pope burlesqued Philips's "elegant dialect" in a pastoral dialogue, purporting to be the work of an "old west-country bard." I quote a brief passage:

> *Cicily.*   Rager go vetch tha kee, or else tha zun
> Will quite be go, bevor c'have half a don.
> *Roger.*   *Thou shouldst not ax ma tweece, but I've a be*
> *To dreave our bull to bull tha parson's kee.*

Pope's eclogues, the essay concluded, must on the whole be excluded from the pastoral class. Lacking Philips's "beautiful rusticity," they are evidently not pastorals at all, "but something better."[11]

The immediate consequences of Pope's essay are somewhat obscure. Pope believed that Philips, incapable of a direct reply, secretly tried to get revenge by alienating Addison from Pope,[12] but there was apparently no open break. When the proposals for Pope's translation of Homer were published (October 1713), the group at Button's gave it at least nominal support, and Philips himself was responsible for collecting the guineas of the Hanover Club members. It is certain, however, that by the beginning of 1714 the "little senate" had openly declared war on Pope. In February he was gazetted as an enemy of the "Grand Société" at Button's; and although this action "was laughed at by the chief of my Whig-friends and my Tory-friends,"[13] it was a clear indication of the attitude among the lesser Whig writers, the friends and supporters of Philips. It was at this time, too, that Philips held up the subscription money, and in April Pope was attacked, along with Gay and Rowe, in Gildon's *New Rehearsal*.[14] *The Shepherd's Week* was published in the same month, and Parnell's squib, *The Bookworm,* in which Philips was laughed at along with Dennis (Pope's other enemy), appeared at about the same time.[15] In view of the time sequence, it is difficult to believe that these pieces, Parnell's and Gay's, do not represent counterattacks by the friends of Pope.

Some critics have treated the warfare between Pope and the "little senate" as a private affair in which Gay could not have been intimately concerned. Austin Dobson, for instance, says that Pope "decoyed" Gay into "his own war" with Philips.[16] W. H. Irving states that, in the letter to Caryll, Pope "sought to suggest" that *The Shepherd's Week* was an attack on Philips and remarks that Gay "indeed may have encouraged Pope to think so."[17]

To my mind, this view has no real plausibility. Even if Philips had been a purely personal enemy of Pope's, Gay had sufficient motive for attacking him. From the beginning of their acquaintance, as Dr. Johnson said, Pope had received Gay into his inmost confidence, and their friendship "lasted to their separation by death, without any known abatement on either part."[18] Gay had already come to Pope's support, in another quarrel, by ironically dedicating his play, *The Mohocks* (April 1712), to John Dennis; he was to support him again in January 1715 by collaborating on *The What D'Ye Call It,* in which Pope and Gay mock Philips's play *The Distressed Mother* and even poke mild fun at Addison. Friendship for Pope was in itself sufficient reason for aiding him in his battles.

But Philips was not merely a personal enemy of Pope's. His friends had identified Gay with Pope and had attacked them both; he was Gay's own enemy as well as Pope's. Furthermore, Philips was both a Whig and a dunce, and in either capacity he was Gay's natural foe; Gay was much more a Tory than Pope, and just as much an enemy of fools. Philips was in fact a favorite butt for the whole Scriblerus Club group; Parnell, Pope, and Swift at one time or another all attacked him, and Gay had the same motives, both literary and political, for doing so. There is no reason, then, to suppose that Pope had to "incite" or "decoy" him into such a project. On the contrary, Philips was a natural target for Gay's wit, and it is entirely credible that Gay, even without encouragement from Pope or Swift, might have conceived and carried out a plan for burlesquing Philips's insipid *Pastorals*. Though Pope oversimplified Gay's motives for such an attack, the biographical evidence makes a strong prima facie case for Pope's description of *The Shepherd's Week* as a satire on Philips. It is plausible, and indeed very likely, that the poem had this purpose. With this probability in mind, we may turn to the poem itself.[19]

ℋℋℋ

The Shepherd's Week consists of six pastoral eclogues accompanied by a rather elaborate critical apparatus: a proeme, a prologue, a number of notes, and a word index. A large part of the poem's charm comes from its vivid rural details—accounts of hobgoblins and gypsies, descriptions of cheese and butter making, of sheep tending and hog feeding, of country wrestling matches, dances, and games. Gay's purpose, however, was not descriptive and realistic but comic, and the rural characters and scenes are distorted and exaggerated for comic effort.[20] Like Shakespeare's artisans, shepherds, and squires, Gay's rustics have a certain naïve charm, but from the sophisticated urban point of view which Gay (like Shakespeare) expected in his readers, these dairymaids and swineherds are ludicrous—delightful but absurd.

Gay's comic pastorals are relevant to Philips in two ways: first through direct verbal parody, and secondly through Gay's adoption of a pastoral formula, a style and manner of treatment, which is meant to be understood as imitating that of Philips. Critics have recognized the element of direct parody in *The Shepherd's Week* but have considered it to be incidental and comparatively unimportant, a superficial factor in a poem with quite different basic purposes. The other aspect of Gay's satire on Philips seems to have escaped attention.

Gay's direct imitations of Philips add little to Pope's ironic analysis in the *Guardian*. In the following tabulation I have tried to indicate both the extent of Gay's parody and the closeness with which it paralleled Pope's attack. To save space I have omitted most of the illustrative passages that might be quoted, but even with a minimum of detail the range and quantity of parody are, I think, impressive.

1. Obsolete or "Doric" language. Pope ironically praised Philips for using antiquated terms like *welladay, whilom, make mock,* and *witless younglings*. Spenserian diction is the most obvious aspect of Gay's parody of Philips. Besides the terms mentioned by Pope, Gay has scores of Spenserianisms such as *adown, erst, dearlings, ween, plain,* and the like, all of which appear in Philips, along with others from the general Spenserian stock. Many of these have comic glosses, evidently burlesquing those contributed by E.K. to the *Shepherd's Calendar.*[21]

2. Rustic names. Pope commended Philips's choice of names "peculiar to the country, and more agreeable to a reader of delicacy; such as Hobbinol, Lobbin, Cuddy, and Colin Clout." Gay uses the same Spenserian names, describing them in the proeme as "right simple and meet for the country," and also invents several comic names analogous to these. The most obvious instance is Blouzelind for the Rosalind of Spenser and Philips, but Grubbinol, Cloddipole, Hobnelia, and Bumkinet have the same comic relevance to Philips. Lightfoot, a dog mentioned by Philips, also appears in *The Shepherd's Week.*[22]

3. Violations of decorum. Pope said that "Mr. Philips hath with great judgment described wolves in England" and praised him for showing flowers of all seasons in bloom at once. Gay says in the proeme that his shepherd does not defend his flock from wolves, because in England there are none. Among several passages imitating Philips's flower descriptions, the following is representative:

> My *Blouzelinda* is the blithest Lass,
> Than Primrose sweeter, or the Clover-Grass.
> Fair is the King-Cup that in Meadow blows,
> Fair is the Daisie that beside her grows,
> Fair is the Gillyflow'r, of Gardens sweet,
> Fair is the Mary-Gold, for Pottage meet.
> But *Blouzelind*'s than Gillyflow'r more fair,
> Than Daisie, Mary-Gold, or King-Cup rare.[23]

4. Platitudinous proverbs. Philips excels in country proverbs according to Pope, who quoted some very flat examples. Gay has six or seven similarly banal maxims, all italicized for emphasis.[24]

5. Pseudosimplicity. Pope: "In the first of these authors [i.e. Philips], two shepherds thus innocently describe the behavior of their mistresses.

> *Hobb.*   As Marian bath'd, by chance I passed by;
> She blush'd, and at me cast a side-long eye:
> Then swift beneath the crystal wave she try'd
> Her beauteous form, but all in vain, to hide.
> *Lang.*   As I to cool me bath'd one sultry day,

> Fond Lydia lurking in the sedges lay;
> The wanton laugh'd and seem'd in hast to fly;
> Yet often stopp'd and often turn'd her eye.[25]

Gay burlesques this rather coy passage as follows:

> *Lobbin.* On two near Elms, the slacken'd Cord I hung,
>   Now high, now low my *Blouzelinda* swung.
>   With the rude Wind her rumpled Garment rose,
>   And show'd her taper Leg, and scarlet Hose.
> *Cuddy.* Across the fallen Oak the Plank I laid,
>   And my self pois'd against the tott'ring Maid,
>   High leapt the Plank; adown *Buxoma* fell;
>   I spy'd—but faithful Sweethearts never tell.[26]

6. Inanity. Pope quoted from Philips' second ecologue:

> Ah me the while! ah me, the luckless day!
> Ah luckless lad, the rather might I say;
> Ah silly I! more silly than my sheep,
> Which on the flow'ry plains I once did keep.[27]

Gay has:

> Ah woful Day! ah woful Noon and Morn!
> When first by thee my Younglings white were shorn,
> Then first, I ween, I cast a Lover's Eye,
> My Sheep were silly, but more silly I.[28]

Pope, again quoting Philips:

> O woful day! O day of woe, quoth he,
> And woful I, who live the day to see.[29]

Gay's parody of this passage:

> I rue the Day, a rueful Day, I trow,
> The woful Day, a Day indeed of Woe![30]

In light of the tabulation given above, it is difficult to accept the traditional view that parody of Philips is superficial or infrequent in *The Shepherd's Week*. The verses quoted are scattered throughout the poem; none of its six eclogues is without some passage of direct burlesque. It seems unlikely that such extensive parody could have been added, as W. H. Irving thinks, "in the later stages of composition."[31]

This brings us to the second aspect of Gay's burlesque, his adoption of a style and manner modeled on those of Philips. The clue to Gay's intentions is

to be found in the proeme, where he explains, for those who can read between
the lines, both his purpose and his comic method. The proeme has been
underemphasized by most critics; it has also been misunderstood through a
failure to realize that it is consistently ironic.[32] Gay does not express his own
views but assumes throughout the proeme the character and attitudes of a
rustic bard, signing himself "Thy loving countryman, JOHN GAY." Not
only the proeme and the prologue but the notes and the eclogues themselves
are assumed to have been written by the "painful hand" of this naïve and
earnest swain. His opinions, it need hardly be said, are very different from
Gay's own.

In the proeme Gay rejects with indignant scorn the sort of pastoral Pope
wrote. He dismisses the theory of the golden age as "a Rout and Rabblement
of Critical Gallimawfry" and describes the diction of contemporary pastoral
as "the fine finical newfangled Fooleries of this gay Gothic Garniture."[33] His
own eclogues, by contrast, combine Theocritan realism and Spenserian
dialect. In his matter, following "the true ancient guise of Theocritus," the
poet claims to represent the scenes and manners of actual country life, as they
exist in his own country and in his own time. As the "Louts" of Theocritus
behold their goats at rut in all simplicity, so Gay's shepherdesses do not idly
pipe on oaten reeds but milk the kine and drive the straying hogs to the sties.
In his diction, however, "thy loving countryman" confesses that he has
departed from Theocritus, who copied genuine vulgar usage, the rural dialect
actually spoken in his time. The poet concedes that the language of his own
eclogues is spoken neither in the country nor at court, that it never has been
spoken, and, "if I judge aright, will never be uttered in Times future." Such
language must soon turn to rubbish and ruins, and the bard can find no rational
motive for adopting it. He has been led into it, he says, by "deep learned
Ensamples." The bard has a good deal of hearty common sense, but he is
simple and modest and wants to do everything in the proper way.[34]

Gay's "ensample," of course, was Philips. Philips had professed to be a
disciple of Virgil, Theocritus, and Spenser.[35] His materials were mainly
Virgilian (as Gay's therefore also were), but he had imitated Spenser's dialect
and had attempted, by the description of English settings and rural customs, to
achieve a Theocritan local realism. Tickell, while accepting the assumptions
of prevailing pastoral theory, had contended that English eclogists should give
their poems a specifically English flavor. Commending Philips as a true-born
son of Theocritus and Spenser, Tickell had praised his "Doric" language, his
simplicity, and his "beautiful rusticity." Pope ironically accepted this
definition of Philips's work and carried it to a ludicrous extreme in the vulgar
and barely intelligible ballad of the "old west-country bard."

The Shepherd's Week has the same relation to Philips that Pope's *Guardian* essay had. With an irony paralleling Pope's, Gay indicates that he takes Philips as his model. His purpose is to reveal the artistic fatuity of Tickell's pastoral theory and of Philips's practice; his method is to illustrate their principles and definitions in a series of comic eclogues. Gay imitates Virgil, Theocritus, and Spenser because Philips had done so. His shepherds are low-comedy bumpkins because he wished to imply that Philips's style, if consistently followed out, could lead to no other effect; if, as Tickell claimed, the rules of pastoral were to be drawn from the practice of Philips, this was the sort of poem which must result. This idea, implicit in Gay's proeme and consistently applied in the eclogues themselves, is the organizing principle of *The Shepherd's Week*. It is this idea which gives the poem a coherent artistic plan.

Johnson remarked, in reviewing Gay's poem, that it had been read with pleasure by "those who had no interest in the rivalry of the poets, nor knowledge of the critical dispute." This is undoubtedly true. The comic formula adopted in *The Shepherd's Week* is sufficiently general to be amusing apart from any specific satiric object; as in *The Beggar's Opera,* the topical allusions may be disregarded. I believe, however, that *The Shepherd's Week* was designed as a burlesque of Philips's *Pastorals* and that its particular combination of qualities, its content, form, manner, and diction, were determined by this purpose. On any other hypothesis, important features of the poem must be disregarded or left unexplained. It can be fully understood—and fully enjoyed too—only against the background of controversy in which it originated.

Notes

1. Gay, *Poetical Works,* ed. G. C. Faber (London: Oxford University Press, 1926), p. xxxvi.

2. Pope to Caryll, 8 June 1714, *The Correspondence of Alexander Pope,* ed. George Sherburn (Oxford: Clarendon Press, 1956), I, 229. This edition will hereafter be cited as *Correspondence.* For Warburton's account of the incident, see Pope, *Works,* ed. Whitwell Elwin and W. J. Courthope (London: J. Murray, 1871-86), VI, 210.

3. Sir Leslie Stephen, *Hours in a Library,* new ed. (New York: G. P. Putnam's Sons, 1904), I, 141; cf. his *Alexander Pope* (London: Macmillan, 1908; first published in 1880). This conception of Pope's character, taken for granted by many critics in Stephen's day, has been undermined by the new evidence and more sympathetic interpretation presented by George Sherburn's *Early Career of Alexander Pope* (Oxford: Clarendon Press, 1934) and later studies.

4. Pope to Swift, 8 December 1713, *Correspondence,* I, 200; also reprinted in Swift's *Correspondence,* ed. Harold Williams (Oxford: Clarendon Press, 1963), I, 414.

5. Since the facts to be summarized here are familiar, I have made my account as brief as possible. For other treatments of this material see Bonamy Dobrée, *Essays in Biography, 1680-1726* (London: Oxford University Press, 1925), pp. 266-70; Robert J. Allen, *The Clubs of Augustan London* (Cambridge, Mass.: Harvard University Press, 1933), pp. 244-46; Sherburn,

Early Career, pp. 115-22; and W. H. Irving, *John Gay, Favorite of the Wits* (Durham, N.C.: Duke University Press, 1940), pp. 82-90.

6. See for example Swift, *Journal to Stella,* ed. Harold Williams (Oxford: Clarendon Press, 1948), I, 129.

7. In a letter to Henry Cromwell, 28 October 1710, Pope gives qualified but sufficiently generous praise to Philips's eclogues; see *Correspondence,* I, 100-101.

8. *Tatler,* no. 10; *Spectator,* nos. 223, 229, 336, 400, 578.

9. Leonard Welsted, *Remarks on the English Poets* (1712) and Thomas Tickell, *The Prospect of Peace* (1712); see also Charles Gildon, *Complete Art of Poetry* (1718), I, 157; cf. Sherburn, *Early Career,* p. 118.

10. Nos. 22, 23, 28, 30, 32; text in *British Essayists,* ed. Alexander Chalmers (London, 1808), Vol. XVI. On the authorship of these essays see R. E. Tickell, *Thomas Tickell and the Eighteenth-Century Poets* (London: Constable & Co., 1931), pp. 25ff.

11. *Guardian,* no. 40; Chalmers, *British Essayists,* XVI, 204-12; also reprinted in Pope, *Works,* X, 507-14.

12. Pope to Jervas, 27 August 1714, *Correspondence,* I, 244-45; see also Jervas to Pope, 20 August 1714, ibid., p. 244. Cf. Joseph Spence, *Observations, Anecdotes, and Characters of Books and Men,* ed. James M. Osborn (Oxford: Clarendon Press, 1966), I, 62-64, 71.

13. Pope to Caryll, 25 February 1714, *Correspondence,* I, 210.

14. Cf. Sherburn, *Early Career,* pp. 125, 163-64.

15. Thomas Parnell, *Poems on Several Occasions* (London, 1770), pp. 102-7.

16. In the *Dictionary of National Biography,* VII, 962-69; cf. Austin Dobson, *Miscellanies,* first series (New York, 1898), pp. 239-74.

17. Irving, p. 83.

18. Samuel Johnson, *Lives of the English Poets,* ed. G. B. Hill (Oxford: Clarendon Press, 1905), II, 268.

19. Perhaps the best evidence in support of Pope, for those who can follow the allusive jests of one intimate friend to another, is furnished by the references to Button's, Philips, and *The Shepherd's Week* in his own letters to Gay on 4 May and 23 September 1714. The first concludes, "Let them also know at *Button*'s that I am mindful of them. I am, divine Bucoliast! *Thy loving Countryman.*" In the later letter, welcoming Gay home from his futile journey to Hanover, he says: "Hast thou not left of thy Issue in divers Lands, that *German Gays* and *Dutch Gays* may arise, to write Pastorals and sing their Songs in strange Countries? Are not the *Blouzelinda*'s of the *Hague* as charming as the *Rosalinda*'s of *Britain?* or have the two great Pastoral Poets of our Nation renounced Love at the same time? for *Philips,* immortal *Philips, Hanover Philips,* hath deserted, yea and in a rustick manner kicked his *Rosalind.*" (*Correspondence,* I, 223, 255.)

20. Cf. R. P. Bond, *English Burlesque Poetry* (Cambridge, Mass.: Harvard University Press, 1932), pp. 110-15.

21. John Gay, *Poetry and Prose,* ed. Vinton A. Dearing and Charles E. Beckwith (Oxford: Clarendon Press, 1974), pp. 96, 104, 105, 109, 113. All quotations from *The Shepherd's Week* follow the text of this edition, I, 90-126.

22. Philips, *Pastorals,* Ecl. II, l. 29, in *Poems,* ed. M. G. Segar (Oxford: B. Blackwell, 1937), p. 11. Gay, "Prologue," l. 43.

23. "Monday,"ll. 41-48; cf. Philips, IV, 5-8. See also "Friday," ll. 83-87 and 133-38.

24. "Monday," ll. 8, 98; "Tuesday," ll. 18, 102; "Wednesday," l. 31; "Friday," ll. 151-52; cf. Philips, II, 55-56, 79-80; IV, 121-22; VI, 16.

25. Philips, VI, 69-76. I quote the text as given by Pope in *British Essayists,* XVI, 208.

26. "Monday," ll. 103-10.

27. Philips, II, 57-58, 61-62; Pope, in *British Essayists,* XVI, 210.

28. "Tuesday," ll. 25-28.

29. Philips, IV, 47-48.

30. "Thursday," ll. 5-6.

31. Irving, p. 83.

32. This point was missed, for example, by Dr. Johnson (*Lives,* II, 269) and by R. P. Bond (*English Burlesque Poetry,* p. 110).

33. Gay, *Poetry and Prose,* I, 90-91. Like the glosses (see above, n.21 and text), the proeme is apparently intended to parody the style of E. K.

34. Ibid., I, 90, 92. In his "Discourse on Pastoral Poetry" Pope contrasts the diction of Theocritus and Spenser along these same lines.

35. See Philips's preface to the *Pastorals,* Segar, p. 3. For an appraisal of the interpretation of *The Shepherd's Week* that has been presented here, see Patricia Meyer Spacks, *John Gay* (New York: Twayne Publishers, 1965), pp. 30-40.

6

Pope's *Eloisa* and the *Heroides* of Ovid

There is a remarkable discrepancy in critical judgments of Pope's *Eloisa to Abelard* between his own period and later times. For almost a century, Emile Audra says, the poem was generally considered in both France and England to be "la plus belle et la plus émouvante des épîtres amoureuses."[1] If anything, he understates the enthusiastic admiration felt for the poem by readers and critics from its publication in 1717 to the end of the eighteenth century. In 1756, *Eloisa* was "in the Hands of all, and in the Memories of most readers."[2] Joseph Warton, who thought that it would outlive all but two or three other poems by Pope, described it as "one of the most highly finished, and certainly the most interesting, of the pieces of our author."[3] Critics of the 1780s praise it in even more superlative terms; Dr. Johnson calls it "one of the most happy productions of human wit," excelling every composition of the same kind. Gilbert Wakefield says that Gray's *Elegy* is more finished and pathetic than any other poem in the world—"'Pope's *Eloisa* alone excepted"—and William Mason regards Pope's epistle as "such a *chef d'oeuvre*, that nothing of the kind can be relished after it."[4]

As Audra's remark implies, this consensus of admiration did not outlast Pope's century. Some nineteenth-century readers, including Byron,[5] continued to believe that *Eloisa* was a beautiful and moving poem, but for the most part its reputation was buried, along with almost everything Pope wrote, in the revolution of taste initiated by Wordsworth's epoch-making *Preface*. In

This essay originally appeared in *Studies in Eighteenth-Century Culture*, Vol. III, ed. Harold Pagliaro (Cleveland and London: Case Western Reserve University Press, 1973), pp. 11-34; permission to reprint it has been granted by the American Society for Eighteenth-Century Studies.

our own century, in spite of the sweeping revaluation of Pope which has been in progress for some forty years, the poem has by no means recovered the critical esteem in which it was held during his age. According to Geoffrey Tillotson, Mason "spoke the enthusiasm of a past century. The modern reader is inclined to overlook or disparage *Eloisa to Abelard*." Tillotson does his best to make the poem sound worth reading, but his remarks about its "rhetoric," "geometrizing," and "operatic flights" seem more likely to discourage any reading at all than to open the way toward a fair and unprejudiced appraisal.[6] A more perceptive and sophisticated reader, Reuben Brower, leaves the poem in little better case. His chapter on *Eloisa* in *The Poetry of Allusion* presents a systematic comparison with Pope's formal model, the *Heroides* of Ovid. Brower knows these poems, in the original, as well as most professed classical scholars, and he reads them as living poetry. Yet his subtle analyses of the language of particular passages in Ovid and in Pope do not add up to any convincing account or defense of the poem as a whole. There are "moments we remember and treasure in *Eloisa to Abelard*," Brower says, but he finds no overall design or formal structure except a succession of coups, tirades, and remembered scenes, following Ovidian patterns of wit and rhythm. If this is all the poem has to offer, Brower is quite right in concluding that *Eloisa to Abelard* may strike us as "remarkable" or "fine," but that in reading it we are not likely to feel "how moving" or "how convincing."[7]

Where a contrast between contemporary opinion and later judgment is so sharp, there is surely some reason to surmise that the fault may lie not in the poem but in us, in our way of reading it. The readers and critics of a poet's own time may, of course, be mistaken in their judgments on his works; as Dr. Johnson says, contemporary opinion is often distorted by local and temporary prejudices, by biases of interest or passion. But biases of another kind may distort the judgment of later ages even more drastically—blindnesses and deafnesses of perception, prejudices of taste, aesthetic principle, or critical method. Wordsworth and his successors put many such blinders on the minds of men, and, though scholars try to remove them, we too often continue to think and read through those distorting glasses. The readers of a poet's own time, who are likely to share his philosophical, artistic, and critical perspectives, are surely in a better position to understand what he is doing and how his poems should be read than those bred in a different intellectual and aesthetic milieu. Critics of a later age, recognizing such a divergence of taste and judgment, should at least ask themselves whether they may not be failing to read the work "with the same spirit that its author writ."[8]

The aim of this paper is to attempt to recover that spirit and to present a reading of *Eloisa to Abelard* which is guided by it. The argument will be in two parts, historical and critical. In the first, after reconstructing from editions and criticisms of Ovid the way of interpreting and judging the *Heroides* which was shared by most competent readers during the Restoration and the early eighteenth century, I shall propose a hypothesis as to the artistic intention controlling Pope's poem. The second part will analyze and appraise the poem in the light of that intention, but using interpretive and critical principles of my own choosing. I hope that Pope's epistle, seen in this perspective, will seem a much better poem than has usually been thought since the time of Warton, Johnson, Wakefield, and Mason.

⟡⟡⟡

In summarizing the conception of Ovid which prevailed generally in both France and England before and during Pope's lifetime, I shall follow for the most part an outline provided by Dryden in his preface to Ovid's *Epistles* and in eight other essays in which he discusses Ovid's poetry. Together Dryden's discussions of Ovid constitute the fullest and most systematic statement of a view that many other critics shared.[9] A few of the latter will be quoted for further illustration of particular points, and additional references will be cited in footnotes.

For readers and critics of that age, the most important of Ovid's poems were the *Metamorphoses* and the *Heroides,* especially the latter. These epistles, Dryden says, are "generally granted to be the most perfect pieces of Ovid,"[10] and he based his general conception of Ovid as a poet on those poems. They were for him the definitive example of Ovid's poetry, and the other writings, including even the *Metamorphoses,* were interpreted as approximations to the same type.

Dryden's criticism of the *Heroides* looks in two directions, taking the poems first as the standard examples of their kind, the heroic epistle, then as works to be judged, like any others, by the extent to which they realize the ideal possibilities of that form. The definition and laws of the heroic epistle must be inferred from Ovid's practice, since he was the inventor of the genre; but his own poems are to be judged by their conformity to the definition and the rules inferrable from it. According to Dryden, the *Heroides* have some defects, which a perfect example of their kind would avoid.

The heroic epistle, as adumbrated though never fully achieved by Ovid, is a kind of poem closely related to the drama. Of all the Romans, Dryden says, Ovid "had a genius most proper for the stage."[11] In his epistles, the poet does not speak in his own person; the words of the poem are those of "feigned persons," dramatic characters.[12] The poet pictures human nature in disorder, "the movements and affections of the mind, either combating between two contrary passions, or extremely discomposed by one.''[13] Ovid is described in very similar terms by Joseph Trapp just six years before *Eloisa to Abelard* first appeared in print. Of all the ancient poets, he says, ''none understood nature more than he, or expressed her various conflicts better.'' In the story of Medea and Jason in *Metamorphoses* VII, for example, ''the poet wonderfully describes the dubious strife between love and shame, reason and affection, as he does in many other places.''[14] In the age of Dryden and Pope, Ovid was read as a dramatist of the emotions, depicting disordered or conflicting passions through the speeches and actions of feigned persons in moments of intense feeling.

In the critical theory of that period, the definition of a genre includes both its subject matter, the particular aspect of nature with which it is concerned, and also its mode of treatment—mimetic or nonmimetic, narrative or dramatic, and so forth. To be complete, however, the definition must also distinguish the poetic effect peculiar to the form—its proper pleasure and instruction and the specific emotional impact it has upon the reader or audience. To achieve these effects is the governing purpose of all works belonging to the given genre, and therefore also the poetic intention of the writer of such a work.

Trapp arrives at a rather vague description of the effect and purpose of the Ovidian epistle through a contrast between poems of the sublime and the marvelous, which impress on the mind something great, unusual, and portentous, and other kinds, which excite ''grief, pity, terror, and work upon other passions.'' Asserting that the ''great art of Poetry'' is to move the passions, he cites ''Phyllis to Demophoön'' in the *Heroides* as particularly affecting, ''wonderfully adapted to move compassion.''[15] Dryden had previously expressed the same notions more clearly and forcefully. Ovid, he writes in the *Essay of Dramatic Poesy,* ''had a way of writing so fit to stir up a pleasing admiration and concernment, which are the objects of a tragedy, . . . that, had he lived in our age, . . . no man but must have yielded to him.''[16] The poet's dramatic representation of a soul in conflict moves the soul of the reader through imaginative identification and sympathy to a parallel emotional response. ''I will appeal to any man, who has read this poet,'' Dryden says in the preface to *Ovid's Epistles,* ''whether he finds not the natural emotion of the same passion in himself, which the poet describes in his feigned persons?''[17] This tragic or quasi-tragic effect is the proper pleasure of a heroic epistle, its poetic purpose and intent.

In most ways, Dryden and others in that age believed, Ovid's epistles were admirably adapted to the aims of their kind. The Roman poet understood the passions, felt them within himself, and represented them truly and vividly, through just and lively images. His poems are also beautifully ordered and unified: ''our Poet has always the goal in his eye, which directs him in his race; some beautiful design, which he first establishes, and then contrives the means, which will naturally conduct it to his end."[18]

But there is an "allay"[19] in the gold of Ovid's poems. As Quintilian and Seneca had observed long before,[20] he did not always know when to give over, when a thought or feeling had been sufficiently expressed, and he was also too often led astray by his overingenious fancy into "unseasonable and absurd conceits," inappropriate to a poem of true and intense feeling. But his worst fault, deplored by dozens of seventeenth- and eighteenth-century critics, is what Dryden calls Ovid's "darling sin"—the love of wit.[21] In an essay on "The Character of Tragedies," St.-Evremond writes:

> The soul when it is sensibly touched does not afford the mind an opportunity to think intensely, much less to ramble and divert itself in the variety of its conceptions. It is upon this account that I can hardly bear with Ovid's luxurious fancy. He is witty in his grief, and gives himself a world of trouble to show his wit when we expect nothing but natural thoughts from him.[22]

Ovid was Addison's favorite classical example of false or mixed wit, and Dryden repeatedly speaks of his "boyisms" and "puerilities," his verbal turns and puns. Even in the *Heroides,* the most perfect of his poems, "he often writ too pointedly for his subject, and made his persons speak more eloquently than the violence of their passion would admit: so that he is frequently witty out of season."[23] In a poem of tragic emotional quality, wit is out of place; it breaks the reader's pity and thus destroys the very thing the poet is building.[24]

This way of reading the epistles is probably far off the mark, if the standard for validity in interpretation is the "real" or "Roman" Ovid, the *Heroides* of Ovid's own intention. In the *Amores* he himself contrasts majestic and haughty tragedy with his own more delicate elegiac muse:

> sum levis, et mecum levis est, mea cura, Cupido;
> non sum materia fortior ipsa mea.[25]

Modern scholars, especially in the last thirty years or so, have tended to consider Ovid's wit not as an accidental defect, at odds with the poet's artistic purpose, but as essential to his poetic aim.[26] There have been many Ovids in the two millennia since his death, and the Ovid of the seventeenth century may have been just as chimerical as the medieval *Ovide moralisé*.

Our concern, however, is not with Ovid himself but with the *Heroides* as conceived and read by Pope. The hypothesis I want to propose is that he interpreted and judged them very much as his predecessors and contemporaries did—as dramatic poems of tragic quality and effect—and that in the letters of Abélard and Héloïse, as transmitted to him through the intermediaries so meticulously described by Audra, he saw materials which might be shaped into an epistle more beautiful and moving than any of Ovid's own. It would avoid the errors of the Roman poet, his repetitions, conceits, and unseasonable wit, but in other respects would conform to the idea of the kind which Ovid founded. Such a poem, following Dryden's principles, would represent nature in disorder, the mind of a feigned person torn by contrary passions. Its effect would be to stir pity, and it would have a beautiful unity of design, driving always to one end—a resolution of the speaker's conflict and a catharsis of the reader's feeling. If *Eloisa to Abelard* is to be read "with the same spirit that its author writ," I believe it should be judged in the light of these aims.

❦❦❦

Before turning to the poem itself, we should recognize that both the *Heroides* and *Eloisa to Abelard* can be called either dramatic or tragic only in a qualified sense. Such poems are dramatic, in a literal definition, because none of the words are the poet's—all must be understood as spoken by an imagined person; the subject of the poem is the thoughts and feelings of that person, as arising from his or her character and situation. But these poems are not meant to be acted, and the epistolary device removes them one degree from direct representation. They are not plays, for there is only one speaker, the poem is a single, self-contained speech, and there is no external action. Their effect, too, cannot be fully tragic. Pity may certainly be aroused, if the speaker suffers, but since she is not in danger, our fear for her must be much less intense than that produced by a fully tragic dramatic action; it would be, at most, a kind of moral concern, lest the speaker's mind break down or think and feel in self-destructive ways. Granting these reservations, I should like to take Pope's poem seriously as both dramatic and tragic, in the limited sense indicated.

In a poem of this kind, we may distinguish four essential elements: a dramatic situation, a speaker with a distinct individual character, a sequence of thoughts and feelings arising from the reaction of the speaker to the situation, and finally the style or artistic medium through which all these are expressed. In reading the poem, we may not be conscious of them as separate aspects; the poem, if successful, has a single massive effect. But for purposes of analysis and criticism, we may differentiate these elements, taking them in turn and testing each to determine its value in relation to the poet's intention, as postulated above; the organizing principle which binds them together should emerge in the course of the analysis. As a whole and in all its parts, the poem should be informed and animated by the pervasive influence of its poetic purpose.

For twentieth-century readers, the greatest barrier to appreciation of Pope's poem is its style. To ears trained to a different music, its diction and syntax may well seem artificial and cold, the chime of its couplets monotonous and jingly. To Root and Tillotson, both defenders of the poem, its manner seems "rhetorical," by which they apparently mean something like "artificial" or "ornamental"—suited perhaps to analysis and aphoristic statement, but poorly adapted to the expression of feeling.[27] These prejudices die slowly; thirty years after those critics, Murray Krieger is still asking whether any style could be less suited to convey the immediacy of Eloisa's passionate struggle than "Pope's most polished version of that most finished verse-form, the heroic couplet."[28] One wonders what he would say of the alexandrines of Corneille and Racine as a vehicle for tragic expression.

For some years, however, several scholars have been helping us to see that the couplet, as Pope used it, is capable of a wide range of effects, and to discriminate those effects more subtly and perceptively. The general thesis of John A. Jones's book, *Pope's Couplet Art,* is that the styles of Pope's major poems tend in each case toward a dominant pattern, the "couplet norm," which is different for each poem and appropriate to its particular subject and genre. "For his passionate nun," Jones says in his chapter on *Eloisa,* "Pope created a distinctive stylistic decorum; and artist that he was, he used it in this poem alone." Sharply differentiating the styles of *Eloisa,* the *Rape of the Lock,* and the *Essay on Criticism,* Jones analyzes nine long passages in Pope's epistle in minute detail; of one pair of verses, for example, he says that it "is not like Pope's typical balanced couplet: it has no pivotal caesura, it lacks chiastic syntax, or meaning, and the negating climax overwhelms and canals all three preceding statements" in the twenty-line verse paragraph of which it is a part. Granting that Eloisa sometimes "makes points and creates a kind of emotional symmetry based on the oppositions of nature and grace," Jones argues that this occurs in passages which express the intellectual aspect of her deeper emotional conflict; the antithetical statements, only one element in the poem's style, "release powerful emotions, which . . . engulf and transcend antithesis and debate."[29] The concept of the couplet norm may be open to question, and some of Jones's descriptions are perhaps too rhapsodical, but he does a good deal to lessen those blindnesses and deafnesses which are still too much with us.

Although Jones's chapter assumes that *Eloisa* is a poem of inward conflict, told and experienced from the first-person point of view, and moving throughout toward a final resolution, his argument is not explicitly or systematically guided by a generic definition such as I am proposing here. In a more theoretical approach, deriving the qualities of style appropriate to a heroic epistle from the definition of that form, I believe we could assert that the essential requirement for any tragic style is simply the power to express thought, feeling, and character.[30] Since drama is not life but art, since tragedy is serious and intense, since its characters have moral stature and human importance, and since their fates concern us deeply, its language not only may but should depart quite widely from the norms of colloquial speech as used in ordinary life, so long as it remains clear, expressive, flexible, and actual. In applying such criteria to Pope's poem, we should remember that it is a letter, not literally a speech, and also that both the writer and its recipient are "two of the most distinguished persons of their age in Learning and Beauty," as Pope notes in his "Argument" to the poem. One sign that the style of *Eloisa* does vividly communicate thought, feeling, and character is that we really forget, after the first few lines, that we are reading a letter; our awareness of ink and paper magically dissolves, and even voice is almost forgotten, so that we think we are within the very mind of Eloisa, as her soul reaches out to her absent lover.

Without attempting to emulate Jones's detailed analyses, I may comment briefly on three representative passages. The first expresses Eloisa's resignation to her lot and looks forward, unconsciously, to the vision of her death at the end of the poem. The language is simple and direct, an intensified and elevated, yet natural, way of writing:

> Yet here for ever, ever must I stay;
> Sad proof how well a lover can obey!
> Death, only death, can break the lasting chain;
> And here ev'n then, shall my cold dust remain,
> Here all its frailties, all its flames resign,
> And wait, till 'tis no sin to mix with thine. (ll. 171-76)

In this there is nothing epigrammatic; it is neither stiff nor pointed, but fluid, supple, and intense.

In another passage, the manner is different:

> Oh happy state! when souls each other draw,
> When love is liberty, and nature, law:
> All then is full, possessing and possest,
> No craving Void left aking in the breast:
> Ev'n thought meets thought ere from the lips it part,
> And each warm wish springs mutual from the heart.
> This sure is bliss (if bliss on earth there be)
> And once the lot of Abelard and me. (ll. 91-98)

These words are not "rhetoric," in the pejorative sense of that much-abused word, so often applied to the style of *Eloisa* by old-fashioned critics. If the second and third verses have a strongly marked caesura and a balance of subject-predicate against subject-predicate and of active against passive participle, the reason is that Eloisa's mind is sufficiently keen and clear to think in such terms naturally. The passage as a whole is alive with feeling and with character; the words are those of a thoughtful and intelligent woman, generalizing in a brief moment of fond remembrance about the great experience of her life.

Still different, though not more suited to the changing moods of a tragic monologue, is Eloisa's account of her dreams:

> I wake—no more I hear, no more I view,
> The phantom flies me, as unkind as you.
> I call aloud; it hears not what I say;
> I stretch my empty arms; it glides away:
> To dream once more I close my willing eyes;
> Ye soft illusions, dear deceits, arise!
> Alas no more—methinks we wandring go
> Thro' dreary wastes, and weep each other's woe;
> Where round some mould'ring tow'r pale ivy creeps,
> And low-brow'd rocks hang nodding o'er the deeps.
> Sudden you mount! you beckon from the skies;
> Clouds interpose, waves roar, and winds arise.
> I shriek, start up, the same sad prospect find,
> And wake to all the griefs I left behind. (ll. 235-48)

The contrast in style between these dramatic lines and any passage in the *Essay on Criticism,* the Horatian imitations, or the *Dunciad* should be evident to the most tone-deaf ear; the shifting tones and speeds of the language express vividly the fluctuating moods of Eloisa's waking and dreaming, the sharpness of her frustrated longing, the sadness of her loneliness and grief. In these passages and many others, with their varying tones and tempos, we find a style which preserves a tragic dignity and elevation, is entirely in character for the speaker, and yet is capable of expressing a wide range of tragic emotions. The style is not Shakespearean, but it is a style worthy of tragedy and adapted to its needs.

Of the "situation," as I have called it, much less needs to be said. Like all the great love stories of the world, the love of Abélard and Héloïse is essentially tragic. The obstacle to the lovers' happiness, more final and complete than in the other great love stories, makes the suffering of Héloïse more terrible than Isolde's or Juliet's. At the same time, it makes impossible any resolution in action. This fact, which for the novelist or playwright constitutes a fatal defect in the story, is an advantage to Pope, since in a tragic epistle there is no external action; what is needed is a static situation and an internal resolution.

Eloisa's immediate situation, as Pope represents it in the poem, is that of a woman still deeply in love but absent from her lover, living in a cloister, and cut off from him both by his emasculated condition and by her own religious vows. Pope pictures her at the most poignant moment, as she tries to answer the letter which has reawakened all her old passions. This situation, as it interacts with her character, creates the conflict which the poem must finally resolve: that struggle of "grace and nature, virtue and passion" of which Pope speaks in "The Argument."

Some readers have felt that the conflict is one-sided—that the pull of religion on Eloisa is far weaker than the pull of her sexual desire. Brower finds that "The Christian experience expressed in *Eloisa to Abelard* is curiously external, and curiously generalized." Eloisa has little of the mystic about her, he thinks: "Indeed her chief religious emotion is guilt, the pang of conscience, rather than positive love of God or any vivid experience of salvation."[31] The question is important, because the poem collapses as drama if Brower is right.

It may be readily conceded, since Pope is very explicit about it, that Eloisa's original motives for taking vows were not religious: "Not grace, or zeal, love only was my call" (l. 117). The length of time since her separation from Abelard and her entrance into monastic life is not specified, but is clearly very long; through all those years, she has lived as her sisters live, trying sincerely not only to do penance for her sin but to obey and love her God. Yet even at the moment of writing, she cannot give herself wholly to religion:

> All is not Heav'n's while *Abelard* has part,
> Still rebel nature holds out half my heart;
> Nor pray'rs nor fasts its stubborn pulse restrain,
> Nor tears, for ages, taught to flow in vain. (ll. 25-28)

She is, as Brower says, fully conscious of the sinfulness of her love, both past and present, and the prevailing impression of her life as a nun is one of penitence, renunciation, and "voluntary pains" (l. 18).

But a basic purpose of that life, part of its daily rhythm, is contemplation—"heav'nly-pensive" contemplation, Eloisa calls it in the second line of the poem. She practices it, too: "No more these scenes my meditation aid,/ Or lull to rest the visionary maid" (ll. 161-62). Though she contrasts her own divided heart with the serenity of the blameless vestal, she recognizes the joy which flows from that kind of commitment, and there are times when her own heart fully responds:

> But let heav'n seize it, all at once 'tis fir'd,
> Not touch'd, but rapt; not waken'd, but inspir'd! (ll. 201-2)

Her vision of the whispering angels and winged seraphs, the white virgins and the Spouse himself who welcome the vestal to heaven (ll. 216-22), expresses her religious feelings eloquently, as does her own acceptance, near the close, of grace, hope, and faith (ll. 297-300). If rebel nature holds out half her heart until the end of the poem, the other half not only knows the joy and peace of heavenly love, but is powerfully drawn to it. This side of her nature seems to me fully realized in dramatic terms.

Eloisa's character, though foreshadowed in the sources, is largely Pope's own creation. Many of the details can be paralleled in the writers analyzed by Audra, but in Bayle, Bussy, and Hughes, as in the original Latin letters, these details lie scattered, mixed with much that is alien and irrelevant.[32] Pope has shaped this material to his own idea, selecting those elements which contribute to his aim. Some of the finest touches have no parallel in the sources, and all are transformed by his art.

In the interpretation of drama, character must be inferred by the reader or audience from signs—from what each person seeks and avoids, approves and disapproves, from the way he thinks and the emotions he expresses. Only a few salient traits of Eloisa's character can be mentioned here—those most basic to our sense of her as tragic—and even these can be illustrated by only a small sampling of the signs from which we infer them.

Eloisa is "good" in the Aristotelian sense; that is, we feel her to be far superior ethically to ourselves, to average humanity. This is true not only in the sense that she fully accepts the moral values which condemn her past and present passion, judging herself more severely than any of us would wish to judge her. It is also shown in a certain magnanimity and generosity of spirit. The pain she has suffered for so long has not made her self-centered, blind to the feelings of others, resentful of those who are free from such suffering; she shows this in her attitudes toward "the wedded dame," toward her sisters, the blameless vestals, toward Abelard himself. She states, as a fact well known to him, that he was the seducer: "Thou know'st how guiltless first I met thy flame" (l. 59). But she does not use this fact to blame him, nor to excuse herself; it is simply the truth, though it has its effect on our opinion of both lovers. The penalties have fallen more heavily on her than on him, since passion is still alive in her; but if she could, she would take the whole punishment upon herself: "Ah more than share it! give me all thy grief" (l.

50). This goodness is the basis of our pity for her, since her suffering so far exceeds her fault, and it also makes clear from the beginning the impossibility for her of any action which would be injurious to him.

A quality in Eloisa which has been overlooked or unmentioned by critics is her high intelligence. This might be taken for granted from known history, and Pope himself draws attention to it in his "Argument," but it is also manifested dramatically throughout the poem. Pope has eliminated all the theological argument that takes up so much space in the Latin letters, but at a purely human level his Eloisa is the most clear-sighted of women. Unlike most of Ovid's heroines, she is never befuddled, never deceived by her feelings. When she feels most intensely, she continues to see everything as it is and in its true proportions. An aspect of this quality of mind is her honesty with herself. When she calls on heaven for help, she immediately asks herself: "but whence arose that pray'r?/ Sprung it from piety, or from despair?" (ll. 179-80). And she knows that her tears are sometimes "too soft," arising not from sincere repentance but from grief for her lost love (l. 270; cf. l. 194). It is this clarity of mind that defines her dilemma so sharply—for herself and for us—and it is an essential psychological cause, along with her goodness, of her final decision to give up all hope for even the most minimal realization of her love in this life.

But perhaps the most basic of all her extraordinary qualities, for the tragic effect of Pope's small internal drama, is Eloisa's wholeheartedness, her complete lack of any self-protective reservations or qualifications; she has given herself totally, once and for all. It was for this love that she had become a nun, "When, warm in youth, I bade the world farewell" (l. 110). Pope is following the sources when Eloisa says that, though often pressed to marriage by Abelard, her desire was to follow no laws but those which love has made (ll. 73-90); as Tillotson observes, however, Pope purifies the issue by omitting the practical argument (present in Hughes) that marriage would have injured Abelard's career and by basing her refusal wholly on the nature of a "true passion," undiluted by human ties, legalisms, and worldly considerations.[33] The depth, intensity, and unexpungeable quality of her love is manifested by the whole texture of her impassioned letter—by her longing for his presence, by the almost inextricable mixing within her mind of the idea of God and the image of Abelard, by her dreams and the painful wakening from them, by her faith that her love was and still is returned, "mutual from the heart" (l. 96). When she hopes near the close that saints will embrace Abelard "with a love like mine" (l. 342), the wish does not seem to us blasphemous or bombastic; we feel that she has earned the right to make such a comparison.

The last and most important of the four elements in Pope's poem is the sequence of thoughts and feelings through which Eloisa passes. Here we should recognize, I believe, that there is one sense in which the poem may truly be called "rhetorical"; it is the sense in which all of Ovid's *Heroides* are rhetorical, and for that matter many speeches in almost all plays—that is, they are attempts to persuade, addressed by one fictitious person to another. Although Eloisa is certainly expressing herself throughout her letter, she is also pleading with him (as most of Ovid's heroines do) first to write to her, then to come to her. These pleas, eight times repeated, are the structural backbone of the drama.

Eloisa's pleas are entirely different from the rhetoric of Ovid's deserted women, because her own character and her relation to her lover are fundamentally different. Though Ovid's heroines differ from each other in character, most of them are self-centered, self-pitying, morally weak, hurt, angry, and much afraid that they have been betrayed. But Eloisa shows none of these traits, and she is completely confident that she is still loved; she assumes that there is truth, honesty, and unselfish concern for the other on both sides. It is characteristic of her personality, of the nature of her love, and of the tone of her appeals to Abelard that when she slips, just once, into an argument that is not quite candid—

> Ah, think at least thy flock deserves thy care,
> Plants of thy hand, and children of thy pray'r, (ll. 129-30)

—she quickly recognizes that this is unfair to him and unworthy of herself:

> See how the force of others' pray'rs I try
> (O pious fraud of am'rous charity!)
> But why should I on others' pray'rs depend?
> Come thou, my father, brother, husband, friend! (ll. 149-52)

Hers is a rhetoric which Plato himself might approve, since it is based on truth and understanding.

In this plotless kind of poem, the action is a movement of the soul from one state to another—from reawakened desire, through pleas for his coming, to a renunciation of all desire for reunion with him on this earth, and a final acceptance of death and a hope for spiritual union in heaven. This sequence is that goal, which directs the poet in his race: that "beautiful design, which he first establishes, and then contrives the means, which will naturally conduct it to his end." As plot, according to Aristotle, is the "soul" of a play, its organizing and individuating principle, so this movement of the soul, unfolding in time, is the principle which unifies and binds together all the elements of Pope's plotless inner drama.

Following the broad sequence outlined above, we may divide the poem into four main sections. The first fifty-eight lines are expository; they establish the immediate situation (the convent setting, her receipt of Abelard's letter), and indicate the conflicting elements in her feeling: love and religion, Abelard and God. In lines 59-118, with admirable economy and dramatic propriety, Pope reveals through Eloisa's own thought the main outline of the preceding events, giving us everything we need to know about the past: their clandestine happiness, the terrible vengeance of her family, and her entrance into the religious life.

The central section of the poem (ll. 119-288), continuing her pleas for Abelard's return, reaches its climax, and the crisis of the drama, in her despairing cry:

> Come, if thou dar'st, all charming as thou art!
> Oppose thy self to heav'n; dispute my heart;
> Come, with one glance of those deluding eyes,
> Blot out each bright Idea of the skies.
> Take back that grace, those sorrows, and those tears,
> Take back my fruitless penitence and pray'rs,
> Snatch me, just mounting, from the blest abode,
> Assist the fiends and tear me from my God! (ll. 281-88)

But this wish reveals to her, even as she speaks, the full destructiveness of her plea—the impossibility for her of this solution, and above all the spiritual ruin it would bring to him. Abruptly, then, in a revulsion of feeling which Pope has solidly grounded in her character, she completely reverses her plea:

> No, fly me, fly me! far as Pole from Pole;
> Rise *Alps* between us! and whole oceans roll!
> Ah come not, write not, think not once of me,
> Nor share one pang of all I felt for thee.
> Thy oaths I quit, thy memory resign,
> Forget, renounce me, hate whate'er was mine. (ll. 289-94)

The last seventy-seven lines of the poem, beginning with the passage just quoted, present the gradual resolution of her conflict and the dying away of her tragic passion. She renounces all rights to his presence or even to his memory, bids adieu to all her "long lov'd, ador'd ideas" of him, welcomes heavenly grace, foresees her death, imagines that she is called to eternal rest and peace by the spirit of a sainted sister, hopes that Abelard will perform the last rites, envisions his later ascent into heaven, welcomed by angels and saints, and prays that they may at last be laid together in "one kind grave"—reunited without sin, conflict, or penalty. She has one last spasm of desire, hoping that when he returns as she is dying Abelard will "Suck my last breath, and catch my flying soul!'' But she immediately rejects the thought; he must come in "sacred vestments," holding the cross, not as lover but as priest (ll. 324-28). Three additional consoling thoughts close the poem: that lovers in future ages will visit their common grave and be moved to "mutual pity," that a devoted worshiper may sometime drop "one human tear" for them, and be forgiven, and that "our sad, our tender story" may some day be told by a future bard (ll. 343-66). For the reader as well as for Eloisa, these final thoughts complete the tragic catharsis. Her grief will end in the grave, and her love, sanctified by penitence and sacrifice, will be reconciled with her piety. The poem ends, as a tragedy should, not in pain but in peace.[34]

༒༒༒

For almost a century and a half, from the beginning of the nineteenth century until well into the twentieth, it was difficult for anyone to do justice to the literature of the eighteenth century, and most conspicuously to its poetry. The radical changes begun both in the writing of poetry and in poetic theory and criticism by Blake, Wordsworth, and Coleridge—a by-product of the even more profound and sweeping revolution in philosophy initiated by Kant—brought a flood of poems, wonderfully beautiful in themselves, but organized on new formal principles and employing conventions wholly unknown to their eighteenth-century predecessors. They also introduced alien standards of critical judgment and a different habit in reading, so that the poetic assumptions, techniques, intentions, and effects of Pope and others were misunderstood or condemned, the ability to perceive and appreciate his poems on their own terms almost wholly lost.

In the last four decades, literary scholarship has done much to correct these misunderstandings. Partly through a process of historical reconstruction, as in Audra's seminal study, partly through fresh critical readings guided by twentieth- rather than nineteenth-century aesthetic principles and methods of interpretation, as in Brower's sensitive and illuminating book, scholars and critics have reopened the case for Pope as a poet, producing many valuable new insights and judgments. In his preface to *Essential Articles for the Study of Alexander Pope,* in fact, Maynard Mack is bold enough to say that the process of critical revaluation, begun in the 1930s, was virtually complete by the early 1960s.[35]

Whatever may be the case with Pope's other poems, I do not believe that any canonical interpretation and evaluation is attained either in the two articles on *Eloisa to Abelard* which Mack included in his anthology or in more recent essays by other critics, though all of them illuminate the text in varying aspects and degrees.

Here I have tried to recover Pope's own intention. Since Audra, everyone has recognized the fact that the epistle is a poem "traitant à la manière d'Ovide une matière nouvelle"[36]—the new matter, of course, being the story of Héloïse and Abélard, as reinterpreted by French and English translators and adaptors in the latter part of the seventeenth century. I have followed the same clue, but have raised several questions not previously asked. How did Pope and his contemporaries read the *Heroides?* If Pope took Ovid as his formal model, what kind of a poem did he suppose himself to be writing? If *Eloisa* is a poem of that kind, what are the parts of which it is composed, by what organizing principle are the parts bound together in a unified poetic whole, and what kind of emotional effect is the poem designed to produce? If it is governed by such aesthetic intentions, how did Pope select and shape the *matière nouvelle* to those ends? And finally, how well does the poem realize concretely the formal and affective potentialities inherent in its kind?

It would be absurd to claim that the reading presented here is final and definitive. The whole argument is hypothetical, resting on the series of if-clauses stated above, and any or all of these hypotheses might be challenged. The if-clauses, in turn, depend upon theoretical assumptions as to interpretive method and evaluative criteria which have not been explicitly formulated in this essay, much less examined and defended philosophically, and which many present-day critics do not accept. Such an argument will surely not be convincing to a critic like Krieger, who finds in the poem almost the same dramatic movement that I have described, including the "all-passion-spent acceptance that Eloisa has achieved" at the end, but who regards all that as merely the "official rhetoric" of the poem; Pope's language, Krieger claims, has a life of its own, anarchic or chaotic, which subverts his rational design and makes the poem a partial failure, though an attractive one to post-Freudian taste.[37] We are arguing from different premises, as Sydney Smith said in a famous joke, and I fear we could never reach agreement.

But there is some comfort in the knowledge that Warton and Johnson, Wakefield and Mason, intelligent critics of Pope's own century, believed *Eloisa to Abelard* to be a most beautiful and touching poem, a unique masterpiece in its own kind. I like to think they would approve if I conclude by saying, "Yes, I do feel, when I read this poem, 'how moving' and 'how convincing.' "

Notes

1. Emile Audra, *L'Influence française dans l'oeuvre de Pope* (Paris: Champion, 1931), p. 443.

2. Advertisement to *An Elegy Written in an Empty Assembly-Room* (1756), quoted by Geoffrey Tillotson, ed., *The Rape of the Lock and Other Poems,* Twickenham edition (London: Methuen, 1940), II, 399. All citations of *Eloisa to Abelard* will refer to this edition, giving line numbers within parentheses in the text.

3. Joseph Warton, *An Essay on the Writings and Genius of Pope* (London, 1756), I, 333-34.

4. Samuel Johnson, *Lives of the English Poets,* ed. G. B. Hill (Oxford: Clarendon Press, 1905), III, 235-36; Gilbert Wakefield, *The Poems of Mr. Gray* (London, 1786), p. 167; William Mason, Preface to *Poems by William Whitehead* (London, 1788), III, 35.

5. Byron, *Letters and Journals,* ed. R. E. Prothero (London: John Murray, 1900), IV, 489.

6. Tillotson, pp. 288-91.

7. Reuben A. Brower, *Alexander Pope: The Poetry of Allusion* (Oxford: Clarendon Press, 1959), pp. 83-84. For other discussions of the poem, see Henry Pettit, "Pope's *Eloisa to Abelard:* An Interpretation," *University of Colorado Studies,* no. 4 (Boulder, 1953), pp. 67-74; Brendan P. O'Hehir, "Virtue and Passion: the Dialectic of *Eloisa to Abelard," Texas Studies in Literature and Language,* II (1960), 219-32; Robert P. Kalmey, "Pope's *Eloisa to Abelard* and 'Those Celebrated Letters,' " *PQ,* 47 (1968),164-78; Rebecca Price Parkin, *The Poetic Workmanship of Alexander Pope* (Minneapolis: University of Minnesota Press, 1955), especially pp. 12-16, 145-46; idem, "Alexander Pope's Use of Biblical and Ecclesiastical Allusions," *Studies on Voltaire and the Eighteenth Century,* 57 (1967),1183-1216, especially pp. 1193-1200; also the works referred to in notes 27, 28, and 29 below.

8. Pope, *Essay on Criticism,* II, 34. Pope applies this principle in his postscript to the *Odyssey,* where he defends the poem against Longinus: "Whoever reads the Odyssey with an eye to the Iliad, expecting to find it of the same character, or of the same sort of spirit, will be grievously deceived, and err against the first principle of Criticism, which is to consider the nature of the piece, and the intent of his author." He goes on to argue that if Homer has "accomplished his own design, and done all that the nature of his Poem demanded or allowed, it still remains perfect in its kind, and as much a master-piece as the Iliad" (*Poems,* Twickenham ed. [London: Methuen, 1967], X, 382,384).

9. See especially the prefaces to *Annus Mirabilis, Ovid's Espistles,* and the *Fables,* and the dedication of *Examen Poeticum.* Briefer comments occur in the *Essay of Dramatic Poesy,* the prefaces to *Troilus and Cressida* and to *Sylvae,* the *Discourse on Satire,* and the *Parallel of Poetry and Painting.*

10. Preface to *Ovid's Epistles,* in *Essays,* ed. W. P. Ker (Oxford: Clarendon Press, 1926), I, 236. Cf. *Les XXI epîtres d'Ovide* (Lyon, 1556), pp. 9-10; Henry Peacham, *The Compleat Gentleman* (1622), in *Critical Essays of the Seventeenth Century,* ed., J. E. Spingarn, (Oxford: Clarendon Press, 1908), I, 125-26; and Gaspar Bachet, Sr. de Méziriac, *Commentaires sur les épistres d'Ovide* (La Haye, 1716; originally published 1626), I, 73.

11. *Essay of Dramatic Poesy,* Ker, I, 53. Bachet says: ". . . Entre tous les ouvrages de ce grand poëte, le livre de ses epistres est celui qui est la plus remply de belles conceptions, le mieux limé, et le plus poly (*Commentaires,* I, 73).

12. Preface to *Ovid's Epistles,* Ker, I, 233. Warton says that Ovid deserves much credit for inventing "this beautiful species of writing epistles under feigned characters. It is a high improvement on the Greek elegy; to which its dramatic nature renders it greatly superior. It is indeed no other than a passionate soliloquy; in which, the mind gives vent to the distresses and emotions under which it labours: but by being directed and addressed to a particular person, it gains a degree of propriety, that the best-conducted soliloquy, in a tragedy, must ever want" (*Essay on Pope,* I, 286).

13. Preface to *Annus Mirabilis,* Ker, I, 15; cf. pp. 53, 233-34. According to Audra, Pope "eut

alors écrit quelque chose comme la miniature d'une tragedie française, où les incidents ne sont rien, et où la marche de l'action est faite de ces alternances dans le coeur des personnages'' (p. 432).

14. Joseph Trapp, *Lectures on Poetry* (Latin version 1711; English trans. 1742), Lect. VIII, in *Eighteenth-Century Critical Essays,* ed. Scott Elledge (Ithaca: Cornell University Press, 1961), I, 242-43.

15. Ibid.

16. Ker, I, 53.

17. Preface to *Ovid's Epistles,* Ker, I, 233. Cf. Ovid, *Epistolarum Heroidum Liber* (London, 1702), A2 verso; Samuel Garth, *Ovid's Metamorphoses, in Fifteen Books,* 2d ed. (London: J. Tonson, 1720), I, xxiii.

18. Preface to *Ovid's Epistles,* Ker, I, 235. Cf. Garth, I, xix; René Rapin, *Reflections on Artistotle's Treatise of Poesy in General* (1674), in *The Continental Model,* ed. Scott Elledge and Donald Schier (Minneapolis: Carleton College and the University of Minnesota Press, 1960), p. 282.

19. Ker, I, 234.

20. Marcus Annaeus Seneca, "The Elder," *Controversiae,* ix. 5, 17; Quintilian *Institutes of Rhetoric* X. i. 88, 98.

21. Ker, I, 233-35. Cf. Garth, I, xxvii-ix; Rapin, p. 275; Trapp, in Elledge, I, 231-32.

22. Charles de Saint-Evremond, "On the Character of Tragedies" (1672), in Elledge and Schier, p. 150.

23. Ker, I, 233-35; cf. II, 9, 193-94, 255-57. See also Addision, *Spectator,* nos. 62, 279, and *Miscellaneous Works,* ed. A. C. Guthkelch (London: G. Bell, 1914), I, 145. Garth and Trapp raise the same objection.

24. In the preface to the *Fables,* Dryden says: "On these occasions the poet should endeavour to raise pity; but, instead of this, Ovid is tickling you to laugh. Virgil never made use of such machines when he was moving you to commiserate the death of Dido; he would not destroy what he was building" (Ker, II, 257). Cf. Addison, *Miscellaneous Works,* I, 145-46.

25. Ovid *Amores* III. i. 41-42.

26. E. K. Rand says that the *Heroides* should be regarded "not as unsuccessful attempts at tragic monologue, but as thoroughly competent studies of women's moods" (*Ovid and his Influence* [New York: Longmans, Green, 1928], p. 22). L. P. Wilkinson calls Ovid a "baroque spirit before his time" and says that "The Heroides were probably not intended to move; they are a display of virtuosity designed to entertain" (*Ovid Recalled* [Cambridge: Cambridge University Press, 1955], pp. 97-99). See also T. F. Higham, "Ovid: Some Aspects of his Character and Aims," *Classical Review,* 48 (1934), 105-16, and Herman Fränkel, *Ovid: A Poet between Two Worlds* (Berkeley and Los Angeles: University of California Press, 1945), pp. 36-46.

27. R. K. Root, *The Poetical Career of Alexander Pope* (Princeton: Princeton University Press, 1938), pp. 94-102; Tillotson, pp. 288-91.

28. Murray Krieger, " 'Eloisa to Abelard': The Escape from Body or the Embrace of Body,'' *Eighteenth-Century Studies,* (1969),28-47.

29. John A. Jones, *Pope's Couplet Art* (Athens: Ohio University Press, 1969), Ch. 6. William Bowman Piper, *The Heroic Couplet* (Cleveland: Case Western Reserve University Press, 1969), also contributes greatly to appreciation of the wide range of effects possible to the couplet form, though he concentrates on the style of Pope's discursive and satirical poems, from the *Essay on Criticism* to Dialogue II of the *Epilogue to the Satires.* He does not discuss *Eloisa to Abelard.*

30. For fuller development of this conception of a tragic style, see Moody E. Prior, *The Language of Tragedy* (Bloomington: Indiana University Press, 1966), Ch. 1; and Elder Olson, *Tragedy and the Theory of Drama* (Detroit: Wayne State University Press, 1961), pp. 88-89, 112-25.

31. Brower, p. 82. Dr. Johnson does not seem to find any lack of religious feeling in Eloisa: "The mixture of religious hope and resignation gives an elevation and dignity to disappointed

love, which images merely natural cannot bestow'' (*Lives*, III, 236). Héloïse's problem, Etienne Gilson says in his remarkable series of lectures, is ''to find in the passion this man inspires the strength required for a life of sacrifice which is both meaningless and impossible save on the level of the love of God.'' He suggests that Héloïse was perhaps ''far closer to divine charity than many others who dethrone God for a great deal less than Abelard'' (*Héloïse and Abélard*, tr. L. K. Shook [Ann Arbor: University of Michigan Press, 1960], p. 96). For Gilson's comment on Pope's poem, see pp. ix-x.

32. Nothing could be further from Pope's treatment than the ironic and cynical, even comic account given by Bayle in his articles on Abélard and on Héloïse. Pope's selective use of his sources is recognized by Root (p. 96), and Tillotson (p. 280), but since they do not define the aims which guide his choice and shaping of details, they give only a vague sense of his independence and originality. A better, though very brief, comment on his use of his sources is that of George Sherburn, ed., *The Best of Pope* (New York: T. Nelson & Sons, 1929), pp. 404-5.

33. Tillotson, pp. 404-5n.

34. Warton's comment is perceptive: ''ELOISA, at the conclusion of the EPISTLE . . . is judiciously represented as gradually settling into a tranquillity of mind, and seemingly reconciled to her fate'' (*Essay on Pope*, I, 332).

35. Maynard Mack, *Essential Articles for the Study of Alexander Pope*, rev. ed. (Hamden, Conn.: Archon Books, 1964), p. xii.

36. Audra, p. 402.

37. Krieger, pp. 45-47.

PART THREE

Four Philosophical Critics

7

Joseph Warton's Classification of English Poets

An interesting feature of Joseph Warton's *Essay on the Genius and Writings of Pope* (1756) is a classification of English poets into four groups according to poetic merit. The first and highest group includes "our only three sublime and pathetic poets"—Shakespeare, Milton, and Spenser. The second includes "such as possessed the true poetical genius, in a more moderate degree, but had noble talents for moral and ethical poesy." In the third are placed "men of wit, of elegant taste, and some fancy in describing familiar life," and in the lowest class are ranked "the mere versifiers, however smooth and mellifluous some of them may be thought."

The definitions of these classes remain substantially the same through the *Essay's* five editions, but W. D. MacClintock has shown that in Warton's second edition (1762) so many poets are shifted from one class to another that the character of the grouping is radically changed.[1] He tabulates these changes as follows:

	1756	1762
Class 1	Spenser	Spenser
	Shakespeare	Shakespeare
	Milton	Milton
	"And then, at proper intervals,"	

Reprinted with permission of the Johns Hopkins University Press from *Modern Language Notes*, 51 (1936), 515-18.

	1756	1762
Class 1	Otway	
(continued)	Lee	
Class 2	Dryden	Dryden
	Donne	Prior
	Denham	Addison
	Cowley	Cowley
	Congreve	Waller
		Garth
		Fenton
		Gay
		Denham
		Parnell
Class 3	Prior	Butler
	Waller	Swift
	Parnell	Rochester
	Swift	Donne
	Fenton	Dorset
		Oldham
Class 4	Unchanged	

MacClintock includes this revision among those which imply "a genuine growth in taste, in critical acumen or range, and in the use of new information to modify preceding points of view." The first version, he says, contains critical mistakes which "are many and reveal sad limitations in his critical attainments. It will be seen, however, that he shows marked improvement in his revision six years later."[2]

Unfortunately for his thesis, this revision—the most plausible example MacClintock is able to provide of the growth of Warton's critical ability—exactly follows suggestions made in a magazine review of the *Essay's* first edition. MacClintock mentions this review—in the *Monthly Review,* 14 (1756),528-54, and 15 (1756),52-78—and quotes a sentence from it,[3] but he seems not to have noticed two most striking facts: first, that a dozen or more of its critical judgments are plagiarized from a review by Dr. Johnson which had appeared a month earlier in the *Literary Magazine;* and second, that its criticism of Warton's classification of the poets was the basis for his revision in 1762.

A few examples will show the dependence of this reviewer upon Johnson's earlier notice:

Warton, on Pope's *Windsor Forest:* ''Rural beauty in general, and not the peculiar beauties of the forest of Windsor, are here described'' (*Essay,* 1756, p. 20).

Johnson:	*Monthly Review:*
''He must inquire, whether Windsor Forest has, in reality, any thing peculiar'' (*Works* [London, 1816], ii, 359).	''But it ought first to be inquired, whether Winsor-Forest has in reality any peculiar beauties, and whether Pope has omitted these'' (14, p. 546).

Other parallels: The mind, not the ear, is offended by repeated rhymes on the same vowel (Johnson, p. 363: *Review,* 15, p. 56). Somerville's *Chace* is more detailed than the chase passage in *Windsor Forest* because that was Somerville's whole subject (Johnson, p. 359); *Review,* 14, p. 545).

The identity of these remarks with Johnson's would lead one to suspect that Johnson had written both reviews, were it not that Griffiths, editor of the *Monthly,* ascribed the notice to Dr. James Grainger, author of *The Sugar Cane*.[4] Furthermore, the reviewer says, in making one of his borrowed criticisms, ''as another writer words it,'' thence continuing with Johnson's remark.'[5] He also speculates on the possibility that Warton may be the author of the anonymous *Essay,* concluding that he probably is not;[6] Johnson knew that Warton was the author.[7]

Grainger's notice is not entirely plagiarized. Johnson's review is twelve pages long; that in the *Monthly,* expanded by quotation from the *Essay* and by several original criticisms, is fifty-two pages long. Its most valuable original comment is on Warton's classification of the poets. The review suggest five possible changes, involving eight poets; all of these changes, and no others, are made by Warton in 1762. These suggestions and Warton's changes in reponse to them are here summarized:

1. The reviewer objects to placing Otway and Lee in Class 1, where they are ahead of Dryden. In 1762 the two dramatists are dropped from the list.

2. The reviewer remarks that in one place Warton refers to Donne as a mere man of wit or man of sense, but that in the classification of poets he is ranked in Class 2. In 1762 Donne is demoted to Class 3.

3. Denham, the reviewer says, ought certainly to be ahead of Donne, though below Prior and Fenton. In 1762 Denham is allowed to remain in class 2, but Donne is moved down and Prior and Fenton are moved up into Class 2, so that Denham is below them.

4. The reviewer thinks Congreve much overrated by inclusion in Class 2. Warton removes him entirely in the second edition.

5. Finally, Parnell ought to be higher, but not too high. He is raised from third place in Class 3 to the last place in Class 2.[8]

Warton's indebtedness to his critic seems to be demonstrated by a sentence he adds to the classification in the second edition. The reviewer had said that Warton was not only unfortunate in his arrangement of the poets but had also left out many of the most important ones; in 1762 Warton replies to this charge, saying, "This enumeration is not intended as a complete catalogue of writers, and in their proper order [i.e. within the classes, although they are now in fact exactly in the order suggested by the reviewer], but only to mark out briefly the different species of our celebrated authors."

That Warton's revision should so exactly follow the reviewer's suggestions may be thought to imply a commendable willingness to take advantage of criticism, but such a growth in taste and critical acumen as MacClintock finds is certainly dubious. The revision is interesting too as it illustrates Warton's lack of independence—one may almost say of respect for his own abilities and judgments—which appears with almost equal clarity elsewhere in the *Essay* and in his other writings.

Notes

1. W. D. MacClintock, *Joseph Warton's Essay on Pope: A History of the Five Editions* (Chapel Hill: University of North Carolina Press, 1933), pp. 57-58.

2. Ibid.

3. Ibid., pp. 24-27.

4. John Nichols, *Illustrations of the Literary History of the Eighteenth Century,* vii (London, 1848), p. 226, note. Confirmed by B. C. Nangle, *The Monthly Review* (Oxford: Clarendon Press, 1934), p. 18.

5. *Monthly Review,* 14, 548.

6. Ibid., p. 536.

7. John Wooll, *Biographical Memoirs of Joseph Warton* (London, 1806), pp. 238-39.

8. *Monthly Review,* 14, 534-36.

8

Joseph Warton on the Imagination

Joseph Warton's conception of the imagination and its functions breaks apart quite clearly into three separate definitions. In that to be discussed first, Warton relates imagination to the marvelous, to the remote and strange; in the second, to originality or invention; and in the third, to visual imagery.

Throughout his critical writing, from 1753 to 1797, he expresses excited delight in the strange and fanciful, and especially in the bizarre and faraway past. In his last book, published when he was seventy-five, Warton writes:

> We live in a reasoning and prosaic age. The forests of Fairy-land have been rooted up and destroyed; the castles and the palaces of Fancy are in ruins; the magic wand of Prospero is broken and buried many fathoms in the earth.[1]

Similarly, at the very beginning of his critical career, writing in the *Adventurer* as a young clergyman thirty years old, Warton praises Shakespeare's "boundless imagination," particularly as it is shown in *The Tempest*, where the poet "has carried the romantic, the wonderful, and the wild, to the most pleasing extravagance."[2] This is Warton's first clearly distinguishable definition of the term "imagination."

In his second definition Warton makes the term equivalent to originality. In connection with Pope's *Eloisa to Abelard*, he says that "POPE was a most excellent IMPROVER, if no great original INVENTOR."[3] Of the *Rape of the Lock* he writes:

Reprinted, with permission of the University of Chicago Press, from *Modern Philology*, 25 (1937), 73-87.

It is in this composition, POPE principally appears a POET; in which he has displayed more imagination than in all his other works taken together. It should however be remembered, that he was not the FIRST former and creator of those beautiful machines, the sylphs; on which his claim to imagination is chiefly founded.[4]

Thus Pope displayed his imagination by inventing, or half-inventing, the sylphs; in the *Eloisa* he showed his lack of it by depending upon Abelard's letters, which he merely "improved" into verse. In the same way Warton declares that the greatest poems "strike the imagination with what is Great, Beautiful, and New,"[5] and he often complains that modern poets "fail of giving their readers new images."[6] It seems quite clear, then, that Warton thought of novelty or originality as one of the functions of imagination.

In his third definition Warton gives the term an entirely different twist of meaning. In this definition the central quality of imagination is the power of conceiving or vividly responding to visual images. Here he follows Addison's analysis in the *Spectator,* where "the pleasures of the imagination" are defined as those which "arise from visual objects, whether when we have them actually in our view, or when we call up their ideas into our minds by paintings, statues, or any of the like occasions."[7]

With this analysis in mind Warton praised the effects Pope achieved in *Windsor Forest* by "selecting such circumstances, as are best adapted to strike the imagination by lively pictures; the selection of which chiefly constitutes true poetry."[8] This theory of poetry and the imagination is summarized in a very significant sentence: the power, Warton says, "of all others most essential to poetry" is that of "turning *readers* into *spectators*."[9]

This principle had three main lines of specific application. The first of these is personification and allegory, whose general importance in Warton's theory and in Collins's practice has been emphasized by A. S. P. Woodhouse.[10] Warton speaks of personification as "one of the greatest efforts of the creative power of a warm and lively imagination,"[11] and his biographer Wooll speaks of the high spirit with which Warton used to comment to his classes at Winchester "on the prosopopeia of Oedipus or Electra."[12] Similarly he contends that two "paintings," or allegorical figures, in the first book of Lucretius are alone sufficient to prove him a great poet.[13]

The second application of this principle, by a natural extension of the metaphor "painting," gives great prestige to picturesque landscape as material for imaginative poetry. Thomson's descriptive scenes, Warton says, "are frequently as wild and romantic as those of Salvator Rosa, pleasingly varied with precipices and torrents, and 'castled cliffs,' and deep vallies, with piny mountains, and the gloomiest caverns.''[14] Here there is an interesting fusion of the visual principle with interest in the bizarre and "wild."

The third application of this principle, and by far the most important, is a demand for circumstantiality as against abstraction and generality in the poet's descriptions, epithets, and the like. "The use, the force, and the excellence of language," Warton writes, "certainly consists in raising *clear, complete,* and *circumstantial* images, and in turning *readers* into *spectators.*"[15] After illustrating through eight pages of quotation, Warton concludes: "I have dwelt the longer on this subject, because I think I can perceive many symptoms, even among writers of eminence, of departing from these *true,* and *lively,* and *minute* representations of Nature, and of *dwelling in generalities.*"[16] The contrast of this view with that of men like Johnson and Reynolds need not be labored. Poetry, said Johnson, "cannot dwell upon the minuter distinctions, by which one species differs from another, without departing from that simplicity of grandeur which fills the imagination."[17]

❧❧❧❧

Warton is a transition figure, and his *Essay on Pope,* as Saintsbury once wrote, is "a real document, showing drift, but also drifting. The Time-Spirit is carrying the man along, but he is carried half-unconsciously."[18] Such a view of Warton's historical place is certainly sounder than that of Sir Edmund Gosse, who believed that Warton had created the theory of aesthetics according to which Wordsworth, Byron, and Keats wrote, and who saw the two Warton brothers as "bicyclist scouts who prophesied of an advance that was nearly fifty years delayed."[19] Yet Saintsbury's conception of Warton may be misleading, for he goes on to say that the critic's inclination "is evidently towards something new—perhaps he does *not* quite know what—and away from something old, which *we* at least can perceive without much difficulty to be the Neo-classic creed."[20] The error in such a view is its exaggeration of drift away from neoclassicism, its underemphasis of backward pull. For in everything Warton wrote no fact is more obvious than the dominance in his thought of a traditional body of doctrine—a set of ideas which continually limited and bounded his own views and controlled his taste.

At the basis of his thought lay the cornerstone of all neoclassical doctrine—the belief that art imitates nature. This dogma, Lovejoy has shown, was subject to almost endless variations of interpretation, some of which are not characteristically eighteenth century. Warton's reading, while not extreme or unnecessarily rigid, was representative; it was, in fact, very much like that of Dr. Johnson. Lovejoy cites Warton as an examplar of what is perhaps the most widespread and liberal of neoclassical conceptions of nature, that which defines it as "the universal and immutable in thought, feeling, and taste; what has always been known, what everyone can immediately understand and enjoy."[21] This definition is well illustrated by Warton's contention that theories of philosophy and theology "are maintained and exploded in different ages; but true and genuine pictures of nature and passion, are not subject to such revolutions and changes. . . . Homer, Sophocles, Terence, and Virgil, being felt and relished by all men, still retain and preserve, unaltered and undisputed, admiration and applause."[22] The same belief lies behind Warton's conclusion to the first volume of his *Essay on Pope:* "WIT and SATIRE are transitory and perishable, but NATURE and PASSION are eternal."[23] This belief was the basis of his central criticism of Pope, most of whose work, being moral and satiric, dealt not with nature and passion, which are eternal, but with temporary and local aberrations from them, with the affectations and mannerisms and beliefs of a particular time and place.

As to the nature of imitation, Warton accepts the very careful and exhaustive analysis of the term made by Richard Hurd in 1751. Hurd argues that, since poetry is an imitation or "original copying" of nature, and since "in any supposed combination of circumstances, one train of thought is, generally, most obvious, and occurs soonest to the understanding; and, it being the office of poetry to present the most *natural* appearances," it is inevitable that poets should resemble one another.[24] Warton accepts this definition and writes:

> The works of those who profess an art, whose essence is imitation, must needs be stamped with a close resemblance to each other, since the objects material or animate, extraneous or internal, which they all imitate, lie equally open to the observation of all, and are perfectly similar. Descriptions therefore that are faithful and just, MUST BE UNIFORM AND ALIKE. . . .[25]

Both Warton and Hurd seem to reduce imitation to description—though to description very broadly defined, as appears from the phrase, "objects material or animate, extraneous or internal." Quite clearly Warton is attempting here to make an inclusive generalization, one which will cover all sorts of poetry and poetic material—persons as well as things, ideas as well as objects; in short, "reflection" as well as "sensation." In identifying imitation with observation and description Warton is far from the Aristotelian conception of mimesis, but the view is thoroughly representative of his period; its essential feature is the emphasis upon uniformity, upon "what has always been known, what everyone can immediately understand and enjoy."

The pull exerted by these ideas is well illustrated in Warton's three definitions of imagination. It was upon the first of these that Phelps, Beers, Gosse, and other early students of "preromanticism" based their contention that he was a revolutionary critic, the first in his time to defy cold rationality and exalt the imagination. It is certain that Warton's taste was often for "the romantic, the wonderful, and the wild"; and yet it would be very erroneous to suppose that he was thoroughly committed to a poetry of pure fancy. The theory of imitation, even very liberally and generally interpreted, prevented any such systematic exaltation of the bizarre and mysterious.

It might have been supposed, for example, in view of the delight Warton took in Shakespeare's "vast exuberance of fancy," that he would approve strongly of Ariosto, the great master of marvels and romantic adventure. Instead he attacks Ariosto as an "extravagant and lawless rhapsodist," and says, quoting Hume, that Ariosto pleases

> not by his monstrous and improbable fictions, by his bizarre mixture of the serious and comic styles, by the want of coherence in his stories, or by the continual interruptions in his narration. He charms by the force and clearness of his expression, by the readiness and variety of his inventions, and by his natural pictures of the passions, especially those of the gay and amorous kind.[26]

A still more interesting example, in view of the very high rank Warton assigned to Milton, is furnished by his paper in the *Adventurer* on "Blemishes in Paradise Lost." Here he criticizes the "glaring pictures" of Paradise and argues that it takes very little strength of mind to paint such scenes, in which are brought together "the greatest variety of the most splendid images, without any regard to their use or congruity." These, he says, "are easily feigned; but having no relative beauty as pictures of nature, nor any absolute excellence as derived from truth, they can only please those who, when they read, exercise no faculty but fancy, and admire because they do not think."[27]

In both of these passages the pressure upon Warton of a traditional aesthetics is very clear. He objects to Milton's romantic picture because it is not natural, not derived from truth, and praises (by quotation from Hume) the one element of natural picture which is to be found in Ariosto. Thus Warton differs from some of his contemporaries—Reynolds and Johnson, for example—chiefly in being more willing than they to suspend disbelief, to forget propriety and restraint upon occasion. More than a hundred years earlier Thomas Hobbes had written: "In a good poem . . . both judgment and fancy are required: but the fancy must be more eminent; because they please for the extravagancy; but ought not to displease by indiscretion."[28] From this generalization Warton's enthusiasms represent no significant departure—except perhaps in one respect, that he never synthesized the two qualities, never worked out a systematic or consistent theory. It is typical of him that instead he should have extolled extravagancy in one essay and in another a few weeks later, with equal confidence, have demanded discretion.

The doctrine of imitation, as interpreted by Warton, was equally powerful in controlling his views on poetic originality. We have seen that he often regretted the lack of it in modern poets and agreed with Addison that the imagination delights not only in what is great and beautiful but also in what is new. Yet according to his own conception of artistic imitation of nature, poetic originality was hardly possible. Hurd's central argument had been that "common sense directs us, for the most part, to regard resemblances in great writers, not as the pilferings, or frugal acquisitions of needy *art,* but as the honest fruits of genius, the free and liberal bounties of unenvying *nature.*"[29] Warton declares himself sensible of "what a late critic has urged, that a want of seeming originality arises frequently, not from a barrenness and timidity of genius, but from invincible necessity, and the nature of things."[30] Nor was this a mere gesture of polite approval for a recent and brilliant statement of traditional doctrine. Warton was essentially conservative on this whole question, for here, again, he was controlled by the belief that art communicates "the universal and immutable in thought, feeling, and taste."

His conservatism is especially clear in his rejection of Edward Young's ideas on this subject. Young's *Conjectures on Original Composition* (1759) had not been published when Warton dedicated the first volume of his *Essay on Pope* to him, but in the second volume and in his edition of Pope Warton made clear his rejection of his friend's views. He rejected them on several different grounds, the most frequently expressed of which was an objection to Young's belief that modern poets could and ought to surpass the ancients; with this heresy Warton, as a thoroughgoing admirer of the classics, could of course not agree.[31] He felt, moreover—and this objection is still more significant—that the studious cultivation of originality had grave dangers. He wondered whether "when just models . . . have once appeared, succeeding writers, by ambitiously endeavouring to surpass those just models, and to be original and new, do not become distorted and unnatural, in their thoughts and diction."[32] Thus Cowley, because he attempted to be novel, "abounds in false thoughts; in far-sought sentiments; in forced, unnatural conceits."[33] The recurrence of the word "unnatural" in these two passages indicates how closely Warton followed the prevailing views of his time. Here, as so often, he wavered between two extremes, though drawn toward both. He did not quite believe that poetry consists wholly in "Nature to Advantage dress'd,

What oft was thought, but ne'er so well express'd.'' And yet he felt that poets
"must needs be stamped with a close resemblance to each other" and
believed that the conscious pursuit of difference and originality must result in
affectation, eccentricity, and unnaturalness.

A related but somewhat different conflict is involved in his plea for
circumstantiality. We have seen that he believed in a uniform nature and in an
art which, imitating nature, had a universal, eternal appeal. According to "the
high neo-classical dogma," Lovejoy finds, "the germ of improvement or
reform was one of simplification, standardization, the avoidance of the particular, the elimination of local variations and individual diversities. . . ."[34]
That Warton accepted some such conception is shown by his belief, already
referred to above, that Pope's enduring works were not the satires and moral
essays—which deal with local oddities and philosophical ideas which will
change—but his poems of nature and passion, *Eloisa to Abelard* and the *Elegy
to an Unfortunate Young Lady*.

From this conception, however, a more questionable corollary was often
drawn. It was argued that if nature, which poetry imitates, is defined as the
invariant, the universal and uniform, then the poet must treat not the variable
individual but the constant species. Poetry, therefore, cannot dwell upon the
minuter distinctions, number the streaks of the tulip, or, in Reynolds' phrase,
"finish every hair."[35] Clearly there is no place in such a view for Warton's
"*true, lively,* and *minute* representations of Nature.''

The curious and significant fact about Warton is that he should have failed
to see this incompatibility. He accepted, as fully as anyone in his time, the
more or less Horatian doctrine that poetry, if it is to have a permanent
audience, must deal with eternal and unchanging materials. But at other
times, quite disregarding this principle, he based his contentions on the more
or less Longinian doctrine that poetry must be exciting, vivid, and expressive
of an unusually live, warm, and sensitive personality. Occasionally, as in
Warton's demand for vivid particularity, the inconsistencies between the two
traditions are only too apparent.

Such contradictions, resulting from shifting the terms of an aesthetic
analysis in the light of one or another critical tradition, could be traced in most
of the eighteenth-century critics. On this particular point, however,
contemporaries of Warton like Johnson and Reynolds were more clearheaded.
Thus Johnson defended a generalized style—the "grandeur of generality"—not only because he liked it better but also because it was more consistent with the bases of his aesthetic theory. Warton, accepting the same
basic assumption, defended a poetic style which departed radically from it. It
is not surprising, therefore, that Johnson should sometimes have been irritated

(as he was) by the diffuseness, the rambling, and the excessively eclectic enthusiasms of his friend.

ↃↄↃↄↃↄ

The second section of this paper has shown the unsoundness, in view of the large element of strictly neoclassical theory in Warton's criticism, of any conception that makes him a revolutionary critic. In this final section the sources of some of his most characteristic views will be presented, with the particular purpose of showing that even his most characteristic and unusual positions had precedent and sound authority in their support. Where Gildon was not with him, Addison was.

His leading principle—the definition of imagination as the power of "turning *readers* into *spectators*"—may be taken as an example, The locus classicus for this idea is a famous passage in Longinus. Warton quotes the sentence: Upon occasion, Longinus writes, the poet or orator "by reason of the rapt and excited state of his feelings, imagines himself to see what he is talking about, and produces a similar illusion in his hearers."[36] How familiar this passage was to seventeenth- and eighteenth-century readers may be judged from the following echoes of it:

Dryden [1677]: Imaging is, in itself, the very height and life of Poetry. It is, as Longinus describes it, a discourse, which by a kind of enthusiasm, or extraordinary emotion of the soul, makes it seem to us that we behold those things which the poet paints, so as to be pleased with them, and to admire them."[37]

John Dennis [1704]: For the Spirits being set in a violent Emotion, and the Imagination being fir'd by that Agitation; and the Brain being deeply penetrated by those Impressions, the very Objects themselves are set as it were before us, and consequently we are sensible of the same Passion that we should feel from the things themselves.[38]

Leonard Welsted [1712]: The next thing then the Critick points at is that happy boldness and mastery which Euripides discovers in the designing of his Images; but here I must remind you, that by the word "Images" he understands no other than those enthusiasms and transports where the Poet seems to see the thing he is speaking of. . . .[39]

Addison [1712]: [Livy] describes everything in so lively a manner, that his whole history is an admirable picture, and touches on such proper circumstances in every story, *that this reader becomes a kind of spectator,* and feels in himself all the variety of passions which are correspondent to the several parts of the relation.[40]

John Hughes [1715]: The Power of raising Images or Resemblances of things, giving them Life and Action, and presenting them as it were before the Eyes, was thought by the ancients to have something in it like Creation: And it was probably for this fabling Part, that the first Authors of such Works were call'd *Poets* or *Makers*. . . .[41]

Pope [1715]: What he [Homer] writes is of the most animated Nature imaginable; every thing moves, every thing lives, and is put in Action. If a Council be call'd, or a Battel fought, you are not coldly inform'd of what was said or done as from a third Person; the Reader is hurry'd out of himself by the Force of the Poet's Imagination, and turns in one place to a Hearer, in another to a Spectator.[42]

Pope [1715]: Homer makes us Hearers, and *Virgil* leaves us Readers.[43]

Joseph Spence [1726]: ''Nothing can be more beautiful to the Eye, than these Landscapes are in the Poem: they make every thing present to us; and agreeably deceive us into an Imagination, that we *actually See, what we only Hear.*[44]

Richard Hurd [1751]: To be able, on all occasions, to exhibit what the Greek Rhetoricians call Phantasion; which is, as Longinus well expresses it, when ''the poet, from his own vivid and enthusiastic conception seems to have the object, he describes, in actual view, and presents it, almost, to the eyes of the reader,'' this can be accomplished by nothing less, than the genuine plastic powers of original *invention.*[45]

Warton [1756]: The whole train of imagery in this stanza is alive, sublime, and animated to an unparallelled degree; the poet [Dryden] had so strongly possessed himself of the action described, that he places it fully before the eyes of the reader.[46]

Henry Home, Lord Kames [1762]: Writers of genius, sensible that the eye is the best avenue to the heart, represent every thing as passing in our sight; and, from readers or hearers, transform us as it were into spectators. . . .[47]

Johnson [1781]: [Pope] had Imagination, which strongly impresses on the writer's mind and enables him to convey to the reader the various forms of nature, incidents of life, and energies of passion. . . .[48]

From this evidence it is obvious that Warton's central definition of imagination, which made it the power of turning readers into spectators, was far from original or even newly introduced. Nor were Warton's applications of this principle without precedent. It has been shown, in the first section of this paper, that he applied it, at various times, to picturesque "painting," to personification, and to circumstantial detail in description. Since the fad for the picturesque is well recognized to have been established in both poetry and criticism at least fifteen years before Warton's *Essay,* this aspect of his theory need not detain us here.[49] The second application is more illuminating, but since Woodhouse has already given an interesting account of the place assigned to personification in the criticism of Addison, Hughes, and Warton, and in the verse of Collins,[50] this too may be quite briefly dismissed. One of Addison's leading points in the essays on the imagination had been a defense of personification, simile, and allegory, through which, he says, "a truth in the understanding is, as it were, reflected by the imagination; we are able to see something like colour and shape in a notion, and to discover a scheme of thought traced out upon matter."[51] The same idea is to be found in Hughes and in Pope.[52] A still more direct influence on Warton, which Woodhouse does not mention, was that of Joseph Spence, under whose roof the *Essay on Pope* was begun.[53] Spence says that metaphor and allegory are the light of poetry, and that their chief use and beauty is "*to give Light and Perspicuity to a description;* to cloath Words . . . with Substance; and to make *Language visible.* . . ."[54] Spence writes of Pope, very much as Pope had done of Homer:

> But all these Beautiful Pictures, are only Pictures of *still Life;* this Gentleman's Excellency reaches farther; he is as masterly in all his Motions, and Actions; he can teach his Pencil to express Ideas yet in the Mind; and to paint out the Passions of the Soul.[55]

That Warton read these ideas of personification into Longinus we know from two very interesting essays, purporting to be translations from newly discovered Longinian manuscripts, which he contributed to the *Adventurer.* That there is much more of Addison and Spence in them than there is of Longinus seems particularly clear in the second paper, where Warton writes:

> It is the peculiar privilege of poetry, not only to place material objects in the most amiable attitudes, and to clothe them in the most graceful dress, but also to give life and motion to immaterial beings; and form, and colour, and action, even to abstract ideas; to embody the Virtues, the Vices, and the Passions; and to bring before our eyes, as on a stage, every faculty of the human mind.[56]

Warton's views on personification, by lending critical support to the "allegorical odes" written by himself, by Collins, and by Gray, helped to produce original creative work; the views themselves were anything but revolutionary.

Thus Longinus and Addison provide the sanction for Warton's love of personification. Quintilian is his authority for demanding concreteness and minuteness in description. Here Warton had no support from his chief master, Addison, who made no contention on this subject one way or the other. Quintilian, though emphasizing persuasion rather than poetic excitement as the end of speaking and writing, agreed with Longinus that writing should be more than bare narration, that facts should be "displayed in their living truth to the eyes of the mind."[57] Longinus was content to quote some especially vivid passages; Quintilian goes on to expound a method by which such vividness may be achieved:

> So, too, we may move our hearers to tears by the picture of a captured town. For the mere statement that the town was stormed, while no doubt it embraces all that such a calamity involves, has all the curtness of a dispatch, and fails to penetrate to the emotions of the hearer. But if we expand all that the one word "stormed" includes, we shall see the flames pouring from house and temple, and hear the crash of falling roofs and one confused clamour blent of many cries: we shall behold some in doubt whither to fly, others clinging to their nearest and dearest in one last embrace, while the wailing of women and children and the laments of old men that the cruelty of fate should have spared them to see that day will strike upon our ears. . . . For though, as I have already said, the sack of a city includes all these things, it is less effective to tell the whole news at once than to recount it detail by detail.[58]

In this respect, as in so many others, Warton had the support of his friend Spence. In his *Essay on Pope's Odyssey,* Spence cites the chapter in Quintilian which has been quoted just above, remarking that

> With Poets and in History, *there may be some Fraud in saying only the bare truth.* In either, 'tis not sufficient to tell us, *that such a City,* for Instance, *was taken and ravag'd with a great deal of Inhumanity:* There is a *Poetical Falsity,* if a strong Idea of each particular be not imprinted on the mind; and an *Historical,* if some things are passed over only with a general mark of Infamy or Dislike.[59]

Warton finds in Pope's *Windsor Forest* a parallel for Quintilian's ravaged city. In this passage, he says, the influence of peace and commerce are expressed by selecting such circumstances, as are best adapted to strike the imagination by lively pictures; the selection of which chiefly constitutes real poetry. An historian or prosewriter might say, "Then shall the most distant nations crowd into my port:" a poet sets before your eyes, "the ships of uncouth form," that shall arrive in the Thames.[60]

This quotation makes a fitting conclusion to a survey of Warton's theory of the imagination. The selection of "lively pictures," he says, "chiefly constitutes real poetry"; and it will be remembered that one allegorical "painting" by Lucretius—"beautiful to the last degree, and more glowing than any figure painted by Titian"[61]—was enough to prove to Warton that its author was a supreme poet. It was this delight in and insistence upon the visual image, rather than his love for "the castles and the palaces of Fancy," which was the characteristic feature of his poetic theory. In one result of this delight, his demand for particularity, the future was certainly on Warton's side: soon we hear no more of the "grandeur of generality"; the poet is told to keep his eye on the object. But even in this contention, the only one that was unusual in his time, both Hurd and Spence were before him and Quintilian provided a classical sanction. And all his views, to repeat the conclusions of this paper's second section, fall within that broad and flexible framework of ideas whose central arch was "imitation of nature" and which dominated the criticism of Warton and his contemporaries.

Notes

1. Joseph Warton, ed. *Works of Pope* (London, 1797), I, lv.
2. Warton, *Adventurer*, No. 93. Addison also found Shakespeare to excel in "that noble extravagance of fancy" (*Spectator*, No. 419). Cf. Philip Mahone Griffith, "Joseph Warton's Criticism of Shakespeare," *Tulane Studies in English*, 14 (1965),17-27.
3. Warton, *Essay on the Writings and Genius of Pope* (London, 1756), I, 298.
4. Ibid., p. 248. Warton's critic, Owen Ruffhead, commenting on these remarks, contends very reasonably that Warton is confusing two different terms, "invention" and "imagination," and wishes that before passing "these hasty censures" the critic "had previously defined the words. . ." (*Works of Pope*, ed. Ruffhead [London, 1769], V, 346).
5. Warton, *Essay* (1782, 1st issue), II, ii; also *Adventurer*, No. 80. The three adjectives are Addison's (*Spectator*, No. 412).
6. Warton, *Essay* (1756), I, 49.
7. Addison, *Spectator*, No. 411.
8. Warton, *Essay* (1756), I, 27.
9. Warton, *Essay* (1806), II, 160.
10. A. S. P. Woodhouse, "Collins and the Creative Imagination," *Studies in English by Members of University College, Toronto* (Toronto, 1931), pp. 58-130.
11. Warton, *Adventurer*, No. 57.

12. John Wooll, *Biographical memoirs . . . Joseph Warton* (London, 1806), p. 100.

13. Warton, ed., *Works of Virgil* (London, 1753), I, 416.

14. Warton, *Essay* (1756), I, 43. Cf. Elizabeth Manwaring, *Italian Landscape in Eighteenth-Century England* (New York: Oxford University Press, 1925), pp. 101-8.

15. Warton, *Essay* (1806), II, 160.

16. Ibid., pp. 160-68.

17. Samuel Johnson, *Rambler*, No. 36. For other quotations see J. E. Brown, *The Critical Opinions of Samuel Johnson* (Princeton: Princeton University Press, 1926), pp. 115-18. George Sherburn finds Warton's love of particularity his only unusual position (*The Early Career of Alexander Pope* [Oxford: Clarendon Press, 1934], pp. 9-10).

18. George Saintsbury, *A History of English Criticism* (Edinburgh and London: W. Blackwood, 1925), p. 260.

19. Edmund Gosse, "Two Pioneers of Romanticism," *Proceedings of the British Academy* (1915-16), pp. 146-47.

20. Saintsbury, p. 261.

21. A. O. Lovejoy, " 'Nature' as Aesthetic Norm," *MLN*, 42 (1927), 444-50.

22. Warton, *Works of Pope*, I, 254n.

23. Warton, *Essay* (1756), I, 334; cf. Johnson, *Rambler*, No. 36.

24. Richard Hurd, "A Discourse on Poetical Imitation," in Horace, *Epistola ad Augustum*, ed. Hurd (London, 1751), pp. 133-34.

25. Warton, *Essay* (1756), I, 89ff.; see also *Adventurer*, No. 63, and *Works of Pope*, I, 21.

26. Warton, *Essay* (1806), I, 238n.; cf. Hume, "Of the Standard of Taste" (1757), in *Essays, Moral, Political, and Literary*, ed. T. H. Green and T. H. Grose (London, 1898), I, 270.

27. Warton, *Adventurer*, No. 101.

28. Thomas Hobbes, *Leviathan*, I, viii, in *English Works*, ed. William Molesworth (London: J. Bohn, 1839), III, 58. See note by F. B. Kaye, "Current Bibliography, 1660-1800," *PQ*, 7 (1928), 178; and Donald Bond, " 'Distrust' of Imagination in English Neo-Classicism," *PQ*, 14 (1935), 54-69.

29. Hurd, p. 136.

30. Warton, *Essay* (1756), I, 89.

31. In reply to Young, Warton writes, it might well be said, "You, indeed, have given us a considerable number of original thoughts in your works, but they would have been more chaste and correct if you had imitated the ancients more" (*Works of Pope*, I, 65-66n.). Elsewhere he quotes at length from Reynold's plea, in the third lecture of his *Discourses*, for knowledge of the classical masterpieces (*Works of Pope*, I, 257-59n.) Young himself did not deny that "the classics are forever our rightful and revered masters in composition" (*Conjectures*, ed. E. J. Morley [Manchester, 1918], p. 16). Warton also objects against Young that "he had, perhaps, done better if he had followed" Pope's advice: "Learn hence for ancient rules a just esteem; To copy nature is to copy them" (*Works of Pope*, I, 252-53n.).

32. Warton, *Essay* (1756), I, 204.

33. Warton, *Essay* (1806), II, 349; cf. pp. 39-45. In his edition of Pope (I, 267, 270), Warton quotes Johnson's similar view of Cowley (*Lives of the English Poets*, ed. G. B. Hill [Oxford, 1905], I, 20-21), praising it as the best of Johnson's criticism.

34. A. O. Lovejoy, "Optimism and Romanticism," *PMLA*, 42 (1927), 943.

35. Reynolds, *Discourses on Art*, ed. Robert R. Wark (San Marino, Calif.: Huntington Library, 1959), Discourse XI, p. 195. For a searching analysis of Reynold's views on this subject, see Walter J. Hipple, Jr., "General and Particular in the *Discourses* of Sir Joshua Reynolds," *Jounal of Aesthetics and Art Criticism*, 11 (1953), 231-47, and idem, *The Beautiful, the Sublime, and the Picturesque in Eighteenth-Century British Aesthetic Theory* (Carbondale: Southern Illinois University Press, 1957), Ch. 9.

36. Longinus *On the Sublime* 15 (trans. H. L. Havell [London, 1890]), pp. 31-32.

37. Dryden, "Apology for Heroic Poetry," in *Essays of John Dryden*, ed. W. P. Ker (Oxford:

Clarendon Press, 1926), I, 186. This essay is generally agreed to represent the first impact of Boileau's translation of Longinus, which had appeared three years earlier.

38. Dennis, "The Grounds of Criticism," in *Critical Works of John Dennis,* ed. E. N. Hooker, Vol. I (Baltimore: Johns Hopkins University Press, 1939), p. 363.

39. Welsted, "Remarks on Longinus," in *The Works in Verse and Prose, of Leonard Welsted, esq.,* ed. John Nichols (London, 1787), p. 415.

40. Addison, *Spectator,* No. 420 (my italics).

41. Hughes, "Essay on Allegorical Poetry," in *Works of Spenser,* ed. Hughes (London, 1715), I, xxiii.

42. Pope, Preface to *Iliad,* in Durham, p. 324.

43. Ibid., p. 330.

44. Spence, *Essay on Pope's Odyssey* (London, 1726), I, 66; Longinus 15 is cited in a footnote.

45. Hurd, p. 122.

46. Warton, *Essay on Pope* (1756), I, 55.

47. Henry Home, Lord Kames, *Elements of Criticism,* 7th ed. (Edinburgh, 1788), II, 351.

48. Johnson, *Lives,* ed. Hill, III, 247.

49. Manwaring finds Thomson the chief literary influence in the picturesque movement (pp. 101-8).

50. Woodhouse, pp. 101-2, etc.

51. Addison, *Spectator,* No. 421. Personfication is discussed at more length, ibid., No. 273.

52. Hughes writes that allegory "frequently gives life to virtues and vices, passions and diseases, to natural and moral qualities, and represents them acting as divine, human, or infernal persons" ("Essay on Allegorical Poetry," in Durham, p. 95, cited by Woodhouse, p. 103; cf. Addison, *Spectator,* No. 419).

Of Homer's "allegorical fable" Pope writes: "How fertile will that Imagination appear which was able to cloathe all the properties of Elements, the Qualifications of the Mind, the Virtues and Vices, in Forms and Persons" (Durham, p. 327; Woodhouse does not mention the place of Pope in this tradition).

53. Warton mentions this fact three times (*Essay* [1756], I, 154, and *Essay* [1806], II, 233; *Works of Pope,* I, xxvi; see also Wooll, p. 30.)

54. Joseph Spence, *Essay on Pope's Odyssey,* I, 38; see also II, 72. Spence also shared Warton's interest in the picturesque, giving warm praise to the descriptions in Pope's Homer, "especially hanging Woods, Slopes, and Precipices" (I, 64). For Spence on the "sister arts" see I, 75-76, 83-86, and II, 191.

55. Ibid., I, 68.

56. Warton, *Adventurer,* No. 57.

57. Quintilian *Institutes of rhetoric* (trans H. E. Butler) viii. 3. 62. Cited by Warton, *Essay* (1806), II, 168.

58. Quintilian *Inst.* viii. 3. 67-70.

59. Spence, *Essay* (1727), II, 121. The passage is cited by W. D. MacClintock, *Joseph Warton's Essay on Pope, a History of the Five Editions* (Chapel Hill: University of North Carolina Press, 1933), p. 10.

60. Warton, *Essay* (1756), I, 27; *Windsor Forest,* ll. 400 ff. Hurd made very similar contentions. For the poet, he says, "every minute mark and lineament of the contemplated form leaves a corresponding trace on his fancy." Conveying the liveliest ideas of these forms "is what we call *painting* in poetry; by which not only the general natures of things are described, and their appearances shadowed forth; but every single *property* marked, and the poet's own image set in distinct relief before the eyes of his reader" ("Discourse," pp. 121-22).

61. Warton, *Works of Virgil,* I, 416; see n. 13.

9

Richard Hurd's *Letters on Chivalry and Romance*

Richard Hurd was one of those eighteenth-century English divines, remote descendants of Erasmus, who added an interest in the literature of their own country to the traditional combination of classical scholarship with ecclesiastical duties and Christian teaching. Born in Staffordshire in 1720, Hurd was educated in Brewood Grammar School in that county and at Emmanuel College, Cambridge (B.A., 1739). In a conventional but uniformly successful career in the church, he was ordained deacon and priest, was elected a fellow of Emmanuel, took the degrees of M.A., B.D., and D.D., was Preacher of Whitehall and Lincoln's Inn and preceptor to the Prince of Wales, served as archdeacon of Gloucester and for six years as bishop of Lichfield and Coventry, and died in his sleep at the age of eighty-eight after almost twenty-seven years as bishop of Worcester (1781-1808). He had declined the primacy, offered to him by the king in 1783, as "a charge not suited to his temper and talents, and much too heavy for him to sustain, especially in these times."[1]

It is characteristic not only of Hurd's own interests but of his type and his time that his first two books, both published before he was thirty, were an *Enquiry into the Rejection of the Christian Miracles by the Heathen* and an

---

Reprinted, with permission of the William Andrews Clark Memorial Library, University of California, Los Angeles, from Richard Hurd, *Letters on Chivalry and Romance,* ed. Hoyt Trowbridge, Augustan Reprint series, nos. 101-2 (Los Angeles: William Andrews Clark Memorial Library, 1963), pp. i-xi. A few passages have been lifted, also with permission, from my essay "Bishop Hurd: a Reinterpretation," *PMLA,* 58 (1943), 450-65.

edition of Horace's *Ars poetica* with an English commentary and notes. Besides the *Letters on Chivalry and Romance* (1762), his best-known book, his later writings include an edition of the *Epistola ad Augustus,* several volumes of sermons, polemical works against Jortin, Leland, and Hume's *Natural History of Religion,* editions of the works of Warburton and Addison, a number of moral and political dialogues, and essays or prefaces on "Poetical Imitation," "The Provinces of the Drama," "The Idea of Universal Poetry," and other literary subjects. Hurd was a protégé of William Warburton, editor of Pope and Shakespeare and author of *The Divine Legation of Moses,* and his friends included Joseph and Thomas Warton, William Mason, and Thomas Gray.[2]

The *Letters* are written in the easy style of literary criticism popularized by Addison. Since the friend to whom they are addressed is not identified or given any individual character, the epistolary device serves chiefly to rationalize the cultivated but almost ostentatiously amateur style and tone, a vulgarization of the Horatian manner and the French tradition of the *honnête homme,* long since acclimated in England. Hurd's argument, described with humorous self-deprecation as "this profound system" (Letter IV), is as thin as it is polite.

The occasion, subject, and purpose of the work have not always been clearly understood. As the title pages of later editions indicate, the *Letters* were written "to illustrate some Passages in the THIRD DIALOGUE." In the dialogue, "On the Age of Queen Elizabeth" (1759), Dr. Arbuthnot is represented as defending that reign, against the whiggish political criticisms of Addison, by praising its manners. He discusses three virtues, "convivial, gymnastic, and musical"—the hospitality, bravery, and "elegance of art and genius" which were manifested in festivals such as Leicester's entertainment of the queen, the exercises of the tiltyard, and the poetical fictions of Elizabethan and Jacobean masques, traces of which are still evident to liberally educated men in the ruins of Kenilworth, scene of the debate.[3] In the course of his argument, Arbuthnot suggests that what has been censured as incredible and fantastic in the works of the old poets and romance writers "was frequently but a just copy of life, and that there was more of truth and reality in their representations, than we are apt to imagine," and that in the bold fictions and high figurative manner of some of the Elizabethan poets we find "the essence of the truest and sublimest poetry."[4] These are the ideas which Hurd thought worth developing further, and which provide the basic intellectual content of the *Letters*. Hurd is not defending the medieval romances, which he candidly confesses that he has not read (Letter IV), nor is he attacking the critical principles or general theory of poetry which were accepted in his time. The subject of the *Letters* is Renaissance narrative literature, including the Italian epics as well as Spenser, Milton, Shakespeare, and Hurd's purpose was to defend the romance element in that literature as conducive to the sublime.

To the early students of eighteenth-century literature and criticism, beginning in the 1890s and continuing into the 1930s and 1940s, Hurd was one of the heroes of "preromanticism"—another "bicyclist scout," as Edmund Gosse fancifully put it, who heralded a great aesthetic advance that was delayed for fifty years.[5] One of the irritating shortcomings of J. W. H. Atkins's monumental history of literary criticism is its perpetuation of the idea advanced by Phelps, Beers, Saintsbury, and others that Hurd was launching "a frontal attack upon the whole system" of prevailing critical theory, a "concise and searching attack on the neo-classic creed."[6] The plausibility of this interpretation of the *Letters* depends partly on the misconception of Hurd's subject and purpose, partly on a mistaken opinion that eighteenth-century criticism, "the neo-classic creed," was too rationalistic to admit any function for imagination or emotion in either the creation or the enjoyment of poetry. A more fundamental defect, however, is the methodological bias resulting from an unhistorical imposition of nineteenth-century issues and categories on eighteenth-century writings, those of Hurd and others. This kind of distortion permeated all the old studies of "preromanticism," but it certainly ought not to have been continued by a scholar writing in 1951, when Atkins's volume on Hurd's period was published.

A useful corrective to this view is a brief and unpretentious paper by Victor M. Hamm, "A Seventeenth-Century French Source for Hurd's *Letters on Chivalry and Romance*," published in 1937 but not mentioned by Atkins. Following a clue provided by a reference in the fourth letter, Hamm shows not only that many of Hurd's ideas about chivalry and romance had been anticipated in two *Mémoires* by Ste.-Palaye which had appeared in Volumes XVII and XX of the *Histoire de l'académie des inscriptions et belles-lettres* (1743 and 1746), but that Ste.-Palaye in turn was indebted to a dialogue by Jean Chapelain, *De la lecture des vieux Romans,* written before 1650. As Hamm remarks, "Much of the 'new' and 'radical' in Hurd's work must seem strangely tame and derivative when we realize that it had already been uttered more than a hundred years before, and by the founder of French classicism itself!"[7]

The most profitable approach to the interpretation of the *Letters,* in my opinion, is not through Hurd's supposed anticipation of romantic ideas but rather through his relation to two currents of thought in his own time. One of these tendencies was primarily historical and scholarly, the other philosophical; they were almost entirely independent of each other and were developed by different groups of writers. In the first Hurd was associated with his friends the Wartons, as well as Thomas Percy and many others, and in the second with such contemporaries in criticism as Edmund Burke, Lord Kames, Sir Joshua Reynolds, and even David Hume, with whom Hurd had much more in common as an aesthetician than he did in religion. Hurd's chief claim to originality probably lies in the combination he effects in the *Letters* between these two tendencies in eighteenth-century thought.

The first component, a complex movement not yet fully charted by historians of ideas, has been variously described as "the historical point of view," "the rise of English literary history," and "the Elizabethan revival." Risking a considerable oversimplification, I believe that the movement was dominated by two rules or slogans, one concerned with the interpretation of the literature of past ages, the other with its critical evaluation. Both concepts were clearly stated by Hurd's friend Thomas Warton:

1. Interpretation

In reading the works of an author who lived in a remote age, it is necessary that we should look back upon the customs and manners which prevailed in that age; that we should place ourselves in his situation, and circumstances; that we may be the better enabled to judge and discern how his turn of thinking, and manners of composing was biass'd, influenc'd, and, as it were, tinctur'd, by very familiar and reigning appearances, which are utterly different from those with which we are at present surrounded.

2. Evaluation

But it is absurd to think of judging either Ariosto or Spenser by precepts which they did not attend to. We who live in the days of writing by rule, are apt to try every composition by those laws which we have been taught to think the sole criterion of excellence. . . . We require the same order and design which every modern performance is expected to have, in poems where they never were regarded or intended.[8]

Neither of these ideas was at all novel. In their excellent studies of the movement, Wellek, Wasserman, and Wimsatt and Brooks show that similar statements were made by sixteenth-century Italian defenders of Ariosto, by Chapelain and Dryden in the seventeenth century, and by Hughes, Upton, and other commentators on Shakespeare, Spenser, and Ben Jonson in the eighteenth. The same slogans were applied to Hebrew poetry by Lowth, to Homer by Blackwell and Wood, and to the Greeks and Romans generally by Gibbon,[9] but the finest statement of these ideas, as well as their most impressive exemplification in practice, was the preface and notes of Dr.

Johnson's edition of Shakespeare (1765). Among students of this movement, Wellek is primarily interested in the development of narrative literary history, of which Warton's *History of English Poetry* was the first large-scale example. Wasserman, chiefly concerned with editions and commentaries, says that the historical point of view, though long current in a scattered way, did not become a continuous, effective movement until "a practical method of scholarship was borrowed from editors of the classics for application to native products."[10] Both would agree that the main impact of these ideas was felt by scholars; in a more sophisticated form, the same ideas are at work in most literary scholarship today—as they are, indeed, in this essay.

A second movement in eighteenth-century thought, at least equally relevant to the *Letters,* has been less studied by historians of literary criticism; the most useful account is that of Walter J. Hipple.[11] This movement, one of the many consequences of the seventeenth-century revolution which shifted the emphasis in philosophy from things to the mind, is a tradition in aesthetics—or in "philosophical criticism," to use the terminology of the period—which began in England with Addison's influential *Spectator* papers on the pleasures of the imagination and culminated in Hurd's generation with such elaborate and systematic works as Burke's *Philosophical Enquiry into the Origins of Our Ideas of the Sublime and Beautiful* (1757), Alexander Gerard's *Essay on Taste* (1759), the *Elements of Criticism* by Henry Home, Lord Kames (1762), and the *Discourses on Art* of Sir Joshua Reynolds (1769-90). Although these writers differ among themselves, they are alike in attempting to establish criticism as a rational science by grounding it on universal laws of mind. Their reasoning, as Hipple observes, often follows the procedure described by Mill as the "historical" or "inverse deductive" method, in which tentative generalizations drawn by induction from observed phenomena are then explained and verified by principles deduced from laws of human nature.[12]

In the *Letters,* Hurd combines the historical point of view with a rather superficial version of the method and principles of the philosophic critics. Letter I, summarizing the subject and plan of the work, begins by asserting that "Nothing in human nature, my dear friend, is without its reasons." Hurd's first purpose is to determine the causes of the institution of chivalry, which in Letters II and III he traces to the anarchic political and social conditions of feudal Europe. In Letters IV and V he confirms this analysis by showing that there was a close resemblance between civil conditions in the Gothic age and in the heroic age of Greece, and consequently between the romances and Homeric epics, the chief literary manifestations of those two eras. In letters VI to X, shifting from historical sociology to a more intriguing problem of aesthetic value, Hurd seeks an explanation of the appeal which romance fictions continued to have, notably for Ariosto, Tasso, Spenser, Milton, and other Renaissance poets, long after chivalry had spent itself as a social institution. This phenomenon, too, must have its reasons. "May there not be something in the Gothic Romance peculiarly suited to the views of a genius, and to the ends of poetry? . . . The circumstances in the Gothic fictions and manners, which are proper to the ends of poetry (if any such there be) must be pointed out." Finally, the inquiry is completed in Letters XI and XII by determining the causes which, in spite of the aesthetic potentialities of romance materials, led to the decline and rejection of "the Gothic taste" in later times.

Hurd's sympathy with the historical critics is evident in his assertions that "readers do not usually do, as they ought, put themselves in the circumstances of the poet, or rather of those, of whom the poet writes" (Letter I), and that "the Gothic architecture has it's own rules, by which when it comes to be examined, it is seen to have it's merit, as well as the Grecian" (Letter VIII). In the last Letter he uses the same rather crude historical schematism which had been advanced by both Joseph and Thomas Warton, a decline of imagination with the growth of reason and civilization.[13] But Hurd was not a scholarly antiquarian like his friend Warton,[14] and he was not really at all interested in avoiding errors of literary interpretation by laborious study of the customs and manners which prevailed in former ages. What did interest him was the aesthetic justification of the romance element in Renaissance writings, a question of evaluation that could not be resolved by historical techniques but required an appeal to some kind of aesthetic principles.

Hurd says in Letter I: "The only criticism, indeed that is worth regarding is, the philosophical." His conception of truly philosophical criticism is expressed in several of his other writings. It is by means of philosophy, he states in the dedication of his edition of the *Epistle to Augustus,* that criticism, "which were otherwise a vague and superficial thing, acquires the soundness and solidity of science." Criticism, as a form of didactic writing, "is employed in *referring particular facts to general principles.*" Its final perfection "would consist in an ability to refer *every* beauty and blemish to a separate class; and *every* class, by a gradual progression, to some *one* single principle."[15] Hurd was only half joking, in a passage added to the fourth Letter in later editions, when he spoke of himself as one of the "system-makers."[16]

The principles of his aesthetics, merely implicit in the *Letters,* are developed systematically in his essay "On the Idea of Universal Poetry," first published in 1766. The end of poetry, he says, is pleasure: "When we speak of poetry, as an *art,* we mean *such a way or method of treating a subject, as is found most pleasing and delightful to us.''* Since the end of all poetry is to ''gratify the desires of the mind,'' a knowledge of the laws of mind is required for the derivation of its rules, which are ''but so many MEANS, which experience finds most conducive to that end.'' Human beings are uniformly constituted and have, in the main, a similar experience; we are ''all furnished with the same original *properties and affections,* as with the same stock of *perceptions and ideas.''* Without this similarity of mind there could be no philosophical criticism, but since uniformity does exist a scientific art of poetry is possible. With characteristic thinness of argument, Hurd proceeds to show that all poetry requires the use of figurative language, fiction, and numbers. The essay concludes:

> And THUS much of the idea of UNIVERSAL POETRY. It is the art of
> treating any subject in *such* a way as is found most delightful to us; that
> is, IN AN ORNAMENTED AND NUMEROUS STYLE—IN THE
> WAY OF FICTION—AND IN VERSE. Whatever deserves the name of
> POEM must unite these three properties; only in different degrees of
> each, according to its nature. For the art of every *kind* of poetry is only
> this general art so modified as the *nature* of each, that is, its more
> immediate and subordinate end, may respectively require.[17]

The peculiar flavor of Hurd's historico-philosophical mode of criticism is perceived most piquantly in his discussions of Spenser and Tasso (Letters VIII and X). Both raise central questions of critical judgment—the unity of the *Faerie Queene,* the naturalness of the events represented in *Jerusalem Delivered.* In both cases the argument is partly historical: Spenser's poem is to be criticized ''under the idea, not of a classical but Gothic composition,'' and in judging the fictions of Tasso we must remember the age in which he wrote. In resolving the questions he has posed, however, Hurd appeals to philosophical principles and distinctions, arguing deductively not only from the universal end of all poetry (pleasure) and two of its universal attributes (fiction and figurative language, as in Dialogue III), but also from the specific literary kind (epic, ''the greater poetry'') and its subordinate ends (sublimity and admiration).

The rule of unity, Hurd says in Letter VIII, ''is drawn from the nature of Epic composition itself, and holds equally, let the subject be what it will, and whatever the system of manners be on which it is conducted. . . . Every work of art must be *one,* the very idea of a work requiring it.'' But unity—as Hurd says of other universal qualities in ''The Idea of Universal Poetry''—is of various kinds and may be achieved by various means, according to the subject, the subordinate purpose, and the particular method employed. Spenser's poem exhibits a general plan or design, derived from its Gothic subject matter, which is unified by the common origin of all its events in the feast of the Faerie Queene and by a common end, fulfillment of her injunctions to the knights. To the extent that he followed this design, Spenser's method is consistent with the laws of the kind, arose out of his material, and gives the poem "that sort of unity and simplicity, which results from its nature."

Tasso's "*Lyes* of Gothic invention" are defended in Letter X by an analogous line of argument. The need for truth or naturalness in poetry is granted, as a valid universal rule. But the *degree* of nature appropriate to any work depends upon its kind. "The reason of the thing" shows that the epic muse ("the more sublime and creative poetry") is not bound by the cautious rules of dramatic credibility; far from being a fault, the golden dreams of Tasso are his chief glory, since it is through them that he fired the mind with admiration, the proper effect of the greater poetry. Yet these dreams must have some basis in fact, or at least in popular belief, for "we must first *believe,* before we can be *affected.*" Historically, we must recognize that a sufficient basis did exist in Tasso's time, to his great advantage. We do not believe those golden dreams ourselves, in our more rational and enlightened age, but if we put ourselves "in the circumstances of the poet, or rather of those, of whom the poet writes," as sound critical evaluation requires, we will acknowledge that they are justified by beliefs still current among Tasso's original audience. That basis does not exist any longer, and for that reason, Hurd says, "I would advise no modern poet to revive these faery tales in an epic poem."[18]

Philosophically, "nature" is a term of systematically varied meaning. It is not a fixed standard but a shifting proportion, a ratio between truth and fiction, the probable and the marvelous, which varies with every age and for every genre. The term has no single, fixed meaning, for its significance is determined, at any point, by the particular context in which it is used. Like fiction, figures, and numbers, "nature" is essential to every poem, but like them it must be present "in different degrees" according to the kind. In its systematic dialectical manipulation of this and similar terms, few passages in Hurd's critical writings are more typical of his method than the tenth Letter.[19]

Hurd is not a critic of major status or significance. He is never very weighty. In philosophical scope and penetration he cannot be compared with Burke or Gerard, to say nothing of Hume, and as historian he does not pretend to compete with Thomas Warton, Ste.-Palaye, or Dr. Johnson in the "ungrateful task" (Letter IV) of quarrying the primary sources. Preferring the amateur tone and relaxed standards of the easy style, he was usually content with facile generalizations and ingenious conjectures in both aspects of his criticism. Granting all this, however, we may still claim a certain position for him as an interesting minor writer. In the *Letters on Chivalry and Romance* he produced one notable book, still highly readable and entertaining, not quite like any other of that day or since. Though a relatively small element in the whole tradition of British literary criticism, it is one that we should be sorry to be without.

Notes

1. Hurd, "Some Occurrences in my Life," in *Works of Richard Hurd* (London, 1811), I, vii ff.; reprinted in Edith J. Morley, ed., *Hurd's Letters on Chivalry and Romance, with the Third Elizabethan Dialogue* (London, 1911), pp. 20-33. See also Francis Kilvert, *Memoirs of the Life and Writings of Richard Hurd* (London, 1860), and the article on Hurd by J. M. Rigg in the *Dictionary of National Biography*, X, 314-16.

2. Cf. *The Correspondence of Richard Hurd and William Mason and Letters of Richard Hurd to Thomas Gray*, ed. E. H. Pearce and Leonard Whibley (Cambridge: Cambridge University Press, 1932), and James Nankivell, "Extracts from the Destroyed Letters of Richard Hurd to William Mason," *MLR*, 14 (1950), 153-61. On Hurd's friendship with Thomas Warton, see "The Correspondence between Warton and Hurd," *Bodleian Quarterly Record*, 6 (1932), 303ff., and Edwine Montague, "Bishop Hurd's Association with Thomas Warton," *Stanford Studies in Language and Literature* (1941),233-56. Hurd's correspondence with Warburton is preserved in *Letters of a Late Eminent Prelate to One of his Friends* (Kidderminster, 1808)—a collection described by Macaulay as "Bully to Sneak." See also Leslie Stephen, *History of English Thought in the Eighteenth Century*, 3d ed. (London: John Murray, 1927), I, 347-51; and A. W. Evans, *Warburton and the Warburtonians: A Study in Some Eighteenth-Century Controversies* (Oxford: Oxford University Press, 1932).

3. Hurd, *Moral and Political Dialogues; with Letters on Chivalry and Romance* (London, 1765), I, 158-202; in Morley, pp. 48-74.

4. Ibid., pp. 171-72, 197-99; in Morley, pp. 48-74.

5. See Edmund Gosse, "Two Pioneers of Romanticism," *Proceedings of the British Academy* (1915-16), pp. 146-47; W. L. Phelps, *The Beginnings of the English Romantic Movement* (Boston: Ginn, 1893), pp. 112-15; H. A. Beers, *A History of English Romanticism in the Eighteenth Century* (London: Kegan Paul, 1899), pp. 221-26; George Saintsbury, *A History of Criticism* (Edinburgh and London: W. Blackwood, 1922-29), III, 75-78; Aisso Bosker, *Literary Criticism in the Age of Johnson* (Groningen: Walters, 1930), pp. 216-22, 231-32; Audley L. Smith, "Richard Hurd's *Letters on Chivalry and Romance*," *ELH*, 5 (1939), 58-81.

6. J. W. H. Atkins, *English Literary Criticism: 17th and 18th Centuries* (London: Methuen, 1951), pp. 215-24.

7. Victor M. Hamm, "A Seventeenth-Century French Source for Hurd's *Letters on Chivalry and Romance*," *PMLA*, 52 (1937),820-28.

8. Thomas Warton, *Observations on the Faerie Queene of Spenser*, 1st ed. (1754), p. 217; 2d ed. (1762), I, 21; cf. 1st ed., p. 142.

9. René Wellek, *The Rise of English Literary History* (Chapel Hill: University of North Carolina Press, 1941), Chs. 3-7; idem, *A History of Modern Criticism: 1750-1950* (New Haven: Yale University Press, 1955), Ch. 6; Earl R. Wasserman, *Elizabethan Poetry in the Eighteenth Century* (Urbana: University of Illinois Press, 1947), Ch. 5; William K. Wimsatt, Jr., and

Cleanth Brooks, *Literary Criticism: A Short History* (New York: Alfred A. Knopf, 1957), Ch. 24. These studies have largely superseded earlier treatments such as those by G. M. Miller, *The Historical Point of View in English Criticism* (Heidelberg, 1913); Odell Shepard, "Thomas Warton and the Historical Point of View in Criticism," *JEGP,* 58 (1943),450-65; D. N. Smith, *Warton's History of English Poetry* (London: H. Milford, 1929), and Francis S. Miller, "The Historic Sense of Thomas Warton, Jr.," *ELH,* 5 (1938),71-92.

10. Wasserman, pp. 216-17.

11. Walter J. Hipple, Jr., *The Beautiful, the Sublime, and the Picturesque in Eighteenth-Century British Aesthetic Theory* (Carbondale: Southern Illinois University Press, 1957), pp. 7-9, 312-20. Cf. R. S. Crane, "English Neo-Classical Criticism: An Outline Sketch," *Critics and Criticism, Ancient and Modern,* ed. Crane (Chicago: University of Chicago Press, 1952), pp. 372-88; Robert Marsh, *Four Dialectical Theories of Poetry* (Chicago: University of Chicago Press, 1965), pp. 6-11; James S. Malek, *The Arts Compared* (Detroit: Wayne State University Press, 1974), pp. 60-83, 139-56.

12. Hipple, p. 81. On the "inverse deductive" method, see John Stuart Mill, *A System of Logic, Ratiocinative and Inductive,* 9th ed. (London, 1873), Book VI, Ch. 10.

13. Cf. Wellek, *History of Modern Criticism,* I, 128-30.

14. Cf. Wellek, *Rise of English Literary History,* p. 179.

15. Hurd, *Works,* I, 282, 390-91; cf. II, 105, 110. For a fuller development of this aspect of Hurd's thought, see Hoyt Trowbridge, "Bishop Hurd: a Reinterpretation," *PMLA,* 58 (1943), 450-65.

16. Hurd, *Dialogues and Letters,* 1765 ed., III, 214; in Morley, p. 156.

17. Hurd, *Works,* II, 3-26.

18. A. L. Smith says: "It was in his insistence upon the superiority of Gothic manners over classic *for the purposes of modern poetry* that Hurd was the most original and the most anti-neoclassical" ("Hurd's *Letters,*" p. 67; italics mine). On the contrary, Hurd states emphatically that "the success of these fictions will not be great, when they have no longer any footing in the popular belief." Milton therefore did well, even a hundred years before Hurd's time, in replacing Gothic fables with more believable fictions—the Christian machinery of angels and devils. Elsewhere Hurd commends Davenant for rejecting the Italian prodigies and enchantments: "These conceits, he rightly saw, had too slender a foundation in the serious belief of his age to justify a relation of them" ("Discourse on Poetical Imitation," *Works,* II, 237-38).

19. Cf. the treatment of "beauty" in "Notes on the *Art of Poetry,*" *Works,* I, 110-16, and of "pleasure" and "instruction," *Works,* II, 16. A striking instance of this way of using terms is the treatment of "universality" or "the general" in Hurd's essay on the drama. Lessing, who devotes four numbers of the *Hamburgische Dramaturgie* to the exposition of Hurd's dramatic theory, is puzzled by the apparent inconsistency between Hurd's statement that all poetry imitates general truth, or the universal, and his contention that in tragedy the characterization should be "particular." In Hurd's context, this contention means that tragic characters should be *more* particular than those of comedy: "In calling the tragic character *particular,* I suppose it only *less representative* of the kind than the comic, not that the draught of so much character as it is concerned to represent should not be *general*" (*Works,* II, 49; cf. I, 255-61). In attempting to fix the meaning of "the general," Lessing pursues Hurd around an endless circle, but in Hurd's own terms these different propositions are not inconsistent.

10

Edward Gibbon, Literary Critic

During a period of almost six weeks early in 1762—8 February to 18 March—Gibbon devoted most of his time for study to writing an extensive summary and critical discussion of Richard Hurd's commentaries on the epistles of Horace to the Pisos and to Augustus.[1] This "Extrait raisonné," unpublished during his lifetime, was selected for inclusion, along with Gibbon's autobiography, other material from his notebooks and journals, and some previously published essays, in the two-volume *Miscellaneous Works of Edward Gibbon,* edited after his death by his friend and executor, John Holroyd, Lord Sheffield.[2] Gibbon's manuscript, totaling thirty folio pages, is now in the British Museum (Add. MSS. 34,880, fols. 188-218).

The criticism of Hurd is the work of a young man, still some weeks short of his twenty-fifth birthday (27 April), but a remarkably precocious one in certain respects. Gibbon had lost "my litterary maidenhead"[3] a year earlier, with the publication of his *Essai sur l'étude de la litterature,*[4] and he was already a thinker and scholar with well-established interests and habits, substantial reading, and considerable experience in the weighing of evidence and arguments. Above all, he had a mind eager to be used and to prove itself further.

The discussion of Hurd is dated at the beginning from Devizes and at the end from Blandford. During those weeks Gibbon was still engaged in his two and half years of service as captain in the south battalion of the Hampshire militia. As he tells us in the *Autobiography,* the regiment was stationed in the

This essay originally appeared in *Eighteenth Century Studies,* 4 (1971), 403-19; permission to reprint it has been granted by the American Society for Eighteenth-Century Studies.

"populous and disorderly" town of Devizes from October 1761 to the end of February 1762, moved briefly to Salisbury, 28 February—9 March, and then returned to "our beloved Blandford," where they had been during the summer of 1760 and where they remained through the spring until the colors were moved to Southampton on 2 June 1762. The militia was finally disembodied at the end of that year, on 23 December.[5]

It is somewhat astonishing that an officer on active duty, even in the militia in time of peace, should have carried out such a substantial piece of intellectual work—all the more so since he continued to do other reading concurrently.[6] But Gibbon was, to say the least, a most unusual officer. During the first seven or eight months of his service he was almost wholly absorbed in military business (though he characteristically instructed himself in his new trade by reading a book, Charles Guischardt's *Mémoires militaires sur les Grecs et les Romains,* [1758]), but thereafter he was always able to secure a separate lodging, necessary books, and some leisure to think, read, and even write: "in the life most averse to study, some hours may be stolen, some minutes may be snatched."[7] How successfully he managed to do so is attested not only by the thirty pages on Hurd's Horace but by other additions to his commonplace book and the reading he recorded day by day in his journal.

That the work he had done on Hurd was of lasting importance to Gibbon is indicated by the fact that he mentioned it specifically in his autobiography, drafted almost thirty years later.[8] He seems to have remembered especially the amount of time and effort involved and the pleasure and pride of the intellectual exercise. His memory actually exaggerated the former, increasing the number of pages he had written from thirty to fifty—an error silently corrected by Sheffield in preparing the notes for publication.[9] But those "closely written pages in folio" were most memorable, undoubtedly, because in writing them the young Gibbon had "presumed to think for myself."[10] The "Extrait" is an original piece of literary criticism, the most sustained and substantial that Gibbon was ever to write.[11]

∂∂∂

Hurd's edition of the two epistles is an unconventional book, as he acknowledges.[12] His text is basically a reprint of Bentley's, originally issued in 1711, although Hurd rejects a few Bentleian emendations, on interpretive rather than textual grounds. There are also very few verbal glosses, identifications of allusions, or other explanatory notes of the usual sort. The editorial matter is of three kinds: a "Commentary," printed below the texts, a running paraphrase of each poem designed to show its argumentative structure and unity of design; copious and often lengthy ''Notes'' on particular passages, most of them offering ''disquisitions'' suggested by ''hints'' in the text; and three ''Dissertations,'' extended essays on questions of literary theory.[13] His models, Hurd says, had been ''foreign, particularly the Italian critics,'' but especially the commentary of Bishop William Warburton on the English Horace, Alexander Pope.[14] To Warburton, who soon became his lifelong mentor and patron in the church, Hurd paid fulsome tribute in his dedication of the *Epistola ad Augustum* and in several of his notes.[15]

There is some discrepancy in Gibbon's overall judgment of Hurd's achievement between the ''Extrait'' itself and his reference to it in the *Autobiography*. In the latter he says that all those pages ''could scarcely comprise my full and free discussion of the sense of the master and the pedantry of the servant.''[16] If Horace is the master and Hurd the servant, the charge of pedantry is quite foreign to the attitudes Gibbon expressed in 1762. He had reservations about Hurd's execution, specifically his ''harsh and affected manner,'' the style clouded with obscure metaphors and exotic or technical expressions, and he thought that the excessive praises of Warburton would be disgusting to any sensible reader.[17] But at that time the commentary had seemed of great interest and its author a man of real scope and ability. Hurd is ''one of those valuable authors who cannot be read without improvement,'' a writer with a fund of well-digested reading, clearness of judgment, and ''a niceness of penetration, capable of taking things from their first principles, and observing their most minute differences.'' Gibbon did not regret the time he had spent, for it had ''started a new train of ideas upon many curious points of criticism.''[18] Such comments do not necessarily imply agreement with Hurd on specific issues, but they do manifest respect and even admiration for the total quality of his performance.

Gibbon's general outlook as a literary critic can be characterized by comparing it with Hurd's. As I have shown in the preceding essay, Hurd belonged to that school of ''philosophical'' or ''scientific'' criticism, the dominant critical mode in England and Scotland during the second half of the eighteenth century, which grounded the canons of literary judgment on universal laws of mind.[19] Among many programmatic statements of his views, particularly apposite in the present context is a seven-page note on verses 210-14 of the *Epistle to Augustus*. Observing that in this passage Horace makes his own feeling the test of poetical merit, Hurd asserts that this is philosophically correct, since all the varied emotional effects of different species of poetry are ''the object not of *reason* but *sentiment*,'' so that ''feeling or sentiment itself is not only the surest but the sole *ultimate* arbiter of works of genius.'' It is possible, however, to establish general rules by an appeal to experience, drawing conclusions from ''wide and general observations of the aptness and efficacy of certain *means* to produce those *impressions*'' on the mind.[20] By ''criticism,'' Hurd says:

> I understand that *species* of didactic writing, which *refers to general rules the virtues and faults of composition*. And the perfection of this *art* would consist in an ability to refer *every* beauty and blemish to a separate class; and *every* class, by a gradual progression, to some *one* single principle.

At present the critical art is far short of perfection, for many beauties and blemishes cannot be referred to any general rule, while many accepted rules are unconnected and not reducible to a common principle. Hurd concludes by evaluating the achievements in criticism of Longinus, Bouhours, and Addison in the light of these concepts. He finds that although they have followed the proper *''scientifical''* method by referring particular beauties to appropriate genera and species, their actual accomplishment is disappointing because their categories are too broad and indeterminate and because the beauties they identify are not traced to ''those *peculiar* qualities in *sentiment*'' which are their source and justification. These much-admired writers advance the science of criticism very little, since they do not ''lay open the more secret and hidden springs of that *pleasure,* which results from poetical composition.''[21] At the end of the note he thus returns to feeling as the ultimate arbiter.

It would have been convenient for purposes of comparison if Gibbon had commented on the note summarized above, but he did not choose to do so; in the ''Extrait'' he was engaged in the practice of criticism, not in theorizing about it. He had, however, discussed the question not long before in his *Essay on the Study of Literature,* where he was concerned not only with literary criticism but with the nature and value of belleletristic study as a whole:

> Criticism is, in my opinion, the art of forming a judgment of writings and writers; of what they have said; of what they have said well; and what they have said truly. Under the first head are comprehended grammar, a knowledge of languages, and manuscripts; a capacity of distinguishing supposed from genuine performances, and of restoring the true reading of corrupted passages. Under the second, is included the whole theory of elocution and poesy. The third opens an immense field, the enquiry into the circumstances and truth of facts. Thus the whole generation of critics may be distinguished under three kinds, grammarians, rhetoricians, and historians.[22]

The common ground between Hurd and Gibbon lies, of course, in the second category, in which the aim is to judge what writers have said well, on the basis of rhetorical or poetic theory. Gibbon was much more interested than Hurd in the third or historical kind of criticism, of which he gives several illustrative demonstrations in the *Essay* itself.[23] Both Hurd and Gibbon deplored the exclusive identification of criticism with textual and grammatical scholarship, which both regarded as a necessary but lower and less admirable element in humanistic study.

The purpose of Gibbon's *Essay* is to defend the study of ancient literature, in a mathematical and scientific age, by showing that the highest faculties of the mind are required for its successful pursuit.[24] All the sciences, he argues, depend on both reasonings and facts: "Without the latter, the objects of our study would be chimerical; and without the former, our most scientific acquirements would be implicit and irrational."[25] A talent for philosophizing is rare in any field of study. As exemplified in the writings of Cicero, Tacitus, Bacon, Leibniz, Bayle, Fontenelle, and Montesquieu, it

> consists in the capacity of recurring to the most simple ideas; in discovering and combining the first principles of things. . . . There are many men capable of forming particular ideas with precision; but there are few who can comprehend, in one abstract idea, a numerous association of others, less general.[26]

The materials of criticism, both literary and historical, are the books which surround a man of letters in his study, but the task of the critic has scarcely begun when his mind has been filled with "'all that relates to what men are, or have been; all that creative genius hath invented, that the understanding hath considered. . . .'"[27] The critic deliberates, compares, hesitates, and decides; "ready and fertile in resources, but void of false refinement," he must have a clear head, a fine taste, and acute penetration.

In judging the beauties and defects of literature, more specifically, the true critic is not content with insipid admiration, but "searches into the most secret emotions of the human heart, to discover the causes of his pleasure or disgust." Aristotle was the father of literary criticism; his metaphysical system has been exploded because he was destitute of observations and advanced chimeras instead of facts, but time has confirmed his decisions as a critic because "he hath drawn his rules from the nature of things, and a knowledge of the human heart; illustrating them by examples from the greatest models of antiquity."[28] Gibbon is very close to Hurd in his beliefs that criticism worthy of the name is philosophical, combining particular observations and perceptions with an ability to explain phenomena by tracing them to their causes, their first principles and most simple ideas, and that the rules by which literary judgment is guided must be drawn from the causes of pleasure or disgust, which lie in the emotions of the human heart. Gibbon had no quarrel with Hurd's general conception of the nature of criticism, the spirit in which it should be conducted, or its theoretical basis in psychology. Both operate within the same world of critical discourse.

If there is any difference between Hurd and Gibbon at this rather rarefied level of abstraction, it is one of emphasis. Gibbon is less inclined to stress the ultimate goal of tracing everything back to "some *one* single principle," and he is well aware of the risks of premature or inadequately supported generalization. The true critic is philosophical, certainly, but also diffident and sensible, serving reason and fact, seeking always "that kind of proof his subject admits of." He refuses to offer conjectures as truths, reasonings for facts, or probabilities for demonstrations, and must always be ready to sacrifice "the most brilliant, the most specious hypotheses to truth."[29] As one would expect, Gibbon also gives more weight than Hurd to the need for solid historical knowledge. Throughout the *Essay* he insists that an acquaintance with antiquity is the only valid comment on the writings of the ancients; their delicacies and graces can be appreciated at their true value only by those with a "portion of antique taste," derived from a thorough and circumstantial knowledge of the conditions and manners of the past.[30] These ideas do not clearly separate Hurd's philosophy from Gibbon's, for Hurd accepted all of them in principle, but in the actual practice of critical thought Gibbon's insistence on methodological caution and scholarly self-discipline could make a good deal of difference. These attitudes did, in fact, influence his response to Hurd's arguments at several points.

Gibbon's coverage of the various elements of Hurd's edition, though selective, comprehends a wide range of subjects and critical problems. Either by abstract or by counterargument (most often by a combination of the two), he considers Hurd's theses on the design or plan of both epistles, as set forth in their respective Commentaries; nine separate Notes on the *Art of Poetry* and two on *To Augustus;* and the two main Dissertations, on drama and on poetical imitation, with a briefer allusion to the letter to Mason on the marks of imitation. The types of problem involved may be summarized as follows:

1. Questions of historical fact (development of satire as a genre in Roman literature, the general character of ancient wit).

2. Questions of interpretation and evaluation of particular works and writers (the purpose of Virgil's third *Georgic,* consistency of characterization in the *Iphigenia* and *Electra* of Euripides, the unity and coherence of argument in Horace's two didactic epistles).

3. Questions concerning the validity or aesthetic utility of particular

rules or devices in certain genres (the chorus in tragedy, figurative language in poetry, the practice of beginning an epic narration at a climactic moment, in the midst of things).

4. Questions concerning the definition of species and general laws of a major genre (the drama), or still broader questions of poetic theory (definitions of beauty, the nature of poetic imitation).

All these questions were, of course, initially posed by Hurd, but Gibbon selected them for discussion because he too found them legitimate and significant. They are representative, though not exhaustively, of the kinds of problem which seemed important to this school of critics, and which their methods were designed to resolve.

Within their common critical mode, the conceptual tools available to Gibbon and Hurd in dealing with such questions were numerous, varied, and highly flexible. Reasoning might be either inductive or deductive, moving upward from observed particulars to empirical generalizations or downward from principles to account for phenomena. In either case it is explicitly probabilistic, true only for the most part, though there is no effort toward nor expectation of statistical precision; both men recognize higher and lower degrees of probability, but without any stated canons for comparing weights of evidence. In deductive arguments, the concept of ''principle'' is vaguely defined, being applied indifferently to premises or hypotheses at all levels of generality and with widely varying rigor of antecedent proof. Inductions, similarly, are often carried out in token fashion, by identifying sources or classes of potentially observable instances; both Hurd and Gibbon frequently appeal for confirmation of their generalizations to the testimony of experts (''every man of letters''), majority opinion (''it has been often observed''), or the common experience of all men (''I appeal to the breast of every one'').[31] On questions of value, discussion turns on ends and means—a poetic technique, practice, or concrete handling of materials is justified or censured by its efficacy or inefficacy in fulfilling aesthetic purposes determined by reason, tradition, established convention, or individual choice.

The rich resourcefulness of this kind of criticism arises in part from the variety and pliability of these devices of argument, in part from the innumerable combinations which could be effected within its working vocabulary, a set of terms and distinctions familiar to all students of the period: beauties or graces, pleasure, sublimity, verisimilitude, the epopoea; fable, manners, arrangement, and style; the circumstances and maxims of an age; reason and fact, reason and sentiment, passion and imagination, vividness and propriety, a subject and its management, and others far too numerous to list. If this whole world of discourse appears, from this account, as loose and uncontrolled as it is versatile, it is true that one cannot claim any high order of rigor for such a way of reasoning. We may observe, however, that eighteenth-century critics of this school were at least better trained logically, more conscious of the problems, principles, and techniques of argument with which they worked, and more sophisticated about the limitations of their own methods than many critics, including those of our own day. I wonder, indeed, whether standards of proof in literary criticism have been much more rigorous in any period.

ℨℨℨ

In the preceding section, I was describing a way of reasoning in criticism which was practiced not only by Gibbon and Hurd but by others in their time as well. We would not do justice to these writers, however, if we did not attempt to convey some sense of the very different ways in which minds as diverse as Gibbon's and Hurd's could operate within that mode of discourse. Since this can best be done by following the actual processes of thought, as the critic reasons on particular problems, I propose to devote the rest of this essay to an analysis of two of Gibbon's more extended comments on Hurd, his examination of the essay "On Poetical Imitation" and his discussion of the rule of *in medias res* in epic poetry.[32]

In his dissertation on imitation, Hurd had undertaken to consider two questions, though Gibbon discussed only the first:

> *Whether that Conformity in Phrase or Sentiment between two writers of different times, which we call* IMITATION, *may not with probability enough, for the most part, be accounted for from general causes, arising from our common nature; that is, from the exercise of our natural faculties on such objects as lie in common to all observers.*

The only way to resolve this question, Hurd says, is "by taking the matter pretty deep, and deducing from it its *first principles*."[33] The argument is very elaborate, covering almost a hundred and fifty pages in the 1766 edition (III, 1-146), but its basic structure is simple. Gibbon says that Hurd "accounts for resemblances of works, by resemblances of things";[34] it would be more accurate to say, by resemblances of things *and* minds, objects and natural faculties. Nature is always the same, and human beings respond to it in uniform ways; hence their representations of nature in art are inevitably similar, and men widely separated in time and space must arrive independently at identical sentiments and images. Except where there are very special circumstances, therefore, Hurd contends that similarities between writers "may, for the most part, and with the highest probability, be accounted for from . . . the same common principles of nature."[35]

In this as in other parts of Hurd's commentary on Horace, Gibbon finds the subject well worth discussing ("extremely curious"), and the treatment highly original and interesting; the author has shown great learning and ingenuity, cites many ancient and modern examples, and criticizes them with taste. Nevertheless, Gibbon "must decline subscribing to Mr. Hurd's theory."[36] His reasons are presented in three separate arguments.

He begins by pointing out the extreme and unqualified character of Hurd's thesis: not merely that the ideas and methods employed by the ancients were natural, but actually "the *sole natural ones*," and consequently that later poets, if endued with judgment, not only "*might,* but *must*" rediscover them independently. Gibbon is quite willing to allow that there may be similitude without imitation, but he cannot believe that this is true in all cases; if some resemblances in writings can be explained by resemblances of things, certainly there must be others which result, intentionally or unintentionally, from the intimate knowledge of the ancients, engraved on our minds by education, and from our veneration for them as models. There is, therefore, a strong prima facie case for suspecting that where a resemblance is striking, there is imitation. This is the easiest and most natural explanation, and in the absence of contrary evidence it should be preferred.

In the second phase of his argument, Gibbon offers one of those token inductions mentioned above.[37] To offset Hurd's deductions a priori, the question may be examined a posteriori by citing two kinds of example: striking similarities between writers who had no knowledge of each other, and images and sentiments in modern writers which are original and without ancient parallels. The first category would tend to support Hurd, but such instances are hard to find; some of them might be explained (as in the case of Shakespeare) by the general diffusion of learning in the writer's age, and those remaining would prove only what Gibbon concedes, that resemblances may occur without imitation. Instances in the second category would be much easier to find, even in writers who practice "an open, perpetual imitation of the ancients." From such examples it would follow a fortiori that these writers would have been still more original if they had written from their own natural feelings and observations. Gibbon recognizes that such evidence cannot be decisive, but he thinks that the advantage would not be on Hurd's side if the induction were carried out.

In the last part of his comment on the dissertation, Gibbon makes "two or three general observations, which may give an idea, both of his method of reasoning, and of my objections to it." These observations go to the root of Hurd's argument, suggesting that his whole enterprise is overambitious, because the principles from which he deduces his solution of the problem could never be convincingly proved:

He enters upon a task, in my opinion, far above human abilities. To examine the origin of our ideas is the business of metaphysics, and the greatest philosophers have failed in the attempt. But it is perhaps still more difficult to embrace them all at one view, and to class them according to their different objects, in so accurate a manner as to assure ourselves that we have suffered no material species to escape. This is, however, what Mr. Hurd undertakes.

This basic objection is developed and supported by three supplementary arguments. In the first of these, interestingly, Gibbon makes the same criticism that Hurd raises against Longinus, Bouhours, and Addison: "his smallest species are yet too general to prove anything," for it is on highly particularized similarities that a charge of imitation is founded, not on such broad, categorical resemblances as Hurd's theory might explain. In his two final objections, Gibbon once again shows his preference for inductive over deductive arguments, his desire for facts as well as reasonings. "Let us, for a moment, abandon fiction, and enter into historic truth." The annals of any nation will show that character, passion, and situation, in their effects on manners, can "combine in such a variety of ways, as no algebra could reach." When we add that human nature, modified by changing manners, government, religion, and other variables, appears in a different shape to the writers of every age and country, the shifting picture of mankind seems to afford "a most extensive and infinite range of ideas, almost sufficient of itself to preserve genius from imitation." In these last remarks, Gibbon is himself making deductions from first principles—from general causes of variation in human life—but the principles are drawn from abundant empirical evidence, preserved in the factual accounts of history. In the face of this evidence, we should be cautious about supposing that "the operations of human nature are easily classed, or circumscribed."

Our final example, Gibbon's discussion of the traditional rule that the epic poem should begin in the midst of things, is particularly worth examining because only a small portion of it is devoted to Hurd's note on the subject.[38] Here Gibbon "presumes to think for himself" in an independent consideration of an important critical question, a crucial precept for both the composition of poems by writers and their evaluation by readers and critics. In the course of his argument he also reveals something about his own responses as a reader, the affective as well as the intellectual dimensions of his critical capacity. I shall pass over his brief but cogent remarks on Hurd, confining my analysis to Gibbon's own reasons and conclusions.[39]

The first of his four arguments is similar to one of his criticisms of Hurd's thesis on poetical imitation: the proposition is too broad and general to provide a solution in particular cases. To say that the epic poet should rush into the midst of things, leaving antecedent events to be revealed by way of episode through the mouth of the hero, gives little help to a writer trying to decide on his narrative strategy. The principal subject can be stated in general terms—the anger of Achilles or the establishment of Aeneas in Italy—but all such actions consist of many events which contribute to the final outcome. The rule assumes that there is a self-evident distinction between the main action and its subordinate parts, but offers no criterion for making this distinction. Since all the events have some connection with the subject, one could go through a long sorites, asking of every incident whether it was part of the principal subject or merely preparatory to it, should be related first or later; the rule would never provide an answer. Even if founded on reason, it is too vague to be reduced to practice.

The second and third of Gibbon's arguments could be well described as studies in the rhetoric of fiction, since they concern the response of readers to a narrative organized as the traditional rule prescribes. When we are thrown at once into the midst of the subject, without any preparation, we are surprised and perplexed. Having only a faint idea of the characters or the situation of the hero, we cannot be greatly moved by his misfortunes or concerned for his fate; there may be beauties, but not those powerful emotional effects which are the aim and proper pleasure of an epic poem. When these initial difficulties have been worked through and the reader begins to enter fully into present events, the rule requires the poet to interrupt the momentum of his story and turn his reader's attention to antecedent events about which he has little or no curiosity at that point. "Is this consulting the pleasure of the reader? and that pleasure ought to be the aim of every writer."

This analysis is supported both by general reasons drawn from laws of the mind and by an account of Gibbon's own response in two particular cases, the *Aeneid* and *Iphigenia in Aulis*. In the first, Gibbon is almost as bold and self-confident as Hurd in his assertions about the workings of the human mind. "In every operation of the mind," he says, "there is a much higher delight in descending from the cause to the effect, than in ascending from the effect to the cause." In reading a fable, consequently, it is the event we are anxious about, and "our anxiety increases, or diminishes, as that event is known or unknown to us." The principle is plausible enough, and perhaps could be confirmed by evidences of the kind which Gibbon found convincing, but he does not attempt to prove its validity here. The passage illustrates rather neatly the seductive attractions of this way of reasoning, as well as the risks inherent in its use.

Gibbon uses the *Aeneid* to illustrate the disadvantages of the narrative method he is attacking, but he reveals himself as a great admirer of Virgil's power over the emotions. If we have read his poem as it deserves, by the end of the first book our feelings have been fully engaged, "taking the greatest part in the important scene which begins to disclose itself." After the interruption of the action for a long recital of the sack of Troy and the voyages of Aeneas, "when we finally return to Dido, we have almost forgotten who she was." This sequence of feelings is a tribute to Virgil's imaginative mastery, but not to his judgment in the choice of narrative methods or the arrangement of his fable. The *Iphigenia* (which Gibbon knew in the version ending with the Messenger's report of the heroine's miraculous escape, rejected as spurious by modern scholars) is cited to support his claim that even on second or later perusals of a great work, when the reader is aware of the final outcome, his absorption in the action and anxiety to know the catastrophe are almost as great as they were on the first reading:

> Although, when we can coolly reflect, we are acquainted with the event, yet the true poet, by interesting our passions, chains us down to the present moment, and prevents our seeing any thing beyond it. When I read the tragedy of Iphigenia for the twentieth time, I know Iphigenia will not be sacrificed; but the struggles of Agamemnon, the rage of Achilles, the despair of Clytemnestra, make me ignorant, and tremblingly anxious for the event.

Those who do not understand this, Gibbon suggests, have a very inadequate idea of "the power of imagination." In his own case, clearly, the imaginative and emotional engagement was intense.

Gibbon's fourth and final argument, which concerns the stylistic consequences of the Horatian precept, shows once again that he operated within the critical mode of his time, but in his own way. The argument turns on the nature of the epopoea, as a poetic species, on the psychological bases of the special pleasure it is designed to give, and on stylistic decorum, appropriateness of expression to the character and situation of speakers. Transport is the aesthetic purpose of an epic poem, and bold figures and poetic imagery are essential to its effects. There are two natural sources of such figures, "strong passion, and a fine imagination":[40]

> The first can operate, in any strong degree, only during the actual influence of the misfortune which gave birth to it; and though the recollection of the latter may call forth some sparks of the former, yet it will be a faint, reflected heat, very unequal to the great effect of transporting both the speaker and the hearer.

As for the second source, a fine imagination is no essential part of a hero's character, but it is the poet's most essential gift, which he properly uses to the fullest extent in those portions of the story which he relates himself. The consequences to be inferred from these positions may be summed up in a dilemma: in reporting past actions through the mouth of the hero, the poet must either violate propriety by expressing the hero's thoughts and feelings with unnatural eloquence or sacrifice the aims of his poem and the imaginative satisfaction of his readers by representing events in simple, unadorned words, "far inferior, as to style, to the rest of the poem." It is a strong proof of the inconveniences of the inverted narrative method, demanded by the rule of *in medias res,* that Virgil had to make Aeneas as great a poet as himself, preferring to avoid the second horn of the dilemma and thus to offend the judgment rather than the imagination of his readers. The dilemma, like the sorites, is a form of syllogism not highly regarded by severe logicians, but it expresses very well the hypothetical and probabilistic character of Gibbon's principles and the paired disjunctive terms through which he reasoned both here and in many other places.

Gibbon did not write his "Extrait raisonné" on Hurd for publication, but to preserve a record of his readings and as a test of his own critical capacity. Though he reaches some original and even startling conclusions on specific issues, he offers no novel fundamental ideas and breaks no new ground in subject or method. But he does show in those thirty folio pages how highly he rated literary criticism, as one of the essential tasks of a complete man of letters, and that he had mastered at an early age the facts and reasonings needed to think for himself on such questions. His approach is philosophical, but the empirical temper of his mind saves him from the kind of "scientifical" hubris which is so characteristic of Hurd. He is "ready and fertile in resources, but void of false refinement," and he checks the flights of abstract speculation by returning to historic truth, the annals of nations, and by testing his psychological hypotheses against his own sensitive perceptions and feelings as a reader. He might have been an excellent critic, if he had not chosen to make his name primarily as a historian. In any case, we may be glad that he preserved his criticism of Hurd among his papers, and that his friend Sheffield had the good judgment to put it into print in the *Miscellaneous Works* after Gibbon's death.

Notes

1. Hurd's edition of *Epistola ad Pisones* was originally published separately in 1749, followed in 1751 by a separate edition of *Ad Augustum*. They were first published together in two volumes in 1753. Gibbon used the Cambridge edition of 1757, which I have not been able to see. References in this paper are to the fourth edition, 3 vols. (London, 1766), hereafter cited as Hurd.

2. *Miscellaneous Works of Edward Gibbon* (London, 1796); hereafter cited as *Miscellaneous Works*. For the "Extrait Raisonné" on Hurd see II, 27-50.

3. This is Gibbon's phrase in the manuscript of his autobiography, also in the British Museum (Add. MSS. 34,874, fol. 45v), for which Sheffield substituted a colorless paraphrase (*Autobiography*, ed. Bernard Groom [London: Macmillan, 1957], p. 99. This conveniently accessible edition, a reprint of Sheffield's text, is hereafter cited as *Autobiography*). The sexual metaphor appealed to Gibbon, for in several other contexts he uses variations of it which Sheffield allowed to stand. He speaks of the unfinished *Decline and Fall* in a letter as "my wife" and of his books in the *Autobiography* as "my seraglio." He "consummated my first labour" by completing the *Essai*, but its publication was delayed because he "shrunk from the press with the terrors of virgin modesty." The *Decline and Fall* was also his child, and in two famous passages he marks both the moment of its conception and the hour of its deliverance (*Private Letters*, ed. Rowland E. Prothero [London, 1896], 2: 143; *Autobiography*, pp. 96, 175, 168). Gibbon did not conceive of himself as a celibate monk—an abhorrent idea—but rather as a man of the world who had found a moral and emotional equivalent of marriage in the life of the mind, in the reading and writing of books.

4. Gibbon had begun to write the *Essai* before leaving Lausanne in April 1758, and he completed the first draft soon after his return to England. It was thoroughly rewritten in the winter of 1758-59 but then kept in his desk until the spring of 1761, when it was published in London by T. Becket and P. A. de Hondt (*Autobiography*, pp. 84-98). References in this paper are to the first edition in English (London, 1764), hereafter cited as *Essay*.

5. *Autobiography*, pp. 104-6.

6. He mentions (*Miscellaneous Works*, II, 26) the *Argentis* of John Barclay (1621) and the edition of Ovid by C.G. Bachet, Sieur de Méziriac (1716). Both titles are listed among the books he owned in Geoffrey L. Keynes, *The Library of Edward Gibbon* (London: Jonathan Cape, 1940), pp. 62, 211.

7. *Autobiography*, pp. 106-8.

8. *Autobiography*, pp. 109-10. Draft B, from which this portion of the *Autobiography* was taken by Sheffield and all subsequent editors, is dated 1788-89 by George A. Bonnard, ed., Edward Gibbon, *Memoirs of My Life* (London, 1966), pp. xiv-xix. The six drafts have been published in *The Autobiographies of Edward Gibbon*, ed. John Murray (London, 1896).

9. B.M. Add. MSS. 34,874, fol. 52v. Cf. Bonnard, pp. 119n. and 297.

10. *Autobiography*, p. 110.

11. He did, however, write an "Extrait raisonné" on Longinus, an "Examination" of Juvenal's satires, an "Enquiry" on catalogues of armies in epic poems, an essay on Ovid's *Fasti*, and "Critical Observations on the Design of the Sixth Book of the Aeneid," a reply to Warburton's interpretation in the *Divine Legation of Moses* (*Miscellaneous Works*, II, 78-87, 95-120, 313-19, 342-46, and 497-525).

12. Hurd, I, xv-xvi.

13. The three dissertations are "On the Provinces of Dramatic Poetry," "On Poetical Imitation," and "On the Marks of Imitation, in a letter of Mr. Mason." A fourth dissertation, "On the Idea of Universal Poetry," not included in 1753 or 1757, was added in later editions.

14. Hurd, I, xv-xvi. Warburton's edition of Pope's *Works* was published in 1751. I have not been able to identify the Italians Hurd refers to.

15. Hurd, II, iii-xix.

16. *Autobiography*, p. 110.

17. In his scathing rebuttal of Warburton's interpretation of *Aeneid* VI, referred to in n.11 above, Gibbon remarks ironically that it may be some "foolish fondness of antiquity, which inclines me to doubt, whether the BISHOP OF GLOUCESTER has really united the severe sense of ARISTOTLE with the sublime imagination of LONGINUS," as Hurd had asserted (*Miscellaneous Works*, II, 522-23).

18. *Miscellaneous Works*, II, 27, 50.

19. See chapter 9, above; Hoyt Trowbridge, ed., Richard Hurd, *Letters on Chivalry and Romance*, Augustan Reprint Series, nos. 101-2 (Los Angeles: William Andrews Clark Memorial Library, 1963), pp. i-xi; idem, "Bishop Hurd: a Reinterpretation," PMLA, 58 (1943),450-65.

20. In these statements Hurd anticipates by six years three of the main theses of David Hume's essay, "Of the Standard of Taste," first published in 1757. A discussion of the companion essay, "Of Tragedy," was added by Hurd in the 1766 edition of his commentary on Horace (Hurd, I, 97-102).

21. Hurd, II, 107-15.

22. *Essay*, pp. 46-47. For other discussions of this work see Georges A. Bonnard, "Gibbon's *Essai sur l'étude de la literature,*" *English Studies,* 32 (1957),145-53; and Ronald S. Crane, "Shifting Definitions and Evaluations of the Humanities," in *The Idea of the Humanities* (Chicago: University of Chicago Press, 1967), I,91-93.

23. In another article, "Le deuxième séjour de Gibbon à Lausanne," in *Mélanges d' histoire et de littérature offerts à Monsieur Charles Gilliard* (Lausanne: Université de Lausanne, 1944), pp. 400-420, Bonnard argues that at this period Gibbon had not yet settled between literary and historical studies as his main talent and interest. It is sufficient for our purposes here to recognize that Gibbon, while eventually devoting most of his energy to history, always believed that literary criticism was of equal dignity and equally necessary in a complete humanistic scholarship.

24. *Autobiography*, pp. 94-95.

25. *Essay*, p. 77.

26. Ibid., pp. 86-91.

27. Ibid., p. 48.

28. Ibid., pp. 45-46, 50.

29. *Essay*, pp. 48-50.

30. Ibid., pp. 25-26; cf. pp. 29-30, 32, 91, and passim.

31. These examples are cited from *Miscellaneous Works,* II, 29, 30, 45, but they could easily be paralleled by similar statements elsewhere in the "Extrait" and in Hurd's commentary.

32. These two comments, as well as the one on "Provinces of the Drama," run to five or six printed pages each. Gibbon's discussions of the origins of Roman satire, figurative language in tragedy, and the uses of the chorus are briefer, two to three pages each.

33. Hurd, III, 1-2.

34. *Miscellaneous Works*, II, 46.

35. Hurd, III, 6-7; cf. 51-52, 79, 100-101, 115-16.

36. *Miscellaneous Works*, II, 45-50; specific page references will not be cited.

37. An elegant example of this kind of argument is the series of affirmative and negative instances offered by Hume to confirm his theory in "Of Tragedy," in *Of the Standard of Taste and Other Essays,* ed. John W. Lenz (Indianapolis: Bobbs-Merrill Co., 1965), pp. 33-37.

38. Note on the *Art of Poetry,* verse 148, in Hurd, I, 121-24.

39. *Miscellaneous Works*, II, 30-35; specific page references will not be cited.

40. The theory of figurative language in poetry is discussed more fully in another comment on Hurd, *Miscellaneous Works*, II, 28-30.

11

Platonism and Sir Joshua Reynolds

It has sometimes been said that neoclassical critics like Johnson and Reynolds, who held that art derives its value in part at least from a representation of general and enduring truth, were "Idealists" and subscribed to a Platonic or pseudo-Platonic aesthetics.[1] Louis I. Bredvold, citing Reynolds among others, has discussed an "affinity between Neo-Classicism and Platonism," a relationship in spirit and theory which, he believes, may help us to understand the special inspiration of eighteenth-century art. The basis of this affinity, Bredvold says, lies in a similarity of aim: "The whole effort of Neo-Classicism was to express ideal truth and ideal beauty; the Platonists saw in the finished art, so far as it was great and genuine, a revelation of a transcendent truth and beauty, a visible embodiment of the unseen Idea." Although he finds a "general indifference towards transcendental metaphysics" in the eighteenth-century writers, Brevold sees in Reynolds's *Discourses on Art* a conception of ideal beauty "which leads beyond Aristotle, and which Reynolds, like Bellori, Père André, Winckelmann, and other men of similar tendencies, definitely thought of as Platonic rather than Aristotelian." If, he suggests, men like Reynolds had been metaphysicians, they would have been Platonists.[2]

Certainly it would be a mistake to deny that eighteenth-century aesthetic and critical theories show some similarity to various types of idealism, or that Platonic theory, as the archetypal idealism, is sometimes echoed by writers of that period. Nevertheless there were strong anti-Platonic currents in

Reprinted, with permission of Swets Publishing Service, Lisse, Holland, from *English Studies,* 21 (1939), 1-7.

eighteenth-century thought, as Bredvold recognizes, and because of the British empirical tradition, this was particularly true in England; for that reason, any attempt to trace a "tendency towards Platonism" through the period is likely, even with so cautious a scholar as Brevold, to be misleading. I hope to show in the succeeding pages that Reynolds, who is taken as a representative figure, shows a tendency away from Platonism much more prominently than any attraction towards it. More specifically, it will be argued that the true philosophical affinity of Reynolds's aesthetic system is not Plato but John Locke.

Two quotations will illustrate the element of "idealism" in Reynolds's thought. The first occurs in the third of his *Discourses:*

> The poets, orators, and rhetoricians of antiquity are continually enforcing this position; that all the arts receive their perfection from an ideal beauty, superior to what is to be found in individual nature. They are ever referring to the practice of the painters and sculptors of their times, particularly Phidias . . . to illustrate their assertions. As if they could not sufficiently express their admiration of his genius by what they knew, they have recourse to poetical enthusiasm. They call it inspiration; a gift from heaven. The artist is supposed to have ascended to celestial regions, to furnish his mind with this perfect idea of beauty.[3]

The second illustration is from a note written by Reynolds for William Mason's translation of du Fresnoy's *De Arte Graphica:*

> There is an absolute necessity for the Painter to generalize his notions; to paint particulars is not to paint nature, it is only to paint circumstances. When the Artist has conceived in his imagination the image of perfect beauty, or the abstract idea of forms, he may be said to be admitted into the great council of Nature, and to
>
> > Trace beauty's beam to its eternal spring,
> > And pure to man the fire celestial bring.[4]

These two passages express clearly one of Reynolds's most fundamental conceptions: the belief that the sublime artist is not a mechanical copyist like the camera obscura, but an imitator of "the idea of that central form, if I may so express it, from which every deviation is deformity."[5] The painter must absolutely generalize his notions.

That these remarks approach somewhat closely to Platonism, in a nontechnical sense, need not be denied. On the other hand, it should be noted that Reynolds makes them with an air of deprecation, in a conditional or "as if'' tone. This is particularly clear in the first passage, where the remark that ancient critics ''have recourse to poetical enthusiasm'' suggests that their extravagance should be discounted. With the general principle of selection and generalization Reynolds of course had no quarrel, but he conceived this principle in commonsense terms. In the second passage, too, Reynolds is careful to state that the artist ''may be said to be'' admitted into the great council of nature. Furthermore, the word ''abstract'' which he applies to the ''idea of forms'' implies an empirical epistomology.

Reynolds was in fact far from accepting an idealist conception of the universe or of nature. The genuinely idealistic Renaissance view was that the value of art and the source of aesthetic pleasure lay in the representation of ideal forms. Reynolds's view, though historically derived from the earlier theory, lacked this universal validation, this sanction from the eternal, transcendental Idea: he simply sheared away the transempirical realm behind the artist's conception. It was for this reason that he declared, in one of the most eloquent passages in the *Discourses,* that the artist's idea ''subsists only in the mind; the sight never beheld it, nor has the hand expressed it; it is an idea residing in the breast of the artist. . . .''[6] It was for this reason too that he explicitly rejected the doctrine expounded in the remarks on Phidias quoted above, and warned his hearers that ''such enthusiastic admiration seldom promotes knowledge.'' The student, Reynolds declares:

> Examines his own mind, and perceives there nothing of that divine inspiration, with which, he is told, so many others have been favoured. He never travelled to heaven to gather new ideas; and he finds himself possessed of no other qualifications than what mere common observation and a plain understanding can confer. . . . This great ideal perfection and beauty are not to be sought in the heavens, but upon the earth. They are about us, and upon every side of us.[7]

It was in this very un-Platonic spirit, holding himself, like others, to have no qualifications but what ''mere common observation and a plain understanding'' could give, that Reynolds approached the problems of aesthetics. If, he says,

> In order to be intelligible, I appear to degrade art by bringing her down from the visionary situation in the clouds, it is only to give her a more solid mansion upon the earth. It is necessary that at some time or other we should see things as they really are, and not impose on ourselves by that false magnitude with which objects appear when viewed indistinctly as through a mist.[8]

In this spirit Reynolds rewrote traditional theory of painting, taking over from his predecessors some terms, the general conception of beauty that was not photographic, that was in some way heightened, purified, or clarified, and a prejudice against such styles as the Dutch, which give "exact representation of individual objects with all their imperfections."[9] He adopted these attitudes and principles but reinterpreted them in such a way that they were consistent with an empirical metaphysics and psychology.

❦❦❦

In this reinterpretation, the idea imitated by the artist is not conceived as universal at all but rather as "general"—that is, as representing the widely distributed, the customary. The particular is for Reynolds the "local and temporary," a deviation not from any hypothetical ideal but from empirical nature's "accustomed practice."[10] The power, he says,

> of discovering what is deformed in Nature, or, in other words, what is particular and uncommon, can be acquired only by experience; and the whole beauty and grandeur of the art consists, in my opinion, in being able to get above all singular forms, local customs, particularities, and details of every kind.[11]

The resemblance between this view and the teachings of Locke is very close. Locke maintained that the substantial forms or transcendental ideas of the schoolmen were meaningless and unintelligible. All our ideas "terminate in" or are "ultimately founded upon" ideas of sensation or reflection; experience is therefore always concrete and particular. Reality itself, quite apart from our ideas of it, is wholly made up of particulars, and consequently "*general* and *universal* belong not to the real existence of things; but are the inventions and creatures of the understanding, made by it for its own use, and concern only signs, whether words or ideas."[12] This explains Reynolds's more eloquently worded assertion that the ideal "subsists only in the mind" and must be "an idea residing in the breast of the artist."

Locke's nominalism was, however, not complete. Nature was not for him indeterminate and chaotic; objects possessed real similarities which provided a basis for arranging them into classes:

> Many particular substances are so made by Nature, that they have agreement and likeness one with another, and so afford a foundation of being ranked into sorts.[13]

Thus it was possible for "sortal names," though made by the mind and not by nature, to "signify or represent many particular objects."[14] They were signs representing the idea of a class, and they could represent many particular objects because from them, by a process which Locke called "partial consideration," irrelevant individual variations had been abstracted.

Reynolds's "great ideal perfection and beauty" are the analogue in painting of Locke's sortal names or nominal essences. Being derived by the elimination of local variations in experienced particular objects, they are, of course, "not to be sought in the heavens, but upon the earth," as Reynolds wrote in a passage already quoted. On the other hand they are fictions of the mind and consequently not to be found in individual real objects, but rather in the minds of men.

At this point the only significant difference between the two theorists lies in the degree of emphasis they give to natural similarities. Locke was inclined to minimize them, to insist that since "the real internal . . . constitution of things" is hidden from us, generalization must be merely approximate. Reynolds, on the other hand, returned again and again to the idea of uniformity; he was more confident than Locke that the minds of men, as the external forms of objects, were genuinely similar to each other and therefore susceptible to generalization and abstraction. Locke's belief that we are limited to probabilities in the comprehension of external things prevented dogmatism on this question. But Reynolds, being a painter and not a metaphysician, was not interested in the "real internal constitution of things." He was satisfied to accept similarities at the perceptual level as absolute.

At the same time he bolstered his belief in uniformity, which in itself was not characteristically Lockeian, by appeals to Locke's empirical psychology:

> The internal fabrick of our minds, as well as the external forms of our bodies, being nearly uniform; it seems then to follow of course, that as the imagination is incapable of producing any thing originally of itself, and can only vary and combine those ideas with which it is furnished by means of the senses, there will be necessarily an agreement of the imaginations, as in the senses of men.[15]

Thus even while emphasizing a uniformity which Locke would have minimized, Reynolds grounded his belief on Locke's epistemological position. This dependence may also be illustrated by Reynolds's definition of truth:

> The natural appetite or taste of the human mind is for TRUTH; whether that truth results from the real agreement or equality of original ideas among themselves; from the agreement of the representation of any object with the thing represented; or from the correspondence of the several parts of any arrangement with each other.[16]

What is this but an application of Locke's definition of knowledge:

> Knowledge then seems to me to be nothing but the perception of the connexion and agreement, or disagreement and repugnancy of any of our ideas.[17]

To Locke and to the British empirical tradition in general, then, we may confidently ascribe Reynolds's considered and reiterated definition of the universal or ideal as the common, the usual, the widely distributed—a definition which makes his aesthetics predominantly conceptualistic, empirical, and anti-Platonic.

✖✖✖

But since Reynolds did demand that the artist select and clarify nature as it was presented to him by sense, the distinction which has been drawn here between his conceptualism and a true idealism, though accepted as valid, may still be thought merely technical. Bredvold concedes that "the eighteenth century did not focus its attention on Platonic ideas, preferring something more definite and less atmospheric," but he believes that "a philosophical influence is none the less real because it has ceased to operate as a doctrine and become an inspiration and a mode of enjoyment."[18]

For several reasons, it does not seem possible to agree even with this statement of indirect and diffused influence. I have said that Reynolds's aesthetic theories were historically derived from the Renaissance Platonizers; but to identify his views with theirs is to obscure one of the central phenomena of English aesthetic theory in the eighteenth century—a process which may be called the empiricization of Renaissance terminology and concepts. Bredvold refers to Dryden's "suspicious admiration" for the confused pseudo-Platonism of Bellori.[19] In Reynolds, who was more strongly influenced by Renaissance Platonism than any other important English writer of his time, this suspicion had increased, had become a conviction that "such enthusiastic admiration seldom promotes knowledge."

The same process of bringing down to earth may be observed in eighteenth-century discussions of inspiration, genius, invention, and so on. It can be seen, I hope without reading in too broad an implication, in a sentence of Pope's:

> Imagination has no limits, and that is a sphere in which you may move on to eternity; but where one is confined to truth, or, to speak more like a human creature, to the appearances of truth, we soon find the shortness of our tether.[20]

It was always the aim of these men to "speak more like a human creature," or, as Reynolds himself said, to give art and thought "a more solid mansion upon the earth." To most eighteenth-century thinkers, Platonism could seem nothing but enthusiasm, an untenable, extravagant counsel of perfection. To men like Locke and Pope and Johnson, art did well if it portrayed the "appearances of truth."

In the second place, the association of Reynolds with idealism tends to obscure an entirely different and at least equally important aspect of his views. In idealistic theory, as we have seen, art can be defended on the ground of its revelation of eternal truth and beauty. For Reynolds this transcendental sanction was not possible. In a few passages—those which provide the substantial basis for Bredvold's sense of an affinity between Platonism and neoclassicism—Reynolds makes use of an analogous argument, declaring the mere representation of "general truth" to be a sufficient validation for art. But frequently he expresses a different belief, and one which seems to leave representation, though not nature, quite out of account:

> My notion of nature comprehends not only the forms which nature produces, but also the nature and internal fabrick and organization, as I may call it, of the human mind and imagination.[21]

And again:

> Whatever pleases has in it what is analogous to the mind, and is, therefore, in the highest and best sense of the word, natural.[22]

This shift in definition from the external world to the mind of man has profound significance for the artist. It means, in the first place, that his focus of attention is turned away from representation and toward his audience. Consequently,

> Everything is to be done with which it is natural for the mind to be pleased, whether it proceeds from simplicity or variety, uniformity or irregularity; whether the scenes are familiar or exotic; rude and wild, or enriched and cultivated; for it is natural for the mind to be pleased with all these in their turn.[23]

This shift means too that the artist must consult "common sense deciding upon the common feelings of mankind,"[24] and that along with appeals to which all men will respond, the artist will not hesitate to exploit "what we have called apparent or secondary truths, proceeding from local and temporary prejudices, fancies, fashions, or accidental connection of ideas." Of these secondary truths, Reynolds says:

If it appears that these last have still their foundation, however slender, in the original fabrick of our minds; it follows that all these truths or beauties deserve and require the attention of the artist, in proportion to their stability or duration, or as their influence is more or less extensive.[25]

Nothing could be much less idealistic than this.

Finally, the association of neoclassicism with idealism tends to conceal what seems to me the most distinctive feature of eighteenth-century art—its public and social character. Accepting human limitation and imperfection, the neoclassical artist achieved his satisfaction from a belief that "a general union of minds, like a general combination of the forces of all mankind, makes a strength that is irresistible."[26] Human beings do not ascend to celestial regions; they have no insight but what "common observation and a plain understanding" can furnish them with. The individual is weak, but the tradition is greater than any member of it. If their art was grounded neither in a misty and incomprehensible ideal nor in the aberrations and imperfections of the single individual, Reynolds believed that poets and painters, by a general union of minds working in the spirit of public service, might gradually effect social progress. So conceived, art may at last

be so far diffused, that its effects may extend themselves imperceptibly into publick benefits, and be among the means of bestowing on whole nations refinement of taste: which if it does not lead directly to purity of manners, obviates at least their greatest depravation, by disentangling the mind from appetite, and conducting the thoughts through successive stages of excellence, till that contemplation of universal rectitude and harmony which began by Taste, may, as it is exalted and refined, conclude in Virtue.[27]

It was from such a faith, rather than from any diluted idealism, that eighteenth-century English art derived its special depth and dignity.

Notes

1. E. N. S. Thompson writes: "The doctrines of the ideal form and universal truth are as old as Plato and Aristotle. From his early teacher, Zacharia L. Mudge, 'the wisest man' he ever knew, Reynolds had imbibed Plato's teaching, and the theory of the ideal had become an artist's commonplace through the teaching of du Fresnoy, Dryden, Bellori, and other critics'' ("The *Discourses* of Sir Joshua Reynolds," *PMLA*, 32 [1917], 339-66). Cf. A. Bosker, *Literary Criticism in the Age of Johnson* (Gronigen: Walters, 1930), pp. 80-85; W. P. Ker, ed., *Essays of John Dryden* (Oxford: Clarendon Press, 1926), I, lix; and Michael Macklem, "Reynolds and the Ambiguities of Neo-Classical Criticism," *PQ*, 31 (1952), 383-98.

2. L. I. Bredvold, "The Tendency towards Platonism in Neo-Classical Esthetics," *ELH*, 1 (1934), 91-119. See also his *Selected Poems of Alexander Pope* (New York: F. S. Crofts, 1926), pp. xxi-xxiv.

3. Reynolds, *Discourses on Art*, ed. Robert R. Wark (San Marino, Calif.: Huntington Library, 1959), Lect. III, p. 42.

4. *The Works of William Mason* (London, 1811), III, 81. The couplet is quoted from lines 19-20 of Mason's translation of du Fresnoy.

5. *Discourses*, III, 45. According to René Bray, "il y a deux états de nature pour les théoriciens classiques, d'abord la nature materielle, 'la grossiere nature,' puis la nature idéale, rationnelle, choisie, ordonnée, organisée par l'esprit. Et c'est celle-ci que l'art doit imiter. Nous voici loin du naturalisme" (*La Formation de la doctrine classique* [Paris: Librairie Hachette, 1927], pp. 156-57). It should be noted that nature "selected, ordered, and organized" is not necessarily "ideal" in a technical sense.

6. *Discourses*, IX, 171.

7. Ibid., III, 43-44.

8. Ibid., VII, 119.

9. Ibid., p. 124.

10. Ibid. Lovejoy therefore cites Reynolds as an exponent of the view that art should imitate general or average, as against ideal, types (A.O. Lovejoy, " 'Nature' as Aesthetic Norm," *MLN*, 42 [1927],444-50). Wark, while continuing to associate Reynolds with a tradition going back to Plato and Aristotle, says that he "is more empirical than many of his predecessors; that is, he relies more on direct observation and a sort of averaging process rather than on what might be called inspiration" (*Discourses*, pp. xix-xx).

11. *Discourses*, III, 44.

12. Locke, *Essay concerning Human Understanding*, ed. A. C. Fraser (Oxford: Clarendon Press, 1894), Bk. III, Ch. iii, sec. 11.

13. Ibid., III, vi, 30; cf. III, iii, 13.

14. Ibid., III, iii, 11. Locke's conception of nominal essences helps to explain Reynolds's insistence both on imitation of classical models and on observation and the practice of painting from life. The classical models, being permanent, help the painter to discover the qualities which are general and enduring; to paraphrase Pope, Phidias and Nature were, he found, the same. Yet the great paintings of the past are only guides, and the ultimate basis of the artist's conception of his subject must always be "many particular substances," observed in experience.

15. *Discourses*, VII, 132.

16. Ibid., VII, 122.

17. Locke, *Essay*, IV, i, 1. A serious weakness of Kenneth MacLean's *John Locke and English Literature of the Eighteenth-Century* (New Haven: Yale University Press, 1936) is its failure to discuss influences of this sort. His method is too much that of the classical source-study, emphasizing verbal resemblances and the recurrence of illustrative detail, to reveal these much more interesting and significant philosophical analogies.

18. Bredvold, *Selected Poems of Alexander Pope*, p. xxiii.

19. Ibid. See Dryden, "Parallel of Poetry and Painting," in *Essays*, ed. Ker, II, 123-24.

20. *Works of Pope*, ed. W. Elwin and W. J. Courthope, VII, 330.

21. *Discourses*, VII, 124.

22. Ibid., p. 127.

23. Ibid. Cf. W. J. Hipple, Jr., *The Beautiful, the Sublime, and the Picturesque in Eighteenth-Century British Aesthetic Theory* (Carbondale, Ill.: Southern Illinois University Press, 1957), Ch. 9, pp. 136-37.

24. *Discourses*, VII, 131.

25. Ibid., p. 141; cf. 122, 139. In Reynolds's system, Hipple observes, "opinion as well as truth must be regarded by the artist, and its authority is proportioned to the universality of the prejudice." Such concessions mark the difference of his system from Plato's, in which "the highest art of Reynolds would be second-best" (p. 146).

26. *Discourses,* VII, 132.

27. Ibid., IX, 171. In a sense quite different from Bredvold's, Reynolds may justly be called a Platonist. In his brilliant paper, "Literary Criticism and the Concept of Imitation in Antiquity," *MP,* 34 (1936),1-35, Richard McKeon distinguishes between the *methods* of Plato and Aristotle. The latter proceeded by literal definition of terms and the division of knowledge into a number of distinct sciences. Plato, however, by reason of his special approach or method, found it impossible to consider art without regard to its moral and political effects; the different sciences coalesce and terminology is not literal or univocal but varies with the context. Cf. Elder Olson, ed., *Longinus on the Sublime and Sir Joshua Reynolds' Discourses on Art* (Chicago: Packard & Co., 1945), pp. vii-xxi; and Hipple, especially pp. 136, 138, 141.

PART FOUR

The Theory and Practice of
Probable Reasoning

12

Scattered Atoms of Probability

In his *Life of Dryden,* after several paragraphs surveying his author's knowledge of literature, Dr. Johnson concludes that Dryden owed less to profound or systematic study than to conversation, desultory reading, and a remarkably quick and vigilant mind. He immediately adds:

> Of all this however if the proof be demanded I will not undertake to give it; the atoms of probability, of which my opinion has been formed, lie scattered over all his works: and by him who thinks the question worth his notice his works must be perused with very close attention.[1]

This brief passage implies some interesting facts of intellectual and cultural history. Johnson assumes—as a writer today surely could not assume—that his readers are familiar with the technical or semitechnical vocabulary of logic, the skill or science concerned with proofs and evidences, so that a phrase like "atoms of probability" will be readily intelligible. The word "opinion," too, appears to carry a more precise and definite meaning than it would bear in most other ages. He also takes for granted a certain attitude of mind, an understanding of his way of reasoning sympathetic enough to assure his readers' acceptance of his refusal as reasonable—neither lazy nor ungracious, but fully warranted by the methodological complexities involved in proving such a proposition. A branch of logic particularly concerned with a kind of empirical reasoning which gropes toward truth, sometimes attaining a fair approximation to it but never full intellectual clarity and certainty, must have been quite well known to the educated reading public of Johnson's day.

This essay originally appeared in *Eighteenth-Century Studies,* 5 (1971), 1-38; permission to reprint it has been granted by the American Society for Eighteenth-Century Studies.

Similar passages occur nearly everywhere in eighteenth-century British writings—not only in biography and criticism, but also in works on religion, philosophy, morals, history, politics, and almost every subject of general human concern. Butler's *Analogy of Religion* begins with an "Introduction" on probable evidence, and Hume's *Treatise* and *Enquiry* both include chapters on the same subject.[2] The true critic, Gibbon says in his youthful *Essay on the Study of Literature,* does not offer "conjectures as truths, reasoning for facts, or probabilities for demonstrations. . . . Geometry is employed only in demonstrations peculiar to itself: Criticism deliberates between the different degrees of probability. It is by comparing these we daily regulate our actions, and often determine our future destiny."[3] Burke makes the same kind of distinctions in his attack on political "speculatists":

> The science of constructing a commonwealth, or renovating it, or reforming it, is like every other experimental science, not to be taught *a priori*. . . . The pretended rights of these theorists are all extremes; and in proportion as they are metaphysically true, they are morally and politically false. The rights of men are in a sort of middle, incapable of definition, but not impossible to be discerned. . . . Political reasoning is a computing principle; adding, subtracting, multiplying, and dividing, morally and not metaphysically or mathematically, true moral denominations.[4]

Though he does not use the word itself in this passage, Burke is saying that politics is a probable rather than a demonstrative science. It is based on experience, not on abstract, a priori principles. Its premises, arguments, and conclusions are no more exact or certain than its definitions, but a rough outline of truth and right is "not impossible to be discerned."

Even the novelists are full of the language of probable reasoning. Jane Austen, whose heroes and heroines aspire to be rational creatures, is continually dramatizing that kind of thinking in the mental processes of her characters. In his firm but kindly correction of Catherine Morland's fantasies about his father, Henry Tilney says:

> Dear Miss Morland, consider the dreadful nature of the suspicions you have entertained. What have you been judging from? Remember the country and the age in which we live. Remember that we are English, that we are Christians. Consult your own understanding, your own sense of the probable, your own observation of what is passing around you . . . Dearest Miss Morland, what ideas have you been admitting?[5]

Elizabeth Bennet's agonizing reappraisal, after she receives Darcy's letter of explanation, is a process of rational interpretation and judgment, based on a comparing of probabilities: she "weighed every circumstance with what she meant to be impartiality—deliberated on the probability of each statement." Even after concluding that she had been terribly mistaken—that she had "courted prepossession and ignorance, and driven reason away"—she is still "re-considering events, determining probabilities, and reconciling herself as well as she could, to a change so sudden and important."[6]

The hypothesis suggested by these few but diverse examples seems to me very inviting. It is new; students of Hume and Butler have not entirely overlooked their statements on probability, which are extensive, explicit, and central to the arguments of the works in which they appear, but the pervasiveness of these terms, distinctions, and concepts has escaped the attention of scholars. The subject is important historically, if probabilistic reasoning was in fact widely understood and widely practiced in the period, since it was not nearly so characteristic of the preceding and following periods, the renaissance and the nineteenth century. I believe, too, that an understanding of this way of reasoning might illuminate the actual processes of thought in many fields during the eighteenth century, not only clarifying the meaning of terms and the structure of arguments but also explaining why those writers reasoned as they did. Finally, the quality of their thinking can be fairly judged only by the standards appropriate to their own mode of thought, as applied to the range of problems arising in their various disciplines.

An adequate test of these hypotheses, analyzing even a small sampling of works representing four or five different fields of thought, would require a study of at least monograph length. In this paper, I can attempt no more than a first, illustrative treatment of a single instance, Johnson's *Preface to Shakespeare*. To provide some insight into the logical principles underlying probabilistic reasoning, its methodological rationale, I shall first summarize the theoretical treatment of the subject that was most familiar to eighteenth-century writers and readers, Locke's discussion in Book IV of *An Essay concerning Human Understanding* (1690). My primary interest, however, is in the practice of probable reasoning, not in its theory; what is to be said about Locke, though necessarily extensive, is instrumental to the analysis of Johnson which will follow. My examination of the *Preface* is offered as a limited test of the claims tentatively made above for this approach to the understanding of eighteenth-century thought.

Locke on Probable Reasoning

In a frequently quoted passage in his prefatory "Epistle to the Reader," Locke explains the occasion and purpose which led him to undertake the inquiry that finally terminated in the *Essay*. In a discussion on some thorny question—unnamed but evidently of substantive philosophical interest—a small group of his friends found themselves blocked by difficulties arising on every side. Locke then suggested that they had been taking a wrong course; before the inquiry could be conducted with any prospect of success, it was necessary first to "examine our own abilities, and see what *objects* our understandings were, or were not, fitted to deal with." Epistemology, that is to say, is prior in the order of thought to metaphysics, ethics, political theory, natural science, and all other fields of substantive investigation. The *Essay,* therefore, is a propaedeutic to rational inquiry in every intellectual discipline, and Locke himself (in his own modest phrase) is not a master builder in the sciences but only "an under-labourer in clearing the ground a little, and removing some of the rubbish that lies in the way to knowledge."[7]

Negatively, Locke's aim in the *Essay* is to discover the limit or boundary between the knowable and the unknowable: "the horizon . . . which sets the bounds between the enlightened and dark parts of things." By so doing, he will refute both the skeptics, who "question everything, and disclaim all knowledge, because some things are not to be understood," and at the opposite extreme those overconfident reasoners who presume that the whole vast ocean of being is "the natural and undoubted possession of our understandings, wherein there was nothing exempt from its decisions, or that escaped its comprehension." More positively and constructively, his purpose is to establish the grounds of knowledge and opinion, and the "measures" by which truth may be attained or approximated in all things which the human understanding has the capacity to comprehend.[8]

The plan or design of the *Essay,* as Locke explains in the "Introduction," is to "inquire into the original, certainty, and extent of *human knowledge;* together with the grounds and degrees of *belief, opinion,* and *assent.*" Following a "historical, plain method," he will give an account of the origin of our ideas, then show what knowledge the understanding has through those ideas, and finally inquire into the nature and grounds of faith or opinion.[9] Books I and II, constituting the whole first volume of Fraser's standard edition, are devoted to the first part of the investigation, the origin of our ideas. Book III, "Of Words," is transitional to the treatment of both knowledge and opinion in Book IV. Criticism of the *Essay* has centered mainly on the first two Books, in which Locke lays the foundation of his empirical epistemology with the famous attack on innate ideas, the distinctions between sensation and reflection, simple and complex ideas, primary and secondary qualities, the analysis of mixed modes, substances, relations, cause and effect, and other fundamental problems. It is in the last Book, however, that he finally fulfills his original propaedeutic purpose.

The first thirteen chapters of Book IV are concerned with "knowledge," a term reserved by Locke for those truths which can be apprehended with certainty. Since our concern in this paper is with probable reasoning, leading to "opinion," "faith," or "judgment," his treatment of certain knowledge must be almost as drastically foreshortened as Books I-III were just above. But a few of his basic concepts and conclusions must be explained in order to clarify, by contrast, his views on probability.

In general, Locke's theory of knowledge may be described as intuitional.[10] In his system, truth inheres solely in propositions; all propositions are constituted by two terms, a subject and a predicate; each of these is the sign of an idea; and the way to advance both knowledge and right judgment is by comparing ideas, either directly or through intermediary ideas, to determine their agreement or disagreement with each other.[11] Knowledge is possible wherever this agreement or disagreement is immediately and certainly perceptible:

> Sometimes the mind perceives the agreement or disagreement of two ideas *immediately by themselves,* without the intervention of any other: and this I think we may call *intuitive knowledge.* . . . Such kinds of truths the mind perceives at the first sight of the ideas together, by bare intuition; without the intervention of any other idea: and this kind of knowledge is the clearest and most certain that human frailty is capable of. This part of knowledge is irresistible, and, like bright sunshine, forces itself immediately to be perceived, as soon as ever the mind turns its view that way; and leaves no room for hesitation, doubt, or examination, but the mind is presently filled with the clear light of it. (ii, 1)

Even in demonstrative reasoning, in which the agreement or disagreement is not directly perceived but must be established by the intervention of other ideas, each step of the argument is intuitively clear and certain:

> Certainty depends so wholly on this intuition, that, in the next degree of knowledge, which I call demonstrative, this intuition is necessary in all the connexions of the intermediate ideas, without which we cannot attain knowledge and certainty. (ii, 1; cf. xv, 3)

A third source of knowledge is sensation, by which we intuit the existence of particular external things, when they are present to our senses (iii, 2).

From the first of these three sources, direct intuition, each of us has certain knowledge of his own existence, since in "every act of sensation, reasoning, or thinking, we are conscious to ourselves of our own being; and, in this matter, come not short of the highest degree of certainty" (ix, 3). The mathematical relations of geometry and algebra (iii, 2; iii, 29; and passim); the principles of abstract morality (iii, 18; xii, 8; cf. I, ii, 1 and III, xi, 15-16); and the existence of God (x, 1-19) may all be proved by reasoned demonstration, while the existence of external things when actually present to the senses is, of course, known by sensation (xi, 1-14; cf. iii, 5, 21).

These are fundamental truths, of the most vital importance for our existence and well-being both here and hereafter, but obviously they do not take us far into the vast ocean of being and life:

> The understanding faculties being given to man, not barely for speculation, but also for the conduct of his life, man would be at a great loss if he had nothing to direct him but what has the certainty of true *knowledge*. For that being very short and scanty, as we have seen, he would be often utterly in the dark, and in most of the actions of his life, perfectly at a stand, had he nothing to guide him in the absence of clear and certain knowledge. . . . Therefore, as God has set some things in broad daylight; as he has given us some certain knowledge, though limited to a few things in comparison . . . so, in the greatest part of our concernments, he has afforded us only the twilight, as I may say so, of probability; suitable, I presume, to that state of mediocrity and probationership he has been pleased to place us in here. (xiv, 1-2)

This twilight zone—the realm of judgment, assent, opinion, or faith—is explored in chapters xiv-xx of Book IV. As Locke had sought in the preceding chapters to determine the degrees and extent of knowledge, strictly defined, here he considers *"the several degrees and grounds of probability"* (xv, 2).

Several interpreters and critics have observed that Locke's treatment of probable reasoning is too superficial and unsystematic to be adequate philosophically; Aaron, for example, says that Locke missed a golden opportunity to become the founder of the modern logic of probability.[12] Locke has much to say about the grounds of judgment in the hundred pages devoted to the subject in Fraser's edition, but he does not offer any clear fundamental principle or principles to guide himself or us through the maze of observations, distinctions, and classifications which he sets forth. To use one of his own favorite terms, he fails to "bottom" the inquiry on any "place of rest and stability."[13]

That being the case, his theory is perhaps best approached negatively, by establishing first of all what probable reasoning is not. We may say with confidence that it is not intuition, for probability "wants that intuitive evidence which infallibly determines the understanding and produces certain knowledge" (xv, 5). The ideas with which it deals are not adequate and determinate, but incomplete and obscure, and their agreement or disagreement is not immediately evident to the mind. We know by sensation, for example, that external objects exist while they are actually present to the senses, and by memory that they have existed in the past, but we do not have certain knowledge, either immediately or by demonstration, of their "real essences," their internal fabric and constitution (III, vi, 9: IV, vi, 4-15). Concerning the species of natural substances, such as "man" or "gold," our information consists of nothing more than an "imperfect collection of those apparent qualities our senses can discover" (vi, 10, 15)— a bundle of simple ideas, coexisting together in one subject, but carrying with them no "*visible necessary* connexion or inconsistency with any other simple ideas, whose co-existence with them we would inform ourselves about" (iii, 9-10; cf. II, xxiii; III, vi). It is impossible, therefore, either to know the "precise bounds and extent" of any such species or to grasp the causal relationships among their various observable qualities and powers, including the power of their primary qualities to produce in us the ideas of their secondary qualities (vi, 4). The best we can do is to combine these unconnected simple ideas into one complex idea, not the "real" but only the "nominal" essence of that particular substance, to which we give a "sortal name" of our own invention (III, iii, 11-15; vi, 30). Propositions concerning such substances can merely assert, as an inductive generalization, that such-and-such qualities have been regularly observed to coexist in a given subject; that in the presence of a certain complex idea, we expect from experience that another complex idea will be created, generated, made, or altered (II, xxvi); and the like. These propositions can be more or less probable, but they can never be intuitively certain.

Up to this point, I have followed the sequence of topics in Locke's own exposition of his theory. From here on, though I hope the account will be faithful to the letter and spirit of Locke's epistemology, the chapter-by-chapter review will be dropped in order to emphasize the issues which are most important for intellectual history and particularly pertinent to the reasoning of Johnson and other writers of the period.

DEFINITIONS OF PROBABILITY

Probability is defined or described twice in chapter xv of Book IV. It is the *appearance* of agreement or disagreement between two ideas, "by the intervention of proofs, whose connexion is not constant and immutable, or at least is not perceived to be so, but is, or appears for the most part to be so, and is enough to induce the mind to judge the proposition to be true or false, rather than the contrary.'' In the second passage, it is described as ''likeliness to be true, the very notation of the word signifying such a proposition, for which there be arguments or proofs to make it pass, or be received for true.'' It is that which ''makes us presume Things to be true, before we know them to be so'' (xv, 1-3).

In these phrases—''*appears* for the most part,'' ''make it *pass*,'' ''*be received* for true,'' and ''*presume* to be true''—Locke emphasizes the weakness, obscurity, and uncertainty of all probable arguments and conclusions. But they are all we have both for the conduct of daily life and in most of the arts and sciences, and one of Locke's most basic aims is to defend this kind of reasoning not only as necessary for lack of better, but also as legitimate and valid, within its proper sphere and admitted risks of error, and to improve its use by clarifying its nature, conditions, methods, and standards.

SCOPE OF PROBABLE REASONING

In general, the subjects and problems falling within the sphere of probability include everything in the vast ocean of being which human understanding has the capacity to comprehend, except for those which are certainly known by intuition, demonstration, or sensation. Following for convenience Locke's own much-criticized ''Division of the Sciences'' into three main branches (Ch. xxi), we may summarize more specifically as follows:

1. Geometry and algebra are demonstrative sciences. Otherwise, the whole of ''Physica,'' or natural philosophy, is probabilistic. Locke is very explicit in many passages of the *Essay* on the merely probable status of physics, chemistry, and biology (iii, 29; xii, 9-12, etc.).

2. The second division, ''Practica,'' is concerned with ''that which man himself ought to do, as a rational and voluntary agent, for the attainment of any end, especially happiness'' (xxi, 1). These sciences, unlike those in the first group, seek speculative truth not only for its own sake, but also as a guide to the conduct of life. Religion falls within this division, since in Locke's view human happiness is impossible without it.

(a) The existence of God and the necessity of obeying his Commandments, according to Locke, are certainly known through demonstration (xi, 13; xiii,

4), and are therefore outside the sphere of probability. Revealed religion is, of course, not a science, but natural reason is required to determine that Scripture actually is the voice of God, and also to interpret the holy writings correctly; in both cases, the reasoning is probable (xvi, 14; xvii, 8, 10). This is the classic position on the relation between faith and reason, in the tradition of Aquinas and Hooker.

(b) The status of ethics and politics is complicated by Locke's belief that the principles of abstract morality could be established demonstratively; in one passage (iii, 8), he also suggests that some political and legal principles might be demonstrable. But he never developed the demonstrated science of ethics which he thought possible, and his successors assumed that both ethics and politics were limited to probabilities, as Aristotle had argued long before.[14]

(c) The third branch of science, "Logica," includes the theory of signs, ideas, and words as instruments of knowledge (xxi, 4). This is the field to which the *Essay* itself belongs, and its method is partly demonstrative, partly probable.

4. One of the objections to Locke's threefold classification is that it makes no place for history, perhaps on the ground that it is concerned with particulars and consequently is not a science. It is clear, however, that Locke valued history highly, and he frequently cites historical propositions to illustrate probable reasoning (e.g. xvi, 7-8). Criticism, the evaluation of works of art, literature, and oratory, cannot be placed anywhere in Locke's scheme, but it could not be demonstrative.

5. Finally, the reasonings of everyday life—by which, as Gibbon says, "we daily regulate our actions, and often determine our future destiny"—are of course wholly probabilistic. Locke says: "He that, in the ordinary affairs of life, would admit of nothing but direct plain demonstration, would be sure of nothing in this world, but of perishing quickly" (xi, 10).

THE GROUNDS OF PROBABILITY

There are two general "Grounds of Probability": the conformity of anything with our own knowledge, observation, and experience; and the testimony of others, vouching their observation and experience (xv, 4). The main intention of these rather vague general statements is to reaffirm the empirical origin of all evidence, and to add a simple distinction between firsthand and secondhand evidence. The implications of the word "conformity" will be discussed below.

With regard to secondhand evidence, Locke suggests six specific criteria which may be applied in weighing testimonies; the number of witnesses; their integrity; their skill; the author's design, when the testimony is cited from a book; the circumstances and internal consistency of the report itself; and contrary testimonies. These might perhaps be reduced to three criteria: the number of testimonies for and against the proposition in question; the moral and intellectual character of each witness as an individual, as well as the presence or absence of any special interest which might bias his judgment in the particular case; and the credibility of the testimonies themselves. The testimony of others is essential to history and in the affairs of ordinary life, but the natural and moral sciences must also depend upon it for the dissemination and comparison of empirical findings; hence the strict rules and conventions governing such communications.

REASON AND PROBABILITY

"Reason" is defined by Locke as a power of the mind, an active faculty which finds, compares, and orders ideas to "draw into view the truth sought for" (xvii, 2). In some passages he seems to distinguish between "reason" as the faculty operative in demonstration and "judgment" as a different faculty concerned with probabilities. The two *processes* are distinct, because their conditions, grounds, and measures are different, but in his chapter "Of Reason," Locke states emphatically that they are equally rational:

> [Through reason] the mind comes to see, either the certain agreement or disagreement of any two ideas, as in demonstration, in which it arrives at *knowledge;* or their probable connexion, on which it gives or withholds its assent, as in *opinion.* . . . In both these cases, the faculty which finds out the means, and rightly applies them, to discover certainty in the one, and probability in the other, is that which we call *reason* (xvii, 2).

EXPERIENCE AND PROBABILITY

Locke's basic thesis throughout the *Essay* is that all achieved truth, whether general or particular, certain or probable, has its ultimate source and warrant in sensation or reflection, the two avenues in experience which provide us with our ideas, the fundamental data of all thought. If this is true of intuitive, demonstrative, and sensitive knowledge, it is doubly true of probable reasoning, which not only originates in observation and experience but must be continually checked and rechecked against them. Combining this point with the preceding, we may observe that the disjunction often made by historians between "Rationalism" and "Empiricism" is wholly without basis in Locke's epistemology, and could not be applied to it without serious distortion.[15]

INDUCTION AND DEDUCTION IN PROBABLE REASONING

Locke does not use these terms, because he regards all reasoning as a comparison of ideas, either directly or through intermediate ideas. But probable reasoning may move upward from observed particulars to generalizations or downward from general propositions to confirm and explain phenomena:

> For in *particulars* our knowledge begins, and so spreads itself, by degrees, to *generals*. Though afterwards the mind takes the quite contrary course, and having drawn its knowledge into as general propositions as it can, makes those familiar to its thoughts, and accustoms itself to have recourse to them, as to the standards of truth and falsehood. By which familiar use of them, as rules to measure the truth of other propositions, it comes in time to be thought, that more particular propositions have their truth and evidence from their conformity to these more general ones, which, in discourse and argumentation, are so frequently urged, and constantly admitted. (vii, 11)

It "comes in time to be thought" that our assent to particular propositions depends upon their conformity with more general propositions, and this is correct both in the restricted sense that any proposition becomes more probable through its conformity with others and also in the broader sense that truths at all levels of generality are confirmed by their mutual consistency. But here again Locke reiterates the fundamental importance of direct observation, the rooting of the general in the particular. It is not the general rule that is known first and clearest, he says, but the particular instance: "it is that gives life and birth to the other" (xii, 3).

ANALOGY IN PROBABLE RREASONING

The word "conformity" in the general definition of probability, repeated in the passage quoted just above, implies a concept that is basic to Locke's whole account of probability—the concept of analogy. He uses the term, as well as several synonyms like "concurrence," "consonancy," "agreement," and "proportion," in an undefined and unanalyzed way. In its simplest application, analogy refers to conformity between a particular fact, observed or reported, and what is usually observed to happen in similar cases. The highest degree of probability, which Locke calls "assurance," occurs when "the general consent of all men, in all ages, as far as it can be known, concurs with a man's constant and never-failing experience in like cases, to confirm the truth of any particular matter of fact attested by fair witnesses" (xvi, 6). A neat example—almost a paradigm for historical propositions—is the statement that Tiberius preferred his private advantage to that of the public (xvi, 7). If all historians concur in the particular fact, and if experience in all ages has shown that men frequently and usually behave in the same manner, the proposition is extremely probable. Gibbon's *Decline and Fall* is full of such arguments, in which the testimonies to an event are first weighed for their credibility, and the alleged event is then compared with general observations about human motivation and conduct.

Analogy has a similar probative force in determining the probability of propositions concerning the manner of operation of things in nature, in which the causal nexus does not fall within the reach of our senses:

> Concerning the manner of operation in most parts of the works of nature: wherein, though we see the sensible effects, yet their causes are unknown, and we perceive not the ways and manner how they are produced. We see animals are generated, nourished, and move; the loadstone draws iron; and the parts of a candle, successively melting, turn into flame, and give us both light and heat. . . . These and the like, coming not within the scrutiny of human senses, cannot be examined by them, or be attested by anybody; and therefore can appear more or less probable, only as they more or less agree to truths that are established in our minds, and as they hold proportion to other parts of our knowledge and observation. *Analogy* in these matters is the only help we have, and it is from that alone we draw all our grounds of probability. (xvi, 12)

This is the typical mode of reasoning in both the natural and the moral sciences, if they are conducted on empirical and probabilistic lines.

MAXIMS AND PRINCIPLES

In the chapters (vi-viii) concerned with these elements in the reasoning process, Locke's main purpose is to show, once again, that no universal propositions are innate, all being derived from sensation or reflection, and that the only ones which can be certain are those in which the agreement or disagreement of abstract ideas can be intuited, either directly or through intermediary ideas. The mind, Locke says in his chapter on "The Improvement of Our Knowledge," is always seeking to penetrate into the causes of things, and to find principles to rest on. But those who begin their inquiries from "general maxims, precarious principles, and hypotheses laid down at pleasure" set out from the wrong end (xii, 12-13)—an interesting echo, as Fraser notes, of the statement in the "Epistle to the Reader" that Locke and his friends had taken a wrong path in their discussion, had begun at the wrong end.[16] Maxims and principles must be appealed to in deductive reasoning, but Locke defines both in terms recognizing their probabilistic status and empirical origin as inductive generalizations.

HYPOTHESES

A hypothesis is a general proposition (maxim or principle) presumed or postulated as the premise of an argument. Locke has no objection to their use so long as their tentative, provisional status is recognized. They may, and indeed must, be used to explain the phenomena of nature, but real advances are possible only when we are continuously aware that our hypotheses are probable at best—not unquestionable truths but conjectures grounded on experience:

> He that would not deceive himself, ought to build his hypothesis on matter of fact, and make it out by sensible experience, and not presume on matter of fact, because of his hypothesis, that is, because he supposes it to be so. (II, i, 10; cf. IV, xii, 13)

Gibbon and Burke are saying the same thing in the passages quoted in the first section of this essay.

AUTHORITY IN PROBABLE REASONING

In his attitude toward authority, Locke distinguishes between the weight to be given to it in determining questions of fact and matters of opinion. On the former, we tend to believe a "sober fair man," even when he is the only witness, and "as the relators are more in number, and of more credit, and have no interest to speak contrary to the truth," the testimony becomes more and more probable (xv, 5). On matters of opinion, the testimony of experts and learned men rightly carries considerable weight, especially with those who are not themselves expert on the questions at issue. But Locke emphatically and repeatedly warns against the dangers of regulating our assent entirely by the opinions of others:

> I mean the giving up our assent to the common received opinions, either of our friends or party, neighbourhood or country. How many men have no other ground for their tenets, than the supposed honesty, or learning, or number of those of the same profession? As if honest and bookish men could not err; or truth were to be established by the vote of the multitude: yet this with most men serves the turn. (xx, 17)

Of the four sorts of arguments commonly used by men in their reasonings with others, Locke asserts, the feeblest and most contemptible is an appeal to respected authority, *argumentum ad verecundiam.* The only kind of argument that brings true instruction with it, advancing us in our way to understanding, is that which "uses proofs drawn from any of the foundations of knowledge or probability"—*argumentum ad judicium,* which brings to the question "proofs and arguments, and light arising from the nature of things themselves, and not from my shamefacedness, ignorance, or error" (xvii, 19-22).

Locke was not a skeptic—his epistemology as a whole is a refutation of those who "disclaim all knowledge, because some things are not to be understood" (Fraser, I, 30)—but he was well aware that "there is much more falsehood and error among men, than truth and knowledge" (xv, 6), and consequently that nothing is more likely to mislead us than unquestioning faith in the opinions of others, including those we know and like most.

THE DEGREES OF ASSENT

In probable reasoning, according to the definitions given in chapter xv, the connection of the available proofs is never constant and immutable, but always to some extent obscure, uncertain, and variable. The probability of any proposition whose truth cannot be determined by intuition or demonstration is, therefore, a matter of degree. If we are to proceed rationally on such questions, we must review all the evidences and proofs on both sides, carefully weighing and balancing them before reaching a conclusion:

> The great excellency and use of the judgment is to observe right, and take a true estimate of the force and weight of each probability; and then

casting them up all right together, choose that side which has the overbalance. (xvii, 16; cf. xvi, 9; xx, 5)

Upon a due balancing, the degree of assent should be given "proportionably to the preponderancy of the greater grounds of probability on one side or the other" (xv, 5).

By way of summary, we may conclude this account with an example, given by Locke in chapter xv to illustrate reasoning based on the two general grounds of probability: the conformity of any proposition with our own observation and experience, and the testimony of others. The proposition is one of particular fact: *In the midst of a sharp European winter, a man walked upon water hardened with cold.* Such an assertion, Locke says, would have different degrees of probability for different judges:

1. For one who observed the event himself, the proposition is "past probability; it is knowledge" (that is, "sensitive" knowledge).

2. For one who had not seen the particular event but who was familiar with European winters, the proposition would have a high degree of probability because of its analogy with past experience. He would have observed many times that water hardens into ice under certain temperature conditions, that such conditions often occur in Europe during the winter, that ice becomes solid enough to bear a man's weight if the cold is severe and continues long enough, and so forth. In the particular case, however, he might still legitimately reject the proposition if there were something manifestly suspect about the reporter or his testimony.

3. For one born between the tropics, the proposition would be extremely difficult to credit because he had never seen or heard of any such thing before—his experience would have been quite contrary. He might allow it a low degree of probability, nevertheless, if the fact were attested by numerous and reliable witnesses, having no motive for saying anything but the truth.

4. On the other hand, it would not be entirely irrational for such a judge to conclude that the witnesses must be lying, as the king of Siam is said to have done when the Dutch ambassador put the same proposition to him. To the king, it seemed more likely that apparently trustworthy witnesses would have some unknown reason to deceive him than that the whole course of nature, as he knew it, should be reversed. So great is the weight given—and on the whole properly—to what is usually observed to happen, to the analogy between a particular alleged event and the nature of things as known to us through observation and experience (xv, 5).

In his notes on this passage, Fraser stresses the subjectivity of judgments of probability, since in Locke's account they depend on "the custom and analogies of personal experience,'' the amount and kinds of experience a particular judge happens to have had.[17] This is correct if we are thinking exclusively of judgments made by individuals at the level of common sense, based on unsystematic observations in the course of ordinary life. It is this very subjectivity, in fact, which makes sound judgment in everyday affairs such an admirable human trait; it is all one's own, a fund of practical wisdom which is the mark of a sane and mature humanity. But Fraser seems to forget that, for Locke, the same logic of probability which operates in personal judgments and decisions is also the basis for all nondemonstrative sciences. On many questions the element of subjectivity can obviously be greatly reduced, if not wholly eliminated, when the observations are collective, public, and systematic, are recorded and compared, are made under stated conditions which can be repeated by others, are given precision by standardized quantitative measures, where that is possible, and with many other safeguards against personal bias, human error, and limitations of experience, long since familiar in all inductive sciences.

Though Locke does not say so, it would be true to the spirit of his philosophy to observe that the Dutch ambassador gave up too easily. He might well have been able to convince even a seventeenth-century king of Siam by drawing his attention to a number of additional analogies, within his own experience or attested by consistent and repeated observations by disinterested and unimpeachable witnesses. The king was already familiar, for example, with a second state of water, namely steam; the alteration of water to that state occurs in the presence of increased temperature, as his daily tea service informed him. He was surely aware, too, that other substances, such as metals, existed in two states, solid and liquid, again varying with temperature.[18] All this he knew from his own experience, though it may not have occurred to him to conclude, from these analogies, that the full range of possible states appeared to be three, solid, liquid, and gaseous. In Europe, however, the boiling and freezing points of water had been exactly measured, and, if allowance were made for another measurable variable, barometric pressure, had been shown to be invariably accompanied by changes of state from water to steam or water to ice. These analogies could not prove the original proposition to be certainly true, but if the king of Siam were a rational man he could escape from the limitations of his subjectivity by acknowledging that the analogies gave the ambassador's assertion a very high order of probability.

Locke set out to show—against the skeptics on one side and overconfident reasoners from a priori principles on the other—that a beneficent Creator has placed some things beyond the reach of human comprehension, but also has endowed us with faculties capable of grasping a few essential truths with certainty and many others with sufficient probability for belief and action. In the bright sunshine of knowledge, we are certain of the existence of God, ourselves as individuals, and external things, as well as our duty of obedience and the truths demonstrated in pure mathematics. Probability is twilight by comparison, but through it we can discover with varying degrees of assurance many truths about nature, man, society, and the facts of history. Guided by reason and revelation, learning from observation and experience, it is open to men to advance understanding of the world around us far beyond present knowledge, and also to be wise and good in the affairs of this life of probationership. The great ethical appeal, heard throughout the *Essay,* is a ringing call to all men to use their God-given powers to those great ends.

As a preliminary test of our hypothesis, it should be evident that several specific ideas in Locke's account of probable reasoning do shed light on the passages cited or quoted in the opening section of this paper. The basic distinction between demonstration and probability is explicitly stated by Gibbon and Burke; both criticism and politics are probable sciences, grounded on experience, while history depends on the critical evaluation of testimonies and the conformity or analogy of particular events with what is usually observed to happen in like cases. The concept of analogy provides Butler not only with the title of his book but with the overall structure of his argument on natural and revealed religion. Burke's statement that political reasoning is a "calculating principle" is a version of Locke's rule that the degree of assent should be proportional to the preponderancy of evidence, after weighing and balancing all the probabilities on both sides. Hume reiterates the idea in his chapter "Of Probability" in the *Enquiry:*

> There is certainly a probability, which arises from a superiority of chances on any side; and according as this superiority increases; and surpasses the opposite chances, the probability receives a proportionable encrease, and begets still a higher degree of belief or assent to that side, in which we discover the superiority. (sec. vi)

In Johnson's statement about the sources of Dryden's learning, the word "opinion" is used just as Locke used it in the *Essay;* in Johnson's *Dictionary* (1755) it is defined as *Perswasion of the mind, without proof or certain knowledge.* In reaching his conclusion, Johnson implies, he had weighed all the atoms of probability, scattered throughout his author's writings, and then chose that side which had the overbalance. And Elizabeth Bennet was doing exactly the same thing, in a crucial problem of personal life, when she read and reread Darcy's letter, deliberating on the probability of each statement until the preponderancy in favor of his new interpretation of people and events was unmistakable.

It seems safe to say, even from these few instances, that thought in the eighteenth century was often self-consciously probabilistic both in the empirical sciences, natural and social, and also in the day-to-day problems of human living. If that is so, can we doubt that an understanding of the logic of probability, as conceived in that period, would help us to interpret and evaluate the writings which employ that method of reasoning?

Probable Reasoning in the *Preface to Shakespeare*

If space permits more thorough analysis of only one work to illustrate the logic of probability in actual operation, the choice of Johnson's *Preface to Shakespeare* is perhaps debatable.[19] As tests of our hypothesis, it would of course be desirable to analyze a piece of historical writing, a political or economic argument, a treatment of ethical questions, a work on chemistry or biology; important and illuminating examples would not be hard to find in any of these fields. But Johnson's representativeness, his stature as writer and thinker, and his easily documented familiarity with the theory and terminology of probable reasoning are considerations favoring the selection of one of his works. The *Preface* has a special advantage for present purposes, since its three main divisions—critical, historical, and editorial[20]—illustrate the application of probable reasoning to three different disciplines, each raising distinct kinds of problem.

That Johnson was thoroughly acquainted with the logic of probability is evident from definitions and illustrative quotations for pertinent terms in his *Dictionary*. His first definition of the word "opinion" has already been cited above; the term must be understood in that sense if we are to interpret correctly his refusal to offer proofs of the conclusion he had reached about Dryden's learning. "Probability" is defined as *Likelihood; appearance of truth; evidence arising from the preponderation of argument; it is less than moral certainty,* a series of phrases which neatly summarizes several of Locke's basic concepts on the subject. The meaning of "Judgment" is illustrated by quoting one of Locke's own definitions of the term:

> The faculty which God has given man to supply the want of certain knowledge, is *judgment,* whereby the mind takes any proposition to be true or false, without perceiving a demonstrative evidence in the proofs. (*Essay,* IV, xiv, 3)

Other passages from the fourth Book of the *Essay* are cited to illustrate definitions Johnson gives for "probability," "reason," "opinion" (two quotations), and "assent" (two quotations). Locke is not the only source, of course; Johnson cites parallel passages from Hooker, South, Tillotson, Dryden, Glanvill, Watts's *Logic,* and others. The language of probability had become part of the ordinary vocabulary of educated Englishmen at least a generation before Locke published the *Essay,* though his extensive theoretical discussion of probability, and its central role in his epistemology, undoubtedly had a far-reaching influence throughout the following century.

The *Preface to Shakespeare* is filled from beginning to end with the nouns, verbs, adjectives, and adverbs of probable reasoning. Critical discourse, cultural history, and the tasks of an editor all fall within the realm of "opinion," "judgment," and "belief." The critic and textual scholar may "doubt" or "know not" in some matters, in others may "credit," "estimate," or "suppose," "think" or "be inclined to think," "believe" or "have reason to believe." Some of the questions he considers have "no sufficient ground of determination," are "impossible to decide" or "not easy to determine," but a good many of them can be resolved with "proof enough." Some facts are "doubtful," "uncertain," or "improbable," others "likely," "probable," "more probable." The premises from which reasoning proceeds are often hypothetical—assumptions which are "commonly supposed" or "reasonable to suppose"—but they may be drawn from and confirmed by "experience," "observation," and "comparison." The critical, historical, and textual conclusions Johnson reaches "seem" or "appear" to be the case, are "perhaps" true or valid "on the whole"—but they "never become infallible."

These terminological facts are, of course, merely external clues to the actual processes of Johnson's thought. As direct examples of his way of reasoning, I shall briefly consider three specific arguments in the historical section of the *Preface;* examine Johnson's application of the general theory of probability to the techniques of textual scholarship; and conclude with a detailed analysis of Johnson's main critical argument on the "peculiarities of excellence" which establish Shakespeare's superiority as a writer, with a final glance at one aspect of the refutation of traditional views on the unities of time and place. Most of Johnson's typical devices of argument will emerge from analysis of these central and representative passages.

JOHNSON AS PROBABILISTIC HISTORIAN

"Probabilistic history" is really a tautological phrase, since no one has ever supposed that historical propositions were capable of demonstrative proof;

there are, nevertheless, numerous philosophies of history and many works of historiography which take no systematic account of that very obvious fact. In a Lockean view, history is radically factual, and the records and testimonies by which even a single fact can be established are never complete and unambiguous. The interpretation of events is even more precarious, since their causes are not open to observation and can be surmised only by appeal to psychological, economic, political, or other principles, which are themselves doubtful. The most that can be asked of any historian is that the evidences for each fact be critically evaluated and as complete as possible, that the many facts supporting any inductive generalization, though never exhaustive, be as nearly so as circumstances permit, and that the principles appealed to in explaining and interpreting events be as thoroughly grounded in systematic experiments as the state of the relevant sciences allows. If we extrapolate slightly, these are the standards implicit in Locke's general theory of probability and in his scattered remarks about history. It would also seem fair and appropriate, since Johnson's reasoning in the historical part of the *Preface* is of the kind described, to apply those criteria in judging the quality of his thought as a historian.

The middle section of the *Preface,* which I have referred to as historical, is linked to the opening section of critical evaluation by the characteristic Johnsonian notion that "every man's performance to be rightly estimated, must be compared with the state of the age in which he lived, and with his own particular opportunities" (p. 81). This kind of comparison does not alter the objective value of the performance itself, the book or other work,[21] but it does enable us to distinguish what the artist owes to "original powers" from what is due to "casual and adventitious help," the assistance given him by the cultural conditions of his time.

Since the greatest help any age can give a poet is knowledge of books, as an aid to understanding man and nature, Johnson's main purpose in these ten pages is to determine the state of learning in Shakespeare's period and secondarily Shakespeare's own opportunities to share in whatever benefits it had to offer. These are both questions of historical fact, the first highly general, the other more particular. Johnson's method in answering these questions involves (1) simple induction from particular facts to a general proposition, (2) the use of maxims to confirm or explain observed facts, and (3) critical evaluation of testimony. Along with other arguments not mentioned here, all three contribute to Johnson's general conclusion that "the greater part of his excellence was the product of his own genius" (p. 87).

The first method may be illustrated by the evidence Johnson adduces in determining knowledge of the learned languages and the development of

English drama before Shakespeare. Both might be described as proofs by example—not an exhaustive induction from all pertinent facts potentially knowable by Johnson, but a listing, in the first case, of ten writers and scholars who had made the learned tongues accessible through editions, translations, grammars, and teaching, and, in the other case, an even more scattered and incomplete reference to a few plays known or believed to antedate Shakespeare. From the first set of facts he concludes that the English nation was beginning to emerge from barbarity, but that most of the public was still "gross and dark." From the second, even scantier evidences, he infers that Shakespeare found the stage in "a state of utmost rudeness" (pp. 82, 87).

Among several axiomatic propositions in this part of the *Preface,* the following is typical: "As knowledge advances, pleasure passes from the eye to the ear, but returns, as it declines, from the ear to the eye" (p. 83). The observed fact is the predominance in Shakespeare's plays of action over sentiment, argumentation, and style. Johnson explains the fact as resulting from the playwright's effort to please an uncultivated audience, and the maxim confirms the causal explanation by analogy with a general observation. As with other arguments from analogy, the proposition states a proportion: action is to sentiment as the eye is to the ear. Johnson asserts, as an unproved maxim, that pleasure shifts from eye to ear as knowledge increases.

In estimating the advantages Shakespeare owed to education, Johnson proceeds for the most part as he was to do later in the *Life of Dryden,* by perusing the author's works with close attention, then drawing his conclusion from those scattered atoms of probability. But he does examine one famous piece of testimony, Ben Jonson's statement that Shakespeare had "small Latin, and less Greek." Johnson finds three reasons for accepting this judgment: Jonson was in a position to be well informed, since the two men were friends; he had "no imaginable temptation to falsehood"; and the statement, when published in the First Folio, would surely have been refuted by many people if it had not been correct. This evidence, Johnson concludes, "ought therefore to decide the controversy, unless some testimony of equal force could be opposed" (p. 85). It is a textbook case for the weighing of testimony, according to Locke's criteria.

If we evaluate these arguments by the criteria stated above, there is nothing wrong with them from a formal point of view. The three methods illustrated in these passages are all valid as probable proofs of significant historical propositions, leading to a more general conclusion, and Johnson reasons with characteristic intellectual energy and resourcefulness; he is a great finder of arguments. But there are serious weaknesses on the factual side, always basic in an empirical method of proof. We must allow, of course, for the state of pertinent historical knowledge in Johnson's time; he lacked much "casual and adventitious help," available to later scholars, which his age was not yet prepared to give. Nevertheless, the few facts he adduces to support his generalizations about the state of learning and the drama seem patently inadequate. The list of classical scholars is not too bad, but surely he might have known and cited other pre-Shakespearean plays besides *Gorboduc* and *"Hieronnymo"* (undated and unattributed). On the proposition about the predominance of action over sentiment and style in Shakespeare's plays, we might well challenge both the observation itself and the general maxim by which he explains it. The logic is acceptable—though some might balk at the proportion which identifies action with the eye and sentiment with the ear—but it would certainly not be at all unreasonable to ask that he discuss at least one play, as a token example of the relative weight of action and sentiment in Shakespeare's dramaturgy, and produce some kind of historical evidence to show that in all ages lesser degrees of knowledge are correlated with pleasure from the eye, greater with pleasure from the ear. Or the evidence might be psychological, drawn from observations of children: is it a fact that the locus of pleasure shifts from eye to ear as they mature? I'm afraid it would be difficult to prove, even with a low degree of probability.

The reader may not concur in this mixed judgment of Johnson's reasoning as an historian, but I hope he will agree that the criteria I have applied are appropriate, since they are derived from the logic of probability, the method of reasoning that Johnson is actually using.

TEXTUAL SCHOLARSHIP AND THE LOGIC OF PROBABILITY[22]

The two main elements in any edition of a noncontemporary writer have always been text and gloss, the words themselves and interpretation of their meaning. "The business of him that republishes an ancient book," Johnson says in his *Proposals* for an edition of Shakespeare, "is, to correct what is corrupt, and to explain what is obscure" (p. 51). The purpose of an editor is to serve both the author and his readers by establishing a text as close as possible to the writer's intentions and to recover meanings and references which have been obscured by time.

In the *Proposals* and the *Preface* itself, Johnson presents a well-developed theory of the problems, methods, and standards of editorial scholarship, based on the logic of probability. Although Locke's *Essay* includes no reference to editing, the religious and moral overtones of his account of judgment and probability pervade Johnson's discussion. Both text and gloss exist on "the dark side of things," presenting an extreme example of the contrast between the twilight of probability and the broad daylight and bright sunshine of knowledge. Johnson shares Locke's feeling that the obscurity in which God has left many things is suitable to "that state of mediocrity and probationership he has been pleased to place us in here" (*Essay*, IV, xiv, 2). He is saddened by "the unsuccessfulness of enquiry, and the slow advances of truth," the frequency with which opinions prevalent in one age are rejected in the next. But alterations of light and dark are inseparable from the human condition:

> The sudden meteors of intelligence which for a while appear to shoot their beams into the regions of obscurity, on a sudden withdraw their lustre, and leave mortals again to grope their way. (p. 99)

In the closing paragraphs of the *Preface*, lamenting that so great a writer as Shakespeare should have any need for a commentary, Johnson acknowledges the sad but inescapable truth: "But it is vain to carry wishes beyond the condition of human things; that which must happen to all, has happened to Shakespeare, by accident and time." The editor must, then, do what he can to repair those ravages, but always recognizing—the final sentence of the *Preface*—that "every work of this kind is by its nature deficient" (p. 112).

The darkness is not total, however, for text and gloss are not among those things of which we must ever remain ignorant because they are entirely beyond the reach of human comprehension. Some readings and interpretations are more probable than others, and there are guidelines which reason can follow to improve the text and clear up at least some of the obscurities of meaning.

In determining the text, there are several degrees of assurance as to the correctness of readings. The highest degree is when a work is published, seen through the press, and corrected by its author; if the text is published after the author's death, but based on copy written or revised by him, it is in the next degree, its faults being those of only one descent (*Proposals*, p. 51). Unfortunately neither of these degrees of assurance is possible in Shakespeare's case, since he did not supervise any of the printed copies (even those published during his lifetime), the intermediaries between his manuscript and the printers are unidentified and were probably incompetent, and the printers themselves were negligent (*Proposals*, p. 52; *Preface*, p. 92).

In dealing with such corrupt texts, an editor has two available methods, collation and conjectural emendation. The first gives a higher degree of assurance, even with bad copy and ignorant or careless printers, because "they who had the copy before their eyes were more likely to read it right, than we who read it only by imagination." It is Johnson's own settled principle that "the reading of the ancient books is probably true" (p. 106). Collation involves a comparison of extant texts, to determine their variant readings, and an evaluation of their relative degree of authority by their closeness to the author in the line of transmission. Collation is a very dull part of an editor's task, as Johnson acknowledges in a famous passage, but it is very necessary when works exist in multiple versions; like Pope before him, Johnson knew what should be done but did not carry it out to the end—a defect for which he has been well castigated by his critics. He did collate all the Folio texts, however, and established the authority of the First Folio over all the others, since "the rest only deviate from it by the printer's negligence" (p. 96).

Johnson's low opinion of conjectural emendation, perhaps the most striking feature in this part of the *Preface,* is a direct consequence of his probabilistic conception of textual scholarship. It is sometimes necessary, when none of the versions offers a possible reading, but it is a last resort when all else fails. Conjectures are not totally without probability of correctness if they are governed by two restraints: the solution proposed should vary as little as possible from a reading attested by one or more of the extant texts ("with the least possible violation of the text," [p. 97]), and the emendation must conform to "the state, opinion, and modes of language prevailing in every age [or, rather, in the particular author's age], and with his author's particular cast, and turn of expression" (p. 95). The latter is Locke's rule—"conformity with our knowledge, observation, and experience"—as applied to language. Conjecture may sometimes be right, if these restraints are accepted, but the burden of Johnson's discussion is its extreme danger of error and the folly of overconfidence in so risky an enterprise. His own rule, proportioned to the low probability that such emendations will be correct, is *quod dubitas ne feceris*—when in doubt, don't (p. 109).

The need for interpretive comment, once the text has been established with as close an approach to certainty as the case admits, is explained by the "causes of obscurity" which operate in reading any work that has outlived its writer's time. These causes, more fully reviewed in the *Proposals* than in the *Preface,* are of two kinds, linguistic and cultural. Both result from changes brought by time. The author himself may be responsible for some semantic and syntactical difficulties, because of his peculiar cast of style, but changes in the general usage of his language are the main source of ambiguity; every age has its own mode of speech, which becomes increasingly unintelligible to later ages. The other source of obscurity is change in customs, opinions, and traditions (*Proposals,* pp. 52-54). As Johnson puts it in the *Preface:*

> All personal reflections, when names are suppressed, must be in a few years irrecoverably obliterated; and customs . . . , such as modes of dress, formalities of conversation, rules of visits, disposition of furniture, and practices of ceremony, which naturally find places in familiar dialogue, are so fugitive and unsubstantial, that they are not easily retained or recovered. (p. 103; cf. p. 97)

But here again the darkness is not wholly impenetrable. There are guidelines which linguistic and historical inquiry may follow to reduce these obscurities—not clearing them completely, but in many instances; and not certainly, but with "proof enough."

On the linguistic side, the best guides in explaining a particular passage are general knowledge of the state of the language in the author's time, and specific parallels in books contemporary with the author, "illustrations" by which the difficulty is explained (*Preface,* p. 102; cf. *Proposals,* pp. 56-57). Both are applications of Locke's principle of analogy, the confirmation of a particular fact (the meaning of a word or construction) by its conformity with "what is usually observed to happen in like cases," but with emphasis on the temporal variable; the cases are "like" if they occur in the same period, and especially if the parallel is in a book read by the author (*Proposals,* p. 56).

The clarification of obscure allusions, implicit ideas, and minutiae of social custom is even more difficult, since most of the references are to particular facts, almost limitless in number and variety, with few general analogies to go by. Of this kind of information, Johnson says, "every man has some, and none has much." The best hope is for a gradual accumulation of data, from "the recesses of obscure and obsolete papers," by the joint contributions of many scholars (*Preface,* p. 103).

Johnson's critical review of his editorial predecessors (pp. 93-102) is a striking manifestation of his probabilistic philosophy of textual and interpretive scholarship. He treats the previous editors as witnesses, their various texts and glosses as testimonies. They are judged by four criteria, all following from the nature of the problems faced by an editor and the qualities of mind which make for probable success or failure in solving such problems:

1. General native ability—basically, that excellence of judgment which observes right, makes a true estimate of the weight of each

probability, and chooses that side which has the overbalance. This general power of mind must, of course, be specifically adapted to judging the probabilities of text and gloss.

2. Acquired knowledge of language and history—to provide the general analogies necessary to determine the probability of particular readings and interpretations.

3. Industry—collation is only one of the tasks of an editor requiring labor and patience.

4. Scholarly prudence or caution—especially needed to resist the temptations of conjectural emendation, but more generally because all editorial work carries high risks of error.

Theobald, for example, was "a man of narrow comprehension and small acquisitions," but he was "zealous for minute accuracy, and not negligent in pursuing it." He accomplished little, but he deserves credit for being one of the first to collate the ancient copies, and what little he did was commonly right. Upton was skilled in languages and acquainted with books, but he too was deficient in genius and taste; lacking Theobald's caution, he failed to "restrain the rage of emendation." Hanmer and Warburton were much superior to Theobald and Upton in talent and learning, but they underrated the difficulties and risks of their task and overrated their own abilities to make right decisions. Hanmer seems never to have suspected that critics can be fallible, neither himself nor his predecessors, and Warburton was too impatient and presumptuous to do "what labour only can perform, by penetrating to the bottom."

Johnson's acceptance of the testimony of previous editors, as shown by his use of their textual decisions and explanatory notes in his own edition, is roughly proportional to this assessment of their reliability. With regard to textual emendations, his editorial practice distinguishes four degrees of probability:

1. Readings which are "evidently erroneous" are rejected without mention.

2. Those which seem "specious but not right" are included, but with an "animadversion"—contrary evidence of some sort.

3. Those "resting in equipoise between objection and defence" are included in the notes, but not in Johnson's own text.

4. Readings incorporated in his text are "to be considered as in my opinion sufficiently supported" (p. 105).

In another passage, Warburton's interpretive notes are graded on a similar scale, though with a stronger statement of the extreme degrees: (1) censured without reserve; (2) left to the judgment of the reader, as "doubtful, though specious"; (3) deserving of highest approbation.

As an editor, Johnson was well aware that he was part of a tradition, with predecessors on whom he built and with future successors who would build similarly on what he had done. To some extent, the principles stated in the *Proposals* and the *Preface,* as well as some of the practices adopted in his text and notes, are addressed to the scholars who will succeed him and are designed to give them theoretical and factual information necessary to evaluate his work critically, as he had evaluated those who went before him. That is the way scholarship and learning may be advanced, through critical evaluation of the tradition and the gradual accumulation of findings by many contributors.

But I believe that the edition of Shakespeare, like Johnson's other works, was addressed primarily to the intelligent common reader. Such a reader, he assumes, does not want to be the slave of an editor or critic, condemned to accept on faith whatever he is told is true and right; he wants to be able to make his own judgments on textual and interpretive questions as well as in the critical appreciation of an author's writing. In laying down the principles on which he has operated as an editor, in identifying and evaluating the contributions of other editors, and in stating explicitly the reasoning which has led to his own decisions, Johnson is giving that kind of reader all the help he can to judge rightly for himself.

THE PROBABILIST AS LITERARY CRITIC

Johnson is very explicit about the probabilistic, nondemonstrative character of his own reasoning in the critical part of the *Preface*. It is a sign of his method that the essay begins by considering the relevance and probative force of time in judging the excellence of works and writers. Demonstration is impossible on such questions, because artistic merit is "not absolute and definite, but gradual and comparative," a matter of degree. Works of art are "not raised upon principles demonstrative and scientifick, but appealing wholly to observation and experience, no other test can be applied than length of duration and continuance of esteem." Drawing his examples of demonstration from mathematics—the round and the square, the Pythagorean scale of numbers—Johnson contrasts its immediacy and certainty with the tentative, relative, and slowly accumulated findings of probable judgment, critical and other:

Demonstration immediately displays its power, and has nothing to hope or fear from the flux of years; but works tentative and experimental must be estimated by their proportion to the general and collective ability of man, as it is discovered in a long succession of endeavours. Of the first building that was raised, it might be with certainty determined that it was round or square, but whether it was spacious or lofty must have been referred to time. The Pythagorean scale of numbers was at once discovered to be perfect; but the poems of *Homer* we yet know not to transcend the common limits of human intelligence, but by remarking, that nation after nation, and century after century, has been able to do little more than transpose his incidents, new name his characters, and paraphrase his sentiments. (p. 60)

In the logic of probability, as Johnson proceeds to argue, time is a valid test of literary merit for at least four reasons: it eliminates local and temporary causes of liking or disliking, adventitious reasons of interest or passion which may bias judgment; whatever "has been longest known has been most considered, and what is most considered is best understood"; a work of genius cannot be judged excellent until opinion in its favor has been confirmed by frequent comparisons with other works of the same kind, and with "the general and collective ability of man," as learned through long experience; and continuance of esteem over an extended period is evidence that a work or body of works has inherent qualities suited to give pleasure to all or most men.[23] These are not certain truths, but they may be asserted with confidence as "acknowledged and indubitable positions" (p. 60).

Though time has given its verdict in Shakespeare's case, it is still proper and useful to inquire, through the application of critical reasoning, "by what peculiarities of excellence Shakespeare has gained and kept the favour of his countrymen" (p. 61). Time reveals continuance of esteem, a strong evidence that the esteem is justified, but criticism can explore the reasons or causes which explain that favor.

The basic structure of the argument on Shakespeare's merits as a playwright (pp. 61-71) is a categorical syllogism. "Nothing can please many, and please long, but just representations of general nature"; Shakespeare is "the poet of nature," the poet who "holds up to his readers a faithful mirrour of manners and of life"; his plays, therefore, not only do please as a matter of fact but have the enduring qualities which explain and justify that pleasure. This argument does not involve any formal or material fallacy, but obviously it makes no claim to the rigor which a demonstrative syllogism would require. There are too many terms in both major and minor, and none of them is explicitly defined; the term "just," a crucial element in the major, is not repeated in the minor, though it is represented by "faithful," an approximate synonym. Such reasoning cannot pretend to certainty, and Johnson is well aware of the fact.

The major premise of the argument is stated without proof. Though it may appear to be dogmatically asserted, its actual status is that of a reasonable postulate, a highly probable hypothesis. The whole syllogism can be readily restated in hypothetical form without changing its logical character; "*If* just representation, *then* please many and long"; the minor affirms the antecedent, and the conclusion validly asserts the consequent. It would, no doubt, have been impossible for Johnson to assemble all the scattered atoms of probability on which the postulated major premise was based in his own mind, but if he had attempted to sketch out the main types of evidence available to support it, they might well have covered almost the whole scope of Locke's outline of legitimate probable arguments. Most basically, the proposition could be defended as an inductive generalization grounded on "our own knowledge, observation, and experience." As Johnson says of Shakespeare's knowledge of mankind, the origin of such a generalization is a lifetime of "gradual acquisition," through sustained empirical observation and thought (pp. 87-88). The proposition could also be confirmed by analogy with "truths that are established in our minds," could be shown to "hold proportion to other parts of our knowledge and observation" (*Essay,* IV, xvi, 12).

"The testimony of others, vouching their observations and experience," might be cited in further support of the premise. In an interesting passage comparing his own age with Shakespeare's, Johnson observes that his period was far more sophisticated in the study of human nature. In Shakespeare's time:

> Speculation had not yet attempted to analyse the mind, to trace the passions to their sources, to unfold the seminal principles of vice and virtue, or sound the depths of the heart for the motives of action. (p. 88)

Some of these inquiries were conducted with "idle subtlety," in Johnson's opinion, but his generalization would certainly have had wide support from the gradually emerging empirical psychology of his age. And as a proposition concerning poetry, it would have been strongly confirmed by the testimony of two unimpeachable witnesses, Dryden in the *Essay of Dramatic Poesy* and Pope in his own *Preface to Shakespeare,* to say nothing of scores of less distinguished critics, who argued, with some variations of phrasing and emphasis, from the same premise. In Johnson's time and in that school of criticism, at least, the proposition needed no proof because it was universally accepted, seeming almost self-evident. Though not demonstrably true, it bordered so nearly on certainty—as Locke says—that reasonable men should have "no doubt at all" about it (*Essay,* IV, xv, 2). Even today, it seems to me, this postulated premise has an entirely different order of plausibility than Johnson's maxim about pleasures of the eye and the ear, and their variation with the state of knowledge in any age.

The minor premise of Johnson's argument is supported by a series of subarguments, showing that in all the major components of his plays Shakespeare does indeed hold up a faithful mirror of manners and life. His characters are the "genuine progeny of common humanity," acting and speaking by "the influence of those general passions and principles by which all minds are agitated"—observations which again assume that the traits and motives of men are sufficiently well understood to warrant highly probable inductive generalizations. Shakespeare's fables, similarly, are those of a poet who "caught his ideas from the living world, and exhibited only what he saw before him." His dialogue is pursued with ease and simplicity, on topics which actually arise in the commerce of mankind, and is so level with life that it seems to have been "gleaned by diligent selection out of common conversation, and common occurrences." Particularly notable, since it suggests that Johnson's linguistic theory was as probabilistic as his psychology, is his paragraph on the style of Shakespeare's comic dialogue. He describes it as drawn from that part of English speech which is used in the common intercourse of life—"a stile which never becomes obsolete, a certain mode of phraseology so consonant and congenial to the analogy and principles of the respective language as to remain settled and unaltered."

Also prominent throughout this part of the *Preface* are the recurrent comparisons between Shakespeare's plays and the works of other writers, a corollary of the principle that literary value is a matter of degree and one of the types of evidence made available by the passage of time. Shakespeare is "above all writers, at least above all modern writers," the poet of nature. The characters of "other authours" are too often individuals, rather than species; "other writers" maze the imagination by raising up phantoms. "Every other stage," "the theatre, when it is under any other direction," is peopled by such characters as were never seen, talking in a language which was never heard. As we can estimate the immense superiority of Homer's poems only by observing how little has been added by all his successors over many centuries, so it is only "by comparing him with other authors" that we can imagine how much Shakespeare excels in accommodating his sentiments to real life.

Johnson's examination of Shakespeare's "peculiarities of excellence" is appropriately concluded by a reassertion of its probabilistic character:

These observations are to be considered not as unexceptionably constant, but as containing general and predominant truth. *Shakespeare's* familiar dialogue is affirmed to be smooth and clear, yet not wholly without ruggedness or difficulty; as a country may be eminently fruitful, though it has spots unfit for cultivation: His characters are praised as natural, though their sentiments are sometimes forced, and their actions improbable; as the earth upon the whole is spherical, though its surface is varied with protuberances and cavities. (pp. 70-71)

Since literary judgment is "not absolute and definite, but gradual and comparative," the critic must be satisfied with "general and predominant truth"—with arguments that fall short of absolute precision and certitude and with conclusions, consequently, that at best can be asserted only as true "upon the whole." But if this is the best that the nature of the subject and the limitations of human understanding allow, we must recognize that in its own sphere this kind of reasoning is legitimate and valid, can be more or less probable, and that we must use our powers to bring all the light we can.

I wish there were space here to examine in detail Johnson's iconoclastic discussion of the unities of time and place. It is a probable refutation of a traditional position, itself based on probable arguments, and Johnson's dissection of the postulates, principles, and inferences on which it rests is a masterly piece of empirical and probabilistic counterargument. In closing this study of his reasoning as a critic, however, I will comment on only one aspect of the discussion, Johnson's attitude toward authority, which did not appear in his treatment of Shakespeare's merits as a playwright.

The laws concerning time and place in the drama, Johnson states at the beginning, "have been instituted and established by the joint authority of poets and of criticks" (p. 75; for the whole discussion, see pp. 74-81). Johnson says that the question is not one of those that are to be decided by mere authority—it is a matter of opinion, not of fact—but he is very conscious of the weight of expert opinion on the other side. In three separate passages he speaks of his "due reverence to that learning which I must oppose," recollects "how much wit and learning must be produced against me," and concludes the whole discussion with a modest disclaimer:

I am almost frightened at my own temerity; and when I estimate the fame and the strength of those who maintain the contrary opinion, am ready to sink down in reverential silence; as *Aeneas* withdrew from the defence of *Troy,* when he saw *Neptune* shaking the wall, and *Juno* heading the besiegers, (pp. 80-81)

There is, surely, an overtone of smiling exaggeration in this statement,[24] but as Locke had said and as Johnson also believed, the number and skill of witnesses are always fundamental considerations in weighing the testimony of others on any debatable question.

But Locke, as we have seen, warned emphatically and repeatedly against the dangers of regulating our assent entirely by the opinion of others; the only kind of argument which brings true instruction with it is that which offers proofs and arguments, "and light arising from the nature of things themselves." Whether learned from Locke or not, these lessons seem to have been woven into the very sinew of Johnson's mind, becoming an ingrained intellectual and moral habit, almost a second nature in his thought. A decent respect was due to the opinions of well-known critics and the practice of famous poets, members of Johnson's own literary profession who had earned esteem by their achievements in thought and art; by their numbers and eminence, any opinion in which they concurred carried with it a considerable weight of antecedent probability. But as Johnson says in another part of the *Preface,* "there is always an appeal open from criticism to nature" (p. 67)—from opinions to the things themselves. The most learned may err, and to have anything like the firm grounds of belief which would remove all reasonable doubt, we must consider proofs and arguments on both sides of any question, probing the principles alleged in support of the proposition advanced, comparing supposed effects with actual experience, and fully exploring alternative explanations. If the foundations prove sandy, when subjected to such close and candid examination, it is proper to lay respect aside and to launch freely and boldly on one's own search for truth.

Adam Smith called the *Preface* "the most manly piece of criticism that was ever published in any country," and other perceptive readers have said much the same thing.[25] I believe they were responding not only to Johnson's powerful personality but to the ethos of probabilism, a temper of mind difficult to define but strongly felt throughout Locke's *Essay* as well as in the *Rambler, Rasselas,* and the *Preface*. Neither Locke nor Johnson ever forgot that all human things are imperfect and evanescent, yet both believed that the human understanding was a light in darkness, capable of attaining truth or a sufficient approximation to it in all matters of real concern to us. That talent was given to us for use. Respecting truth above persons, however august, both men felt in the fullest degree the pleasure and pride of independent thought.

ℐℐℐ

The purpose of this paper has been to test three closely related hypotheses: that eighteenth-century British writers in several fields of thought used a method of reasoning based on the logic of probability, as understood during that period; that the interpretation and evaluation of their thought might be advanced by an analysis taking account of their method as well as of their doctrines; and that the pervasiveness of this mode of reasoning in that age and country might be important for intellectual history, as a fact with far-reaching implications, possibly distinguishing the latter part of the seventeenth century and the whole eighteenth century, in a fundamental way, from the preceding and following periods.

I believe that the first of these hypotheses has been fully confirmed, at least for Dr. Johnson, by our analysis of his *Preface to Shakespeare*. His thorough acquaintance with the principles and terminology of probable reasoning is shown by definitions and illustrative quotations in the *Dictionary;* in the *Preface* itself, he explicitly recognizes and draws attention to the probabilistic character of his own arguments, and the operation of the method in the actual processes of his thought has been illustrated by detailed analysis. It is clear from Locke's theoretical treatment in the fourth Book of the *Essay* that probable reasoning was conceived during the period as the most legitimate and valid method—for Locke, in fact, the only possible method—in most of the arts and sciences and in the everyday thinking of rational people. In the *Preface*, Johnson adapts the principles of that mode of reasoning to the solution of problems in three different fields of thought, cultural history, textual scholarship, and literary criticism. The passages referred to in Butler, Hume, Gibbon, Burke, and Jane Austen suggest that an examination of additional examples would yield similar results in other disciplines, though the treatment here has been too sketchy to confirm the point conclusively.

On the value of this approach for interpretation and evaluation, I believe that an interpretive procedure which takes account of both doctrine and method can hardly help being sounder than more common approaches, which either disregard method entirely or characterize it only as representing some broad a priori historical category, ''rationalistic,'' ''empirical,'' or the like. Method is the dynamic principle in thinking; it is the mind at work, raising questions, finding proofs, inferring and concluding. Method is more basic than doctrine, since it determines the kinds of questions a reasoner can raise and the way they will be formulated, the definition and use of terms, the classes of evidence and types of argument considered admissible, and the intellectual status of the doctrines themselves—of the conclusions, that is, which are reached through these techniques. If we disregard method in interpreting a writer, we are dealing only with the dead bones of his thought; everything seems arbitrary or accidental, because we do not have the clues which will bring the ideas to life, revealing their meaning, connections, and reasons. But there are many different ways of reasoning, and we must be sure that we have correctly identified a writer's method and that we understand its special mode of operation. If we misconstrue a writer's method, or identify it by some foreign category, derived from another way of thinking, the consequences for interpretation can be disastrous. In that case, the distortion is systematic and all-engulfing; the interpretation is guided by an alien principle, so that the clues are all false and everything is twisted from its true meaning and bearing.[26] But how far these dangers have been avoided in this study, and how much its new approach has contributed to the understanding and appreciation of Johnson as a thinker, may best be left—in the probabilistic eighteenth-century manner—to the judgment of candid readers.

The last of our three hypotheses, concerning the significance for intellectual history of the widespread understanding and extensive use of probable reasoning in eighteenth-century Britain, must be left open as a mere possibility. Its confirmation would require far more extensive and substantial evidence, both from that period and from the preceding and following ages, than we have been able to consider in this essay. Even with much fuller evidence the thesis would be difficult to establish. Some eighteenth-century writers did not use probable reasoning, and some writers in other periods did use it. Locke did not invent the logic of probability, which was first described by Aristotle and which was known, under varying interpretations and formulations, in both medieval and renaissance times. The empirical and probabilistic tradition was continued into the nineteenth century and beyond, in the logic of John Stuart Mill, the development (begun in the seventeenth century) of a mathematical theory of probability, and the methodologies of the inductive sciences.

As a conjecture, however, does it not seem plausible that one of the most basic and distinctive features of eighteenth-century British thought might be the conscious acceptance by many writers of probability as the best guide in many fields, their sophisticated understanding of its principles and rules, and their skilled use of it in their searches after truth? These attitudes did not die with the end of their period, but Kant and his successors, in revolt against the whole seventeenth- and eighteenth-century tradition, produced a new epistemology on different principles. From that, inevitably, followed new systems of metaphysics, theology, politics, and ethics, new kinds of literary criticism and even of historiography. This break with the past was surely one of the most crucial turning points in the history of western thought. If we wish to understand the thinking of most eighteenth-century writers, in Britain at least, we must recognize how differently men reasoned before that shattering change.

Notes

1. Samuel Johnson, *Lives of the English Poets,* ed. G. B. Hill (Oxford: Clarendon Press, 1905), I, 418.

2. Joseph Butler, *The Analogy of Religion, Natural and Revealed, to the Constitution and Course of Nature* (New York, n.d.), pp. xlviii-lvi; David Hume, *A Treatise of Human Nature,* Bk. I, Pt. iii, sec. 2, and *An Enquiry concerning Human Understanding,* sec. 6.

3. Edward Gibbon, *An Essay on the Study of Literature* (London, 1764), pp. 50-51.

4. Edmund Burke, *Reflections on the Revolution in France,* 2d ed. (London, 1790), pp. 90-92.

5. *Northanger Abbey,* Vol. II, Ch. 9, *The Novels of Jane Austen,* ed. R. W. Chapman (London: Oxford University Press, 1959), V, 197-98.

6. *Pride and Prejudice,* Vol. II, Ch. 13, *Novels,* II, 205-9.

7. John Locke, *An Essay concerning Human Understanding,* ed. A. C. Fraser (Oxford: Clarendon Press, 1894), I, 9, 14; cf. "Introduction," I, 31. In a manuscript note in his own copy of the *Essay,* now in the British Museum, Locke's friend James Tyrrell indicates that the question debated was the principles of morality and revealed religion. Cf. Fraser, I, xvi-xvii, and W. von Leyden, ed., *Locke's Essays on the Law of Nature* (Oxford: Clarendon Press, 1954), p. 61.

8. "Introduction," Fraser, I, 30-32.

9. Ibid., 26-28.

10. Cf. Richard I. Aaron, *John Locke,* 2d ed. (Oxford: Clarendon Press, 1955), p. 277, and James Gibson, *Locke's Theory of Knowledge and Its Historical Relations* (Cambridge: Cambridge University Press, 1960), pp. 124-25.

11. All references and quotations will be from Fraser's edition, giving book number in Roman capitals, chapter number in lowercase Roman, and section number in Arabic, within parentheses in the text. Where no book number is given, the reference is to Book IV.

12. Aaron, p. 248. Although Locke was well aware of seventeenth-century developments in mathematics, including the calculus, the *Essay* shows no awareness of the beginnings of a mathematical theory of probability, based on games of chance. In his critique of the *Essay,* Leibniz says that *"a new kind of logic,"* treating the degrees of probability mathematically, would be extremely useful (*New Essays, concerning Human Understanding,* trans. A. G. Langley [LaSalle, Ill.: Open Court, 1949], p. 541).

13. John Locke, *Conduct of the Understanding,* ed. Thomas Fowler (Oxford: Clarendon Press, 1901), sec. xliv. Cf. *Essay,* IV, xvi, 4; xviii, 1.

14. Aristotle *Nichomachean Ethics,* i. 3.

15. This distinction seems to have been first made by Kant, in the final chapter of the *Critique of Pure Reason,* where "empiricists" and "noologists" are listed among the three great perennial divisions with regard to knowledge.

16. Fraser, II, 353, n.4.

17. Fraser, II, 367, notes 1, 3, 5.

18. In another context, discussing the species of corporeal substances, Locke gives the examples of gold, liquid when melted in a furnace, and jelly, congealed when cold, fluid when warm (III, vi, 13).

19. For other recent interpretations of the *Preface,* see W. K. Wimsatt, Jr., *Samuel Johnson on Shakespeare* (New York: Hill and Wang, 1960); M. J. C. Hodgart, *Samuel Johnson and his Times* (London: Batsford, 1962); B. H. Bronson, "Introduction," in Arthur Sherbo, ed., *Johnson on Shakespeare,* Vols. VII and VIII of the Yale Edition of the *Works of Samuel Johnson* (New Haven, 1968), VII, xiii-xxxviii; and Murray Krieger, "Fiction, Nature, and Literary Kinds in Johnson's Criticism of Shakespeare," ECS, 4 (1971), 184-98.

20. Sherbo, VII, 58-81 (criticism), 81-91 (history), 91-113 (scholarly editing). All references

to the *Preface* and to the *Proposals for an Edition of Shakespeare* (1756) will be to Sherbo's edition, with page references within parentheses in the text.

21. According to Johnson, it is of greater dignity to inquire "how far man may extend his designs" than it is to determine "in what rank we shall place any performance," but these are different inquiries and whatever answer we give to the former, it does not make the book worse or better (p. 81). I believe that Bronson is mistaken, therefore, in suggesting that the historical argument "is insinuating a criterion of relativism into critical judgments" (Sherbo, p. xxxii).

22. For other recent discussions of Johnson as editor see Arthur Sherbo, *Samuel Johnson, Editor of Shakespeare* (Urbana: University of Illinois Press, 1956) and R. E. Scholes, *Shakespeare Quarterly,* 11 (1960), 163-71.

23. Sherbo notes (p. 60, n.2) that continuance of esteem, as a test of literary merit, is also discussed in *Rambler* 92.

24. Cf. Donald J. Greene, *Samuel Johnson* (New York: Twayne Publishers, 1970), p. 188.

25. Walter Raleigh, "Johnson on Shakespeare," *Six Essays on Johnson* (Oxford: Clarendon Press, 1910), pp. 75-97; J. W. Krutch, *Samuel Johnson* (New York: Henry Holt & Co., 1944), pp. 333-34; W. J. Bate, *The Achievement of Samuel Johnson* (New York: Oxford University Press, 1961), pp. 41, 195-96, 200-203.

26. This is the defect, in my opinion, of an intelligent and provocative essay on the *Preface* by Murray Krieger, recently published in *Eighteenth-Century Studies* (see above, n.19). Taking three of Johnson's ideas, isolated from their original context, he assimilates them into a Hegelian dialectic of thesis, antithesis, and synthesis, totally foreign to Johnson's thinking. At the beginning of his essay and again at the end, Krieger speaks disarmingly, but too truly, of his "post-Kantian distortions."

13

White of Selborne: The Ethos of Probabilism

Having discussed Dr. Johnson's *Preface to Shakespeare* as an example of probable reasoning in humanistic thought (chap. 12, above), I should like here to examine another example, taken from a quite different area of inquiry: Gilbert White's *The Natural History and Antiquities of Selborne* (1789), a work on the botany, zoology, topography, and climatology of a small rural district—actually, a single parish in Hampshire.

Probable reasoning can legitimately and profitably be considered from a purely technical point of view, as a kind of logic or method of proof, with its own special rules of evidence, types of argument, and criteria of validation. White makes only a few generalizations about method in his book; he is not writing a technical treatise, and he seems to have assumed that the standards for valid biological inference and proof could be taken for granted, as well established by previous naturalists and generally understood by intelligent readers. The criteria governing his own reasoning, however, are quite clearly discernible in his arguments on particular questions, as well as in a number of brief statements and asides. Using a binomial system of classification, as he himself habitually does in identifying plants and animals, we may describe his kind of thinking as Baconian empiricism in genus, Lockeian probabilism in species. His relation to both of those great predecessors will be discussed below.

A paper delivered at the Eighteenth-Century Seminar of the Modern Language Association, New York, December 27, 1974, chaired by Professor Paula Backscheider.

249

But probabilism, as conceived and practiced by many eighteenth-century English writers, has a further, nontechnical dimension, a matrix of religious and ethical concepts and attitudes, as much imaginative and emotional as they are intellectual. In discussing White's *Natural History,* I will begin with the technical aspect, moving at the end of the essay to the extralogical framework, the ethos which suffuses the technical procedures with larger meanings and values.

Gilbert White (1720-93) was an Anglican country parson, classically educated at Basingstoke Grammar School and Oriel College, Oxford (B.A. 1743, elected fellow 1744, M.A. 1746), who was interested from boyhood in the flora and fauna of his native Hampshire. He early developed habits of close and systematic observation of natural phenomena, recorded first in a Garden Kalendar day by day, later in the Journal which became the basis of the *Natural History,* his one published book.[1]

The work is composed in the form of three series of letters. The first two, totaling 110 letters between them, are concerned with natural history; the third, on the antiquities of Selborne, will be disregarded here. The first 44 letters are addressed, under dates ranging from 1767 to 1780, to Thomas Pennant, author of *British Zoology,* a very popular book published by White's brother Benjamin, a London bookseller, who also published *Selborne* itself. The second series, 66 letters dated between 1769 and 1787, is addressed to the Hon. Daines Barrington, a lawyer, antiquarian, and gentleman naturalist (and, incidentally, a member of Dr. Johnson's Club).

The tone and style of the letters are in keeping with the epistolary form and the character of the addressees. Both Pennant and Barrington were well-educated men, fully participating in the Christian-classical culture of the period; White writes as a member of the same culture, who shares with them a special interest in natural history. He speaks throughout in the first person, and one of the chief sources of the much-celebrated charm of the letters is the omnipresence of White's highly individual yet unmistakably eighteenth-century mind and voice. He freely quotes passages in Greek or Latin, usually without translating, and he refers to the works of other naturalists as to writings already familiar to his correspondents. He is also fond of quoting from the poets, especially Milton, Thomson, and Virgil; one of his pleasantest letters speculates on the particular species of *hirundo* Virgil had in mind in a passage of the *Georgics,* concluding from several details that it was probably one of the swallows.[2]

All the letters are short, ranging in the first and most later editions from a single page to a maximum of four or five. Some are extremely miscellaneous, but a number of letters assemble observations, made over a long period of time, on a single subject. Among such "monographies," as White calls them, are the series of four letters on the chief English species of *hirundines* (DB 16, 18, 20, 21)[3] and the remarkable letter on earthworms, scarcely a page long, which anticipates many of the findings in Darwin's classic treatment of the subject (DB 35).[4] Many subjects are returned to again and again; White reaches a definite conclusion on some of the questions raised, but several of the most important of them are left open.

White in the Baconian Tradition

Anything like a full account of Bacon's program for the reform of philosophy and the sciences would obviously be out of place here, but a few of the most basic planks in his platform may be briefly summarized in order to bring out the Baconian strain in White's thought.

A fact that is not much stressed by some students of Bacon, though it seems to me fundamental, is his forceful rejection of both dogmatists and skeptics. After a few cursory observations, he says, the former "lay down the law of nature as a thing already searched out and understood," while the latter "have taken a contrary course, and asserted that absolutely nothing can be known."[5] The attitude of mind that Bacon advocates is not the Acatalepsia of the Greek skeptics, but Eucatalepsia—"not denial of the capacity to understand but provision for understanding truly, for I do not take away authority from the senses, but supply them with helps; I do not slight the understanding, but govern it" (*New Organon*, Aph. 126; cf. Aph. 37; Spedding, VIII, 158, 75). Truth is attainable, but only if it is pursued with a humble submission of mind to the facts of nature, and by means of the proper method, rigorously applied.

Bacon envisioned a New Philosophy to be developed in two distinct stages. The first, the compilation of an encyclopedic natural history, was an immense task, requiring the collaborative effort of many workers over a considerable, though not infinite, period of time—perhaps several generations. Its purpose was to record the results of comprehensive observations and experiments and to draw from them the first tentative, relatively low-level generalizations or axioms which they directly warranted. Bacon came to believe that the natural history, as the basis, starting point, and "true nursing mother" of philosophy, was even more essential than the methodology which he had hoped to develop in the *Novum Organum:*

. . . my Organum, even if it were completed, would not without the

> Natural History, much advance the Instauration of the Sciences, whereas
> the Natural History without the Organum would advance it not a little.
> (*De historia naturali et experimentali monitum,* Spedding, V, 133-34)

It was only in the second phase, nevertheless, that the great Instauration
would be brought to fruition. This phase, the Interpretation of Nature, would
build on the foundation of the natural history a complete philosophy, a
pyramidal theoretical structure of principles and laws in natural philosophy,
physic, and metaphysic (*De Augumentis,* Bk. III, Ch. iv; Spedding, VIII,
507). Bacon believed that the work of the first phase could be done by men of
moderate mental capacity, but that the second phase required a higher kind of
talent. He would have dearly loved to reserve the whole Interpretation of
Nature for himself, if only the natural history had been in existence to build it
on.[6]

In both stages, the method was to be inductive. Bacon's theory of
induction—with its interlocking doctrines of designed rather than random
observations, inclusions and exclusions through comparison of positive and
negative instances, tables for selecting and sorting the mass of historical data,
and so on—is far too complex and debatable to be treated adequately here. For
present purposes, it is perhaps sufficient to illustrate Bacon's most basic
methodological conviction by citing a well-known passage in the *Magna
Instauratio:*

> . . . in dealing with the nature of things I use induction throughout, and
> that in the minor propositions as well as the major. For I consider
> induction to be that form of demonstration which upholds the sense, and
> closes with nature, and comes to the very brink of operation, if it does
> not actually deal with it. . . . Now my plan is to proceed regularly and
> gradually from one axiom to another, so that the most general are not
> reached till the last, but when you do come to them, you find them not to
> be empty notions but well defined, and such as nature would really
> recognize as her first principles, and such as lie at the heart and marrow
> of things. ("The Arguments of the Several Parts," *M.I.,* Spedding, VIII,
> 42)

Bacon's many warnings against trust in authority are in part a consequence
of his conception of the state of learning in his age. Since he believed that the
truths of nature could be discovered only by making a totally new start, using
a different method, all previous philosophy and commonly received opinions
fell under suspicion; they might be good for something, but not for the New
Philosophy. The Idols of the Theatre—the phantasms implanted in the mind
by dogmas, systems, and wrong laws of demonstration—are given that name

because all those principles, axioms, and rules are "but so many stage-plays, representing worlds of their own creation after an unreal and scenic fashion" and received by men through tradition, credulity, and negligence (*N.O.*, Aph. 44; Spedding, VIII 78). But there is a more permanent and philosophical reason for rejecting arguments from authority, for even if the Baconian natural history now existed, the truth of its axioms would depend not on the prestige of its authors but on the observations and experiments from which their generalizations were derived. In the search for truth, we must go not to books but to nature, to the things themselves; if we aspire not to guess and divine, but to discover and know, we must "go to facts themselves for everything" (*M.I.*, Spedding, VIII, 46).

Two other precepts, though less basic, are important as anticipating certain aspects of the new inductive sciences soon to be developed on Baconian principles. One is that the things observed should, wherever possible, be "numbered, weighed, measured, defined." The value of careful measurements is partly utilitarian, because "practical working comes of the due combination of physics and mathematics," but they are also needed in many cases to guarantee the accuracy and dependability of the naturalist's generalizations. The other rule is that no aspect of nature—however ordinary or seemingly trivial, however "mean, illiberal, filthy"—should be neglected by the new philosophy; since the observations to be set forth in the natural history are not collected on their own account, their importance is to be measured not by what the things observed are worth in themselves, but "according to their indirect bearing upon other things, and the influence they may have upon philosophy" (*Parasceve*, Aphs. 6, 7; Spedding, VIII, 365).

Finally, there is Bacon's deeply rooted conviction that scientific knowledge would be "operative to relieve the inconveniences of man's estate" (*De Aug.*, Bk. II, Ch. ii; Spedding, VIII, 415). He distinguishes between experiments of "light" and experiments of "fruit," repeatedly asserting that the aim of the new philosophy is to bring light through axioms concerning the natures and causes of things (*N.O.*, Aph. 99; Spedding, VIII, 135). He warns against overeagerness in the pursuit of immediate practical benefits:

> . . . I wait for harvest-time, and do not attempt to mow the moss or to reap the green corn. For I well know that axioms once rightly discovered will carry whole troops of works along with them, and produce them, not here and there but in clusters. And that unseasonable and puerile hurry to snatch by way of earnest at the first works which come within reach, I utterly condemn and reject, as an Atalanta's apple that hinders the race. (*M.I.*, Spedding, VIII, 48)

Bacon is not a utilitarian or a pragmatist, since use is not for him a sign or test of truth, but the usefulness of scientific knowledge in improving man's condition is a great argument for its value.

In comparing White with Bacon, we must remember that a century and a half had intervened between the posthumous publication of Bacon's last work, *The New Atlantis* (1627), and the publication of White's *Natural History*. It was the same period in which America grew from the Mayflower Compact to the Constitution, and progress in the world of science was similarly spectacular. The main outlines of Bacon's program for science had been adopted and institutionalized by the founding of the Royal Society (incorporated by royal charter in 1662), which Joseph Glanvill saw as the fulfillment of Bacon's "Prophetick Scheam" of Salomon's House.[7] Its official journal, the *Philosophical Transactions,* had appeared continuously for more than a century when White wrote. By his generation, men were at work on scientific studies all over Europe, and a network of learned societies, books and journals, collections, museums, and botanic gardens had been built up, providing naturalists with much accumulated knowledge and many aids and models.

White was by no means isolated from the main currents of life and thought in his time. Though he lived in a small village, not easily accessible, he had responsibilities in London and Oxford which took him regularly to both centers. He was familiar with the major works of seventeenth- and eighteenth-century biology, both English and Continental. In identifying species, and for other purposes as well, he habitually cites John Ray (1627-1705), the first great English naturalist, and the later *Systema Naturae* of Linnaeus (1707-78). He also refers to the writings of Ray's associates, Francis Willughby and William Derham, and to Edward Stillingfleet and Stephen Hales, among British natural philosophers, and to such European biologists as Brisson, Réaumur, and Buffon, all Frenchmen, and Swammerdam, Kramer, and Scopoli, who were Dutch, Austrian, and Italian respectively. White's greatest debt is to men like these, rather than directly to Bacon, but they were all Baconian in working by inductive methods toward a universal natural history.

White describes himself as an "out-door naturalist," one who seeks to achieve the relatively humble aim of observing closely and recording accurately the "natural productions and occurrences" of a single topographical area ("Advertisement," p. 13; cf. DB 1). His most comprehensive biological generalization is the obvious, almost undisputable one that animal behavior is motivated by two instinctual drives, self-preservation and the propagation of the species (DB 8, 11), and his few original discoveries are all of a low order of generalization, very close to the observed phenomena.[8] Bacon would surely have judged him to be a commendable worker in the vineyard of natural history, a man of moderate talent doing essential, though unspectacular, tasks.

But White does not distinguish, as Bacon does, between two stages in the development of the new science. He thought of himself as a "thinking man" (a phrase he uses several times). Though not aspiring to resolve fundamental problems having broad theoretical implications, he did wish to study the world around him philosophically—to connect one observed phenomenon with others, to go beyond description to discover causes and mechanisms, to learn wherever possible not only the fact but the reason for the fact (DB 4, 66). He believed that systematic taxonomy is necessary, for without it nature would be a pathless wilderness, but that the botanist should not be content with a list of names:

> . . . he should study plants philosophically, should investigate the laws of vegetation, should examine the powers and virtues of efficacious herbs, should promote their cultivation. . . . System should be subservient to, not the main object of, pursuit. (DB 40)

White was not satisfied to be a collector and classifier; he hoped in some measure to be not merely an observer, but an Interpreter of Nature.

White's commitment to Baconian induction is everywhere apparent. The very notion of "parochial history" is Baconian, since it rests on the assumption that conclusions must always be grounded on close observation of particulars. As he repeatedly says, generalizations about nature can be asserted with confidence only after "many years of exact observation" (DB 16, 21). It is for this reason that he puts such a high value on "monographies," studies of limited scope dealing either with a single species or genus of animals, like his paper on earthworms, or with a variety of species inhabiting a particular district, like *Selborne* as a whole. Speaking of Scopoli's book on the flora and fauna of the Tyrol, he says:

> Monographers, come from whence they may, have, I think, fair pretence to challenge some regard and approbation from the lovers of natural history; for, as no man can alone investigate all the works of nature, these partial writers may, each in their department, be more accurate in their discoveries, and freer from errors, than more general writers; and so by degrees may pave the way to an universal correct natural history. (TP, 31; cf. DB 7, 10, 16)

White's attitude toward authority is less polemical than Bacon's, but as a good empiricist he "takes his observations from the subject itself, and not from the writings of others" (DB 1). He does need additional observations, to extend his data beyond those he has been able to observe himself, and he kept urging his relatives, friends, and correspondents to observe regularly in their own neighborhoods, to keep records and send him reports, and to send or bring specimens for firsthand study. He is always cautious and discriminating, however, in accepting the testimony not only of lay correspondents but of men like Réaumur, Linnaeus, Ray, and other naturalists. Some of his informants are "nice" or "very exact" observers, but others are less worthy of credit because they are not naturalists, lack ornithological knowledge, report facts at second hand, or observe too carelessly (TP 10, 44; DB 4, 14, 23, 24). White does not give implicit trust even to the fellow scientists whom he respects most, but maintains his independence of judgment and tests their findings against his own observations. Linnaeus's theory that swallows hibernate under water seems to him incredible, and Scopoli, though generally a good naturalist, falls into errors by comparing one animal with another by memory, without specimens before him (TP 32). Even Ray sometimes errs; after procuring and studying several specimens, both alive and dead, of a bird described by Ray, White concludes that it was "strangely classed" by his much admired predecessor, who ranged it under a quite impossible order (TP 25). For White, as for Bacon, the ultimate authority can only be nature itself, the objective phenomena, the facts.

White is also Baconian in his belief that no aspect of nature is unworthy of study. He is never squeamish, and many of the subjects he discusses might be considered "mean, illiberal, filthy" by more fastidious people, such as the burrowing habits of field crickets, the mysterious mechanisms of generation in toads and eels, the copulation of swifts while on the wing, the food of hedgehogs as indicated by their dung, the means by which young birds in the nest are saved from poisoning by their own excreta (TP 17, 27, 40; DB 21). He was well aware, too, that most things in nature are subject to quantitative variation, and that many phenomena can be accurately described only after careful counts or measurements, carried out over a long period of time. Speaking of mean rainfall, an obvious example, White gives figures for total annual rainfall in Selborne during the years 1779-87, which vary from twenty-seven to thirty-nine inches, but he declines even to estimate the average amount: "As my experience in measuring the water is but of short date, I am not qualified to give the mean quantity" (TP 5). He does give dates for the arrival and departure of migratory birds, and also the dates on which various species of birds begin and cease to sing, but he is careful to state that the figures can only be approximate, since the timing varies from year to year (DB 1-3). He remembers, too, that individuals within the same species may vary widely in size, weight, and other features, and that allowance must always be made for sex, age, and other variables. In reporting his most heroic effort of this kind, when he measured the putrefying carcass of a female moose, he apologizes because the stench made a closer and more detailed examination insupportable (TP 28).

On the usefulness of natural knowledge, as on the dangers of trusting to authority, White is more moderate than Bacon but holds an essentially similar view. He thinks, for example, that a full history of noxious insects "would be allowed by the public to be a most useful and important work," and regrets that such knowledge lies scattered, needing to be collected (TP 34). In a similar vein he reports on the raising and harvesting of hops, a principal Selborne crop, and gives an exact account of the process of manufacturing rushlights, as a much cheaper substitute for candles (TP 1; DB 26). He wishes that some future faunist would make a field expedition to Ireland, a country little known to naturalists, because a "person of a thinking turn of mind" would surely draw many just remarks and useful reflections from such a survey (TP 42). White believes that the kind of knowledge presented by a natural historian could be of great practical benefit, and he does not hesitate to point out possible applications of his own observations, but his primary aim in studying nature is simply to know and understand it. Light comes first, though fruits will surely follow.

White as a Lockeian Probabilist

Locke, of course, is another member of the Baconian genus. His theory of human understanding is an autonomous philosophy, with its own internal structural relations, its own vocabulary of concepts and terms; it incorporates many principles and distinctions not to be found in Bacon, and a number of Bacon's most cherished ideas (such as the Tables of Discovery for ordering observed data) have no place in Lockeian epistemology. Locke does subscribe, nevertheless, to several basic planks in Bacon's platform, adapting and restating them in his own terms.

The parallel is particularly close on the attainability of truth. Bacon offers a middle way between the dogmatists and the skeptics. In different words but to the same effect, Locke speaks scornfully of both the Pyrrhonists, who "question everything, and disclaim all knowledge, because some things are not to be understood," and at the opposite extreme those overconfident reasoners who presume that "the whole vast ocean of being is the natural and undoubted possession of our understandings.''[9] Truth in many things is not behond men's grasp, if they will only use properly the powers of understanding which have been given to them.

Because of his view that all reasoning consists in the comparison of ideas to determine their agreement or disagreement, Locke does not speak of induction and deduction, but he is as emphatic as Bacon in asserting that all knowledge begins in particulars, as perceived through observation and experience: ''For in *particulars* our knowledge begins, and so spreads itself, by degrees, to *generals*'' (IV, vii, 11). His attack on the syllogism as useless for the discovery of truth, good only for overcoming an opponent in debate, is as vigorous and eloquent as any of Bacon's many disquisitions on that subject.[10] His attitude toward authority is the same as Bacon's: it is utter folly for anyone who wishes to comprehend truth to regulate his assent by the opinion of others, because the only arguments that give true instruction are those which bring to the question ''light arising from the nature of things themselves'' (IV, xvii, 19-22; cf. xx, 17). Though he has little to say about the need for exact quantitative measurements, his understanding of the role of mathematics in science—thanks partly to Newton, born more than a generation too late to be known to Bacon—is actually much better than Bacon's.

One of the differences between Bacon and Locke is on the usefulness of natural knowledge. While Locke agrees that important material benefits may be expected to flow from inductive science, he does not press that point in defending his revolutionary approach to philosophy; when he speaks of the uses of understanding, he is much more inclined to think of its ethical value, as providing guidance in the pursuit of happiness and the conduct of our moral lives (''Introduction,'' Fraser, I, 30). Like White, he also differs from Bacon in conceiving science and philosophy as a single continuous process, thus collapsing the Baconian distinction between the first and second phases, the natural history and the interpretation of nature.

But the most fundamental difference between Bacon and Locke, at least in the present context, is their sharply divergent attitudes toward probable reasoning. Bacon believed that induction, correctly used, could arrive at clear and certain truth, eventually revealing the natures or forms, the inner causal principles explaining all the things and processes of the world and of man. He was familiar with probable reasoning, which had been discussed at length by Aristotle, Cicero, and other ancients, but he associated it with rhetoric and the wrangling of the schools. He says that the probabilism of the New Academy, allowing ''some things to be followed as probable, though of none to be maintained as true,'' is merely a diluted form of Pyrrhonism, which carries men round in a whirl of arguments and disheartens them for the severe but constructive discipline of inductive investigation (*N.O.*, Aph. 67; Spedding, VIII, 98). The end of the new philosophy is to invent arts, principles, and works, not arguments and probable reasons. Its aim is to comprehend nature in action: "to seek, not pretty and probable conjectures, but certain and demonstrable knowledge" ("Preface," *Magna Instauratio;* "Plan of the Work," *M.I.;* "Preface," *N.O.;* Spedding, VIII, 30-31, 40-41, 63-64).

While agreeing that truth is attainable in many things and that Pyrrhonism is mere nihilism and despair, Locke recognizes two paths toward human comprehension, not one alone. The first, which he calls "knowledge," is far superior because it leads to clear and certain truths: the existence of God and the necessity of obeying his commandments, the existence of external things and of ourselves as individuals, the axioms and conclusions of pure mathematics (IV, i-xiii). But Locke denies that our minds are capable of certain and demonstrable knowledge in any aspect of nature. What Bacon calls the forms or natures of things—in Locke's vocabulary, their "real essences"—are concealed from us. Since we can understand the species of natural substances only through an "imperfect collection of those apparent qualities our senses can discover," we cannot know the "precise bounds and extent" of any such species, nor grasp the causal relationships among their observable attributes and powers. To comprehend nature, therefore, we must fall back to the second path—from the bright sunshine of knowledge to the twilight of probability, a method leading to "*belief, assent,* or *opinion,* which is the admitting or receiving any proposition for true, upon arguments or proofs that are found to persuade us to receive it as true, without certain knowledge that it is so" (II, xxiii; III, vi, 9; IV, vi, 4-15; xv, 4).

For Locke, then, probable reasoning is a legitimate and fruitful method of inquiry, providing a rational basis for accepting or rejecting many propositions of great theoretical and practical importance. Though admittedly second-best, because it can never attain certainty, it is all we have to guide us both in the inductive sciences and in the ordinary affairs of human life.

The *Essay concerning Human Understanding* is, of course, a theoretical treatise on epistemology, not a handbook of practical logic. In the seven chapters devoted to probable reasoning in the fourth Book, nevertheless, Locke does establish the distinctive "grounds and measures" governing such reasoning and develops a number of specific concepts or principles concerning its use for discovery and proof. Since they were summarized at some length in my earlier paper, these ideas will not be reviewed again here. Instead, four of them will be briefly restated below, followed in each case by examples from the *Natural History,* in which White invokes the same principle or rule in reaching conclusions on the various biological problems that he considers.

HOW TESTIMONIES SHOULD BE WEIGHED

According to Locke, the second of two general "Grounds of Probability" is the testimony of others, vouching their observation and experience. In weighing testimonies, he says, we should apply six criteria: the number of witnesses; their integrity; their skill; the author's design, if the testimony is cited from a book; and contrary testimonies (IV, xv, 4). In judging the degree of credence to be given to the reports of lay correspondents and the findings of other naturalists, as we have seen above, White does not give implicit trust to the factual observations, still less to the opinions, of any authority. But the naturalists as a group are more reliable, because of their greater skill and integrity, though some of them are more rigorous than others; Ray is more dependable than Scopoli, but Ray too can err. Among the laymen, some are almost as intelligent, veracious, and exact as the best of the professionals, while others are careless, have too little knowledge, depend on hearsay, fail to mention the circumstances under which observations were made, or claim as fact what other observers have repeatedly denied. White's attitude toward authority is Baconian, but the specific criteria by which he weighs testimonies are those which Locke lays down.

REASONING FROM ANALOGY

The first, and more basic, ground of probability is the principle of analogy, the agreement or conformity of any proposition with *"common observation in like cases"* (xvi,9). Since Locke contends that in "most parts of the works of nature" all that we perceive is the sensible effects, we can only guess and conjecture concerning the "ways or means how they are produced," judging alleged causes to be probable or improbable "as they more or less agree to truths that are established in our minds, and as they hold proportion to other parts of our knowledge and observation. *Analogy* in these matters is the only help we have, and it is from that alone we draw all our grounds of probability." Locke recognizes that analogies can be false and deceptive, but he believes that a "wary" reasoning from analogy can often lead us to "the discovery of truths and useful productions, which would otherwise lie concealed" (xvi, 12).[11]

White frequently reasons from analogy, but he is extremely wary of its possible dangers. His ambiguous attitude is apparent in one of the letters to Pennant, in which he says that a problem which had long puzzled him, the reasons for the early departure of the swifts, might be resolved by analogy with a large species of bat:

> Though I delight very little in analogous reasoning, knowing how fallacious it is with respect to natural history; yet in the following instance, I cannot help being inclined to think it may conduce towards the explanation of a difficulty that I have mentioned before, with respect to the invariable early retreat of the *hirundo apus,* or swift, so many weeks before it's congeners.

Both the birds and the bats fly higher in feeding and emigrate earlier than related species; these are the observed phenomena, the "sensible effects" that Locke speaks of. White conjectures that in both cases the unknown cause is the kind of food available at those high altitudes, "some sorts of high-flying gnats, scarabs, or *phalaenae,* that are of short continuance; and that the short stay of these strangers is regulated by the defect of their food" (TP 26).

In spite of his qualms, White reasons from analogy on dozens of questions. He confesses—"not without some degree of shame"—that in believing that ouzels and fieldfares migrate to Selborne from the north he had reasoned only from analogy with other autumnal birds (TP 25). He confirms observations about the behavior of stone curlews by parallels with the manners of bustards, who also resemble the curlews in aspect and make, and in the structure of their feet (TP 33). He speculates that the relatively rare large bats may not be a separate species from the commoner small variety, but only males of the same species; the discrepancy in numbers might be explained by the ability of one male to serve many females, as among sheep and other quadrupeds (TP 36). He also draws inferences about the fattening of long-billed birds during moderate frosts from observations on rabbits and hogs; about the coloration of young birds by analogy with the lack of sexual differentiation in the young of quadrupeds and men; about a skeletal structure in fallow deer from an apparently similar one in men, and about the physiological function of that structure from facts about asses and horses (DB 5, 6; TP 14).

The dangers of analogous reasoning in natural history are well illustrated by the last of these instances, for modern biologists have shown quite conclusively that the resemblance between the spiracula of the fallow deer and the *puncta lachrymalia* in the human head is superficial and misleading, and that the spiracula are not secondary breathing-places, as White supposed, but outlets for a glandular secretion.[12] But in many of the works of nature, as Locke observes, analogy is "the only help we have, and it is from that alone we draw all our grounds of probability.'' White does not violate Locke's principles in comparing the spiracula with the *puncta lachrymalia,* since he claims no more than that they are ''*probably* analogous'' (italics mine).

Hypothesis in Biological Reasoning

In explaining any phenomenon of nature, Locke says, it is not improper to ''make use of any probable hypothesis whatsoever: hypotheses, if they are well made, are at least great helps to the memory, and often direct us to new discoveries.'' He warns, however, that hypotheses can easily lead us astray. Unless they are grounded on well-examined particulars, take account of negative instances, and are advanced tentatively rather than dogmatically, they can impose upon us by ''making us receive that for an unquestionable truth, which is really at best but a very doubtful conjecture; such as are most (I had almost said all) of the hypotheses in natural philosophy'' (IV, xii, 13; I, iii, vii; IV, vii).

A striking example of White's way of reasoning is his refutation of a hypothesis advanced by Herissant, a French anatomist. The problem is an old one, on which many naturalists had speculated: what prevents cuckoos from hatching their own eggs? Herissant hypothesizes that the placement of the cuckoo's crop, behind the sternum and immediately over the bowels, makes the process of incubation very uncomfortable, if not impossible. Having first confirmed the anatomical observation by making his own dissection of a specimen cuckoo, White then goes on to procure and dissect two other kinds of bird, the fern owl and ringtail hawk, both of which are known to hatch their eggs. Since it turns out that the crops of both birds lie in the same situation as the cuckoo's, Herissant's conjecture falls to the ground, leaving the problem still unsolved (DB 30). White's experiment neatly illustrates Bacon's method of positive and negative instances, as well as Locke's rule that hypotheses, though legitimate and necessary, should always be tested against observed data.

Faced with a problem that ''baffles our searches'' (DB 21), as naturalists so frequently are, a thinking man can only ''hazard a supposition'' (DB 23). In his search for the reason behind the fact, for the unknown causes of visible effects, White offers such conjectures on many occasions. Why should frequently flooded lands be poor? (DB 35). Why has leprosy almost totally disappeared in England? (DB 32). Why do house martins often reappear for a single day in November, after apparently departing, to a bird, early in October? (DB 36). How might we account for the fact that many kinds of birds, unsocial during most of the year, gather in great flocks during harsh winter weather? (DB 10). What motives could explain why "so cruel and sanguinary a beast as a cat" should adopt and foster a baby rabbit, usually its natural prey? (DB 34). To these and other queries, White sometimes offers a single possible solution, sometimes several alternative hypotheses. Whether singular or plural, these conjectures are legitimate, in a Lockeian logic of probability, because White never mistakes them for unquestionable truths. They are always advanced tentatively, almost diffidently, and often with a wish for additional information or an invitation for others to refute or support his proposals with further evidence.

THE DEGREES OF ASSENT

According to Locke, "the principle act of ratiocination is *the finding the agreement or disagreement of two ideas one with another, by the intervention of a third.*" This is the process both in demonstrative arguments, which can lead to certain knowledge, and in probable reasoning, which cannot; the difference is that in demonstration the agreement of the intermediary idea with the two extremes is clear and certain, while in judgments of probability it is only a "*usual* or *likely* one," a connection which is not constant and immutable, but "is, or appears for the most part to be so." Since the usual and the likely admit degrees of frequency—as "for the most part" also implies—a sound judge of probability must "take a true estimate of the force and weight of each probability; and then casting them up all right together, choose that side which has the overbalance." The degree of assent that we give to any probable proposition should be proportional to the extent of the overbalance favoring the more probable side. As the latter may vary "from the very neighborhood of certainty and demonstration, quite down to improbability and unlikeliness, even to the confines of impossibility," so the former should range from "full assurance and confidence, quite down to conjecture, doubt, and distrust" (IV, xv, 1, 2; xvii, 16, 18).

The conception that all thought consists in the comparison of ideas is an essential element in Locke's epistemology, but it arises from philosophical issues which need not concern a working naturalist. White does not speak of the agreement or disagreement of ideas; while always remembering that he knows his plants and animals only through observation and experiment, he assumes in commonsense fashion that he is comparing things with things, facts with facts. He is entirely in accord with Locke, however, in recognizing that biological propositions can never be certain, and that the degree of our confidence in them should be proportioned to the force and weight of the evidence in each case, which varies over a very wide range.

Since White, like Locke himself, has no statistical techniques for quantifying such judgments, he is forced to express the varying shades of assurance by a collection of graduated verbal distinctions. At one end of the scale, propositions so strongly supported that they almost reach the neighborhood of certainty may be described as "very near the truth" or even as "past all doubt," though such endorsements are often qualified by a "seems" or "appears" (TP 21, 22; DB 8, 21). At the opposite extreme are questions which are "too puzzling to answer," on which we are "very much in the dark" (TP 17, 34, 40). In between lies a spectrum from the very probable or more probable to the probable, the improbable, and the very improbable. Some generalizations are "true on the whole," and on some problems we can be "pretty sure," "pronounce with some certainty," or believe with "sufficient show of reason" (TP 17; DB 7, 17, 42). In some cases the evidence "seems to be a full proof" or constitutes "a strong proof to the contrary," but in others we may "have some doubt" or be "ready to doubt" (DB 1, 3, 8, 16). This vocabulary, almost identical with the one Dr. Johnson uses for the same purpose in the *Preface to Shakespeare,* was the only language available for making such discriminations in a prestatistical age. Though imprecise, it expresses very well the shadings appropriate to a second-best method, to the twilight world of probable reasoning.

The Ethos of Probabilism

The "ethos" of probabilism, as I have rather vaguely called it, is grounded on a set of mutually coherent concepts in morality and divinity, "those parts of knowledge that men are most concerned to be clear in" (Locke, ed. Fraser, I, 16), but it is not wholly intellectual; associated with the ideas is an interlocking complex of imaginative and emotional responses or attitudes toward God, nature, and man. Both aspects of this Weltanschauung are manifested in ideas and feelings expressed by Locke, by John Ray, the English naturalist so much admired by White, and by White himself.

LOCKE AND THE ETHOS OF PROBABILISM

Locke's *Essay* is a secular work on a specialized subject. It is based not on revealed truth but on arguments and evidence available to natural reason, and its epistemological conclusions describe human understanding as it operates on this earth and is comprehended by us through observation, experience, and ratiocination. But Locke was a deeply religious man, who saw nature and mankind in a theological perspective. Without violating his empirical methodology or overstepping the boundaries of his specialized concerns, he indicates in many places that the powers and limits of the human mind may be set into a wider context of religious and philosophical truths.

Locke believed that the existence and attributes of God could be proved with demonstrative certainty; his argument is an inference from an intuitively known effect, our own existence as thinking beings, to its cause, the prior existence of *"an eternal, most powerful, and most knowing Being"* (IV, x, 1-6). He also believed, but does not attempt to prove, that from the ideas of a supreme Being and of ourselves as corporeal rational creatures "a great part of morality might be made out with that clearness, that could leave, to a considering man, no more reason to doubt, than he could have to doubt of the truth of propositions in mathematics, which have been demonstrated to him." Since he does not prove this proposition, but merely asserts it as a possibility, he is careful to describe it as a "conjecture" which he has "suggested" (III, xi, 16; IV, iii, 18; iv, 7; xii, 8).

The wise and almighty Being is the creator not only of man but of all existing things. If there are spiritual creatures higher than man in the scale of being—a fact which natural reason can only conjecture from a probable argument by analogy, but which may be certainly known from reve- lation—there must remain an infinite gap between the highest of such crea- tures and the Supreme Being (xvi, 12). As for sublunary things, inanimate or animate, they are all dependent, imperfect, subject to change and dissolution. By the goodness of the Maker, nevertheless, each kind has been given the qualities and powers which fit it for the specific conditions and state of being which have been assigned to it in the divine scheme of the whole (II, ix, 11-14; xxiii, 12-13).

Man is the only corporeal creature endowed with understanding—"an intelligent, but frail and weak being, made by and depending on another" (IV, xiii, 4). His mixed, imperfect nature is suited to the conditions of his life, a "fleeting state of action and blindness," and his understanding, capable of certain knowledge in a few things but for the most part given only the flickering light of probability, is appropriate to that "state of mediocrity and probationership he has been pleased to place us in here." The business of our lives, as intended by God, is to "spend the days of this our pilgrimage with industry and care, in the search and following of that way which might lead us to a state of greater perfection" (xiv, 2; xvi, 4).[13]

In spite of our weakness and frailty, God has given us powers which are sufficient, if we will only use them rightly, to comprehend "whatsoever is

necessary for the conveniences of life and information of virtue''
(''Introduction,'' Fraser, I, 29). The bright sunshine of knowledge is a
marvelous gift, though its extent is very short and scanty. Where it fails, we
must fall back upon probable reasoning; though it will always leave us in
twilight, it is a power we are meant to use actively to understand ourselves,
nature and our place in it, and our duties toward God and our fellow man. In
Lockeian ethics, intellectual sloth is one of the worst of sins, because it shows
an impious ingratitude toward our maker.

This view of God, nature, and man has obvious emotional correlatives,
which Locke expresses at several points. Toward the Creator, if we sincerely
believe in him, the natural and proper feelings are love, reverence, and
humble gratitude. In spite of Locke's belief that *''the proper science and
business of mankind in general''* is morality, he does not disesteem the study
of nature nor dissuade men from it, because nature is God's creation and ''the
contemplation of his works gives us occasion to admire, revere, and glorify
their Author'' (xii, 11-12). Toward man and human understanding, the right
attitude is a mixture of humility for our weakness, an uncomplaining
acceptance of the limits of our powers, gratitude for the capacities which we
have been given, pleasure and pride in their active use, and an untiring love of
truth:

> For though the comprehension of our understandings comes exceeding
> short of the vast extent of things, yet shall we have cause enough to
> magnify the bountiful Author of our being, for that proportion and degree
> of knowledge he has bestowed on us, so far above the rest of the
> inhabitants of this our mansion. (''Introduction,'' I, 29; cf. IV, xii, 12;
> xix, 1)

By such ideas and feelings, Locke places the logic of probability in a religious
and ethical context, which animates the technical procedures with larger
meanings and values.

JOHN RAY AND THE PHYSICO-THEOLOGISTS

John Ray presents the ethos of probabilism in a form that is somewhat
different from Locke's, but is fully consistent with it. He was a contemporary
of Locke, Newton, and Boyle, a fellow of the Royal Society from 1667 until
his death in 1705, and a devout Anglican who gave up his Cambridge
fellowship and the priesthood because he could not bring himself to subscribe
to the Act of Uniformity. In addition to works on ornithology, quadrupeds,

plants, fishes, and insects, Ray published near the end of his life a book, *The Wisdom of God Manifested in the Works of the Creation* (1691), which uses a wide-ranging knowledge of astronomy, zoology, and botany to provide *a posteriori* proofs of the existence and attributes of an Almighty Power, creator of the universe and all things in it. The book, which took its original inspiration from Henry More's *Antidote against Atheism* (1652), belongs to a tradition known to intellectual historians as "physico-theology." In his Preface, Ray mentions More, Ralph Cudworth, Edward Stillingfleet, and Robert Boyle as earlier writers on the same subject; he incorporates ideas, arguments, and examples from all of them along with much additional material from other sources and from his own investigations.

As a scientist, Ray was a Baconian and a probabilist of the same kind as White. Like Bacon, he expresses great scorn for natural philosophers who "endeavor to give an Account of any of the Works of Nature, by preconceiv'd Principles of their own." His example is Descartes, whose theories of the pulse of the heart and the transference of motion from one body to another are "grossly mistaken, and confuted by Experience."[14] Like Locke, he distinguishes between demonstrative and probable proofs (pp. 25-26, 44), argues warily from analogy (p. 71), recognizes that all hypotheses are open to question, but that some are far more probable than others (p. 36), and regulates the degree of his assent to any proposition in proportion to the force and weight of the evidence for and against it (pp. 72, 76, 121-22, 217). White needed no other instructor and model for sound biological reasoning, for all the elements of his method are already clearly present and powerfully operative in Ray.

The common element in the writing of all the physico-theologists is an elaborate, scientifically sophisticated version of the argument from design. Ray's text, quoted at the beginning of Part I of his book, is a passage from the Psalms: "How manifold are thy Works, O Lord! In Wisdom hast thou made them all" (p. 25; Ps. civ. 24). We may "trace the Footsteps of his Wisdom" in the composition, order, harmony, and uses of the visible creation, offering "Proofs, taken from Effects and Operations, expos'd to every Man's View, not to be deny'd or question'd by any" (Preface). In Part I he first reviews the heavenly bodies, then turns to terrestrial inanimate bodies—fire, air, water, including the sea, its tides, and freshwater springs and rivers—and finally to the structures, parts, and behavior of living things. Part II discusses in a similar manner the shape and motion of the earth and the anatomy and physiology of man. Ray believes, again in opposition to Descartes, that final causes can be discovered in organic life, though not with certainty (pp. 42, 182), and that mechanical principles cannot explain the actions of living creatures, which require as their efficient cause some kind of "*plastick Nature,* or vital Principle" (pp. 49-51, 74, 93-94, 243). Since animals and men are not machines or automata, the God to be inferred from them cannot be a mere clockmaker. This rejection of the teaching of "*mechanick Theists,*" like Descartes, is perhaps the most distinctive feature of physico-theological thought (p. 45).

Ray's religious view of nature, as bearing everywhere the "Signatures of the Divine Art and Wisdom" (p. 46), has far-reaching moral implications. Bacon had said that nothing in nature is unworthy of study, because axioms contributing to the primary history can be drawn even from things which in themselves seem mean, illiberal, and filthy. Ray gives a different reason for the same conclusion. When the Psalmist calls upon all creatures to praise God, it is as much as to say:

> Ye Sons of Men, neglect none of his Works, those which seem most vile and contemptible: There is Praise belongs to him for them. Think not that any Thing he hath vouchsafed to create, is unworthy thy Cognizance, to be slighted by thee. It is Pride and Arrogance, or Ignorance and Folly, in thee so to think. There is a greater Depth of Art and Skill in the Structure of the Meanest Insect, than thou art able for to fathom, or comprehend. (p. 156)

It would be pride and folly for such a being as man to admire himself or seek his own glory, for he is, no less than the plants and animals, "a Dependent Creature, and hath nothing but what he hath received; and not only dependent but imperfect; yea, weak and impotent" (pp. 159-60). But the Creator in his goodness has endowed man, alone among his creatures, with the capacity for knowing and understanding his works, and it is our bounden duty to use those powers in his service:

> And therefore those who have Leisure, Opportunity, and Abilities, to contemplate and consider any of these Creatures, if they do it not, do as it were rob God of some Part of his Glory, in neglecting or slighting so eminent a Subject of it, and wherein they might have discovered so much Art, Wisdom and Contrivance. (p. 156)

For Ray, the study of nature is a form of worship, to be pursued with "*Admiration, Humility, and Gratitude*" (Preface)—admiration for the splendor of all God's works, humility for our own weakness, and gratitude for the boundless gifts of a wise and merciful Creator. The greatest of these gifts is the human understanding, imperfect though it is, which is given to us not only so that we can plant and build for our greater comfort, but in order that we may comprehend God's creation and repay him with thanks and praise.

WHITE AS PHYSICO-THEOLOGIST

There is only one explicit reference to physico-theology in White's *Natural History,* but it is a very appealing one. He describes the playful sporting and diving of rooks on an autumn evening, which is accompanied by a continual cawing, softened by the air to "a pleasing murmur, very engaging to the imagination," until they finally retire to the woods for the night. White then comments:

> We remember a little girl who, as she was going to bed, used to remark on such an occurrence, in the true spirit of *physico-theology,* that the rooks were saying their prayers; and yet this child was much too young to be aware that the scriptures have said of the Deity—that 'he feedeth the ravens who call upon him.' (DB 59)

There is also only one reference to Ray's *Wisdom of God* (TP 17), but White must have known the book well, for many pieces of information scattered through the letters can also be found in Ray's book, from which we may presume they were taken.[15] In his biography of Ray, Charles Raven mentions White, along with Bishop Butler and John Wesley, as eighteenth-century Christians who followed Ray in their reverence for nature and in defending its study not only as compatible with religion but as filled with religious meaning and value.[16]

White does not write as a parson, though he was one, and his religious views are not obtruded upon the reader. It is obvious, however, that he shares Ray's belief that the effects and operations of nature reveal an admirable wisdom and contrivance, which White ascribes in his mild, unpreachy manner to Providence. Speaking of the transformations of the frog, from the fishlike tadpole to the tailless but footed adult, he exclaims: "How wonderful is the oeconomy of Providence" in adapting the animal first to an aquatic and then to a terrestrial life (TP 17). Speculating on a suggestion of Barrington's that cuckoos appear to be selective in choosing nursing mothers for their eggs and young, White says that, if the observation is true, it "would be adding wonder to wonder, and instancing, in a fresh manner, that the methods of Providence are not subject to any mode or rule, but astonish us in new lights, and in various and changeable appearances" (DB 4). He finds it curious, too, in comparing the nest building of the sand martin with that of the house martin and swallow, "to observe with what different degrees of architectonic skill Providence has endowed birds of the same genus, and so nearly correspondent in their general modes of life!" (DB 20). The times of blooming of the vernal and autumnal crocuses, which the best botanists have been unable to distinguish by any other attribute, also seem to him strange and wonderful:

"This circumstance is one of the wonders of the creation, little noticed, because a common occurrence: yet ought not to be overlooked on account of it's being familiar, since it would be as difficult to be explained as the most stupendous phaenomenon in nature" (DB 41). White even wrote a short poem on the crocuses; he asks what impels or retards their blooming, and then answers:

> The *God* of *Seasons!* whose pervading power
> Controls the sun, or sheds the fleecy shower;
> *He* bids each flower his quick'ning word obey,
> Or to each lingering bloom enjoins delay.
>   (World's Classics ed., p. 9)

White's reasoning on biological problems is rational and objective, using an empirical and probabilistic method, but his response to nature is far from being purely intellectual. As he frequently remarks, natural phenomena appeal strongly to the imagination. In recommending that some future faunist should pay a visit to Ireland, he predicts that such an expedition would produce not only just conclusions and useful remarks but great aesthetic pleasure from the "picturesque lakes and waterfalls, and the lofty stupendous mountains, so little known, and so engaging to the imagination when described and exhibited in a lively manner" (TP 42). He feels that way himself whenever he sees the majestic sweep of the Sussex downs; though he had known them for thirty years, he still finds new beauties and feels fresh admiration whenever he visits them. Echoes from the wooded hill back of Selborne have a fine effect on the imagination, especially when they cease and then resume, "like the pauses in music"; and the grotesque shapes into which snow was driven during a prodigious storm in 1776 were "so striking to the imagination as not to be seen without wonder and pleasure" (DB 17, 60, 62). Feeling, too, enters strongly into his response to nature, especially toward all kinds of animals. He speaks with great affection of the busy field crickets and curious hedgehogs; of Timothy the tortoise, who lived for many years in the garden of an aunt of White's and was moved after her death to his own; and, above all, of his beloved *hirundines,* those "amusive" swallows, martins, and swifts which he observed with so much attention and pleasure almost all his life (TP 10, 23, 27; DB 6, 13, 46, and passim).

Though of course highly personal, White's imaginative and emotional reactions to nature have an intellectual basis and justification in his conviction that Creation everywhere manifests an order, design, purposiveness, and inexhaustible bounty reflecting its divine Maker. His outlook can perhaps be summed up by a final quotation. As so often in White, it is the swallows and martins which call forth his deepest reflections:

I could not help being touched with a secret delight, mixed with some degree of mortification: with delight, to observe with how much ardour and punctuality those poor little birds obeyed the strong impulse towards migration, or hiding, imprinted on their minds by their great Creator; and with some degree of mortification, when I reflected that, after all our pains and inquiries, we are yet not quite certain to what regions they do migrate; and are still further embarrassed to find that some do not actually migrate at all (TP 23).

Whether these birds migrate or hibernate is one of the questions to which he returns again and again throughout the letters, but which remains unresolved because the evidence for and against both possibilities is so evenly balanced that a conscientious probabilist can make no decision. Though it is mortifying to reach that conclusion after so many pains and inquiries, it is not at all surprising: in the twilight world of probable reasoning, our searches must often be baffled. But whatever the solution to this problem may be, White does not doubt that the cause will finally turn out to be an impulse planted in the minds of his creatures by the great Creator, still another manifestation of his power, wisdom, and goodness, and that is what makes the behavior of those poor little birds so delightful.

To be clear about the thesis of this essay, I should add that I do not mean to argue that there is any necessary connection between a commitment to probable reasoning, in biology or in any other field of inquiry, and the complex of religious and moral ideas and attitudes which I have been sketching. There have been many thinkers in several ages who have accepted probability as the best—even the only possible—method of discovery and proof, but who have not been willing to subscribe to the Weltanschauung within which that method was so intimately integrated by Locke, Ray, White, and Johnson. The obvious exceptions in the same period are Gibbon and Hume, both probabilists though neither was an orthodox Christian, and of course there have been many others in different countries and ages who have divorced the logic of probability from its theological and ethical context. All I want to claim is that for many British thinkers of the seventeenth and eighteenth centuries the technical procedures of probable reasoning were suffused with religious meaning, and that we cannot fully understand their writings unless we recognize that fundamental fact.

Notes

1. The standard biography is by Rashleigh Holt-White, *Life and Letters of Gilbert White of Selborne*, 2 vols. (London, 1901). Selections from the "Naturalist's Journal" have been edited by Walter Johnson, *Gilbert White's Journals* (New York: Taplinger, 1970).

2. *The Natural History and Antiquities of Selborne*, Letter 19 to Barrington. The text I have followed is that of the World's Classics edition (London: Oxford University Press, 1902). References will be given within parentheses in the text; the letters to Pennant will be identified as TP, with the number of the letter in Arabic, and those to Barrington as DB 7, etc. Since the letters are so short, page numbers will not be given.

3. The substance of these letters had previously been published in the Royal Society's *Philosophical Transactions,* but White makes several corrections and additions in preparing them for inclusion in the *Natural History.*

4. See *Darwin on Humus and the Earthworm,* ed. Sir Albert Howard (London: Faber & Faber, 1966); the study was originally published in 1881.

5. "Preface" to *The New Organon, The Works of Francis Bacon,* ed. Spedding, Ellis, and Heath (Boston, 1861 and following years), VIII, 59; hereafter cited as Spedding, with volume and page numbers within parentheses in the text.

6. In the Utopian fictional image of this scheme in the *New Atlantis,* it is striking that only three of the thirty-six fellows in Salomon's House are Interpreters of Nature, who "raise the former discoveries by experiments into greater observations, axioms, and aphorisms," all the rest being engaged in various tasks of the natural history.

7. Joseph Glanvill, *Scepsis Scientifica,* ed. John Owen (London, 1885), p. lxv; first published 1665. Cf. Thomas Spratt, *History of the Royal Society,* ed. Jackson I. Cope and Harold W. Jones (St. Louis: Washington University Press, 1958), pp. 35-36.

8. White's most important contributions were the identification of two new species, the harvest mouse and the noctule owl; the separation of willow wrens into three distinct species; and the conclusions from a variety of evidence that the ring ouzel is migratory and that the genetic ancestor of the domestic pigeon was the blue rock dove (TP 12, 16, 19, 24, 44).

9. Locke, *Essay concerning Human Understanding,* ed. A. C. Fraser (Oxford: Clarendon Press, 1894), I, 30-32. All references and quotations will be from Fraser's ed., giving book numbers in Roman capitals, chapter numbers in lower-case Roman, and section number in Arabic, within parentheses in the text. Where no book number is given, the reference is to Book IV.

10. For Bacon's attack on syllogistic reasoning see, e.g., *De Aug.,* Bk. V, Ch. ii; Spedding, IX, 69-70. Cf. Locke, *Essay,* IV, xvii, 4-8.

11. Cf. Locke's *Conduct of the Understanding,* ed. Thomas Fowler, 5th ed. (Oxford: Clarendon Press, 1901), sec. 40.

12. Cf. *Natural History of Selborne,* ed. Grant Allen (New York: Dodd, Mead, 1923), p. 63n.

13. Cf. the entry on "Theology" in *Conduct of the Understanding,* sec. 23.

14. John Ray, *The Wisdom of God in Creation,* 11th ed. (Glasgow, 1744), pp. 48-49; page numbers will be given within parentheses in the text. The best biography of Ray is Charles E. Raven, *John Ray, Naturalist: His Life and Works* (Cambridge: Cambridge University Press, 1942).

15. A particularly striking example is the discussion of maternal instinct, or *storge,* by Ray, pp. 109-10, and by White (DB 4, 14). White also refers (TP 34) to William Derham's Boyle Lectures, *Physico-Theology: or a Demonstration of the Being and Attributes of God from his Works of Creation* (1712).

16. Raven, pp. 452, 477-78.

PART FIVE

———— ⚜ ————

Jane Austen

14

Mind, Body, and Estate:
Jane Austen's System of Values

Most of Jane Austen's critics mention values in passing, recognizing that something of the kind is woven into the texture of her novels. Ian Watt, for example, speaks of the ''positive norms'' which underlie them. Most readers today, he says, are unlikely either to believe in universal norms or to look for them in fiction, but a definite scheme of values is at work in all her stories: ''Jane Austen's own standards—always present in her use of such abstract terms as 'reason,' 'civility,' 'respectability,' and 'taste'—were, like those of her age, much more absolute; and as a novelist she presented all her characters in terms of their relation to a fixed code of values.''[1] Walter Allen briefly lists the standards of judgment which he finds in the novels: ''These are indeed the criteria by which Miss Austen judges her characters: self-command, just consideration of others, knowledge of the heart, and a principle of right derived from education.''[2] But neither he nor anyone else has attempted to define her values explicitly, examine them as a coherent system of ideas, or discuss their functions in the novels as works of art.

Since the subject is surely an important one for the understanding and appreciation of Jane Austen's six comic masterpieces, the purpose of this essay is to explore it more systematically than has been done hitherto. The values to be discussed here are qualities predicated of human beings, personal traits or attributes by which the characters in the stories are differentiated from each other and judged as admirable and likable or the reverse. Stated baldly, my thesis will be that five basic criteria are operative in Jane Austen's characterization of her fictional people: intelligence, morality, feeling, beauty, and worldly condition (rank and fortune). Other standards are also appealed to—manners, taste, feminine "accomplishments"[3]—but they are less important. My account will be based on *Pride and Prejudice,* with occasional reference to other novels to clarify or confirm particular points.

Since the novels are written in a colloquial style, very close to that of ordinary conversation among educated people in Jane Austen's time, the values are not stated in precise philosophical terms. Yet if one went through *Pride and Prejudice* carefully, collecting all the passages of interpretation and judgment pertinent to the five values, he would find quite a clear, firm, well-thought-out structure of ideas. Let us take them up in the order just listed.

ℑℑℑ

Intelligence

No reader, I suppose, could fail to recognize the high value Jane Austen places on intelligence. The cast of characters in *Pride and Prejudice* can be divided cleanly, right down the middle, on the basis of this single criterion: Mrs. Bennet and the younger girls, Mr. Collins, Lady Catherine de Bourgh,[4] Mrs. Philips, Sir William and Lady Lucas are all stupid people, though in differing ways. Elizabeth and Jane, their father, Bingley and Darcy, Charlotte Lucas, and the Gardiners all have good minds—good "parts," as Jane Austen says in her eighteenth-century vocabulary.

The words commonly used in the novels to describe this capacity of the mind are "understanding" and "sense." It is not speculative ability, genius in philosophy, science, or art; it is certainly not Imagination in a Wordsworthian sense, "reason in its most exalted mood." It is mind operating in mundane but vital concerns, the daily affairs of family and neighborhood—meeting the issues and problems, making the judgments and decisions that determine the quality of human lives and the happiness or unhappiness of the people who live them. The chief use of intelligence, in this context, is the understanding of other human beings, their motives and behavior, but it also involves a sound comprehension of the world in which one lives. Intelligence is needed to grasp even such a legal technicality as the entail on Mr. Bennet's estate, which requires its eventual inheritance by Mr. Collins, not by Mrs. Bennet or any of the Bennet daughters. He and his two elder daughters understand this perfectly, however much they may regret it, but to his wife it is an outrageous, unfathomable mystery.[5]

Intelligence, as conceived by Jane Austen and dramatized in her narratives, includes the practical good sense which can find the solution to real-life problems, small and large. Darcy conspicuously illustrates this ability when he paces up and down in the inn at Lambton, silently thinking out the measures to be taken to find Wickham and Lydia in London, after their elopement, and to persuade Wickham to marry her (III, iv, 278). He goes on, of course, to execute the plan with exemplary competence; it includes, among many other intelligent judgments and actions, a shrewd understanding of Wickham as a human being and of what will be needed to bring him round (III, x, 321-25; xvi, 370; xvii, 377).

Intelligence or the lack of it is manifested from moment to moment in all the actions, thoughts, judgments, and choices of Jane Austen's characters, but its most important expression is the ability, attained by only a few of them, to understand and correct their own faults and errors. The plot of *Pride and Prejudice* turns on the capacity for self-knowledge, achieved gradually and with difficulty, of its two chief characters. Darcy must and does learn that his pride has caused him to alienate Elizabeth and do real harm to her sister and his friend Bingley. Elizabeth must and does learn that prejudice, based on superficial first impressions, has blinded her to Wickham's defects and Darcy's merits. The crucial turning point is her painful reinterpretation of people and events after she receives Darcy's letter. She reads and rereads it, weighing every statement until the truth of his account can no longer be denied:

> She grew absolutely ashamed of herself.—Of neither Darcy nor Wickham could she think, without feeling that she had been blind, partial, prejudiced, absurd.
> "How despicably have I acted!" she cried.—"I, who have prided myself on my discernment!—I, who have valued myself on my abilities! . . . I have courted prepossession and ignorance, and driven reason away. . . . Till this moment, I never knew myself." (II, xiii, 208)

All of Jane Austen's heroes and heroines aspire to be rational creatures: not only to *be* intelligent, that is, but to use their minds actively to understand themselves, other people, and the world around them as they actually are and in their true proportions. In this sense Jane Austen is a rationalist, very much a part of the central eighteenth-century tradition.

She sometimes makes distinctions of degree between the minds of her characters, and these discriminations are always important for the story and our response to it. Though all his daughters are silly and ignorant, according to Mr. Bennet, Lizzy is his favorite because she has "something more of quickness than her sisters" (I, i, 5). Elizabeth's gaiety of spirit may have other sources as well, but her wit and sense of the comic would be impossible without this liveliness of mind. Darcy, too, is "clever," clearly superior in understanding to his friend Bingley. But even in making this point, the narrator is careful to state explicitly—and to show by his actions and speeches—that Bingley is "by no means deficient" (I, iv, 16). If he were, we could not respect him or Jane's love for him, and we would not want the story to end with their marriage as well as with Elizabeth's to Darcy.

A formula for a bad marriage is the union of intellectual unequals, an intelligent person with a stupid one, as in the unfortunate instance of Mr. and Mrs. Bennet. Charlotte Lucas's marriage to Collins is a striking case in point: Elizabeth thoroughly disapproves it, because a marriage without mutual respect is terribly dangerous, and no woman as intelligent as Charlotte could possibly esteem such a fool as Collins. But Charlotte's patience, tact, and good sense, along with her determination to make it succeed, are perhaps enough to make the marriage work tolerably well—well enough, at least, to meet the low level of expectation to which Charlotte has consciously reduced her hopes (I, xxii, 125; II, v, 157; ix, 178; xv, 216). Though her choice is a depressing exception, the intelligent belong together in the world of these novels, and the best of them manage to find each other in the end.

Morality

In a long and perceptive essay on Jane Austen, Richard Whately, a nineteenth-century Anglican archbishop of Dublin, contrasted the unobtrusiveness of her religious and moral principles with Maria Edgeworth's direct attempt at moral teaching, always pressing every circumstance of her story into the service of a principle to be inculcated or information to be given. Miss Austen is an unmistakably Christian writer, and her ethical judgments are clearly and impressively conveyed; but no one could describe any of her novels as a "dramatic sermon." Her values are not offensively put forward or forced upon the reader, but spring incidentally from the events of the story. In her tales, instruction "join[s] as a volunteer."[6]

The good bishop may be suspected of clerical bias, but he is certainly correct both on the nondidactic character of her narratives and on the presence in them of religious and moral values. The religion is clearly Christian, but particular doctrines are absent from the novels and no theological issues are raised. Miss Austen does not separate faith from ethics; she seems to take both as parts or aspects of a single body of belief. The key word is "principle," an umbrella term which firmly asserts the need for a moral standard but does not specify its laws in detail; she apparently takes these for granted, as already

well known to her readers, and specific rules of right and wrong are brought
into play, as Whately suggests, only as the circumstances of the stories call for
them. Typical of the reticent and allusive handling of this whole realm of
values is Elizabeth's recognition, when she reviews all the circumstances of
her acquaintance with Wickham and Darcy, that there had never been
anything in the latter's behavior "that betrayed him to be unprincipled or
unjust—any thing that spoke him of irreligious or immoral habits" (II, xiii,
207). Vague though this is, we are left in no doubt that religious and ethical
principles are applied by admirable characters like Elizabeth in her relations
with others, and also by the narrator in judging all of her fictional people.[7]

In *Pride and Prejudice,* the contrast between the virtuous and the
unprincipled is most clearly illustrated by Jane Bennet and Wickham. Jane's
"rectitude and delicacy" (I, xxiii, 128) shine through everything she does,
feels, and says. Though we cannot conceive of her violating any of the ten
commandments, her goodness is not merely an observance of Christian
shalt-nots.[8] It is a positive, active virtue; Jane has "the most generous and
forgiving heart in the world" (III, xiii, 350), a charity of spirit which makes
her want to think as well as she can of everyone she knows, as well as to
desire their good. Elizabeth, with her satirical eye and shrewdness of
observation, recognizes early in the novel that Bingley's sisters are proud and
conceited, with little real concern for anyone but themselves; yet she loves her
sister for trying, in her unaffected candor, to think them kind and amiable.
"To be candid without ostentation or design," Elizabeth says, "—to take the
good of everybody's character and make it still better, and say nothing of the
bad—belongs to you alone" (I, iv, 14-15). There is an element of illusion in
Jane's charitable outlook, but she is good beyond almost anyone in Jane
Austen's novels, and especially admirable and lovable on that account.

By contrast, Darcy condemns Wickham, by no means too harshly, for his
"vicious propensities" and "want of principle" (II, xii, 200). It is a
humiliating irony, recognized by both Mr. Bennet and Elizabeth, that they
have to be thankful to have Lydia finally married to Wickham, "one of the
most worthless young men in Great Britain" (III, viii, 308; vii, 304). He is
most reprehensible not for his self-indulgent dissipations, his gambling and
sexual laxity—though these habits obviously make it unthinkable for him to
be a clergyman—but rather for his ingrained selfishness, his vengeful hatred
of Darcy, and his unscrupulous exploitation of his own charm of person and
manner to deceive others; as Elizabeth tells her aunt, "he is as false and
deceitful, as he is insinuating" (III, v, 284; vi, 294). In keeping with the
comic spirit which presides throughout *Pride and Prejudice,* Wickham
becomes in the end not a villain but Mr. Bennet's favorite son-in-law, second
only to Mr. Collins as a source of scornful amusement. Elizabeth's father

would not give up the latter's correspondence for any consideration, but he values almost as much the transparent impudence and hypocrisy of Wickham, perpetually simpering, smirking, and making preposterous love to the whole family (III, xi, 330; xv, 364; xvii, 379).

Elizabeth originally dislikes Darcy for his arrogant haughtiness of manner, but her refusal of his first proposal of marriage is based upon much more serious faults: by separating Bingley from Jane he had "been the means of ruining, perhaps for ever, the happiness of a most beloved sister," and he had deprived Wickham of the advantages designed for him by Darcy's father, reducing him to comparative poverty and denying him the independence which was "no less his due than his desert" (II, xi, 190-92). Being a man of principle and integrity, Darcy fully admits that these charges, if true, would be serious indeed; the latter particularly would be a "depravity"—a gross violation of justice, filial duty, and the human ties of early friendship (II, xii, 196). He defends himself so well in his letter that Elizabeth is fully convinced that no such violations had occurred; as she later tells Jane, he had all the goodness, Wickham only the appearance of it (II, xvii, 225; xiii, 207). His part in separating Bingley from Jane, for which he refuses to apologize in his letter, is corrected when he comes to see that the affection on both sides is much deeper than he had thought. And in arranging the marriage of Wickham and Lydia, though he does it in large part for Elizabeth's sake, he goes far beyond the requirements of duty and justice; Elizabeth calls it an "unexampled kindness," an "exertion of goodness too great to be probable" (III, x, 326; xvi, 365-66). In moral as in intellectual qualities, Darcy fully deserves the esteem in which Elizabeth comes to hold him; these qualities are the basis of her love for him and the guarantees of happiness in their life together.

Jane Austen conceives both intelligence and morality as active powers, meant to be put to use. Principles, however sound, are nothing but inert abstractions unless they become a habit of mind, a disposition to think and act in a certain way. The distinction between principle and its use in action, between the theory and the practice of virtue, is drawn very explicitly by Darcy and also by Sir Thomas Bertram in *Mansfield Park,* both speaking or thinking in moments of searching self-criticism. Darcy confesses to Elizabeth: "I have been a selfish being all my life, in practice, though not in principle. As a child I was taught what was *right,* but I was not taught to correct my temper. I was given good principles, but left to follow them in pride and conceit" (III, xvi, 369). Sir Thomas blames the family catastrophe on his own errors in the education of his daughters. First was the unfavorable effect upon Maria and Julia of the totally opposite treatment they received from his severity and from the indulgence and flattery of their aunt, Mrs. Norris. But this was not the most dreadful mistake in his plan of education:

> Something must have been wanting *within*. . . . He feared that principle, active principle, had been wanting, that they had never been properly taught to govern their inclinations and tempers, by that sense of duty which can alone suffice. They had been instructed theoretically in their religion, but never required to bring it into daily practice. . . . He had meant them to be good, but his cares had been directed to the understanding and manners, not the disposition. . . . (III, xvii, 463)

Jane Austen is a rationalist in her belief that principles of truth and right exist objectively, can be known by the human understanding, and should be followed in the conduct of life. But she is far from assuming that intellectual acceptance of sound moral values is enough; principles are dynamic and effectual only when they become an inclination, an active disposition and temper of the mind—a *sense* of duty, a "something *within*," as much a matter of habit and feeling as of reason itself.

Feeling

Since all of Jane Austen's novels are love stories, feeling is obviously essential to them. Her usual terms for it, when referring to liking felt by a man for a woman or a woman for a man, are "inclination," "partiality," "affection," or "attachment." It may be slight and shallow, or it may grow in depth and intensity until it becomes a love which would end only with life itself. If esteem is the rational and ethical basis of love, feeling is its affective dimension, a direct emotional response which may or may not be objectively and rationally justifiable. But to marry without it, as Charlotte Lucas does, is as wrong as it is dangerous, and the final obstacle to the marriage of Elizabeth and Darcy is the belief of her father and sister that her only feeling for him is dislike. "Oh, Lizzy!" Jane cries, "do any thing rather than marry without affection" (III, xvii, 373). She is finally able to convince them that Darcy's affection for her had stood the test of many months' suspense, and that her love for him is everything it should be (xvii, 376-77).

The casual reader might not think of Darcy in this connection, but his attraction to Lizzy begins very early in their acquaintance, though she is totally unaware of it. He is "caught" by the beauty of her dark eyes, by her light and pleasing figure, by the easy playfulness of her manners (I, vi, 23). When Elizabeth is at Netherfield during Jane's illness, he begins to think that he may be in some danger, that his feelings may be carrying him away; he "had never been so bewitched by any woman as he was by her" (I, x, 52). In his letter to Elizabeth, still later, Darcy confesses that only "the utmost force of passion," overcoming all his reservations and objections, had brought him to propose to her (I, xii, 198), and when he proposes the second time he speaks "as warmly as a man violently in love can be supposed to do" (III, xvi, 365). Near the end of the story, when he and Elizabeth have come to an understanding, she reproaches him for being shy and silent when he visited her home: "You might have talked to me more when you came to dinner." He replies, "A man who had felt less, might," and of course she gladly accepts that answer (III, xviii, 380).

Elizabeth's love for her sister, Jane's own tender affection, the affectionate heart of Darcy's sister, Georgiana (II, x, 186; xii, 202), mark all three of them as loving by nature, women of feeling, capable of grief and joy, of misery as well as happiness. A fact about Jane Austen's novels which is often overlooked or too little emphasized by critics is that several of her most feeling heroines endure long periods of suffering: not only Jane Bennet, who has to struggle to suppress her love for Bingley through many weeks when she believes that it is not returned, but Elinor Dashwood in *Sense and Sensibility,* Fanny in *Mansfield Park,* Jane Fairfax in *Emma,* and Anne Elliot in *Persuasion.*[9] Many readers, I suspect, do not sufficiently recognize or respond to the quiet heroism of these less brilliant and vivacious women, but they are missing something of great importance to the total effect of the novels. All are happy in the end, since the stories are comedies, but the pain and fortitude of these tender women give the novels a depth and substance which their gayer and more sparkling sisters could not provide.[10]

As with the other values, Jane Austen uses feeling to differentiate her characters; there are affectionate hearts, people without hearts, people with mean and selfish hearts. The quality and tone of their feelings have much to do with their happiness or unhappiness, both from day to day and in their final state at the end of the story. Jane Bennet's usual frame of mind is serene and cheerful, because she hates no one; she is at ease with herself and with those around her. Miss Bingley, so different in temper from her amiable, sincerely friendly brother, gives pain to no one but herself when she vents her ill-natured feelings in criticisms of Elizabeth's person and dress, finally drawing from Darcy the declaration "It is many months since I have considered her as one of the handsomest women of my acquaintance" (III, iii, 271). The good-hearted may know grief and sorrow, but in the end they are happy; for many of the bad-hearted, the ironically appropriate final state is to be tied forever to someone as mean-spirited as themselves. Mrs. Norris in *Mansfield Park,* a domestic tyrant and toady filled with sour hostilities, ends in a kind of hell, shut up with embittered Maria Bertram, with no affection on one side, no judgment on the other; their tempers are their mutual punishment (*MP,* III, xvii, 465). Similar, though more comically reported, is the final disposition of Robert Ferrars and Lucy Steele in *Sense and Sensibility:* "Setting aside the jealousies and ill-will continually subsisting between Fanny and Lucy, in which their husbands of course took a part, as well as the frequent domestic disagreements between Robert and Lucy themselves, nothing could exceed the harmony in which they all lived together" (*S&S,* III, xiv, 377).

The values which I have called "intelligence" and "feeling," though basic in all the stories, are especially important in *Sense and Sensibility,* as its title implies. The two qualities are not mutually exclusive. The initial characterization of the two heroines and their mother makes it clear that Elinor's sense does not prevent her from feeling deeply, and that Marianne's sensibility is by no means incompatible with a good understanding. The former has an excellent heart, strong feelings, and an affectionate disposition, as well as strength of understanding, and the latter is not only generous, amiable, eager in everything, without moderation in her sorrows and joys, but also sensible and clever, with abilities "in many respects, quite equal to Elinor's." In keeping with Jane Austen's usual method of storytelling, the narrator immediately shows these traits in action, as the women respond differently to a particular event, person, or situation. In this case, the events are the death of the girls' father, the inheritance of the house in which they have lived by John Dashwood, their half-brother, and the arrival, immediately after their father's burial, of John's selfish and narrow-minded wife to take possession of the house. This drastic change is shocking to them all, but to Marianne and her mother it is overwhelming:

> Elinor saw, with concern, the excess of her sister's sensibility; but by Mrs. Dashwood it was valued and cherished. They encouraged each other now in the violence of their affliction. The agony of grief which overpowered them at first, was voluntarily renewed, was sought for, was created again and again. They gave themselves up wholly to their sorrow, seeking increase of wretchedness in every reflection that could afford it, and resolved against ever admitting consolation in future. Elinor, too, was deeply afflicted; but still she could struggle, she could exert herself. She could consult with her brother, could receive her

sister-in-law on her arrival, and treat her with proper attention; could strive to rouse her mother to similar exertion, and encourage her to similar forbearance. (*S&S,* I, i, 7)

The ethical and psychological premises which order Jane Austen's depiction of character and action are not stoical, for it is assumed in all the novels that the capacity to think and the capacity to feel are equally human, that both are necessary to a full and admirable manhood or womanhood. Her views are closer to those of Socrates in the *Republic,* when he says that the truly human response to disaster is not to give way to grief—much less to cultivate and nourish it, as Marianne and her mother do—but rather to seek ways of mitigating its bad effects, saving what can be saved, and starting anew.[11] For Jane Austen, as for Plato, emotion is not an evil to be extirpated; when in harmony with reason and truth, it is a positive good, not only the seat and source of individual happiness but the bond which ties a family or a society together. But it can be excessive, out of proportion to the circumstances which arouse it; if indulged and even sought for, it can be terribly destructive both to others and to the one who feels. The rational principle is the higher and nobler part of the soul, and it must govern.[12] This is the knowledge which Marianne had resolved never to be taught, but which she finally learns through experiences so painful that they bring her to the very edge of death.

Beauty

Beauty, in Jane Austen's vocabulary, is a quality of "person," of face and figure. She seems to distinguish three kinds of beauty. One is ephemeral, an attractiveness springing from youth and health; Lydia Bennet has such beauty, as her mother once did too. Jane Austen's favorite word for this quality, at least in speaking of characters she likes and wishes us to like, is "bloom," a glow of freshness and vitality. Another kind is a formal beauty of shape and proportion, a distinction and harmony of countenance and body. This kind of beauty is more lasting; Jane will be beautiful and Darcy handsome even in old age. The third kind is a beauty not wholly physical, since its source is the power of the body to express the mind within—the thoughts, feelings, and personality which animate the body. This is the kind of beauty which so bewitches Darcy; as he says when Miss Bingley is teasing him about his infatuation with Elizabeth's beautiful eyes, a painter might copy their color and shape, and the remarkable fineness of the lashes, but "it would not be easy, indeed, to catch their expression" (I, x, 53; cf. vi, 23; III, xi, 334).

The heroines of the novels usually unite all three, though in differing degrees; both Jane and Elizabeth have the beauty of youth and health, but Jane has more of the second kind, Elizabeth more of the third. Anne Elliot's bloom vanished early, but she retains a quieter elegance of face and figure which visibly conveys the excellence of her mind and the sweetness of her temper (*Persuasion,* I, iv, 28; vii, 61; xii, 104). The heroine of *Emma,* as described by Mrs. Weston, is surely the loveliest of all the women in these stories:

> "Such an eye!—the true hazel eye—and so brilliant! regular features, open countenance, with a complexion—oh, what a bloom of full health, and such a pretty height and size, such a firm and upright figure. There is health, not merely in her bloom, but in her air, her head, her glance. One hears sometimes of a child being 'the picture of health;' now Emma always gives me the idea of being the complete picture of grown-up health. She is loveliness itself, Mr. Knightley, is not she?" (*Emma,* I, v, 39)

In fiction as in life, beauty is important because human beings respond to it so strongly. Jane Austen was well aware, though she would not make such a point explicitly, that beauty of the first kind has a biological function; Mr. Bennet would never have had his five daughters if he had not fallen in love with his wife's youthful good looks. The second kind of beauty gives an aesthetic pleasure, quite apart from sexual desire, for we all take delight in the beauty of any living creature, above all a human one. As Mr. Knightley says very simply, in reply to Mrs. Weston's praise of Emma's beauty, "I love to look at her." The third kind is still more valuable, and should be even more moving, because it has an ethical quality, reflecting the character and individuality of the unique spirit within. The reverse is true, of course, when a countenance reflects a character that is selfish and cold.

Because beauty does appeal to us so powerfully, it can be dangerous and destructive. Elizabeth is blinded for a long time by Wickham's good looks and engaging manners, helped on by his flattering attentions to herself; they lead her to "court prepossession and ignorance, and drive reason away." Willoughby, in *Sense and Sensibility,* is another deceptively handsome man; he almost kills poor Marianne, when he deserts her to court a woman of fortune. Perhaps the most striking case in any of the novels is Mary Crawford, in *Mansfield Park.* She has everything that should make a woman lovable—not only beauty, but intelligence, taste, a good heart in most things, and a sense of humor almost as delightful as Lizzy Bennet's, though it has an edge of malice to it. She is even morally good, in the conventional sense of the shalt-nots. But all these charms are wasted and spoiled because she cannot free herself from the worldly values of fashionable London. Jane Austen seems to share the feeling of her hero, Edmund Bertram, that it is sad—almost heartbreaking—that such a woman should have this fatal defect. Yet it is absolutely necessary that he break with her, and he is much happier, in the long run, with the far less brilliant and dazzling Fanny than he could ever have been with Mary.

Worldly Condition

The most controversial of the five values is the last, rank and fortune. One school of critics, of which Dorothy Van Ghent and Mark Schorer are the best known, claims that the values of Jane Austen's world are materialistic, snobbish, and mercenary. They base this claim on the style of the novels, or rather on certain expressions which they believe to be a dominant element in her vocabulary. It is a language, Van Ghent asserts, of "acquisitiveness and calculation and materialism," reflecting a culture "whose institutions are solidly defined by materialistic interests—property and banking and trade and the law that keeps order in these matters."[13] Schorer goes even further when he says in his preface to *Pride and Prejudice:* "When moral and emotional situations are persistently expressed in economic figures . . . , we can hardly escape the recognition that this is a novel about marriage as a market, and about the female as marketable."[14]

It is true, of course, that the people in Jane Austen's novels are almost shockingly frank, to our taste, in their awareness of other people's fortunes and incomes and in their willingness to mention the figures openly in ordinary conversation. But Van Ghent and Schorer have got the values all upside-down. Their inferences from Jane Austen's vocabulary are far from convincing, since they do not attempt any complete account of her style but merely list arbitrarily selected words and phrases, quoted without context, and make no distinction between expressions used by a despicable character, by an admirable character, or by the narrator. The deeper fallacy of their argument, I believe, is that of inferring Jane Austen's values, or the values of the culture she depicts, from the attitudes of the characters she dislikes and condemns.

Snobbish and mercenary attitudes are frequently expressed in the novels, but always by bad or foolish people. It is Miss Bingley and Mrs. Hurst who laugh so heartily about the "vulgar relations" of Jane and Elizabeth, ostensibly their dear friends—one of their uncles a country attorney, another living by trade somewhere near Cheapside (I, viii, 36-37; x, 53). It is Mr. Collins, in one of the most delightfully apt of his many unwitting self-revelations, who says of Darcy: "This young gentleman is blessed in a peculiar way, with every thing the heart of mortal man can most desire,—splendid property, noble kindred, and extensive patronage" (III, xv, 362). It is Lady Catherine, sycophantically backed up by Collins, who thinks that a marriage between Darcy and Elizabeth would be "so disgraceful a match," and who angrily denounces Lizzy, to her face, for "the upstart pretensions of a young woman without family, connections, or fortune" (III, xiv, 356; xv, 363). It is Mrs. Bennet, finally, who receives the news of their engagement with the ecstatic cry: "Oh! my sweetest Lizzy! how rich and how great you will be! What pin-money, what jewels, what carriages you will have!" (III, xvii, 378).

The attitude of the wise and good characters toward rank and fortune is exactly the opposite. Bingley impatiently rejects his sisters' snobbery: " 'If they had uncles enough to fill *all* Cheapside,' cried Bingley, 'it would not make them one jot less agreeable' " (I, viii, 37). Marriage is not a market for Jane and Elizabeth. Neither would ever marry a man she did not esteem and love; neither of them could be bought at any price. This is so clear in Elizabeth's mind that she can make a joke about it; when Jane asks how soon she began to love Darcy, Elizabeth says: "I believe I must date it from my first seeing his beautiful grounds at Pemberley." It is just as clear to Jane, who begs her sister to be serious (III, xvii, 373).

The test case is Darcy. He does recognize a large discrepancy in wealth and status between himself and Elizabeth; that is obvious to everyone, including herself. He does struggle to repress his growing attachment to her, because of the inferiority of her connections. But their real inferiority lies not in the lack of rank and fortune but in the "total want of propriety" of Mrs. Bennet and her younger daughters; these defects are a source of heavy chagrin to Elizabeth, too (II, xii, 198; xiv, 212-13). As Darcy's original false pride is gradually eroded by his recognition of the merits of both Jane and Elizabeth, by the humbling shock of Elizabeth's refusal of his first proposal, and by his increasing understanding of himself and of her, all worldly obstacles become of no importance. He comes to love the Gardiners, in spite of their proximity to Cheapside, because they are both cheerful, affectionate, and intelligent people. By the end of the story his values are identical with those of the narrator, and he knows well that in fortuneless Elizabeth he has won a treasure richer than all his tribe.

Lord David Cecil, a different sort of critic, succinctly sums up Miss Austen's views on worldly condition: "It was wrong to marry for money, but it was silly to marry without it."[15] The novels recognize that a moderate income and an independent, self-respecting position in society provide the necessary material basis for a civilized and happy life. But rank and riches, beyond that minimum, have little value either for the narrator of the stories or for the amiable people in them.[16]

❧❧❧

In concluding this account, we may turn briefly to the questions mentioned at the beginning: what should be said about Jane Austen's values as a system of ideas, and how do they function in the novels as works of art? The first question is philosophical, concerning those values in the abstract, isolated from the fictional contexts in which they exist. The second is a literary question, interpretive and critical.

On the philosophical side, we should recognize that the values written into these novels are far from original with Miss Austen; they are actually very ancient. The particular source or sources from which she derived them, which probably could not be determined in any case, is not pertinent to our concerns here; it is sufficient to observe that they are part of the humanistic classical-Christian tradition which she inherited. They are summed up in a phrase of the Anglican prayerbook, a humble request for divine mercy on everyone afflicted or distressed in "mind, body, or estate."[17] In a fuller statement, they could have been found in either Plato or Aristotle, as well as in many later philosophers and moralists. In its classical form, the scheme subsumes human values under three categories: "goods of the soul, goods of the body, and external goods." Goods of the soul are the intellectual and moral virtues, which Aristotle develops in great detail in the *Nicomachean Ethics*. Health and beauty are goods of the body; economic sufficiency and social respect are external goods.[18] Jane Austen gives these ideas a Christian coloring and states them in a nontechnical, eighteenth-century vocabulary, but the classification is the same as hers in all essentials.

Aristotle says that this categorization of values represents the common view, generally accepted outside his own school. It is sufficiently clear and valid to provide a starting point for ethics, an inexact science, and he proceeds to use it as a framework for his own elaborate and sophisticated analysis. From a philosophical point of view, one great advantage of this classification is that it is exhaustive; it includes in principle every kind of good which human beings seek and by which their merit may be distinguished and judged. Feeling may seem to be missing, but its place is between goods of the soul and goods of the body, partaking of both; it has a physical, organic basis, but it depends also upon opinion, an activity and function of the mind. Feeling is a good if the mind is well tempered. If there are minor goods, such as taste or good manners, a place can readily be found for them as subdivisions or combinations within the general three-part scheme.

The classification is not a mere list, like that quoted from Walter Allen at the beginning of this essay. It is systematic, genuinely philosophical because intellectually ordered and coherent. The order is hierarchical, from the highest, most fundamental values to those which are lower, less valuable, and derivative. According to Plato in the *Laws:*

> It shall be laid down that the goods of the soul are highest in honour and come first, provided that the soul possesses temperance; second come the good and fair things of the body; and third the so-called goods of substance and property.[19]

Goods of the soul are ultimate ends, to be sought for their own sake. Goods of the body and external goods are both instrumental, to be desired and pursued in proportion to their contribution as means to the realization of the goods of the soul. The body is more closely bound to the soul and affects it more directly, for good or ill, but some minimal level of material and social support is also needed, and is a good to that extent. Plato tends to minimize the value of external goods; Aristotle is more willing to acknowledge them as true, though strictly limited, goods. Happiness, he says,

> . . . needs the external goods as well; for it is impossible, or not easy, to do noble acts without the proper equipment. In many actions we use friends and riches and political power as instruments; and there are some things the lack of which takes the lustre from happiness, as good birth, goodly children, beauty. . . .[20]

At the end of Jane Austen's stories, her heroes and heroines always receive a generous measure of all such goods, but the true basis of their happiness is the excellence of their minds, the soundness of their principles and tempers, and the kindness, generosity, and nobility of their feelings.

On the artistic side, I believe we should recognize that the six novels were not written for the purpose of inculcating these values. They are not dramatic sermons. Jane Austen's stories are neither allegorical nor didactic; she is not arguing any thesis or preaching any moral. The stories are told for their own sake, for their human interest. We read and enjoy them because we become interested in her fictional people, imaginatively and emotionally engaged in their situations and problems and desires. We want to know what happens to them, how the story comes out, and to engage us in that way is the artist's controlling aesthetic purpose.

Although the novels do not exist for the sake of the values written into them, they would be very different as narratives, and would call forth very different responses from us, if the values were different or were not present at all. I believe that they have at least four important aesthetic functions.

In the first place, it is by means of these ideas that the characters are differentiated from each other, so that we see clearly what each one is; the values order our impressions of Jane Austen's people, giving to their small imaginary society the structured clarity and significance of art. Second, as Watt, Allen, and other critics have observed,[21] they guide our judgment of these people and our feelings toward them, determining which we will like and which we will dislike—those we are glad to see frustrated and put down and those we want to work through their difficulties, find each other, and be happy.

Third, since the novels are comedies, the values define and distinguish the range of comic effects which constitutes their special literary quality and character. The main plot is always a high comedy of love, involving young men and women who are basically deserving and likable, but who fall into some kind of mistake or misjudgment. Those who belong together are separated, and one or more of them may suffer through long stretches of the story, but the errors are finally corrected and the tale ends with a happiness which they have always merited and which we have desired for them from the beginning. Interwoven with but subordinated to this kind of comedy of realistic romance is the almost infinite variety of comic effects arising from characters who in different ways and degrees are neither deserving nor lovable—the derisive, punitive comedy of the Collinses and the Lady Catherines, the Hursts and Miss Bingleys, and their many variants in the other novels.

Finally, the values give to these stories of imagined people a human importance, a seriousness of subject and implication, which makes us feel that what happens to them is no trivial matter, but something that deeply engages our sympathy and concern. As Ronald Crane says in his fine essay on *Persuasion,* "It is a love story but assuredly not a mere love story,"[22] for the values at stake are far more weighty and important than those involved in sentimental love stories or popular magazine romances. That is why we do not feel, in finishing one of Jane Austen's novels, that we have passed a few hours quite agreeably, perhaps gratifying a few fantasies along the way, but rather that we have been absorbed in an intellectual, imaginative, and emotional experience of great intensity and depth.

To many people of our bedeviled century, Jane Austen's system of values undoubtedly seems quaint and old-fashioned; it is certainly very different from the values defended in modern phenomenological, analytic, or existential ethical philosophies. It may be true that our world is so radically corrupt that only by such desperate remedies can we save any values at all. It would be a sad thing for the human race, though, if we had to conclude that values like Jane Austen's are gone forever; I believe they represent a sane, generous, humane view of life, beautifully realized in six wonderful comic novels.

Notes

1. Ian Watt, "On *Sense and Sensibility*," in *Jane Austen: A Collection of Critical Essays,* ed. Watt (Englewood Cliffs, N.J.: Prentice Hall, 1963), pp. 42-43.

2. Walter Allen, *The English Novel* (London: J. M. Dent & Sons, 1954), p. 106.

3. On "accomplishments" see Kenneth L. Moler, *Jane Austen's Art of Allusion* (Lincoln: University of Nebraska Press, 1968), Ch. 4. An amusing range of views on the subject is given in the conversation at Netherfield among Darcy, Elizabeth, Bingley, and the Bingley sisters (*P&P,* Vol. I, Ch. viii).

4. Lady Catherine's case is perhaps debatable. Wickham says that she has the reputation of being sensible and clever, but he ascribes it to her rank and fortune, her authoritative manner, and "the pride of her nephew, who chuses that every one connected with him should have an understanding of the first class" (I, xvi, 84), The last of these explanations is clearly biased and malicious, and the first two may also be colored by Wickham's resentment against Darcy. She does and says many stupid things in the course of the story, but her arrogance may be more to blame than any defect of native intelligence.

5. R. W. Chapman, ed., *The Novels of Jane Austen,* 3d ed. (London: Oxford University Press, 1959), I, xiii, 61-62; cf. xxiii, 130. All references and quotations will be from this edition; volume number within each novel will be given in Roman capitals, chapter number in lower-case Roman, and page number in Arabic, within parentheses in the text.

6. Richard Whately, review of *Northanger Abbey* and *Persuasion,* in B. C. Southam, ed., *Jane Austen: The Critical Heritage* (London: Routledge & Kegan Paul, 1968), pp. 87-105. The essay was originally published in *Quarterly Review,* 24 (1821),352-76.

7. Reuben Brower, while stressing the ironies of *Pride and Prejudice,* says that its "vision is not one of Proustian relativity. . . . For Jane Austen there can be no doubt about the meaning of 'principle and integrity' and similar terms of value" ("Light and Bright and Sparkling: Irony and Fiction in *Pride and Prejudice,*" in *The Fields of Light* [New York: Oxford University Press, 1951], pp. 164-81). For a different interpretation of irony in Jane Austen, see Marvin Mudrick, *Jane Austen: Irony as Defense and Discovery* (Berkeley and Los Anleles: University of California Press, 1968).

8. Jane Austen takes the validity of the Decalogue for granted as an essential element in Christian ethical teaching, but she distinguishes sharply between true goodness and mere propriety of conduct. She says of John Dashwood in *Sense and Sensibility:* "He was not an ill-disposed young man, unless to be rather cold-hearted, and rather selfish, is to be ill-disposed: but he was, in general, well respected; for he conducted himself with propriety in the discharge of his ordinary duties." Even more severe is her judgment of Mrs. John Dashwood and Lady Middleton, alike in their combination of coldhearted selfishness with "an insipid propriety of demeanour" (I, i, 5; II, xii, 229). Mudrick is badly mistaken, in his chapter on *Sense and Sensibility,* when he argues that the ethical values it enforces, "the conscience of the novel," are strict conformity to form and convention, to "that peculiar complex of persistent feudal and supervening bourgeois conventions which to Jane Austen's class seemed the base and guarantee of social order; and the highest virtue is adherence to social forms at whatever personal cost" (pp. 85-86).

9. Watt speaks of "the everyday heroism of Elinor" and the joyful emotion which nearly

overcomes her when she hears that Edward Ferrars is free to marry her, after all ("*On Sense and Sensibility,*" p. 49).

10. Charlotte Brontë says of Jane Austen: ". . . The Passions are perfectly unknown to her; she rejects even a speaking acquaintance with that stormy Sisterhood; even to the Feelings she vouchsafes no more than an occasional graceful but distant recognition; too frequent converse with them would ruffle the smooth elegance of her progress" (Southam, p. 128). Although this was written in 1850, less than forty years after the publication of *Pride and Prejudice,* it illustrates dramatically the great gulf between Miss Brontë's post-Byronic philosophy of passion and Miss Austen's more empirical conception of the role of emotion in day-to-day human living.

11. Plato *Republic* x. 603D-604E.

12. When Mary Bennet says that "every impulse of feeling should be guided by reason" (I, vii, 32), she is uttering an unmeaning platitude, one of those pieces of threadbare morality which she is forever extracting from her bookish studies in human nature. In the moral life of her two elder sisters, these empty words become living truth.

13. Dorothy Van Ghent, "On *Pride and Prejudice,*" in *The English Novel: Form and Function* (New York: Holt, Rinehart, and Winston, 1953), pp. 99-111. Cf. Leonard Woolf, "The Economic Determination of Jane Austen," in Judith O'Neill, ed., *Critics on Jane Austen* (London: George Allen and Unwin, 1970), pp. 50-51.

14. Mark Schorer, ed., *Pride and Prejudice* (Boston: Houghton Mifflin Co., 1956), pp. v-xxi. See also his "Fiction and the Analogical Matrix," in John W. Aldridge, ed., *Critiques and Essays on Modern Fiction* (New York: Ronald Press, 1952), pp. 83-98.

15. David Cecil, "Jane Austen," in *Poets and Story-Tellers* (New York: Macmillan, 1949), p. 116. Cf. R. W. Chapman, Jane Austen: *Facts and Problems* (Oxford: Clarendon Press, 1949), pp. 191-93; and Robert Liddell, *The Novels of Jane Austen* (London: Longmans, Green, 1963), pp. 25-27.

16. These points are clearly made in Mrs. Gardiner's caution to Elizabeth about the imprudence of falling in love with Wickham and in their subsequent discussion of the difficulty of drawing the line between avarice and discretion, between the mercenary and the prudent motive (II, iii and iv). Marianne agrees with Elinor that a "competence" is necessary for happiness, but that "wealth" has nothing to do with it; Elinor's estimate of the amount needed for a competence is only half that which Marianne thinks necessary (*S&S,* I, xvii, 91).

17. "Collect or Prayer for all Conditions of Men," *The Book of Common Prayer* (Oxford: Clarendon Press, 1790), p. C6r. There is an interesting use of the phrase in Gibbon's *Autobiography,* when he reviews the state of his existence, after completion of his great history, under "the threefold division of mind, body, and estate." Under the last heading, expressing an economic philosophy much like Elinor Dashwood's, he says that he is indeed rich, "since my income is superior to my expense, and my expense is equal to my wishes." See Gibbon, *Memoirs of My Life,* ed. Georges A. Bonnard (London: Thomas Nelson and Sons, 1966), pp. 186-87.

18. Plato *Laws* i,631C; iii, 697B; v 738D-E, 743E. Aristotle *Nichomachean Ethics* i. 8, 1098b 10-15; *Politics* vii. 1, 1323a 21.

19. Plato *Laws* iii, 697B.

20. Aristotle *Eth. Nich.* i. 8, 1099b 1-5.

21. For a searching theoretical analysis of the function of "signals of evaluation" in novels and of the legitimacy or illegitimacy of our inferring authorial beliefs from such signals, see Sheldon Sacks, *Fiction and the Shape of Belief* (Berkeley and Los Angeles: University of California Press, 1964), Chs. i and vi.

22. Ronald S. Crane, "Jane Austen: 'Persuasion,' " in *The Idea of the Humanities* (Chicago: University of Chicago Press, 1967), II, 283-302.

INDEX

Aaron, Richard I., 218, 247n10, 247n12
Abélard, 140, 143, 150, 152n31, 152n32
Abrams, M. H.: classification of critical species by, 73, 75n12
Addison, Joseph: definition of the imagination by, 41–42, 43, 44, 162, 170; mentioned, 125, 126, 127, 139, 152n23, 158, 168–69, 172n2, 172n5, 172n7, 174n40, 174n51, 176, 179, 188, 194
Aden, John M., 40, 41, 75n2, 75n8, 75n9
admiration: in Renaissance theory, 55; as response to serious literary forms, 55–57, 59, 60, 181; sources of, 55, 56–57
Aesop, 88, 90, 110
affective fallacy. *See* fallacies
age (cultural conditions in a historical period): Dryden on, 6; Johnson on, 232–34
Alcibiades, 88
Allen, Robert J., 132n5
Allen, Walter, 275, 289, 291n2
Amelius, 96, 101
André, Père, 200
Anytus, accuser of Socrates, 88
Aquinas, St. Thomas: teaching on reason and Revelation as grounds of religion, 115–16, 221
Arbuthnot, John, 176
argument from design: cited by Dryden, 25, 27; cited by Watts, 27; employed by physico-theologists, 267–68, 270
Ariosto, Ludovico, 165, 178, 180
Aristides, 85, 88
Aristophanes, 82, 84, 121n4
Aristotle: on probable reasoning, 25–28, 30n41, 30n42, 258; relation of his critical system to Dryden's, 57–59, 61, 67, 72–73; tripartite classification of human goods by, 288, 292n20
—works: *Nichomachean Ethics*, 26, 30n41, 30n42, 288, 289, 292n18, 292n20; *Poetics*, 57–59, 66–67, 69–70, 73; *Politics*, 292n18; *Posterior Analytics*, 30n41; *Prior Analytics*, 30n41; *Rhetoric*, 60; *Topics*, 30n41
—mentioned: 33, 56, 64, 66, 70, 83, 112, 114, 118, 145, 147, 164, 189, 200, 208n10, 209n27, 221, 246, 247n14, 297n1

art: based on understanding, 28; defined by Dryden, 19–21; necessity of rules for, 20–21; probabilities sufficient for, 24–25
Arundell, D. D., 29n6
Asgill, John, 111, 117
atheism: charged by Bentley, 97, 98, 102, 110; by Swift, 106–7, 123n30
Atkins, J. W. H., 177, 183n6
Atticus, 88
audience: Dryden on, 16–20; in rhetorical criticism, 73
Audra, Emile, 135, 140, 145, 149, 150, 151n1, 151n13
Augustine, Saint, 101
Austen, Jane: comic spirit, 278, 290; depiction of character, 284; humanistic classical-Christian inheritance, 288; rationalism of, 277, 280–81; religious and ethical principles in, 278–79, 291n7; system of values, 275–92
—works: *Emma*, 282, 285; *Mansfield Park*, 280–81, 282, 283, 285–86; *Northanger Abbey*, 214, 247n5; *Persuasion*, 282, 285, 290, 292n22; *Pride and Prejudice*, 214–15, 229, 247n5, 276–89 passim, 291n7, 292n10, 292n13; *Sense and Sensibility*, 282, 283–84, 285, 291n8, 291n9
—mentioned, 245
authority: weakness of all arguments based upon, 225–26, 243–44, 252–53, 255–56, 258

Bacon, Francis, 249, 251–59, 260, 262, 267; against trust in authority, 252–53, 255–56, 258; attack on syllogism, 258, 272n10; on attainability of truth, 251, 275; on dogmatism, 251; on experiments of "light" and "fruit," 253; on Idols of the Theatre, 252–53; on induction, 252, 258; on Interpretation of Nature, 251–52, 272n6; on measurements in natural history, 253; not a pragmatist, 253–54; program for reform of science and philosophy, 251–54, 257, 259; rejection of probable reasoning, 258–59; rejection of Pyrrhonic skepticism, 251, 257; on Tables of Discovery, 252, 257; on two stages of New Philosophy, 251–52, 258; on